IMAGINING THE BIG OPEN

SKI
AREA

IMAGINING THE BIG OPEN

Nature, Identity, and Play in the New West

Edited by

Liza Nicholas

Elaine M. Bapis

Thomas J. Harvey

with a Foreword by

Dan Flores

The University of Utah Press
Salt Lake City

Printed on acid-free paper

08 07 06 05 04 03
5 4 3 2 1

Library of Congress Cataloging-in-Publication Data

Imagining the big open : nature, identity, and play in the new West /
edited by Liza Nicholas, Elaine M. Bapis, Thomas J. Harvey ; with a
foreword by Dan Flores.
p. cm.
Includes bibliographical references and index.
ISBN 0-87480-738-7 (pbk. : alk. paper)
1. West (U.S.)—Civilization. 2. Popular culture—West (U.S.) 3. Regionalism—West (U.S.) 4. West (U.S.)—Social conditions. 5. West (U.S.)—Geography. 6. Landscape—Social aspects—West (U.S.) 7. Natural history—West (U.S.)
I. Nicholas, Liza, 1964– II. Bapis, Elaine M., 1949–
III. Harvey, Thomas J., 1955–

F595.3 .I46 2003
978—dc21

2002152321

CONTENTS

Dan Flores

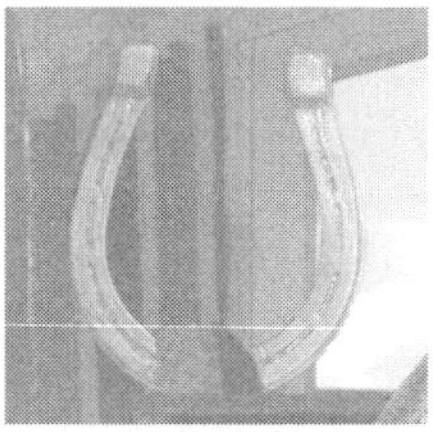

FOREWORD

Through the pointillist stippling of green piñons and junipers rolling away from the patio back of my house outside Santa Fe, the little New Mexican village of Madrid lies just hidden from my view. Only a few decades ago, like dozens—hundreds—of other western places during the heyday of ranching and extraction, which rolled with insatiable hunger across the West from the Civil War on into the twentieth century, Madrid was a going concern, a place even presidents visited. And now? (Since, to truncate history, the mines played out eventually.) Well, to tell the truth, Madrid is a going concern now, too. If any of the old miners are still around, they must have retooled, though, since the hippie residents of the old company shacks and town buildings today seem to be painters, sculptors, furniture makers. You can get a latté in Madrid or shop for New Age attire in a former mining shack now called "Woo-Wear." Or listen to bands from Albuquerque and Texas play Saturday nights in a town where the resident population is under 150. Having somehow wrangled a color graphic of its main (and only) street onto the shopping map that nearby Santa Fe hotels pass out to their guests, Madrid now is evidently a must-see western destination. Magazines like *Texas Monthly* and *The New Yorker* write about it; the place teems with activity. Madrid, New Mexico, in other words, has crossed the Postmodern Divide. It's Way New West.

That's the process the editors and essayists here are serious about, and one is tempted to say, it's about time. Madrid doesn't show up in the pages that follow (it's my own neighborhood example) and probably doesn't work all that well as a case study anyway, since unlike Moab and Red Lodge and Sundance—all places that do appear in these essays—Madrid is less a Bobos in

Paradise town than a Hippies in Paradise one. (Readers who miss my reference in the preceding sentence should immediately buy and waste no time reading David Brooks's book *Bobos in Paradise: The New Upper Class and How They Got There* [Simon and Schuster, 2000], which will not only illuminate *this* book in ways both sobering and funny but is the proper source for a fully rounded definition of the Bobo. I'll simply say it's shorthand for Bourgeois Bohemian and let you make your own guesses about Paradise.) *USA Today* reported in 1997 that 43 percent of baby boomers harbored hopes to retire somewhere in the West. And like every other group of newcomers in the history of region, they're not coming with adaptation on their minds. They're bringing their culture with them and remaking the West in the process.

Montana is the part of the West where I spend the bulk of my time, and in Montana I can think of no examples quite as successful or joyously New West wacky as Madrid. Here ranching and farming and extraction are closer real-life experiences than in the Santa Fe area, which has been New West–bound for nearly a century. History is wrenching Montana direct from extractive colony into the twenty-first century, and for many old Montanans, that shape shifting seems a shocking rejection of too many things. A western economy based on ecotourism and wolf restoration and wilderness has too many Volvos and latté sippers in it for them, too many gawkers, too many chalky-skinned flatlanders with cameras growing from their foreheads, and way too goddamned many environmentalists. Like everyone else in the West, the old Montanans have long commodified the images and the symbols of their place. But when you've spent your life felling trees or running Herefords, an economy based so overtly on turning images and symbols into money just doesn't seem, well, *authentic*. Let's just agree that some of the old Montanans aren't convinced that the Robert Redford Sundance Catalog view of the West (which the essays here show is a stunningly contradictory perspective anyway, even for a movie star) is the one we should all embrace.

Maybe basing the consciousness of your region on a wild native species like, say, salmon, or wolves, is ludicrous. For that matter, maybe the whole notion of regional consciousness is ludicrous. But regional economics aren't, and in that sense many parts of the West—I think not merely of Montana but of the whole Great Plains—really are at a crossroads as we enter the new century. Again and again, that's what's at stake in the essays in this book. Often the issue is less transition than outright survival. One inescapable reflection seems to be: however weird these transformations may strike us, what can we do but embrace human nature? If the only way we can make it in the West is to live with wolves and Woo-Wear shops, why not make the best of it and just be New West Zen? (I haven't used that exact phrasing in Montana bars, I admit.)

On the other hand, we've been here before. Down in New Mexico, if I turn my back on Madrid and walk to my front door, my eyes can follow the winding bed of the Galisteo River westward through gray badlands and horizontal yellow plains to its junction with the Rio Grande. Like Madrid, that confluence is out of sight, but I know it's where the people of Santo Domingo Pueblo go about their lives, functioning and surviving and doing quite well in a country that the outside world has transformed . . . let's see now, how many times?

PREFACE

In May 1998 the *Salt Lake Tribune* praised *The Horse Whisperer*, Robert Redford's nostalgic portrayal of a Montana horse trainer, for paying tribute to the "vision of the West—the real West of unspoiled landscapes and rugged people, not the symbolic West of John Ford's movies." In one of the obligatory promotional appearances on the "Today Show" shortly thereafter, Redford discussed the film he directed, produced, and acted in: "I love the idea of having a blank canvas in front of me," he explained to Katie Couric, "and just filling it with my own thoughts at hand. And—or the way I saw the world. It was a form of sort of social commentary." A week later the Scripps Howard News Service quoted Redford: "My heart's in the West. The view of the West is, therefore, also important to me, the trust of what the West is. We have a lot of mythologizing of the West, either through fiction of fashion or the fiction of some films . . . but a lot of mythologizing comes from a romanticizing of the West, either in oversimplifying characters or making them larger than life or almost cartoon heroes. . . . That didn't interest me. . . . So the idea was to show how it is and also . . . [present] the audience with a view of something that was about to go away."[1]

As native westerners—two of us from Montana and one from Utah—we were both attracted and annoyed by the vision of the West Redford presented. It irritated us that Redford had emerged so uncontested as the West's accepted interpreter and representative, especially since the three of us sometimes found ourselves in conflict with our own New West lifestyles and our rural upbringings. But Redford's ability to reconcile so neatly the "Old" West and its values with the "New" also greatly appealed to us, and we envied how he seamlessly incorporated both sensibilities into his own identity.

We were also drawn to Redford because, for better or worse, his beautiful portrayal of Montana in both *The Horse Whisperer* and *A River Runs Through It* validated Montana as a place important enough to be the setting of major movies, and we realized all too well that such validation had significant ripple effects on the state itself, particularly in the soaring real estate prices for the vistas Redford so gloriously portrayed. Redford's representation of the West clearly matters. *The New Yorker* commented at the release of *The Horse Whisperer*, "Redford's own romance with the West—characteristically obsessive, conscientious and serious—has, in the view of many, gone some way to changing the way we think about it."[2]

And Redford has put his stamp of celebrity ordination on other western spaces as well. Utah, the place he has called home since the late 1960s, has also become an integral part of his identity; he chose the picturesque mountains east of Provo as the setting for his Sundance resort and Park City as the location for his world-famous Sundance Film Festival. We began to see Redford and the western places he helped "produce" and manage as windows into something larger. Our discussions resulted in a panel at the 1999 Western History Association Conference in Portland, "Deconstructing Sundance: Robert Redford's West." Part of the appeal of "Redford's West," we concluded, was how Redford had managed to graft ideas about the Old West to the New in his portrayal of iconoclastic cowboys in his movies, in the sale of the Old West lifestyle and its remnants in the Sundance Catalog, and by the construction of a western playground that harks back to the Old West in its image but relies on New West recreation for its existence.

Redford pragmatically, if not wholly consciously, employs Old West symbols in his imagery and selectively champions the values of the past. Yet his catalog, resort, and films target affluent suburbanites who value the West for its aesthetic attributes, recreational diversions, and spiritual rejuvenating benefits, although many "Old" Westerners who are sustained by ranching, mining, and logging view such uses as disturbing portents of a West in which they have increasingly marginal roles. It fascinated us that Redford has made a successful film and entrepreneurial career out of his ability to reconcile the seemingly contradictory identities of environmentalist *and* champion of an older value system and way of life characterized by a utilitarian approach to the land. In the end, we concluded that the philosophy Redford propagates is as contradictory as the New West itself, and perhaps those very contradictions explained the appeal of his West. Examining his persona seemed a good way to root out these inconsistencies, which we realized surfaced in our own everyday choices and identities—critiquing the New West and its participants, for example, as we sipped double soy lattés on the way to ski in the Wasatch Mountains. This book emerged out of both the panel and our discussions about how we ourselves fit into this New West for which Redford acts as director, merchant, and protector, however self-appointed.

All the essays in this book, whether from a historian, geographer, or literary critic, discuss how the New Western space gets constructed and the repercussions of how we make meaning of this space. By talking about how humans make meaning of a space, we have departed from the dominant methodology of environmental history, which has most often spoken about how humans have affected nature. We are also departing from the New Western history, which focuses on presumptions of loss and seems in the end only to invert the positivist spin of the "Old Western" history. Much recent scholarship preferences race, class, and gender as categories of analysis. In this anthology we have chosen to focus on region and on how the way westerners view and value the landscape they inhabit reflects historical shifts and power relations within the West.

Urbanization, demographic change, and an aesthetic value placed on the western landscape are hardly "new" characteristics of the West. But the phrase *New West* already signified, for better or worse, a number of changes in the West in the last twenty years of which we, and others, have been cognizant. For us the "New West" is less about the loss of local feed stores and the proliferation of espresso shops, as the *Atlas of the New West* would have it,[3] and more about the circulation of a certain kind of knowledge, an emergent taken-for-granted-ness of the "way things ought to be," particularly with regard to the western space.

For the three editors, Robert Redford was simply one window into a New Western discourse in which resilient western symbols are injected with new meanings, a signal of larger regional power shifts. The other writers whose essays are included here have found many enlightening windows of their own into this New Western discourse, but we end this book with Robert Redford because his narrative summarizes so much of the New West sensibility that this volume seeks to examine.

NOTES

1. Sean P. Means, "Redford's Real West: 'The Horse Whisperer' Is a Far Cry from John Ford," *The Salt Lake Tribune*, 10 May 1998, D1, D3; National Broadcast Company, Inc., News Transcripts, "The Today Show," 7:00 A.M. ET, 11 May 1998; Betsy Pickle, Scripps Howard News Service, 1998, Nando.net.

2. Richard Raynor, "Existential Cowboy," *New Yorker*, 18 May 1998, 74.

3. *Atlas of the New West: Portrait of a Changing Region*, gen. ed. William E. Riebsame (New York: W. W. Norton, 1997), 12.

ACKNOWLEDGMENTS

Many people assisted in the creation of this book. Bob Goldberg, Eric Hinderaker, Paul Johnson, J. C. Mutchler, and Mary Strine, all of the University of Utah, commented on individual chapters and helped clarify the themes of the volume. We thank them for their reading time and valuable contributions.

We are also grateful to participants in the panel discussion "Deconstructing Sundance: Robert Redford's West," held at both the Western History Association Meeting in Portland in October 1999 and the Environmental History Conference in Denver in March 2002. We especially thank Phil Deloria, Ann Fabian, Anne Hyde, and Jenny Price for their insights and wisdom.

Dawn Marano, of the University of Utah Press, suggested that we turn our ideas into a book and encouraged us along the way. We thank everyone at the Press, as well as Kimberley Vivier for her patient copyediting. We would also like to thank the contributors for their cooperation and Dan Flores for graciously agreeing to write the foreword.

Part One

POWER SHIFTS

The writers of these three essays use wolves, salmon, and a Wyoming landmark to illuminate shifting power dynamics and values in the West. The debates surrounding these three seemingly disconnected western entities point to larger underlying disagreements about lifestyle and identity. New Westerners can be grouped in part based on perceptions of western space. These perceptions, in turn, are often linked to place of residence, voting patterns, and cultural loyalties. As these three essays illustrate, identity in the New West has to do with a lifestyle that is characterized by the capacity and the disposition to recognize particular western spaces as worthy of admiration, and the conviction that they should be used for recreation rather than work, play rather than production. The cultural privileging of wolves and salmon and the debate over the right way to "experience" Devils Tower all exemplify a shift in the priorities and preferences in the West.

As Joseph Taylor notes, "The salmon crisis of the 1990s was as much about culture as nature." The ability to determine what is aesthetically worthy and to recognize the "right" way to see and experience it defines peoples' identities in the New West today as much as occupation—rancher, logger, attorney—or region—Texas, Montana, Utah—did seventy years ago. And although the impulse to set aside certain spaces for aesthetic appreciation is very old, the ascendancy of a particular "right way to see" western space is indicative of a slow but steady shift from valuing space for the livelihood it provides to valuing it for a purely aesthetic and recreational appreciation.

Karen Jones examines how these shifts in priority have dramatically influenced the cultural assessment of wolves. She points out that "whereas their ancestors had been viewed as worthless vermin whose only redeemable value lay in the pelt, wolves in the modern West were precious alive as servants of the booming recreational economy."

In her look at the differing perspectives on Devils Tower among climbers and Native Americans, Wendy Rex-Atzet notes that although New Westerners often profess their connection to the landscape, they have "no history on the land" and instead are left with typical "sacralized notion(s) of wilderness characteristic of modern Western thought." The recreationalists' West consists of wholly aesthetic places of play that, Rex-Atzet says, are "experientially incorporated into their own identities."

The capacity to view the wolf not as an economic threat but as a vital symbolic western presence, the recognition of the cultural worth of the salmon to the Northwest identity, and the recreational value placed on a western landmark all signify a particular "taste" and the affirmation of a particular lifestyle. This "taste" unites seemingly disparate groups of westerners and provides common cause for nineteen-year-old mountain bikers and sixty-year-old affluent Sierra Club members. But this aesthetic valuing of the West also divides westerners—ranchers from wolf proponents, Native Americans from outdoor spiritualists, and the saviors of salmon from their indifferent neighbors. These three essays examine the differences in lifestyle, taste, and perception that lie at the root of many misunderstandings in today's West.

Joseph E. Taylor III

REGIONAL UNIFIER OR SOCIAL CATSPAW?

A Social and Cultural Historical Geography of Salmon Recovery

How do we assess the currency of a regional symbol of nature? The idea itself is rather paradoxical. Symbols and regions are social constructs. There is nothing natural about either, yet people are forever melding them with nature. Such has been the case with salmon and the Pacific Northwest. In the 1990s people who wanted to save salmon runs from extinction claimed that the fish was a precious symbol of regional nature, but opponents rejected this as wishful thinking. The ensuing debates were often polarized and rather disconnected. Jeff Pampush, of the environmental fishing group Oregon Trout, insisted that "Oregonians overwhelmingly support salmon protections when polled," yet journalist Blaine Harden noted that people "born and raised in the Pacific Northwest are often said to have some special affinity for salmon. . . . But if you grew up in irrigation country, that is nonsense."[1]

The chasm between these arguments was so deep that audiences could be forgiven for wondering whether Pampush and Harden were referring to two different Northwests. In fact, such suspicions would be justified. The salmon wars of the 1990s revealed not only how humans blended nature and culture into competing visions of the environment but also how the Pacific Northwest had become a series of discrete social and cultural landscapes in stark conflict because of declining salmon runs.

Pampush and Harden helped illustrate the polarities of salmon politics, but these extremes were not very useful for understanding public attitudes. In fact, northwesterners who absolutely did or did not care about salmon amounted to but a small fraction of the region's opinions about salmon. Most residents seemed to hold attitudes closer to those expressed by the urban editorialist, rural farmer, county judge, and transplanted retiree who wrote to the Portland *Oregonian* and *Seattle Times* during the 1990s to say that they wanted to save salmon but first needed to know how much it would cost. Northwesterners cared about salmon, but their contingent loyalties revealed important limits to salmon's symbolic power. Resident opinions also suggested a complicated relativity in environmental politics that too often collapsed into caricatures in media headlines.[2]

The contrary passions that swirled around salmon during the 1990s bared critical divisions in the Pacific Northwest. Like the region's mountains and rivers, salmon were a natural feature that separated people and landscapes, and the resulting disagreements about salmon recovery could be mapped several ways. In spatial terms salmon advocates tended to mark themselves not simply as northwesterners but, more concretely, as living west of the Cascade Mountains. Demographic analysis revealed additional nuances: advocates were not only western but predominantly urban, wealthy, and male. Opponents of salmon restoration, if not salmon themselves, tended to live east of the Cascades or in rural areas, and they were disproportionately poorer, less educated, and more politically and economically marginalized than salmon advocates. These social and cultural divisions in turn exposed crucial historical roots. The material and cultural concerns that residents had developed by inhabiting and shaping their landscapes produced radiating interests and beliefs. In the 1990s when polls measured attitudes about salmon recovery, these subregional trends underscored a striking cultural diversity based on northwesterners' disparate historical experiences.[3]

In the Pacific Northwest, in other words, salmon in the 1990s did not unify society so much as pry it apart. Seemingly mundane questions about fish elicited responses that were anything but simple. Residents divided along contingent lines of culture, class, gender, place, and experience, and the region shattered into messy factions with surprising bottom lines. The business concerns that seemed to dominate debates often contained unarticulated worries about the good life that were rarely compatible among stakeholders. These background issues remained salient because subregional rivalries hamstrung all solutions. An environmental problem that seemed the province of biology and political science instead drew ecology, economics, geography, history, and sociology into vexing conundrums. The salmon crisis of the 1990s was as much about culture as nature, and the ongoing contests over these fish yielded lessons that extend far beyond salmon and the Pacific Northwest.

When journalist Tim Egan announced in 1990 that the Pacific Northwest is "wherever the salmon can get to," he articulated a dearly held belief that these fish are an essential component of regional identity, or in historian John Findlay's words, that "Salmon Are Us." Egan was far from alone in his assumptions. Environmentalist firebrand Andy Kerr argued that wild salmon were a "critical indicator of the quality of life" and "sacred to most Northwesterners." Others argued that salmon were a historical link to the frontier past. Oregon's salmon adviser Roy Hemmingway suggested that the "public wants to stay connected to the wild heritage from which American civilization was born," and historian Stephen Ambrose encouraged President Bill Clinton to save salmon because they sustained Lewis and Clark's "Voyage of Discovery during their long winter along the Columbia's estuary." Still others claimed that salmon were an "icon of the Northwest," "a primary symbol of life," and the embodiment "of our homeplaces."[4]

It might be possible to dismiss these claims as impassioned exaggerations made by overzealous advocates, but even dispassionate observers noted broad sympathies for the plight of salmon. In 1997 journalist Jonathon Brinkman reported that salmon decline was the "No. 1 environmental concern of Oregonians." Columnist Rocky Barker was certain that northwesterners would eventually endorse dam breaching to save salmon. Even academics have seen salmonophilia as an essential facet of regional culture. In 1954 geographer Howard Martin argued that salmon held the same symbolic importance in the Pacific Northwest as codfish did in New England. More recently, historians Richard White and William Robbins both claimed that "salmon symbolize nature in the Pacific Northwest."[5]

These were not empty pronouncements. Opinion polls repeatedly documented that a majority of northwesterners supported salmon recovery. In a 1997 poll for the Portland *Oregonian* more than 80 percent of the respondents said that preserving Columbia River salmon was important and 60 percent said that healthy salmon runs were more important than such commercial uses of rivers as electrical generation, irrigation, and barge trafficking. A 1998 poll for the *Seattle Times* showed salmon recovery was a high priority in the Puget Sound region, and two earlier polls by the *Spokane Spokesman Review* revealed that most Washingtonians and Idahoans also favored recovery programs. A fall 2000 poll by the *Seattle Times* indicated that salmon and dam policies were still among the most important issues for Washington voters.[6]

Polls revealed significant cultural sympathies around the region, but their generalizations also implied a false consensus. Pollsters found that many northwesterners had reevaluated their ideas about legitimate uses of natural resources, and the numbers seemed to empower those interest groups that were demanding that governments invest in recovery and restrict activities

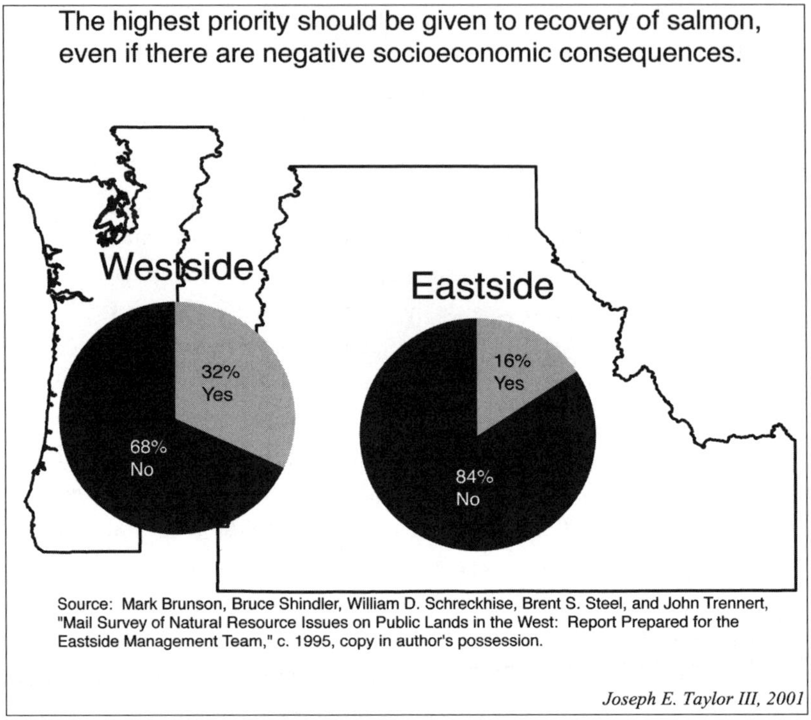

Figure 1

that threatened salmon and salmon habitat. Inferences about regional support masked as much as they revealed, however. Terms such as *northwesterners*, *Oregonians*, *Washingtonians*, and *Idahoans* meant little until grounded in time and place, but once contextualized they could no longer quite support what salmon advocates were claiming. There was in fact no typical Pacific Northwesterner, or even Oregonian, Washingtonian, or Idahoan. It was the lack of situatedness that made regionalisms at once politically potent and materially vague, and it is why we must move beyond labels to ask which particular people did or did not care about salmon and why.

If we scrutinize claims about regional sympathy, we find critical differences. Listen to three statements from the *Seattle Times*. In 1997 two Seattleites claimed, "Poll after poll indicates . . . Northwesterners want to protect and restore salmon. And they have said that they are willing to pay for it"; a year earlier a commercial fisher told a business luncheon, "Several recent polls show that Northwesterners are overwhelmingly in support of restoring salmon and even indicate a willingness to pay for that restoration"; and in 1992 an eastern Washington farmer admitted that altering flows to save

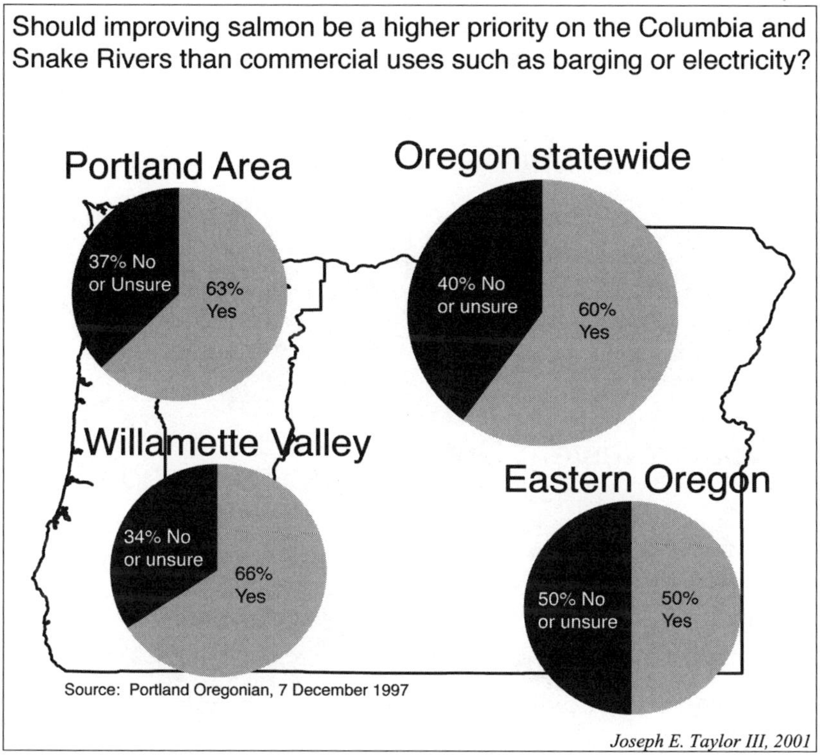

Figure 2

salmon might increase barging costs but that he was willing to support such changes as long as "people are willing to share the burden." Superficially, all seemed in accord with one another and with polls, but there was a rub: implied regional consensus failed the test of specificity because the burdens were not as comparable as speakers suggested. Although the farmer seemed to confirm the others, in reality his risks differed substantially from the inconveniences endured by urban taxpayers, and both veered sharply from the material costs to fishers and the spiritual threats to Indians. Although all lived in the Northwest, each group nurtured a remarkably different relationship with salmon, and claims about salmon's regional importance failed to address this particularity. Much was left unsaid by the pretender labels of regionalism.[7]

When pollsters removed the balancing tendencies of regional generalizations, salmon support tilted dramatically to the left side of the map. People who lived west of the Cascade Mountains were far more concerned with salmon recovery than people east of the mountains. In one survey (Figure 1) westside residents were twice as likely to support salmon recovery as eastside residents. In another (Figure 2), Portlanders and Willamette Valley residents

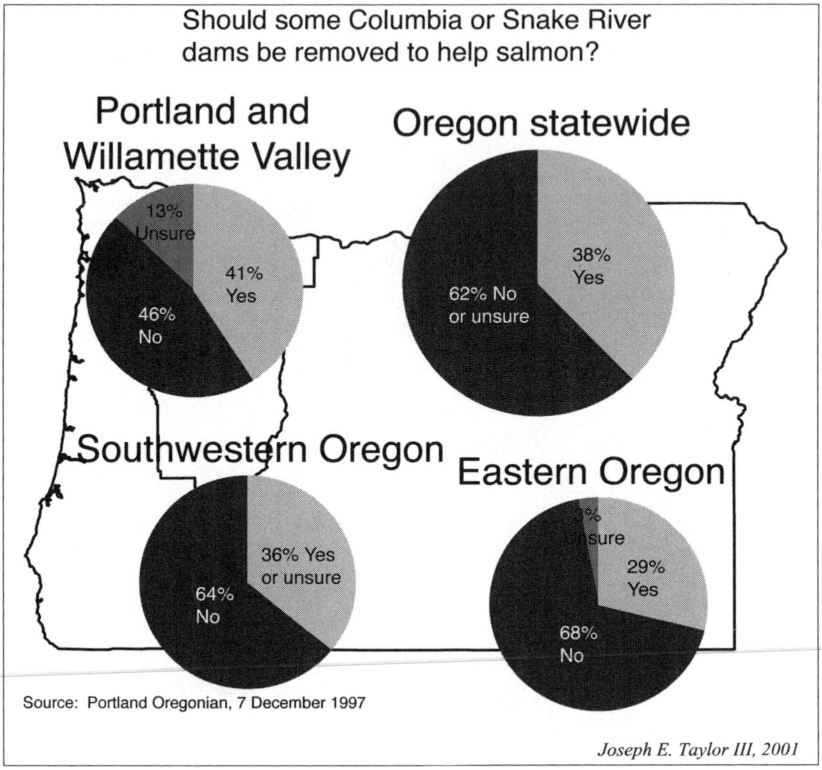

Figure 3

favored salmon over commercial uses of the Columbia and Snake Rivers by 63 percent and 66 percent respectively, but only 50 percent of eastern Oregonians said salmon were more important than commerce. The poll also found (Figure 3) that 38 percent of Oregonians favored breaching, or removing earthen portions of dams to allow streams to flow freely, to help salmon, but this finding too masked subregional divisions. Of Portland and Willamette Valley respondents, 41 percent favored breaching, significantly more than the 29 percent of eastern Oregonians who supported it. Similarly, although a slight plurality of Portlanders (46 percent) opposed dam removal, this again paled before the 64 percent of southwestern Oregonians and 68 percent of eastern Oregonians who rejected breaching. Idaho responses (Figure 4) tossed these generalizations into confusion, however. While 37 percent of Idahoans favored breaching and 50 percent opposed it, urbanites were most resistant (33 percent in favor; 59 percent opposed) because of the impact on their electric bills, and eastern residents were least opposed to breaching (41 percent for; 42 percent against) because it might alleviate demands on their irrigation rights.[8]

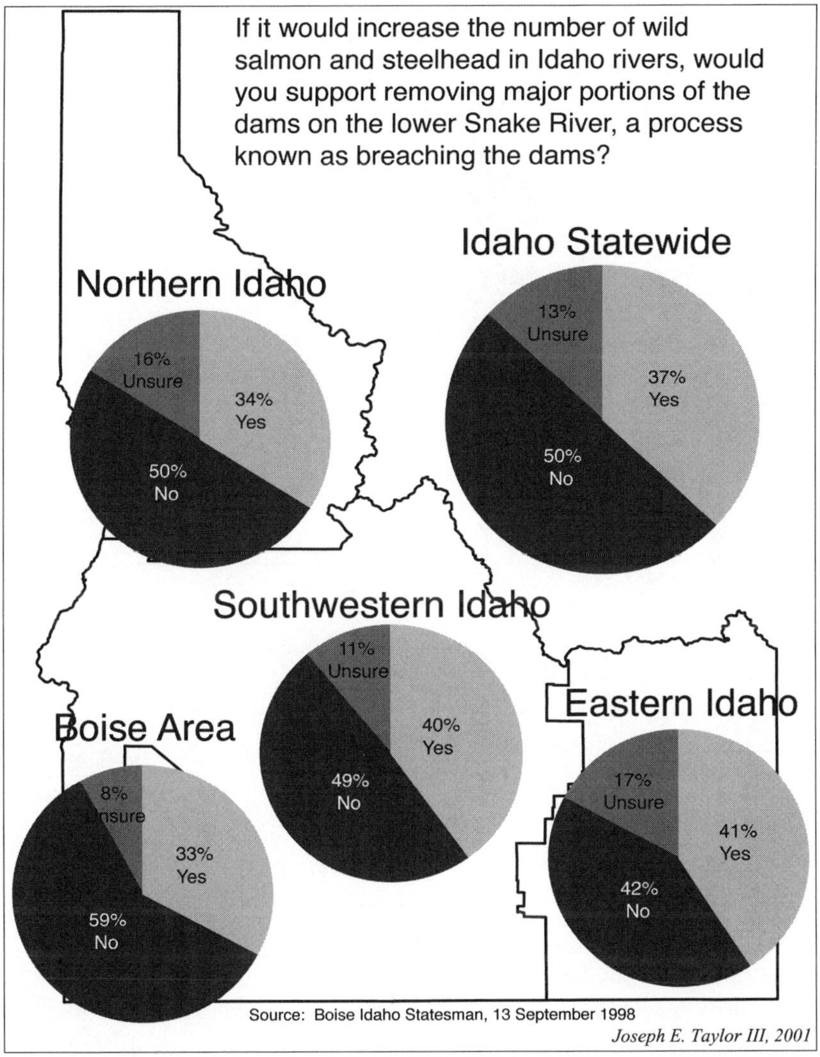

Figure 4

The situatedness of salmon appreciation also shaped how residents explained the salmon crisis. When asked to delimit which factors threaten salmon, respondents consistently blamed external forces. Residents from west of the Cascades focused on foreign trawlers, drift nets, pollution, dams, logging, grazing, and natural predators. They rarely mentioned the effects of urbanization or domestic fishing. Perhaps predictably, eastside residents saw things rather differently. They too condemned foreign trawlers, drift nets, pollution, dams, and logging, but they also named Indian gill netters and domestic commercial fishers. Grazers and irrigators were conspicuously absent

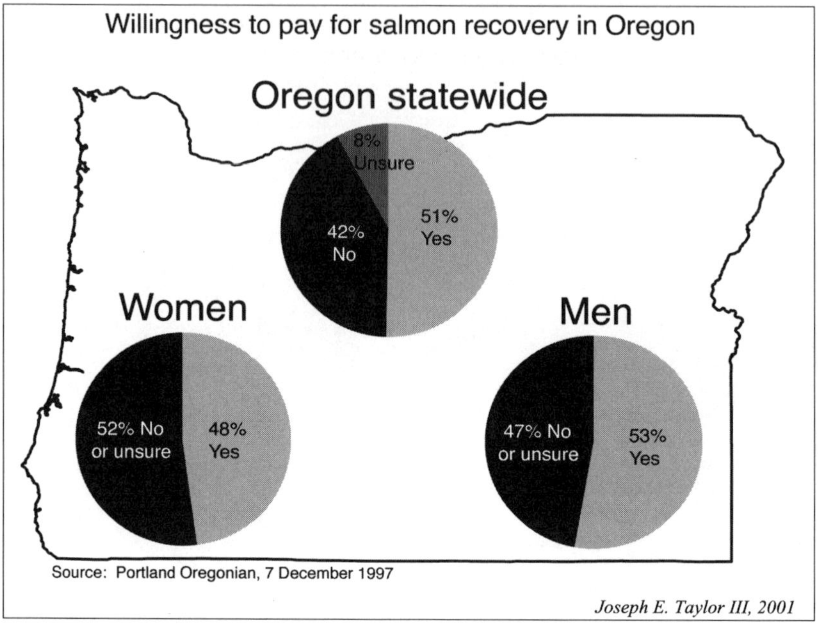

Figure 5

from their list of favored culprits. Rural and eastside residents were also less persuaded that salmon runs were in danger than residents of Portland and Seattle, and they were more willing to heap blame on natural factors such as ocean and atmospheric climate. Yet notice: despite their differences, eastside and westside residents shared the habit of indicting outsiders. This produced the rather silly result that everyone was implicated even though no one admitted responsibility. Blame was spread over the entire map, yet no consensual understanding followed.[9]

Regional generalizations masked these variations, but they exposed one politically salient detail about resource politics. Although urbanites inhabit only a small fraction of Idaho, Oregon, and Washington, they were a plurality in these states by 1900 and a majority by 1930. Moreover, most urbanites lived west of the mountains, and by 1990 over 70 percent of the population lived within fifty miles of Interstate 5 as it ran from Everett, Washington, to Medford, Oregon. By sheer numbers these urbanites dominated salmon politics. As early as 1908, Portland and Willamette Valley residents forever reshaped salmon policy by briefly outlawing all fishing on the Columbia River. Seattle and Tacoma residents achieved a similar coup on the Puget Sound in 1934. Over time urban voters and legislators imposed additional measures that further limited industrial and Indian fishing, and they increasingly insisted on managing not only fish but other natural resources

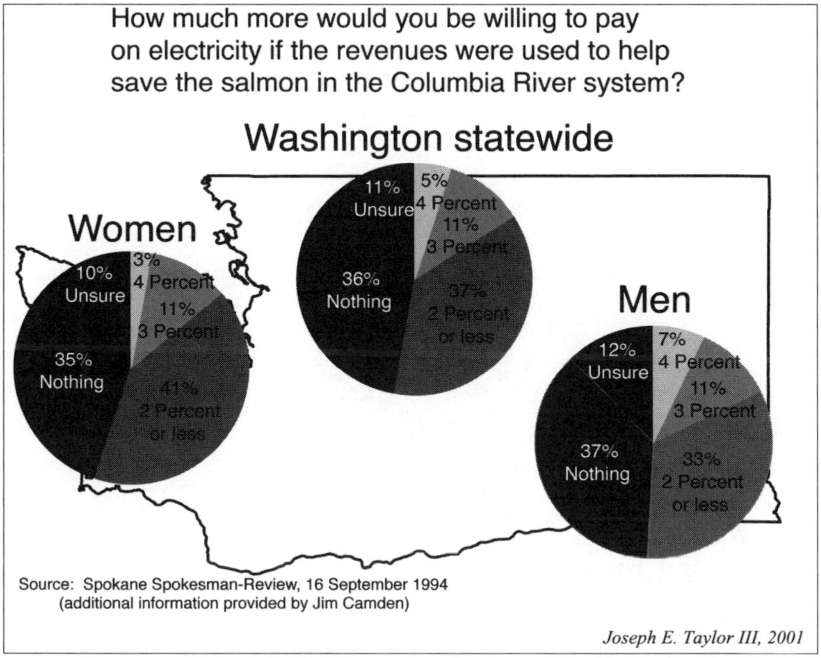

Figure 6

for the benefit of Portlanders and Seattleites. The westside urban perspective might have been spatially constrained, but it possessed tremendous political portent.[10]

This east-west divide was only the opening wedge into claims about regional symbolism in the 1990s. Public opinion polls also exposed nuances about culture and salmon that strengthened some trends but complicated others. When the *Oregonian* asked respondents about paying for salmon recovery, the elderly (52 percent), poor (50 percent), and least educated (54 percent) were least willing. The findings also suggested that divisions between east and west were complicated by differences between urban and rural and between men and women. Whereas 42 percent of urbanites favored dam removal, only 32 percent of ruralites felt similarly, regardless of whether they lived west or east of the Cascades. In addition, more Oregon men than women (Figure 5) were willing to pay for recovery programs (53 percent to 48 percent) and to breach dams (44 percent to 32 percent). In Washington and Idaho, though, some of these trends reversed. The strongest opposition to breaching in Idaho came not from rural residents but from the most urbanized population around Boise, which depended on electricity from dams that would have been affected by recovery efforts. Oregonians' gendered reactions also flip-flopped. In Washington (Figure 6) more women than men supported

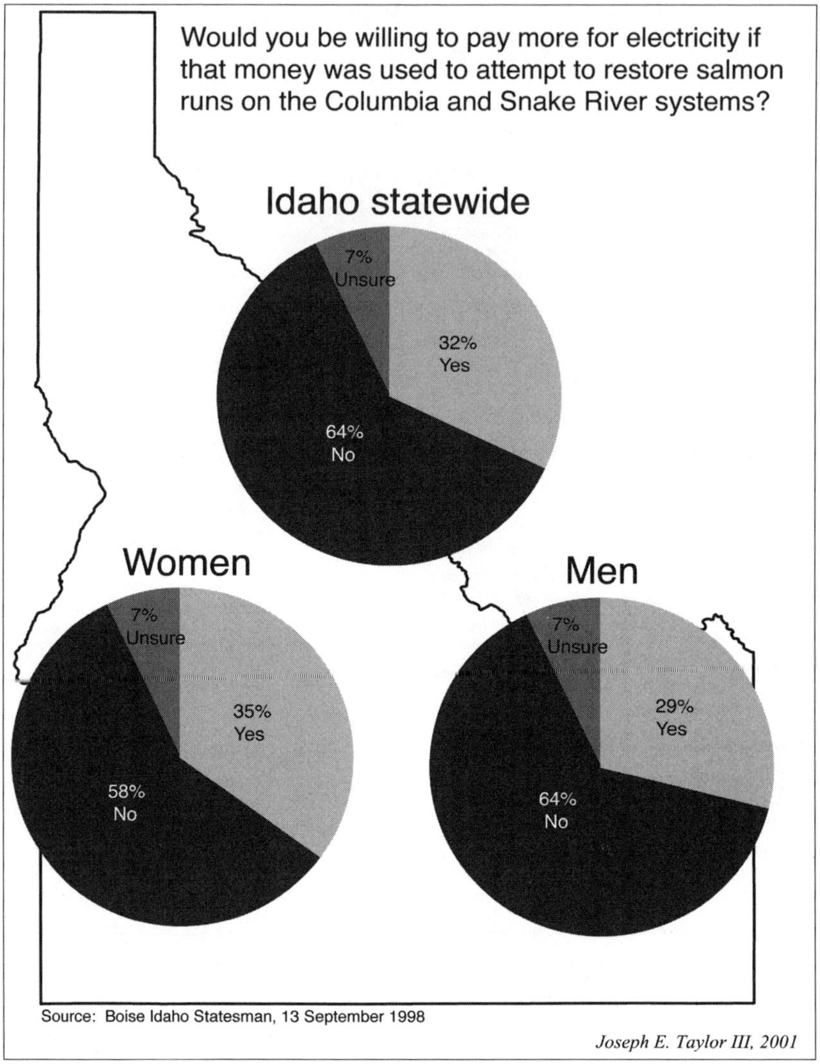

Figure 7

higher electric rates to help salmon recovery, and in Idaho women were more favorable to rate increases (35 percent to 29 percent) (Figure 7) and less opposed to breaching (46 percent to 54 percent) (Figure 8) than men.[11]

Thus questions about fish merged with questions about people, but we should not be surprised that ecology and culture were hopelessly entangled. Scholars regularly note the many ways that cultures divide according to identity and location. Class, race, and gender have long shaped how people interact with the world, and location roots people in particular perspectives. Even the way humans work and play create discrete knowledges of society and na-

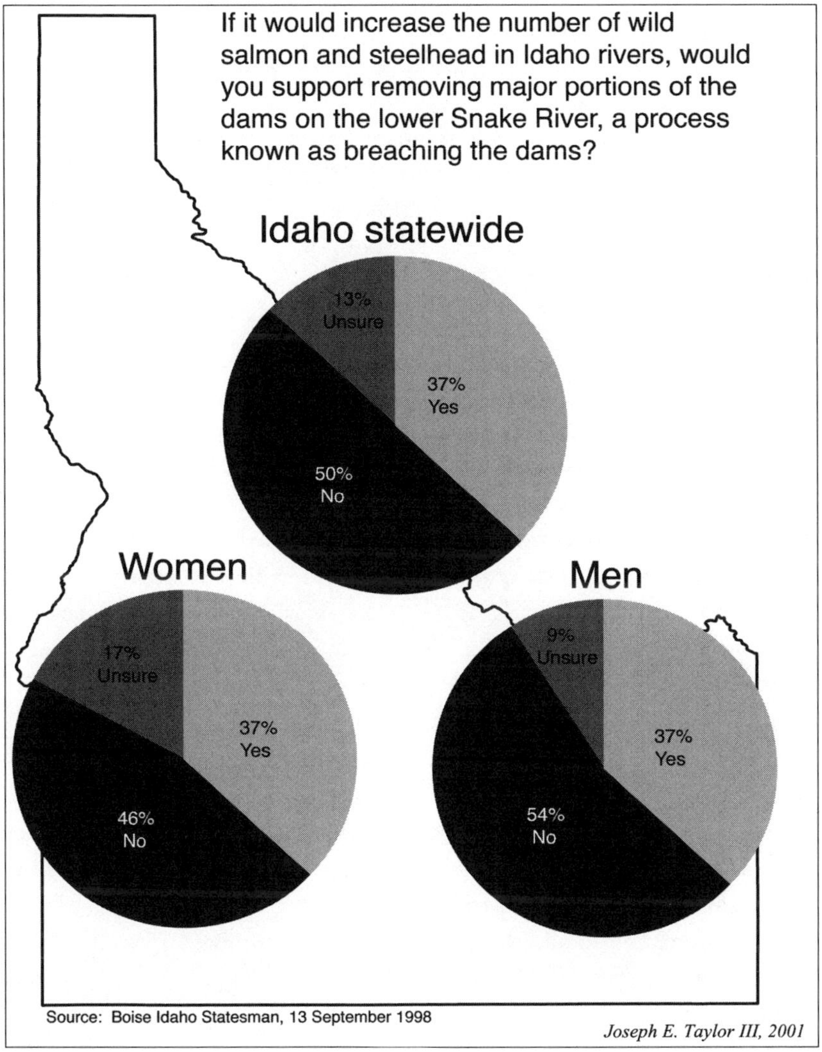

Figure 8

ture. As social conditions mix with individual circumstances, the general and the particular come into tension. There are cultures within cultures, and although drawing lines on maps or between people can help us perceive those divisions, the lines do not explain themselves. For that we have to shift from geography and sociology back to history. For example, opinion polls showed that residents of Seattle, Portland, and the Willamette Valley were consistently more committed to salmon recovery in general and to altering dams in particular than anybody else in the region. What polls could not explain, though, was why this was so. Both support for and opposition to salmon recovery had in fact emerged from long-established relationships between humans and nature. Ultimately, it is history that helps us clarify the human conflicts surrounding salmon.[12]

Perhaps the best way to understand northwesterners' contested relations with salmon is to begin with fish advocates. People cared about salmon for many reasons, but advocacy has historically been shaped more by the interests of fishers than by any other group. Aboriginal and industrial fishers have always expressed concerns about sustaining salmon runs, but in the twentieth century sportfishers were far more influential in shaping salmon politics, especially in cities. Sportfishing was primarily an urban, male, middle-to-upper-class pursuit, and although women participated in increasing numbers after World War II, the stereotypical male angler still prevailed and coveted no fish more than chinook and steelhead salmon, especially if he lived west of the Cascades. For these northwesterners, angling offered a contrapuntal balance to urban life, even when conducted in the shadow of downtown skyscrapers. Westside sportfishers cherished salmon with a passion unmatched by anyone except Indians, and anglers were most adamant and effective in defending their access to fish. As Richard White notes, "Salmon are not so much a means of making a good living as symbols of the good life itself." When salmon advocates insisted that "we need to run the river more like a natural river" or that salmon were an "invaluable indicator of a healthy environment and . . . business climate," they revealed a convergence of cultural and economic assumptions that occurred primarily in westside cities. Throughout the 1990s the urban, gendered, classist face of salmonophilia continued to resonate the values of the westside angling heritage.[13]

In defense of this good life, salmon advocates promoted a variety of self-serving solutions. Urbanites used federal and state funds to restore neighborhood creeks in Seattle, Tacoma, and Portland. Anglers and Republican candidates proposed legislation to end net fishing. Environmental groups and the Seattle City Council endorsed tearing down dams on the Snake River. In each case advocates faced minimal local opposition because the fiscal and cultural costs of their proposals were largely borne by distant governments and nonlocal interests. This could change as a result of recent Endangered Species Act listings on runs that travel through Portland and Puget Sound waters, but urbanites understood that this might also redound to them in higher standards of living, better water quality, and increased property values. Even extreme measures such as breaching dams were less controversial on the westside because few locals depended on any particular dam for their livelihood. This insularity allowed salmon advocates to predict damless futures and regional economic benefits from recreation without anxiety.[14]

Such strategies fostered a constrained form of consensus west of the Cascades, but other issues eroded comity. Despite reams of evidence casting doubt on the impact of hatcheries and predator control, most fishers remained firmly dedicated to artificial propagation and the "management" of pinniped and tern populations. Urban environmentalists opposed these policies, but they too created tensions by purchasing pen-raised Atlantic salmon, which were rapidly displacing Pacific salmon in grocery stores and fish markets. In so doing, urban consumers were also displacing commercial fishers, who were a critical constituency for Pacific salmon. In the end, though, these tensions were minor compared with the fundamental differences over salmon restoration that emanated from elsewhere within the Pacific Northwest.[15]

Outside the urban westside, history and biology discouraged sympathy for salmon. Polls showed that eastside residents were less familiar with salmon issues and less credulous that runs were declining or that dams were responsible. Such findings simply confirmed what historians have known for some time: the inland Northwest is a very different place from the westside.[16] Residents of the arid eastside regarded water as economic lifeblood and were dependent on the very things westside residents criticized. As a result, they conceptualized the landscape very differently than salmon advocates. As Blaine Harden noted, although irrigators studied rivers intensely, they rarely cared about the things that lived in the waters and they readily admitted their ignorance of even basic facts about salmon biology. When Harden questioned his father, a man who had lived his entire adult life near the Columbia, Arno Harden confessed that he "knew next to nothing about salmon." Arno had migrated to eastern Washington during the depression to work on Grand Coulee Dam and then stayed to build a farm and family on the newly irrigated lands near Moses Lake, Washington. His first encounter with salmon happened on the banks of the Columbia near Wenatchee, Washington. Arno saw something flopping in the water and went to investigate. He drew close and saw a huge chinook that "scared the hell out of me. . . . Never seen anything like it. Nobody talked about fish then. I never seen anybody fishing."[17]

Although salmon advocates deplored such ignorance, Harden's experiences represented a rather pervasive and long-standing relationship among humans, water, and fish in the inland Northwest. Plateau Indians fished intensively for salmon for millennia, yet few of them attributed much spiritual significance to salmon. This disparity between material exploitation and spiritual regard contrasted sharply with downstream Indians. Groups who lived and fished west of the eastern edge of the Cascades observed the First Salmon Ceremony—a celebration of the return of spring salmon involving whole villages, elaborate rituals, and restrained fishing—but no group upstream from

Celilo Falls shared this practice. In fact, an inverse relationship seemed to exist in the aboriginal world between the length of salmon migrations and the cultural importance of these fish: the farther upstream a salmon swam, the less likely it carried much spiritual power for Indians. Although no cultural genealogy existed between Arno Harden and Plateau Indians, their shared ambivalence begs explanation.[18]

The answer lies in the bodies of salmon. When Euro-Americans resettled the inland Northwest, they discovered a basic biological fact that Indians already knew but modern observers too often neglected. Though salmon depended on inland streams, they were not particularly useful for the people who lived near those places. Exhausted from living off their bodies during the long inland journeys, salmon were ugly, wasted, and nutritionally worthless by the time they arrived at their spawning grounds. Plateau Indians compensated by relying far more than downstream Indians on deer, elk, bear, and bison. Euro-Americans compensated for the perceived deficiencies of Plateau nature in a different way. Discouraged by the physical limitations of salmon and their poor game qualities, inland settlers tried to replace salmon with exotic species such as bass, perch, crappies, and walleye. When transplanted fish thrived, eastside anglers celebrated the reorganized fishery, and when mainstem dams impounded inland reaches of the Columbia and Snake, exotic fish expanded their ranges throughout the Plateau. Alien fish turned out to be more nutritious, better-adapted, and more challenging prey than salmon, and many eastsiders regarded these fish as more legitimate than native species.[19]

Culturally and materially, this new landscape made sense—only salmon advocacy seemed insane. After more than a century of successful adaptation, eastside residents regarded criticism of their landscape as attacks on their way of life. Salmon advocates were "fish terrorists" and "salmon extremists," and local anglers criticized the Oregon Fish and Wildlife Department's native fish policy as "fish snobbery." This attitude partly explained why gendered reactions to salmon recovery inverted on the Plateau. Eastside male anglers had sworn loyalty to different species. The same went for residents with vested interests in the harnessed river. In 1951 a Pasco, Washington, newspaper called efforts to halt dam building on the lower Snake an "age-old conflict between power and play." The paper reasoned that if "full-scale industrial development is desired, it must be realized that civilization and the primitive are not compatible and some sacrifice of natural resources must be expected." More recently, a Grand Coulee innkeeper said he did not "give a good goddamn about salmon," and a Wamic, Oregon, farmer and barge worker insisted that "the biggest mistake [the federal government] made was putting fish ladders in at Bonneville Dam."[20]

By the late 1990s these cultural and economic conflicts had thoroughly infused recovery politics because the policy of dam breaching seemed increasingly plausible. The Moses Lake and Whitman County Councils declared political warfare on the Seattle City Council after the latter endorsed the idea of breaching four lower Snake River dams. Knowing nothing about salmon did not stop Republican presidential candidate George W. Bush from arguing, "We do not need to breach the dams to save the salmon. Should I become the next president, we won't." And U.S. senator Slade Gorton of Washington, who had previously declared that there was "a cost above which, regrettably, you let species disappear," insisted that it was "time to take dam breaching off the table, lock stock and barrel, once and for all." In water-hungry eastern Oregon, Washington, and Idaho, this was smart politics because salmon had become not a sign of the good life but a threat to it. These northwesterners adamantly opposed even studying the feasibility of breaching dams. If they supported recovery efforts at any level, it was by intensifying such technological responses as barging fish around dams, refining fish passage at dams, or fabricating artificial conduits to flush juvenile fish downstream. East of the Cascades, salmon seemed an anachronism from a preindustrial landscape—it no longer fit.[21]

The contrasts of residency and gender revealed how location and identity shaped people's assessments of salmon, but tenure also played a surprising role. As historian John Findlay noted, the "notion of the Pacific Northwest has been cultivated best by outsiders." Since the 1840s, settlers, railroads, and governments repeatedly redefined the far northwest corner of the United States to enhance their political and economic agendas, and popular ideas about the region were often imposed by nonresidents or recent émigrés. This was equally true of salmon symbolism in the 1990s. With the exception of Indians, the greatest support for salmon came from those who had lived in the region the shortest periods. One poll showed that 58 percent of those most willing to pay for salmon recovery had lived in the region ten years or less, while 93 percent of those aged eighteen to thirty-four favored increased spending for salmon. By contrast, 52 percent of those least willing to pay were aged sixty-three years or older, and 47 percent had lived in the Northwest twenty-one years or longer. Strange as it seemed, salmonophilia was inversely proportional to rootedness. Symbolic affectations paradoxically support Findlay's arguments about alien-imposed constructions of regional identity. For an increasing percentage of northwesterners, salmon was not so much a birthright as an emblem of belonging that was zealously adopted or purchased by those with the least local history.[22]

It is tempting to view correlations of tenure and attitudes and conclude that support for salmon recovery stemmed from regional ignorance, but this charge applied to all parties. More important, the opposite also held true. Advocates on all sides also expressed strong preferences that reflected their intimate knowledge of particular locations and activities. Even recent émigrés were not as ignorant as they appeared. Most had arrived already fully stocked with expectations about what the "real" Pacific Northwest was like because popular media (nature and fishing programs, tourism brochures, corporate recruiting videos) increasingly made explicit claims that salmon were an intrinsic part of the environment and regional culture. Trying to sort among these impressions for hierarchies of legitimacy can obscure the region's complicated environmental politics. There existed within the Pacific Northwest not one or two but many different interpretations of The Good Earth and The Good Life, and each depended on an organization of nature that was in some ways inimical to other relationships.[23]

These tensions were apparent in discussions about the salmon crisis, but weird things happened when people spoke: the unseen became visible and the seen invisible in telling ways. Although humans rarely saw fish in streams, salmon became palpable figures when advocates talked about how rivers *should* work. Listen to Roy Hemmingway describe the spawning ordeal of spring chinook salmon:

> Having swum through thousands of miles of ocean and struggled upstream in fresh water for sometimes hundreds of miles, this most driven of animals reaches the river of its birth. Then it stops, and waits. It finds a deep hole or a spring-fed pool in the stream where cool water remains throughout the heat of summer. Against the slight current in these holes, the salmon swims slowly in place. For months at a time, the fish is still, rarely moving more than a few feet from this chosen place, conserving energy. One can see them crowded together in these holes, their dark gray backs parallel to the current, like a flight of zeppelins, until a disturbance, a shadow, spooks them into dispersal, only to return within minutes one-by-one to their vigil.[24]

This was compelling writing, but it was not literally accurate. A true "deep hole" was too dark to allow one to see the fish, yet salmon's bodies became such critical components of freer-flowing streams that the author made readers see. Other residents performed similar feats of selective vision. Fishers focused on the vulnerable salmon while verbally deracinating rivers of predator species such as seals and terns. Inlanders dwelled on the way harnessed rivers produced cheap electricity, crops, and shipping but ignored the way dams battered fish and flooded spawning beds. Each northwesterner mentally integrated some things not literally perceived (salmon and electricity) while omitting other things readily seen (dams, lakes, birds, seals, working people). What made this even more remarkable was how all referred to the same streams yet cast those waters in strikingly different form and function.[25]

This process of imaging environments was analogous to that of landscape painting. In each case seeing occurred as much in the mind as in the eye, but as philosopher Arnold Berleant explains, what people perceived was never "a purely personal experience . . . but a social one. In engaging aesthetically with environment as with art, the knowledge, beliefs, opinions, and attitudes we have are largely social, cultural and historical in origin. These direct our attention, open or close us to what is happening, and prepare or impede our participation." "The personal," he insists, "is infused with the social." Although northwestern visions of nature were rooted in specific contexts, the dialectic between material nature and cultural meanings transcended time and place. Both salmon advocates and dam proponents conceptualized their ideal environments through an intellectual process that differed little from that of the Romans or eighteenth-century landscape painters. In each case, viewers created a selective impression of nature—by discriminating between what should and should not have been there—that only partially corresponded to what the eye actually saw. In sorting through these visions of salmon and rivers, we encounter depictions of nature that were thoroughly humanized. The discourse surrounding the 1990s salmon crisis was essentially a contest over which rival landscapes should prevail.[26]

In the 1990s public responses to the salmon crisis dramatically qualified the cultural importance of the fish for northwesterners. Salmon were not the tie that binds. They may have been fun to catch and good to eat, but they were hardly transcendent symbols when so many residents turned their backs to one level or another. Moreover, as contestants talked past one another, they revealed that there was no such thing as a homogeneous regional culture. In everyday life there was not one Northwest but many Northwests—not one region but many places—and residents of each place valued their environment in remarkably different ways. The salmon crisis brought people together after a fashion, but their contests were hardly evidence of regional agreement about symbols. Battles about material claims to land, water, and electricity also pitted neighbor against neighbor over rival cultural landscapes.

This lack of consensus highlights a modern paradox about salmon, symbols, and regions. As much as any species, Pacific salmon mapped a coherent natural region. Their genetically coded movements through lakes, rivers, and oceans inscribed spaces that humans long ago learned to exploit. This part of the regional argument was undeniable, but shifting from biological regions to cultural regions created a geographical slippage that exposed a historical problem: culture was never conterminous with salmon's movements. Valuation persisted contentiously only in those cities, towns, and reservations where people still pursued salmon as a way of life or where economies were not threatened by its presence. The paradox of salmon is that they limned a natural space even as they revealed their economic and cultural irrelevance over much of it. When salmon advocates began to invoke symbolism and insisted that their concerns were—or should have been—universal, they unintentionally exposed the region's underlying social and cultural fissures.

The battles that erupted around salmon were hardly unique to fish or the Northwest because no environmental struggle has ever been simply about nature. Debates about salmon recovery pitted human relations with specific landscapes against human relations with rival landscapes. Thus the resulting contests were as much about the future of competing economic and cultural activities as over nature per se. In this vein the political dynamics of salmon cast light on similar wars over public ranges and forests, state and national parks, and wilderness areas around the West. In each case groups have fought tooth and nail over their vested interests in nature, all of which have deep and tangled roots. An analysis of how material and cultural factors have shaped public attitudes about nature in these debates could offer a more nuanced way to understand environmental conflicts than vague assertions about the symbolic importance of nature. Such studies can also help remind scholars and the public that the *New West* is neither quite so new nor separate from that older West that still supplies much of the urban West's food, materials, and power. The Pacific Northwest is thus a microcosm of the modern West. As a region, it is certainly culturally and socially fragmented, yet urban and rural are not worlds apart, nor can they afford to be, for each other's sake and for the sake of salmon.[27]

Although essentialist claims die hard deaths, salmonophiles, and in fact all environmentalists, would be wise to revisit their assumptions about cultural affinities for salmon. Intraregional divisions are real, and residents have fought over these differences for decades. Conciliation will not come easily, yet there is hope for both people and nature. Despite their differences, most northwesterners recognize their interdependence and the fact that the economies of west and east and urban and rural need each other to prosper. They also know that salmon recovery requires broad cooperation. This is a hopeful sign, one that advocates would be wise to pursue. Social and economic interdependency is a more broadly recognizable theme than the dead horse of symbolism. The rhetoric of mutuality is far more likely to generate sympathy than telling people what they ought to feel, and social equity is a far stronger foundation for cooperation than value-laden claims.[28]

It may be appropriate, in other words, to reemphasize progressive-era concerns for social equity in natural resource politics. Americans severed equity from conservation in the 1920s, and it has been sorely missed ever since. Prioritizing claims polarized environmental debates, and notice what resulted: more American nature is officially listed as endangered than at any time since the advent of environmentalism, and the principal means for protecting vulnerable landscapes—the Endangered Species Act—is weaker and more threatened than at any time since its passage in 1973. Continued polarization is a sure ticket to political stalemate and ecological failure. A new politics is in order, and cooperation will be critical for the success of any recovery plan. Cooperation will happen, however, only when participants begin to acknowledge the legitimacy and parity of all interests. The salmon crisis is just one of many environmental problems Americans face, but its history can tell us much about broader directions we should heed or reject. One of the primary lessons of the salmon crisis is the importance of limits—limits of exploitation for certain but also limits of aesthetics. Salmon is not a unifying symbol of nature, and culture cannot be the sole basis for restoring this or perhaps any species.[29]

NOTES

I want to thank Ross Anderson, Rocky Barker, Jonathon Brinkman, Jim Camden, John Findlay, Matt Klingle, and Richard White for their help in preparing this essay.

1. Portland *Oregonian*, 30 November 1997, E5; 4 October 1998, G5; 16 March 1999, B9 ("overwhelmingly support"); *Seattle Times*, 25 February 1992, A1; 24 March 1999, B4; Blaine Harden, *A River Lost: The Life and Death of the Columbia* (New York: W. W. Norton, 1996), 18. For American regionalism, see Edward L. Ayers, Patricia Nelson Limerick, Stephen Nissenbaum, and Peter S. Onuf, *All Over the Map: Rethinking American Regions* (Baltimore: Johns Hopkins University Press, 1996); William G. Robbins, Robert J. Frank, and Richard E. Ross, eds., *Regionalism and the Pacific Northwest* (Corvallis: Oregon State University Press, 1983); and David M. Wrobel and Michael R. Steiner, eds., *Many Wests: Place, Culture, and Regional Identity* (Lawrence: University Press of Kansas, 1997).

2. *Oregonian*, 30 November 1997, E5; 4 October 1998, G5; *Seattle Times*, 25 February 1992, A1; 24 March 1999, B4.

3. The polls discussed in this essay were conducted by and for a variety of organizations, including newspapers, politicians, and government agencies; see *Oregonian*, 7 December 1997, A1; *Seattle Times*, 13 April 1998, B1; *Spokane Spokesman Review*, 16 September 1994, B1, B4; 13 October 1996, A1, A15; 13 September 1998, B8;

Boise Idaho Statesman, 13 September 1998, A22; Mark Brunson, Bruce Shindler, William D. Schreckhise, Brent S. Steel, and John R. Tennert, "Mail Survey of Natural Resource Issues on Public Lands in the West: Report Prepared for the Eastside Ecosystem Management Team," c. 1995, photocopy in author's possession, 29, 38; Peter D. Hart Research Associates, "Winning the Environmental Debate in Swing Districts," January 1999, copy in author's possession. The role of space in shaping human perspective has largely been the province of geographers, but as some scholars increasingly realize, the spatial and the temporal are often intrinsically related. See Anthony Giddens, *The Constitution of Society: Outline of the Theory of Structuration* (Berkeley: University of California Press, 1984), 363; Allan Pred, *Making Histories and Constructing Human Geographies: The Local Transformation of Practice, Power Relations, and Consciousness* (Boulder: Westview, 1990), 5; Edward W. Soja, *Postmodern Geographies: The Reassertion of Space in Critical Social Theory* (London: Verso, 1989), 10–11.

4. Timothy Egan, *The Good Rain: Across Time and Terrain in the Pacific Northwest* (New York: Knopf, 1990), 22; John Findlay, "A Fishy Proposition: Regional Identity in the Pacific Northwest," in *Many Wests*, ed. Wrobel and Steiner, 39; Kerr quoted in Cone, *A Common Fate: Endangered Salmon and the People of the Pacific Northwest* (Corvallis: Oregon State University Press, 1995), 71; Roy Hemmingway, "Salmon and the Northwest," *Open Spaces Quarterly* 1 (Winter 1997–98): 10; Stephen Ambrose, "Honor Lewis and Clark by Saving Rivers, Species," *Seattle Times*, 3 October 2000; "Salmon Forum Report—Keynote Speaker Ginny C.," www.riverdale.k12.or.us/~ginnyc/salmon/htm; Siuslaw Institute of Watershed Arts and Science, "Coho Salmon and Corporate Opportunity," http://www.oregonplan.org/CEG.html#Sundstrom; Tom Jay, "Homecoming," in *Reaching Home: Pacific Salmon, Pacific People*, ed. Natalie Fobes, Tom Jay, and Brad Matsen (Seattle: Alaska Northwest, 1994), 125.

5. *Oregonian*, 7 December 1997, A1; Rocky Barker, phone conversation with author, February 1999; Howard H. Martin, "Fisheries of the North Pacific," in *The Pacific Northwest*, 2d ed., ed. Otis W. Freeman and Howard H. Martin (New York: John Wiley and Sons, 1954), 179; Richard White, *The Organic Machine: The Remaking of the Columbia River* (New York: Hill and Wang, 1995), 90; William G. Robbins, *Landscapes of Promise: The Oregon Story, 1800–1940* (Seattle: University of Washington Press, 1997), 305.

6. *Oregonian*, 7 December 1997, A1; *Seattle Times*, 13 April 1998, B1; 20 September 2000, A1; *Spokane Spokesman Review*, 16 September 1994, B1, B4; 13 October 1996, A1, A15.

7. *Seattle Times*, 25 February 1992, A1; 18 August 1996, B5; 27 April 1997, B7. For Indian concerns, see for example an advertisement by the Confederated Tribes of the Umatilla Indian Reservation in the *Oregonian*, 16 November 1997, E6. Another measure of how shallow and problematic regional salmonophilia may be comes from three works on Pacific Northwest regionalism published during the last three decades: Edwin R. Bingham and Glen A. Love, eds., *Northwest Perspectives:*

Essays on the Culture of the Pacific Northwest (Seattle: University of Washington Press, 1979); Robbins et al., *Regionalism and the Pacific Northwest*; and Paul W. Hirt, ed., *Terra Pacifica: People and Place in the Northwest States and Western Canada* (Pullman: Washington State University Press, 1998). Not one of these volumes features salmon as a central element of understanding regional identity or lists salmon or even fishing in its index.

8. Brunson et al., "Mail Survey," 29, 38; *Oregonian*, 7 December 1997, A1; Boise *Idaho Statesman*, 13 September 1998, A22; *Spokane Spokesman Review*, 13 September 1998, B8.

9. Brunson et al., "Mail Survey," 27–29; *Oregonian*, 7 December 1997, A1; Peter D. Hart Research Associates, "Winning the Environmental Debate."

10. For urbanization, see Earl Pomeroy, *The Pacific Slope: A History of California, Oregon, Washington, Idaho, Utah, and Nevada* (Seattle: University of Washington Press, 1965), 6, 150–51, 193, 372–73; Carlos A. Schwantes, *The Pacific Northwest: An Interpretive History* (Lincoln: University of Nebraska Press, 1989), 4; Harden, *River Lost*, 41. For salmon politics, see Joseph E. Taylor III, "'Politics Is at the Bottom of the Whole Thing': Spatial Relations of Power in Oregon Salmon Management," in *Power and Place in the North American West*, ed. Richard White and John Findlay (Seattle: University of Washington Press, 1999), 233–63; and Taylor, "El Niño and Vanishing Salmon: Culture, Nature, History, and the Politics of Blame," *Western Historical Quarterly* 29 (Winter 1998): 448–57. For urban resource politics, see Carl Abbott, Sy Adler, and Margery Post Abbott, *Planning a New West: The Columbia River Gorge National Scenic Area* (Corvallis: Oregon State University Press, 1997). Since 1990 there have been a number of voter initiatives sponsored by urban environmentalists to convert public forests and ranges into recreational spaces for urban visitors.

11. *Oregonian*, 7 December 1997, A1; *Spokane Spokesman Review*, 16 September 1994; *Idaho Statesman*, 13 September 1998.

12. This discussion draws on many works, among the most influential of which are Denis E. Cosgrove, *Social Formation and Symbolic Landscape* (London: Croom Helm, 1984); Michel Foucault, "Questions on Geography," in *Power/Knowledge: Selected Interviews and Other Writings, 1972–1977*, ed. Colin Gordon, trans. Colin Gordon, Leo Marshall, John Mepham, and Kate Soper (New York: Pantheon, 1980), 62–77; Brian Goodey, "Spotting, Squatting, Sitting, or Setting: Some Public Images of Landscape," in *Landscape Meanings and Values*, ed. Edmund C. Penning-Rowsell and David Lowenthal (London: Allen and Unwin, 1986), 82–99; Donna Haraway, "Situated Knowledges: The Science Question in Feminism as a Site of Discourse on the Privilege of Partial Perspective," *Feminist Studies* 14 (1988): 575–99; Doreen Massey, *Space, Place, and Gender* (Minneapolis: University of Minnesota Press, 1994); Richard White, "'Are You an Environmentalist or Do You Work for a Living?' Work and Nature," in *Uncommon Ground: Rethinking the Human Place in Nature*, ed. William Cronon (New York: W. W. Norton, 1995), 171–85; Michael E. Soulé and Gary Lease, eds., *Reinventing Nature? Responses to Postmodern Deconstruction* (Washington, D.C.: Island Press, 1995).

13. John F. Reiger, *American Sportsmen and the Origins of Conservation*, rev. ed. (Norman: University of Oklahoma Press, 1986); Colleen J. Sheehy, "American Angling: The Rise of Urbanism and the Romance of the Rod and Reel," in *Hard at Play: Leisure in America, 1840–1940*, ed. Kathryn Grover (Amherst: University of Massachusetts Press, 1992), 78–92; Lisa Mighetto, "Sport Fishing on the Columbia River," *Pacific Northwest Quarterly* 87 (Winter 1995–96): 5–15; Barbara Schrodt, "'Taking the Tram': Traveling to Sport and Recreation Activities on Greater Vancouver's Interurban Railway—1890s to 1920s," *Canadian Journal of History of Sport* 19 (May 1988): 52–62; Joseph E. Taylor III, *Making Salmon: An Environmental History of the Northwest Fisheries Crisis* (Seattle: University of Washington Press, 1999), chap. 6; White, *Organic Machine*, 92; *Seattle Times*, 18 August 1996, B5 ("business climate"); 27 April 1997, B7 ("natural river"); Robert Sullivan, "For Northwest, This New War Will Be Harder," *Oregonian*, 22 March 1999, E7.

14. For habitat restoration, see *Seattle Times*, 2 October 1988, B3; 18 August 1996, B5; 13 September 1996, B3; 24 September 1998, B1; 14 October 1998, B8; *Oregonian*, 3 February 1999, B2; 25 February 1999, D1; Taylor, *Making Salmon*, chap. 9. For anti-net campaigns, see *Oregonian*, 1 November 1992, B6; 16 February 1998, D10; *Seattle Times*, 26 October 1999; 8 September 2000; 14 September 2000. For anti-dams, see *Oregonian*, 15 November 1998, B4; 16 November 1998, B10; 20 November 1998, B4; 4 December 1998, C12; 29 January 1999, C8; *Idaho Statesman*, 22 January 1998, 6B; 20, 21, and 22 July 1998; *Seattle Times*, 7 September 2000; *Spokane Spokesman Review*, 22 September 2000. For breached dam images, see Monte Dolack, "Resurrection," 1998, distributed by Idaho Rivers United, Boise; and Oregon Natural Resource Council, "How Will We Save Snake River Salmon?" *Oregonian*, 15 September 1998, B5. For economic benefits, see *Oregonian*, 8 March 1999, B1, B4; Ed Whitelaw, "Breaching Dam Myths: Measuring the Real Costs and Benefits of Breaching Four Dams on the Lower Snake River," *Oregon Quarterly* (Autumn 2000): 16–20; for a critique of recreational economies, see Hal K. Rothman, *Devil's Bargains: Tourism in the Twentieth-Century American West* (Lawrence: University Press of Kansas, 1998).

15. For pro-hatcheries, see *Oregonian*, 11 December 1998, B12; 14 December 1998, B6; 3 February 1999, B12. For anti-predators, see *Oregonian*, 16 November 1998, B10; 1 March 1999, E6. Although commercial and sportfishers seem to share a concern for salmon, rural fishers deeply resent urban fishers for their role in damaging habitat and driving commercial fishers from the water. As one gill netter wrote, "Failing on my own is one thing; failing because someone is destroying your business is another." Another fisher remarked bitterly, "I didn't abandon the fishery. It abandoned me. It's business as usual for everyone except for the gill-netter." *Seattle Times*, 11 February 1996, B1; Irene Martin, *Legacy and Testament: The Story of Columbia River Gillnetters* (Pullman: Washington State University Press, 1994).

16. Judith Austin, "Desert, Sagebrush, and the Pacific Northwest," in *Regionalism and the Pacific Northwest*, ed. Robbins et al., 129–47; Donald W. Meinig, *The Great Columbia Plain: A Historical Geography, 1805–1910* (Seattle: University of Washing-

ton Press, 1968), 3; Katherine G. Morrissey, *Mental Territories: Mapping the Inland Empire* (Ithaca: Cornell University Press, 1997); Carlos A. Schwantes, *The Pacific Northwest: An Interpretive History* (Lincoln: University of Nebraska Press, 1989), 1–14.

17. Brunson et al., "Mail Survey," 27; Harden, *River Lost*, 130, 140, 183–84.

18. Taylor, *Making Salmon*, chap. 1.

19. Harden, *River Lost*, 31; Taylor, *Making Salmon*, chaps. 6 and 7; *Seattle Times*, 20 October 1995, A1; *Oregonian*, 3 August 1998, B9.

20. Harden, *River Lost*, 18, 103, 206–7, 214, 217; *Pasco Columbia Basin News*, 28 February 1951, 2 (I am indebted to John Findlay and Bruce Hevly for this citation); *Oregonian*, 4 August 1997, B13; 3 August 1998, B9.

21. *Spokane Spokesman Review*, 13 September 1998, B8; 30 August 2000 ("off the table"); *Seattle Times*, 16 September 2000 ("next president"); 19 September 2000; *Oregonian*, 14 September 2000; 26 September 2000; Harden, *River Lost*, 237 ("species disappear"); White, *Organic Machine*, 90, 107–8.

22. Findlay, "Fishy Proposition," 44, 69 n. 60; *Oregonian*, 12 November 1996, A1, A6; 7 December 1997, A1. Northwesterners in general, and Oregonians in particular, are notoriously suspicious of outsiders, and newcomers sometimes embrace salmon as a way of becoming "in."

23. For salmon and regionalism, see Findlay, "Fishy Proposition," and White, *Organic Machine*; Joseph Cone and Sandy Ridlington, eds., *The Northwest Salmon Crisis: A Documentary History* (Corvallis: Oregon State University Press, 1996), 165. For theoretical discussions of perspective and place, see Haraway, "Situated Knowledges"; Michael M. Bell, "The Ghosts of Place," *Theory and Society* 26 (1997): 813–36; William Cronon, "A Place for Stories: Nature, History, and Narrative," *Journal of American History* 78 (March 1992): 1347–76; Yi-Fu Tuan, *Space and Place: The Perspective of Experience* (Minneapolis: University of Minnesota Press, 1977); Yi-Fu Tuan, *Topophilia: A Study of Environmental Perception, Attitudes, and Values* (Englewood Cliffs, N.J.: Prentice Hall, 1974); Frederick Turner, *Spirit of Place: The Making of an American Literary Landscape* (Washington, D.C.: Island Press, 1989).

24. Hemmingway, "Salmon and the Northwest," 8.

25. Robert B. Riley, "The Visible, the Visual, and the Vicarious: Questions about Vision, Landscape, and Experience," in *Understanding Ordinary Landscapes*, ed. Paul Groth and Todd W. Bressi (New Haven: Yale University Press, 1997), 200–209; Dell Upton, "Seen, Unseen, and Scene," in *Understanding Ordinary Landscapes*, ed. Groth and Bressi, 174–79.

26. Arnold Berleant, *Living in the Landscape: Toward an Aesthetics of Environment* (Lawrence: University Press of Kansas, 1997), 13 (quotations), and 9–24, 148–55 passim. Christopher C. Sellers guided me to Peter Gallison's usage of image metaphors in *Image and Logic: A Material Culture of Microphysics* (Chicago: University of Chicago Press, 1997). I am drawing my arguments from a number of sources that include Arnold Berleant, *The Aesthetics of Environment* (Philadelphia: Temple University Press, 1992), 1–24, and Henri Lefebvre, *The Production of Space*, trans.

Donald Nicholson-Smith (Cambridge, Mass.: Blackwell, 1991), 113–16. For landscapes, see John Barrell, *The Dark Side of the Landscape: The Rural Poor in English Painting, 1730–1840* (New York: Cambridge University Press, 1980), and Raymond Williams, *The Country and the City* (New York: Oxford University Press, 1973).

27. For "New West," see Neil Campbell, *The Cultures of the American New West* (Edinburgh: Edinburgh University Press, 2000); Peter R. Decker, *Old Fences, New Neighbors* (Tucson: University of Arizona Press, 1998); Tim Egan, *Lasso the Wind: Away to the New West* (New York: Knopf, 1998); Patricia Nelson Limerick, *Something in the Soil: Legacies and Reckonings in the New West* (New York: W. W. Norton, 2001); William E. Riebsame, ed., *Atlas of the New West: Portrait of a Changing Region* (New York: W. W. Norton, 1997); Sharman Apt Russell, *Kill the Cowboy: A Battle of Mythology in the New West* (Lincoln: University of Nebraska Press, 2001). For city and country, see William Cronon, *Nature's Metropolis: Chicago and the Great West* (New York: W. W. Norton, 1991); William Cronon, "Kennecott Journey: The Paths Out of Town," in *Under an Open Sky: Rethinking America's Past*, ed. William Cronon, George Miles, and Jay Gitlin (New York: W. W. Norton, 1992), 28–51.

28. A number of academics have critiqued environmentalists' obsession with pure landscapes: William Cronon, "The Trouble with Wilderness; or, Getting Back to the Wrong Nature," in *Uncommon Ground*, ed. Cronon, 61–90; William M. Denevan, "The Pristine Myth: The Landscape of the Americas in 1492," *Annals of the Association of American Geographers* 83 (September 1992): 369–85; and Michael Pollan, *Second Nature: A Gardener's Education* (New York: Atlantic Monthly Press, 1991). Some people involved in salmon recovery accept portions of the critiques about environmentalism, yet they tend to replace the desire for pristineness with a provincial faith in local wisdom; Mike Connelly, "Home Is Where They'll Lay Me Down," *Orion* 20 (Summer 2001): 15–25; Freeman House, *Totem Salmon: Life Lessons from Another Species* (Boston: Beacon Press, 1999); Jay, "Homecoming."

29. For intraregional economic ties, see Donald C. Meinig, *The Great Columbia Plain: A Historical Geography, 1805–1910* (Seattle: University of Washington Press, 1968), and Carl Abbott, "Regional and Network City: Portland and Seattle in the Twentieth Century," *Western Historical Quarterly* 23 (1992): 293–319. For the fate of equity in conservation, see Clayton R. Koppes, "Efficiency/Equity/Esthetics: Towards a Reinterpretation of American Conservation," *Environmental Review* 11 (Summer 1987): 127–46, and Joseph E. Taylor III, "'Well-Thinking Men and Women': The Battle for the White Act and the Meaning of Conservation in the 1920s," *Pacific Historical Review* 71 (August 2002): 356–87.

Karen Jones

"WAY OUT WEST . . . GHOST TOWNS, GRAY WOLVES, TERRITORIAL PRISONS & MORE!"

Celebrating the Wolf in the New West

The Internet site "Way Out West" celebrates the travels of Bill and his wife on their search for the true West. Photographs document how the couple took to the open road on a gleaming motorcycle, tearing up the asphalt of nine western states. Images of deserted mining towns and abandoned jails figure highly on the site, the gruesome teaser for the "prison gallery" enticing e-browsers to "come and see just how miserable life was in the turn-of-the-century Big Houses of the Territorial West." Pictures of captive wolf facilities in Colorado, Arizona, New Mexico, and Idaho also adorn "Way Out West," digital images capturing alert wolves gazing intently through chain-link fences. Alongside paeans to the life of freedom afforded by a dependable two-wheeled steed, Bill's web page clearly signposts the gray wolf as an enduring symbol of the American West. Canine howls resonate with the cries of luckless prospectors and tortured felons as appropriate refrains to the melodious growl of the motorcycle engine.[1]

In promoting *Canis lupus* as an icon of trans-Mississippi America, Bill ascribed to the ever-popular convention in western circles for mythologizing wild canines. Wolves have captivated the imaginations of generations of Americans, provoking extremes of hatred and adoration from vociferous travelers. In the nineteenth century Euro-American pioneers associated packs of wild canines and their "demonic howls" with the dangers of the savage frontier. Wolf eradication was even promoted as a prerequisite for material prosperity on the Great Plains. In the twentieth-century West the wolf became a symbol of wilderness recreation, the fate of the species connected with ideas of "peaceful coexistence" and ecological diversity. During the 1990s "wolf groupies" gathered seasonally to watch their idols in Yellowstone National Park. Over the span of two centuries images of the ninety-pound predator have been constantly refashioned to suit salient American cultural prerogatives. Attitudes toward the wolf have been invariably linked with perspectives on the winning (or indeed the losing) of the West. With the possible exception of the bison, no other animal has had such profound importance in both Old West and New West paradigms. William B. Mott, director of the National Park Service in the 1980s, pertinently labeled the wolf "not only a marvelous animal, but . . . a symbol of the West."[2] Clothed with multifarious identities, *Canis lupus* represents a totem animal of the changing western landscape.

THE WOLF AND THE OPENING OF THE OLD WEST

A revisit to the Old West reveals material landscapes and human cultures resounding with references to the wolf. Native American folktales cast the wolf as an integral part of western terrain, and the animal denoted an accomplished instructor and shrewd pathfinder. According to the Arikara of the Northern Plains, powerful spirits named Wolf Man and Lucky Man used soft mud from a lake bottom to sculpt the hills and prairies of present-day Missouri. Other stories related how obliging wolf guides accompanied lost travelers and assisted needy tribes. In the Blackfeet legend of the Friendly Medicine Wolf a young woman, disoriented after escaping from enemy captors, was escorted home by an amicable wolf. The tale celebrated how "whenever we are in danger, or distress, we pray to them [wolves] and they often help us."[3] *Canis lupus* signified a familiar, and familial, sight on the western prairie.

Arguably the first Euro-American tourists to penetrate western lands, Meriwether Lewis and William Clark fostered an image of the West as a territory of rolling hills, vast herds of bison, and roving wolves. Near the site of present-day Billings, Montana, Clark expressed a certain incredulousness in his account of faunal plenitude: "For me to mention or give an estimate of the different Species of wild animals on this river particularly Buffalow, Elk, Antelopes and Wolves would be incredible. I shall therefore be silent on the subject further."[4] Other nineteenth-century travelers nurtured similar visions of the West as a landscape teeming with canine vigor. In *The Emigrants' Guide to Oregon and California* (1845) esteemed travel writer Lansford W. Hastings noted how "wolves are very numerous in all portions of this section."[5] Although such reports invariably exaggerated the size of the wolf population (not least as a mechanism to bolster the reputation of the stalwart human narrator), the West was enshrined as the home of the wolf.

Euro-American travelers customarily dressed the wolf in abominable garb.

The proclivity of packs to lurk at the margins of campsites (lured by large and no doubt odoriferous caches of raw meat) was often construed as a threat. Camped at Calfee Creek (in present-day Yellowstone National Park) in 1869, explorer David Folsom was reminded by the sounds of wolves of his own vulnerability in nature: "As darkness approaches, the voice of the night breaks in upon the pervading stillness; the wolf scents us afar and the mournful cadence of his howl adds to our sense of solitude."[6] *Canis lupus* served as a symbol of an uncultivated and terrifying world beyond the frontiers of civilization. Chroniclers made frequent allusions to the "ravages" of wolves and were fixated on the wolf hunt as a carefully orchestrated and grisly execution of innocent herbivores. During his overland excursion to California in 1859 Horace Greeley, editor of the *New York Tribune*, derided the wolf as a "scoundrel . . . of imposing caliber" and betrayed astonishment at the "impudence of these prairie lawyers" in their relentless pursuit of the buffalo.[7] Travelers perceived wolves as audacious and immoral marauders who thrust their bloodied muzzles into the bellies of mortally wounded prey with gusto. In the minds of Euro-Americans the wolf was an archetypal wilderness animal, a brute creation "red in tooth and claw."

The most common reaction of Euro-Americans visiting this untamed, antediluvian West was to kill. The slaughter of wolves was rendered an acceptable, even recreational activity. Alexander Ross, who spent fifteen years working as a fur trader in the Columbia River drainage, explained how trappers idled away their leisure hours, as well as their working ones, killing wolves. Trapping parties scattered "bones or bits of meat on the ground as decoys" and took potshots at any animal hungry enough to take the bait.[8] Late-nineteenth-century tourists perceived the West as a grand arena for sporting endeavor, the abundance of faunal quarry marking the region as prime hunting terrain. The locomotive carrying Horace Greeley westward in 1859 frequently paused to allow hunters to raise their rifles at passing bison, and bullets rained down on wolves who dared come within range. Rocks and buffalo chips provided further ammunition.

Killing for sport or recreation blended easily into economic rationale in the Old West. Between 1860 and 1885 scores of trappers, footloose drifters, and seasonal workers tried their hand at "wolfing" on the Great Plains. Armed with $150 worth of strychnine and supplies, "wolfers" patrolled their own circuits, using poisoned bison meat as bait for local wolves. Enterprising individuals turned wolf killing into an economic boon and an accomplished art to boot, netting two to three thousand dollars for a winter's work.[9] According to Montana rancher Granville Stuart, writing in 1925, "It was a hard and perilous life led by these brave intrepid men but all the more attractive to them because of the dangers encountered."[10] The wolfer represented the archetypal western frontiersman pursuing prosperity, a rugged individualist working alone against the exigencies of a harsh environment and "antagonistic" natives. Between 1870 and 1877 an estimated fifty-five thousand wolf pelts were shipped annually from trading posts such as Fort Benton, Montana, and sold in eastern markets.[11]

The livestock raisers and homesteaders who settled the West from the 1870s onward judged *Canis lupus* according to the lexicon of material progress. The wolf was lambasted as a worthless varmint that threatened the western pioneering endeavor. In 1895 the Montana Bureau of Agriculture, Labor, and Industry warned that "many stock farmers were despondent on account of the great destruction of calves and colts by wild animals, especially wolves, and a number of large owners stated that unless these losses could be diminished, they would have to discontinue breeding cattle."[12] Beleaguered cattlemen grappling with bad weather, outbreaks of disease, and price fluctuations found in *Canis lupus* a tangible target on which to focus their angst. The wolf was demonized as an impediment to the creation of a profitable economy and a thriving western society. Trapper Ben Corbin, in *Corbin's Advice; or, The Wolf Hunter's Guide* (1900), summed up the attitudes of many westerners when he declared that "the wolf is the enemy of civilization, and I want to exterminate him."[13] Settlers galvanized to eradicate *Canis lupus* from local climes. By 1890 most states offered bounties on wolves, and stockmen worked vigorously to eliminate resident packs. As government wolf hunter Stanley Young noted, "There was a sort of unwritten law of the range that no cowman would knowingly pass by a carcass of any kind without inserting in it a goodly dose of strychnine, in the hope of killing one more wolf."[14]

The idea of community and camaraderie in the Old West appeared bound up with the process of wolf extermination. Theodore Roosevelt, who ranched in North Dakota during the late 1800s, reveled in hunting wolves as a social pastime, eagerly pursuing with horse and hounds the animal he labeled "the beast of waste and desolation."[15] National park planners, eager to craft paradises "for the benefit and enjoyment of the people," precluded *Canis lupus* from roaming western landscapes of recreation such as Yellowstone (1872) and Glacier (1910).[16] Meanwhile, organized wolf hunts represented convivial events in fledgling western towns, blithe residents unanimously committed to ridding the country of the "gray peril." Frontier myths grew up around recalcitrant foes. Westerners spun tales of supernatural wolves that destroyed hundreds of cattle and eluded even the most seasoned hunters. Animals known as Old Lefty, Snowdrift, and Three Toes became legendary characters in western popular culture, wily loners who, despite their survival skills, were doomed to fall before the march of national progress. After his eventual capture in October 1920 the Custer Wolf of South Dakota was lionized as "the master criminal of the animal world."[17] Wolves were memorialized as the faunal outlaws of the Old West, animals relentlessly pursued in order to fashion a desired landscape of Texas longhorns and fields of corn. This heady vision of pioneering progress—upstanding Americans overcoming arduous terrain, tenacious animals, and hostile natives in order to build a prosperous and virtuous nation—retained an evergreen allure in twentieth-century American society, as the Hollywood westerns of the 1930s and the 1940s nurtured the mythic Old West in celluloid guise.[18]

THE WOLF AND THE CREATION OF NEW WESTERN IDENTITY

The search for a New Western identity in the late twentieth century allowed scholars to point to a "new" West founded on inclusivity and benevolence, with ethnic minorities, women, and nature all allowed to contribute. The search also encouraged westerners to examine their past priorities and impulses. A solemn critique of Old Western narratives quickly became a hallmark of the New Western canon. The heady truisms of "winning the West" and "taming the wild" were rewritten according to the rubric of a malfeasant rather than a manifest destiny.[19] New Westerners rejected the old iconography of the frontier, of a Wild West of John Wayne, gunfighters, and gumption, in favor of a *Dances with Wolves* zeitgeist. Kevin Costner's West was an epic landscape under siege rather than in the making, with utopian communities of people and animals brutalized by the incursions of the U.S. Army. The wolf remained a symbol of wild, arcadian America, but the death of Costner's wolf Two Socks at the hands of carousing army officers was tragic rather than salutary.[20] In the New Western framework *Canis lupus* was the casualty of a rapacious pioneer ethic that transformed the American landscape. An Internet site named after the four-legged hero of *Dances with Wolves* contained the adage: "To look into the eyes of a wolf is to see your soul. Just be prepared for what you see."[21]

The fate of *Canis lupus* served as a poignant reminder of "white man's guilt," wolf eradication a moral fable about industrial society and its predatory attitude toward western lands. The romance surrounding cowmen and wolfers was tempered in the retelling of the western story. Commentators customarily pointed out how the pursuit of wild canines was marked by a fanatical zeal and extremes of cruelty. Hunters clubbed pups in their dens and hid razor blades in balls of fat so hapless animals bled to death. Scholars described the killing of *Canis lupus* as "an American pogrom" and "a final solution."[22] Secretary of the Interior Bruce Babbitt, himself a westerner, lamented how "our ancestors came to the New World prepared only to conquer."[23] The story of the "winning of the West" was replaced by an affirmative New Western narrative that emphasized themes of subjugation and ecological loss.

Marginalized groups in the twentieth-century West highlighted important parallels between their own experience and the treatment meted out to the much-maligned wolf. Native American writers hailed *Canis lupus* as a common victim of colonialism and the "white man's West." In *On Behalf of the Wolf and the First Peoples* (1995), Lakota writer Joseph Marshall III recalled a conversation with his grandfather, who told him that "they [wolves] were driven from their home . . . just like we were." "It was then that I began to learn that the wolf and I are brothers. That I am more like him than I ever imagined," he recounted.[24] Marshall aligned his people with the wolf as fellow endangered species, viewing the pack and the tribe as misunderstood yet complex communities arbitrarily controlled by modern American society. In the New Western vision, empathy with the wolf represented an act of cultural affirmation, discarding the negative stereotypes imposed on wolves and nonwhites by partisan pioneers. Identification with wolves involved a reassertion of indigenous cultural traditions, the proclaiming of a special connection with the four-legged residents of "Turtle Island" as an act of personal and ancestral pride. Hispanic communities engaged in a similar process of fraternal bonding with the Mexican wolf—with popular 1980s band Los Lobos naming itself after the canine that used to roam the desert Southwest.[25] The celebration of ethnic tradition and wolf lore also appealed to members of the white community. New Westerners seeking to nurture a mystical connection with the land espoused Native American Earth wisdom as their freshly adopted creed. New Agers embraced pantheism and shamanistic rituals as part of an alternative worldview, and Internet sites dedicated to *Canis lupus* frequently quoted Native American maxims or featured tribal art.[26] "Brother Wolf" was a sacred motif in the New West.

Feminist authors in the late twentieth century engaged in a similar exercise in empowerment, appropriating the wolf as a comparable victim of masculine supremacy and frontier violence. Sexism and the persecution of animals were identified as forms of prejudice based on the hierarchical classifications of an entrenched patriarchal society. In the Old West the explorer, the trapper, and the hunter were aggrandized as icons of vigor, courage, and strength. The white Anglo-Saxon male represented the western hero whereas women and wolves were defined as weak, cowardly "others." For ecofeminist geographer Jody Emel, the process of wolf eradication indicated “a dominant construction of masculinity that is predicated upon mastery and control through the hunt.” Emel instead empathized with “the wolf ‘bitches’ who had their dens robbed year after year so that bounty hunters could secure their incomes and identities.”[27] In the New West the wolf represented a powerful role model for female identity, freedom, and fulfillment. In *Women Who Run with the Wolves* (1992) philosopher Clarissa Pinkola Estes argued a need for women to rediscover their spiritual, untamed, and intuitive nature and avoid the “leg traps, cages, and poisoned bait” that historically ensnared wild wolves and wild women.[28] For Estes, learning to run with the wolf pack meant honing instincts and reclaiming inner wildness: “We are all filled with a longing for the wild. . . . We were taught to feel shame for such a desire. We grew our hair long and used it to hide our feelings. But the shadow of Wild Woman still lurks behind us during our days and in our nights. No matter where we are, the shadow that trots behind us is definitely four-footed.”[29]

The sweeping reevaluation of human-canine relations that became an integral part of New Western identity also drew inspiration from the popular environmental movement. The ecophilosophical tenets of modern environmentalism fueled a damning attack on the materialist priorities of the Old West, at the same time providing a blueprint for a New West based on an awareness of the destructive potential of humanity and a desire to protect biotic systems. A generation of Americans raised on *Silent Spring* (1962), Rachel Carson’s exposé of the insidious effects of widespread pesticide use, and *Never Cry Wolf* (1963), Farley Mowat’s roseate portrayal of wolf society, engaged in a heartfelt reassessment of human relations with the rest of the natural world.[30] Ecological science, dating back to the 1920s and 1930s, was instrumental in situating *Canis lupus* as an integral part of a healthy ecosystem. Aesthetic and ethical arguments meanwhile lauded the wolf as an elegant and rightful resident of the American West.[31] Frontier images of wolves as senseless killers were exposed as prevarications, and the story of the Three Little Pigs was rewritten to reveal the wolf as a hapless victim of media hype.[32] Notions of ecological conscience and the need for species coexistence resonated in New Western discourse. Conservationist Aldo Leopold emerged as the patron saint of this environmentally sensitive position, his *Sand County Almanac* (1949) acclaimed as a pioneering biocentric work promoting humility toward the earth. In the famous essay “Thinking Like a Mountain” Leopold described his own road-to-Damascus type of conversion after shooting a female wolf in the American Southwest: “We reached the old wolf in time to watch a fierce green fire dying in her eyes. I realized then, and have known ever since, that there was something new to me in those eyes—

something known only to her and to the mountain. I was young then, and full of trigger-itch; I thought that because fewer wolves meant more deer, that no wolves would mean hunters' paradise. But after seeing the green fire die, I sensed that neither the wolf nor the mountain agreed with such a view."[33] Leopold's epiphany in the White Mountains passed into the realms of environmental folklore. His exchange with the she-wolf appeared in numerous anthologies and was even reenacted as a modern-day ecological parable by the radical environmental group Earthfirst!

Appropriated by a series of different groups seeking to define their own identities, the wolf emerged as a potent mascot of the New West. Highlighting the persecution of wolves and other "minorities" linked with the mission of New Western scholars to reveal the multicultural history of the West, to listen to the voices of the displaced, and to delve beneath the singular narrative of white hegemony.[34] At the same time, the ecological mantra of the New Western agenda offered the wolf as an ideal symbol of biotic vitality.[35]

HOWLS AND MALLS IN THE NEW WESTERN LANDSCAPE

On the 1995-96 official highway map of Montana, Governor Marc Racicot and Theresa Racicot offered visitors a celebration of the beauties of their state: "In so many wondrous ways, Montana is what America used to be—148,000 square miles of vast plains, pure waters, snowy peaks, sprawling forests, rich resources, a staggering array of wildlife. Montana's good-natured, rugged individualists have built a fascinating history beneath these Big Skies. Whatever your recreational interests, you'll find them here in abundance as fresh and intriguing as our recent frontier."[36] The Treasure State was advertised as a veritable goldmine for leisure seekers, a museum landscape where tourists could indulge their favorite western fantasies. On the back of the map, photographs depicted a plethora of activities from trout fishing to whitewater rafting, mountain biking in Yellowstone to riding a bucking bronco at Wolf Point. The Montana map epitomized a New West of play and relaxation, a fantastical landscape of leisure. Whereas the Old West had idealized hard work and individualism on the frontier, modern visions emphasized the exchange between humans and the environment in terms of recreation. The West was construed as a vast wilderness playground that tired and disenchanted metropolitan Americans could visit or even resettle. In place of the frontier visions of Frederick Jackson Turner stood those of media mogul Ted Turner, whose 1.3-million-acre ranch near Bozeman supported bison and wolves rather than cattle and sheep. Rather than work the land, Ted Turner and his ilk wanted to restore the wildness that prior generations had sought to eliminate. The rugged mountains and undulating plains that characterized the West of old still denoted places of limitless opportunity, but for adventure-hungry urbanites with hiking books and sport-utility vehicles rather than prospectors and cowhands.

The wolf played an important part in visions of the New West as a recreational paradise. An ideal visit to "wild America" entailed catching a glimpse of a roving wolf loping effortlessly through the timber. The marked increase in wolf sightings in Glacier National Park, Montana, during the 1970s not only proved that Canadian wolves had decided to frequent the region but also indicated that visitors desperately wanted to spy the famous denizen of the wild. Thrilled vacationers eagerly imagined that any large canine they observed, whether feral dog or coyote, was a wolf. As wildlife biologist Mark Kaley noted, "Due to the popularity of the wolf issue people are more likely to label an unidentified animal as a 'wolf.'"[37] *Canis lupus* possessed an army of supporters with a fervent desire to track the return of wolves to westerly haunts. According to Wisconsin wildlife biologist Adrian Wydeven: "It's almost as if there are wolf *groupies* out there now. It's like the wolf has become a super animal that can't do any harm. . . . For some people it's like wolves are the next best thing to God anymore."[38]

Such idolatry reached its zenith in the recreational elysium of Yellowstone National Park. After two decades of obstreperous wrangling and an environmental impact survey that generated more public comment than any other federal project in U.S. history, wolves were finally restored to Yellowstone in January 1995.[39] Flag-waving children and camera-wielding press greeted the wolves' motorcade as it trundled through the Roosevelt Arch, and thousands of people visited the national park to behold the new arrivals. Enthusiasts armed with spotting scopes set up camp on the Cooke City road to watch the Druid Peak Pack cavorting across the wide sweep of the Lamar Valley, and day trippers bought wolf-watching guides and attended organized wolf howls. Canine allure penetrated beyond park borders, where canny outfitters integrated wolf-viewing escapades into their itineraries. The Where the West Begins Lodge in Ennis, Montana, advertised wolf-watching trips as part of its "Montana Adventure Package," tantalizing tourists with the prospect of "a safari of a different kind," a wild car ride across a primordial landscape roamed by charismatic megafauna. Back at the ranch house, seat-sore adventurers could "enjoy the luxury of soaking in the outdoor hot-tub under the Montana Big Sky while at the same time listening to the coyotes yip and sing."[40] A chance encounter with canine residents appeared an integral feature of the New Western experience. The presence of wolves, coyotes, and other wild animals; the opportunity to barbecue freshly caught trout; and the rustic simplicity of the lodge (with its well-stocked refrigerators and cable television) literally defined "where the West begins."

The appeal of the wolf as a tourist animal reflected New Western desires to experience raw America. Vacationers sought immersion in an untamed landscape free from social strictures and environmental pollutants. *Canis lupus* served as an ideal heritage animal in this "natural" West, a creature whose haunting cries gave substance to the idea of a "howling wilderness." The canine form of communication symbolized the spirit of the wild, as biologist John Theberge noted: "The howl reminds us that our past is deep-rooted in wildness. . . . It epitomizes the wilderness we have fought so successfully to conquer and now must fight to save."[41] The romantic imagery of the West was enhanced by the idea that wolves were once again roaming the Rockies, chasing elk and deer, howling across forested valleys, and picking their way along stony gulches. Allied to this mystical appeal was an ecological tenet that celebrated *Canis lupus* as an environmental savior bringing vibrancy to an emasculated landscape. For New Westerners, the wolf made the landscape whole again, restoring the luminosity of trans-Mississippi America.

At the same time, the return of *Canis lupus* was hailed as a positive western story of American conservationist ethics and national philanthropy. Before his post as head biologist for the Turner Endangered Species Fund, Michael K. Phillips co-orchestrated the Yellowstone program. Phillips lauded wolf restoration in the West as evidence of "a revolutionary change in the way we view ourselves in relation to nature."[42] The unrivaled western canvas, a land of splendid natural wonders, deserved spirited and graceful animals such as the wolf. On an Internet tribute site dedicated to Wolf #10, the enigmatic alpha male of the Yellowstone Rose Creek Pack, M. L. Johnson translated #10's cry to his mate as "Be free with me, live with me, in this new land of plenty."[43] The wealth of the New West lay in its wilderness, big spaces, and national parks. With the West idealized as a magnificent slice of untamed America, canine outlaws became illustrious national heroes whose hangouts naturally appeared on the tourist trail.

There was certainly money to be made from wolf tourism. Financial projections in 1992 estimated that the presence of *Canis lupus* in Yellowstone National Park would generate $43 million per year for the region.[44] Ralph Glidden, the manager of a general store in nearby Cooke City, reported a 20 percent hike in profits during spring 1995.[45] *Canis lupus* represented a recognizable brand in the New West. Whereas their ancestors had been viewed as worthless vermin whose only redeemable value lay in the pelt, wolves in the modern West were precious alive as servants of the booming recreational economy.[46] Nonetheless, a paradox underscored the selling of the latter-day wolf. "The wolf today is for many a potent symbol of the wild, the free, the uncommodifiable," noted Jody Emel.[47] Yet it was precisely such values, this wilderness iconography, that tourists were willing to pay to acquire. In the New West, *Canis lupus* was a nonmaterial but highly marketable commodity, an animal not judged by the dollar but certainly bought with it.

Given the reputation of the wolf as an elusive animal suspicious of sapient presence, most interaction between tourists and wild canines occurred at the mall. If vacationers failed to connect with wolves in the physical West, they could at least purchase a version of the myth to take home as a memento of their wilderness experience. A visit to the store allowed consumers to indulge their fantasies about wolves, to "bring the wolf to life in shimmering gold" as one website lyricized.[48] The modern West of Internet servers and shopping malls provided an ideal habitat for the wolf brand, with burgeoning commercial outlets providing seemingly limitless carrying capacity. On the Defenders of Wildlife Internet site, billboards on a suitably western main street advertised a "Wildlife Mall," "Calendars," "Checks," and "Cards." In the middle of the road stood a wolf, muzzle raised aloft, howling at the sky.[49] The wild animal seemed entirely comfortable in the virtual, urban jungle, and the human species appeared equally at ease in the manufactured West. Browsers experienced the wilderness by mouse and credit card or satisfied their desire for western relics in the simulated nature of the mall.[50] All manner of products were available for lupophiles in the consumer West, from neckties and bracelets to ornaments and stationery. Wolf earrings and necklaces adorned the necks of wolf supporters; serious enthusiasts purchased radio collars worn by the Yellowstone wolves themselves. Consumption provided a way to empathize with the animal, the wearing of the wolf motif a powerful signal of allegiance. A willingness to display such images in public identified the wearer as a wolf advocate, disclosing an affinity with the pack in the same way that individuals affiliated themselves with sports teams. At Hamilton outlets in Yellowstone National Park the walls were hung with T-shirts decorated in various wolf designs, just a few miles from Bottlers Ranch, where ardent wolfers once hung skins out to dry.

Wolf images for sale at the New Western mall ascribed to certain conventions. Posters typically imparted an air of nobility, independence, and energy. T-shirts memorialized the wolf as both an exotic, exceptional species and a native animal in a rugged, authentic setting. The wolf label advertised freedom, strength, sensitivity, and vivacity. Calendar wolves were never underfed, injured, or bloodied but boasted gleaming coats, a charismatic demeanor, and a penetrating gaze. This was wonderful and wild America essentialized in the spirit of the wolf. Honorable traits of vitality and dignity were imprinted on the New Western wolf, exuding a sense of destiny and vigor previously reserved for cowboys. Like the heroic cattlemen memorialized in paintings by nineteenth-century artists Charles M. Russell and Frederic Remington, *Canis lupus* embodied raw and rugged America.[51]

In the desire to capture the essence of a wild, natural West, some portraits strove for realistic poses. Works of art displayed animals roaming, hunting, or attending to their pups. At Kendra's Gifts and Collectibles, the "Wolf Calling His Mate" ornament was advertised with the label, "This sculpture is so finely detailed you can nearly feel the cold."[52] However, the wolf preserved in alabastrite often seemed as far removed from the real animal as the "howling cookie jar" that emitted a wolves' chorus when its lid was opened. Canine paraphernalia sometimes verged on the kitsch, with cheap plastic figurines, sentimental prose, and anthropomorphic portrayals. Wolf trinkets may have characterized an untamed, natural West, but in many cases the products looked decidedly artificial. Often the symbolism behind the wolf brand was more about human conceptions of wilderness and the West, the power to purchase elevated as a therapeutic and redemptive act. An ad for adopting wolves posted on the Internet couched the experience in terms of inner reflection: "What happens when you adopt a wolf? Something magical. Your spirit changes . . . you feel better, like you've done something important—and you have."[53] At the mall consumers purchased meanings of nature as well as products derived from nature itself. The canine hand puppet, the wolf-howl CD, and the beaded choker were all part of a lucrative trade that entwined the majestic creature and the marketable commodity in a powerful New Western identity.

THE BATTLE OVER THE WESTERN WOLF

Wolf merchandise was important in the construction of an alternative western identity for canines in the late twentieth century. However, it was also used to reanimate fears of *Canis lupus* as the fierce killer of Old West folklore. The canine motif was repackaged by wolf haters to convey an entirely different message from that available in national park stores and nature malls. As Hank Fischer, Defenders of Wildlife representative in the northern Rockies, noted: "There have been record numbers of people in Montana, Idaho, and Wyoming wearing baseball caps with wolves on them. Good news? Not really. The wolves have rifle scopes superimposed over them, and the hat's logo reads, 'Wolf Management Team.'"[54] For members of the ranching, hunting, and mining community who still considered the wolf a rapacious killer, T-shirts, bumper stickers, and baseball caps became an important way to articulate Old Western values. At a public meeting regarding the Yellowstone reintroduction, one local unfurled a poster displaying a wolf's head inside a red circle with a bar across it. The poster's caption claimed, "The Wolf Is the Saddam Hussein of the Animal World."[55] Such images conveyed powerful anti-wolf sentiments, suggesting that wolves remained enemies of American progress. Meanwhile, westerners who killed wolves were hailed by some as folk heroes. Jerry Kysar, who shot a wolf a few miles south of Yellowstone National Park in September 1992, produced a print commemorating the event. The poster, which depicted Kysar proudly holding a wolf pelt aloft like the trappers of old, swiftly sold out at the local bar.

Anti-wolf forces perceived themselves as the legitimate occupants of the West, endangered human species under siege from a New Western agenda masterminded by a cabal of environmentalists, animal rights advocates, and New Agers. Pronouncements made by notable wolf critics kept alive the West of old, casting *Canis lupus* as a loathsome varmint and a reprehensible killer. At a public hearing on wolf reintroduction in Helena, Montana, one local testified: "In the early 1900s, the ranchers and rural people found that they could not live with wolves. It is no different now."[56] *Canis lupus* was viewed as a government agent in wolf's clothing, the symbol of a federal agenda unfairly foisted on the West. Ron Marlenee, writing in the *Billings Gazette*, warned that "environmentalists are willing to throw Montanans to the wolves. . . . [Wolf restoration] will give environmentalists the tool they need to stop or appeal power lines, timber sales, road building, hunting seasons, oil and gas exploration, grazing."[57]

The late-twentieth-century American West was a sharply contested landscape, where advocates of the Old and the New West collided. The two sides clashed most vehemently over the issue of wildlife rights, with vociferous individuals from either side expressing their own distinct visions for the land and its residents. Each group articulated its attitude toward the wolf with appropriate imagery, promoting their respective causes on posters and shirts. However, it would be inaccurate to essentialize the debate about *Canis lupus* as a contest between entrenched westerners and recent migrants, ranchers and environmentalists. Appreciation of the wolf was not solely a middle-class, urban phenomenon. Surveys of Montana and Idaho residents in 1990 found 44.7 and 53.3 percent of respondents, respectively, expressing positive attitudes toward wolves.[58] A poll conducted in Wyoming the following year came to similar conclusions.[59] Although many ardent wolf critics heralded from the ranching community, a number of stock raisers appeared willing to adjust to wolves roaming across their land. Demonizing the rancher in the New West proved as erroneous as vilifying *Canis lupus* in the Old West. As environmental historian Richard White pointed out, crafting the West into a landscape of disport, an "organic Disneyland" where those who work the soil are denigrated as ecological despoilers, marginalized environmentalism as the exclusive doctrine of a wealthy, leisured class.[60] The success of the Yellowstone wolf project instead illustrated the importance of listening to all sectors of society, of molding a West that catered to both two-legged and four-legged protagonists.

The wolf appeared permanently caught in the crossfire between Old and New Western discourses. As the West was mythologized, first as a frontier of cultivated progress, then as a renatured wilderness, so too was *Canis lupus*. Wolves were imagined as savage beasts and untamed spirits of the American wilds, variously disparaged and deified as villains and heroes of the western landscape. New Westerners listened to soothing howls on their compact disc players whereas similar sounds chilled the blood of nineteenth-century explorers. Attitudes toward the wolf often reflected changing recreational impulses. Whereas early travelers relished the opportunity to gun down local packs, latter-day tourists preferred to shoot their wolves with cameras. The opportunity to watch wolves at play became an integral part of the romance of the new, wilder West and allowed tourists a rare peek into wolf society. However, even in the New West of ecological ethics and social pluralism the wolf was often defined by the human imagination. At the mall wolf products were attributed traits that owed little to the character of the actual animal. *Canis lupus* was commodified as a symbol of vitality and freedom and confined by plastic. The western wolf tale, in all its renditions, articulated a need to reach beyond human-centered narratives and embrace a more inclusive position. The West represented a complicated landscape where wolf packs as well as humans forged their own trails, dug earthy homes, and played on the prairie. As Aldo Leopold noted, "Only the mountain has lived long enough to listen objectively to the howl of a wolf."[61]

NOTES

1. "Way Out West." Available at http://www.members.tripod.com/~ridingduo [18 December 2000].

2. William B. Mott, quoted in the *Casper Star Tribune*, 20 August 1987.

3. The legend of the Friendly Medicine Wolf was recounted by Piegan Chief Brings-down-the-Sun to trapper Walter McClintock in the late 1800s. See Walter McClintock, *The Old North Trail: Life, Legends, and Religion of the Blackfeet Indians* (1910; reprint, Lincoln: University of Nebraska Press, 1992), 476.

4. William Clark's journal entry for 24 July 1806. Taken from Reuben G.

Thwaites, *Original Journals of the Lewis and Clark Expedition, 1804–6,* 8 vols. (New York: Dodd, Mead & Co., 1904), 5:206.

5. Lansford W. Hastings, *The Emigrants' Guide to Oregon and California* (1845; reprint, Princeton: Princeton University Press, 1932), 98.

6. Charles W. Cook, David E. Folsom, and William Peterson, *The Valley of the Upper Yellowstone,* ed. Aubrey Haines (Norman: University of Oklahoma Press, 1965), 27.

7. Horace Greeley, *An Overland Journey from New York to San Francisco in the Summer of 1859* (1860; reprint, London: Macdonald, 1965), 77.

8. Alexander Ross, *The Fur Hunters of the Far West* (1855; reprint, ed. Kenneth Spaulding, Norman: University of Oklahoma Press, 1956), 114.

9. Figures cited in Edward E. Curnow, "The History of the Eradication of the Wolf in Montana" (master's thesis, University of Montana, 1969), 30.

10. Granville Stuart, *Forty Years on the Frontier* (1925), reprinted in *War Against the Wolf: America's Campaign to Exterminate the Wolf,* ed. Rick McIntyre (Stillwater, Minn.: Voyageur Press, 1995), 58.

11. Figures quoted in Dave Walter, "Wolf Wars," *Montana Magazine* 75 (January/February 1986): 23.

12. Montana Bureau of Agriculture, Labor, and Industry, *Annual Report 1895* (Helena, 1895), 158.

13. Ben Corbin, *Corbin's Advice; or, The Wolf Hunter's Guide* (Bismarck, N.D.: The Tribune Co., 1900), ii.

14. Stanley P. Young, *Last of the Loners* (1970), quoted in Peter Steinhart, *The Company of Wolves* (New York: Vintage Books, 1995), 37.

15. Theodore Roosevelt, *The Wilderness Hunter* (1893; reprint, New York: Charles Scribner's Sons, 1926), 305.

16. The Yellowstone Act of 1872 set aside 3,300 square miles of land in Wyoming as a "public park or pleasuring-ground for the benefit and enjoyment of the people." The tenets of the Yellowstone Act became a blueprint for national park legislation. See *U.S. Statutes at Large* 17 (March 1871–March 1873): chapter 24, 32–33. For a definitive history of national parks in the United States, see Alfred Runte, *National Parks: The American Experience* (Lincoln: University of Nebraska Press, 1979). Informed discussion of wildlife policy in the American preserves can be found in James A. Pritchard, *Preserving Yellowstone's Natural Conditions: Science and the Perception of Nature* (Lincoln: University of Nebraska Press, 1999), and Frederic Wagner, *Wildlife Policies in U.S. National Parks* (Washington, D.C.: Island Press, 1995). For official policy toward predators in particular, see Rick McIntyre, *A Society of Wolves: National Parks and the Battle over the Wolf* (Stillwater, Minn.: Voyageur Press, 1993).

17. Dixon Merritt, "World's Greatest Animal Criminal Dead," U.S. Department of Agriculture press release. Reprinted in McIntyre, *War Against the Wolf,* 242–47. For an intriguing history of the Custer Wolf, written from the point of view of the infamous animal, see Roger Caras, *The Custer Wolf: Biography of an American Renegade* (Boston: Little, Brown, 1966).

18. For the romantic West created by Hollywood, see John G. Cawelti, *The Six*

Gun Mystique (Bowling Green, Ohio: Ohio Popular Press, 1971), and John H. Lenihan, *Showdown: Confronting Modern America in the Western Film* (Urbana: University of Illinois Press, 1980).

19. According to Rick McIntyre, the policy of wolf eradication "became the policy of our emerging nation. Destruction of predators became a heritage passed on for generation after generation. That heritage of conflict and destruction became part of the American way of life." *War Against the Wolf*, 17.

20. *Dances with Wolves* (Majestic Films International, 1990), dir. Kevin Costner.

21. "Two Socks," available at http://www.twosocks.com [31 October 2000].

22. Barry Holstun Lopez, *Of Wolves and Men* (New York: Touchstone Books, 1978), 167; McIntyre, *War Against the Wolf*, 17.

23. "Thoughts from the Field: Bruce Babbitt," in *The Wolves of Yellowstone*, ed. Michael K. Phillips and Douglas W. Smith (Stillwater, Minn.: Voyageur Press, 1996), 52.

24. Joseph Marshall III, *On Behalf of the Wolf and the First Peoples* (Santa Fe: Red Crane Books, 1995), 5.

25. For *el lobo*, the Mexican wolf, see David Brown, *The Wolf in the Southwest* (Tucson: University of Arizona Press, 1983), and Steve Grooms, *The Return of the Wolf* (Minocqua, Wis.: Northword Press, 1993).

26. "Lady Wolf," an Internet site devoted to nature, featured links to wolf- and Native American–related issues; available at http://www.ladywolf.com [31 October 2000]. Kendra's Gifts and Collectibles traded in Native American crafts and wolf merchandise; available at http://www.kendrasgifts.com [31 October 2000].

27. Jody Emel, "Are You Man Enough, Big and Bad Enough? Ecofeminism and Wolf Eradication in the USA," *Environment and Planning, D: Society and Space* 13 (1995): 720, 730. For the links between patriarchy and the conquest of nature, see Carol J. Adams and Josephine Donova, eds., *Animals and Women: Feminist Theoretical Explorations* (Durham: Duke University Press, 1995), and Carolyn Merchant, *The Death of Nature: Women, Ecology, and the Scientific Revolution* (San Francisco: Harper and Row, 1980).

28. Clarissa Pinkola Estes, *Women Who Run with the Wolves: Myths and Stories of the Wild Woman Archetype* (New York: Ballantine Books, 1992), 214.

29. Estes, *Women Who Run*, xiii.

30. Rachel Carson, *Silent Spring* (1962; reprint, Boston: Houghton Mifflin, 1987); Farley Mowat, *Never Cry Wolf* (1963; reprint, Toronto: Seal Books, 1979).

31. For exemplary coverage of the rise of ecological thought and efforts to protect the environment, see Thomas R. Dunlap, *Saving America's Wildlife: Ecology and the American Mind* (Princeton: Princeton University Press, 1988); Lisa Mighetto, *Wild Animals and American Environmental Ethics* (Tucson: University of Arizona Press, 1991); Roderick Frazier Nash, *The Rights of Nature: A History of Environmental Ethics* (Madison: University of Wisconsin Press, 1989); and Donald Worster, *Nature's Economy: A History of Ecological Ideas* (1977; reprint, Cambridge: Cambridge University Press, 1994).

32. Jon Scieszka, *The True Story of the Three Little Pigs* (New York: Viking, 1989).

33. Aldo Leopold, *A Sand County Almanac: With Essays on Conservation from Round River* (1949; reprint, New York: Ballantine Books, 1970), 138–39.

34. Patricia Nelson Limerick, *Legacy of Conquest: The Unbroken Past of the American West* (New York: W. W. Norton, 1987), remains the classic exposition of New Western history.

35. The Yellowstone to Yukon Initiative (Y2Y), an ambitious and visionary scheme begun in 1997 to preserve a vast swathe of wilderness country in western North America, hailed large carnivores as vital agents for a healthy ecosystem. According to President Harvey Locke: "The wolf is a symbol to many of us of wild country and wilderness. The wolf is a fundamental aspect of how Y2Y came to be. So is the grizzly bear. These are the species with which it is hardest for humans to live. . . . These are the species that inspire us." Harvey Locke, "The Yellowstone to Yukon Vision," in *Connections: Proceedings from the First Yellowstone to Yukon Conservation Initiative*, ed. Stephan Legault and Katherine Wiebe (Canmore, Alberta: Yellowstone to Yukon Conservation Initiative, 1998), 33.

36. *Official Highway Map*, 1995–96, produced by Travel Montana, Department of Commerce, and the Montana Department of Transportation.

37. Mark Kaley, "Summary of Observations Since Spring 1975," 23 August 1976, Box 10, George C. Ruhle Library, Glacier National Park, Montana.

38. Adrian Wydeven, quoted in Jay Robert Elhard, *Wolf Tourist: One Summer in the West* (Logan: Utah State University Press, 1996), 33.

39. For the wolf's return to Yellowstone, see Hank Fischer, *Wolf Wars: The Remarkable Inside Story of the Restoration of Wolves to Yellowstone* (Helena, Mont.: Falcon Press, 1995); Thomas McNamee, *The Return of the Wolf to Yellowstone* (New York: Henry Holt, 1997); Phillips and Smith, *Wolves of Yellowstone*; and Paul Schullery, ed., *The Yellowstone Wolf: A Guide and Sourcebook* (Worland, Wyo.: High Plains Publishing, 1995).

40. "Where the West Begins"; available at http://www.wherethewestbegins.com [15 December 2000].

41. John Theberge, quoted in Steinhart, *Company of Wolves*, 92.

42. Michael Phillips, quoted in Phillips and Smith, *Wolves of Yellowstone*, 16.

43. M. L. Johnson, "He's the First"; available at http://www.ladywolf.com/wolfr101a.html [31 October 2000].

44. The figure of $43 million per annum "positive regional economic impact" is cited in John W. Duffield, "An Economic Analysis of Wolf Recovery in Yellowstone: Park Visitor Attitudes and Values," in *Wolves for Yellowstone? A Report to the United States Congress, vol. 4: Research and Analysis*, ed. John Varley and Wayne Brewster (Yellowstone National Park: National Park Service, 1992), 2–82.

45. *Denver Post*, 28 August 1995.

46. For the role of "industrial animals" (beaver, cattle, sheep) and "animals of leisure" (horses, grizzly bears) in the western economy, see Richard White, "Animals and Enterprise," in *The Oxford History of the American West*, ed. Clyde A. Milner II,

Carol A. O'Connor, and Martha A. Sandweiss (New York: Oxford University Press, 1994), 237–73.

47. Emel, "Are You Man Enough," 709.

48. Comment written about the "Running Wolf Pendant," for purchase at the International Wolf Center Gift Store; available at http://www.wolf.org.catalog_00/jewelry/jewelry.shtml [15 December 2000].

49. "Defenders Shopping Village"; available at http://www.defenders.org/village/village.html [31 October 2000].

50. For advertising and consumption in the modern West, see Jennifer Price, *Flight Maps: Adventures with Nature in Modern America* (New York: Basic Books, 1999); Elliott West, "Selling the Myth: Western Images in Advertising," *Montana, the Magazine of Western History* 46 (Summer 1996): 36–49.

51. For insight into the work of Charles Russell and Frederic Remington, see Brian W. Dippie, "The Visual West," in *The Oxford History of the American West*, 675–705.

52. Kendra's Gifts and Collectibles; available at http://www.kendrasgifts.com/heritage/wolves.html [31 October 2000].

53. "North American Wolf Association"; available at http://www.nawa.org.small_miracles.html [31 October 2000].

54. Hank Fischer, "Discord over Wolves," *Defenders* 66 (July/August 1991): 35.

55. Poster reprinted in Grooms, *Return of the Wolf*, 141.

56. John Murphy, president of the Montana Woolgrowers Association, cited in "Public Hearing on Wolf Environmental Impact Statement, Helena, Montana, 1992," in McIntyre, *War Against the Wolf*, 385.

57. Ron Marlenee, "Environmentalists Represent Wolves," *Billings Gazette*, 14 June 1988.

58. Alistair Bath and Colette Phillips, "Statewide Surveys of Montana and Idaho Resident Attitudes Toward Wolf Reintroduction in Yellowstone National Park" (September 1990), report submitted to Friends of Animals, National Wildlife Federation, U.S. Fish and Wildlife Service, and National Park Service, 10. Education, age, knowledge about wolves, gender, and location of the respondents (rural or urban) all emerged as important factors affecting western attitudes toward *Canis lupus*.

59. In a survey conducted by Tom Thompson and Walt Gasson, 44 percent of Wyoming residents polled favored wolf reintroduction. See Tom Thompson and Walt Gasson, "Attitudes of Wyoming Residents on Wolf Reintroduction and Related Issues," Wyoming Game and Fish Department, Cheyenne (15 May 1991), 5.

60. Richard White, "'Are You an Environmentalist or Do You Work for a Living?' Work and Nature," in *Uncommon Ground: Toward Reinventing Nature*, ed. William Cronon (New York: W. W. Norton, 1995), 171–85.

61. Leopold, *Sand County Almanac*, 137.

Wendy Rex-Atzet

NARRATIVES OF PLACE AND POWER

Laying Claim to Devils Tower

> There are things in nature that engender an awful quiet in the heart of man; Devils Tower is one of them.
>
> N. Scott Momaday, *The Way to Rainy Mountain*

Devils Tower National Monument is one of those rare places that catches narratives and meanings the way a tree, having fallen into a river, nets a portion of whatever is traveling downstream: stories seem to drape themselves over its branches, rippling in the currents of time with both grace and tenacity. The striking stone tower that rises alone like a massive stump above the Belle Fourche River valley in northeastern Wyoming seems to demand both explanation and contemplation from the humans who have encountered it over the centuries (Figure 1).[1] Both Native American and Euro-American peoples have laced the rock with many interweaving narratives—from mythic to scientific to spiritual—and their meanings continue to endure.

Euro-Americans named this rock Devils Tower only 125 years ago, but the place has for many centuries been vibrantly meaningful to the Indian peoples of the Northern Plains and the West. White locals and visitors enjoyed the exotic native legends of the tower's origins, but they overlaid their own cultural meanings on the tower, a process that was formalized and expanded after the tower became a national monument. Most recently, rock climbers attracted to this world-renowned climbing destination have invested still more meanings in the rock. During the 1990s Devils Tower became the focus of a heated battle among Native Americans, rock climbers, and the National Park Service (NPS). As a place that carries multiple significances and as

Figure 1. Devils Tower National Monument, west face. *Courtesy of the National Park Service.*

a site of recent cultural conflict, Devils Tower offers a prime opportunity to consider the ways that meaning, identity, and power can be deeply implicated in western landscapes.

THE MAKING OF A PUBLIC TREASURE

Nineteenth-century Americans had known about the wondrous landmark deep within Sioux territory for several decades before a scientific expedition brought back the first written description of the tower in 1875.[2] As a geologist, Henry Newton noted the unusual striations on the tower's sides and the way it was "perched on the crest of a high, flat-topped ridge." But his scientific eye was awed by the sheer drama of the place. "Once seen," he gushed, the tower is "so singular and unique that it can never be forgotten. Its remarkable structure, its symmetry and its prominence make it an unfailing object of wonder. . . . Its summit is so entirely inaccessible that the energetic explorer . . . standing at its base could only look upward in despair of ever planting his feet on top."[3]

Here, in the first words written about the tower, some of its most enduring Euro-American meanings were set out. In Newton's report the uniqueness of the feature as a western landmark and geological phenomenon combines immediately with a desire—made more intense by its impossibility—to plant one's feet on the top. In 1893 booted feet did reach the top, when local ranchers William B. Rogers and Willard Ripley made the climb using a 350-foot ladder attached to wooden stakes pounded into a vertical crack. The July Fourth stunt drew more than a thousand spectators to the tower.[4] This event also marked the beginning of another of the major stories of the tower's white history: a narrative of climbing, adventure, and conquest.

When President Theodore Roosevelt designated Devils Tower the country's first national monument in 1906, the twin narratives of science and scenic wonder that Henry Newton had first articulated justified its protection from private exploitation. Roosevelt proclaimed that this "lofty and isolated rock in the State of Wyoming . . . is such an extraordinary example of the effect of erosion in the higher mountains as to be a natural wonder and an object of great scientific interest."[5] The movement in the late nineteenth and early twentieth centuries to protect the nation's monumental landscapes within national parks and monuments reflected not simply scientific and aesthetic appreciation but also, argues Alfred Runte, cultural insecurity. The spectacular landscapes of the West answered a reactive desire to counter historic European high culture with uniquely American natural antiquities. As dramatic landscapes and natural wonders were preserved for and opened to the use and enjoyment of "all Americans," they became public treasures and important components of American cultural nationalism and national identity.[6]

After the tower had been enveloped within a federal apparatus, the narratives associated with it were employed, integrated, and developed as part of the park's administrative and interpretive functions. The three narratives of science, scenic wonder, and conquest remained primary interpretive themes at Devils Tower National Monument throughout the twentieth century. Of course, since the nineteenth century Euro-Americans have identified Indian legends with the tower as well.[7] It would be erroneous, however, to assume that the white Americans who recorded and repeated Indian narratives also adopted and understood the tower's complex significance to Indian people. For whites, the Indians' legends were just that—primitive but charming folklore. Nevertheless, such picturesque fictions added character to the tower,

Figure 2. The Legend of Devils Tower. *Painting by Herbert Collins, 1936; courtesy of the National Park Service.*

and by incorporating these stories into their own representations of the place, Euro-Americans were also able to integrate romantic Indian imagery into their own identities as Americans.[8]

These widely shared and largely unquestioned cultural assumptions have been expressed and perpetuated in monument literature until the very recent past. The tourist *Handbook* published in 1981 uses the Lakota words *Mateo Tepee* ("Bear's Lodge") as the title for a chapter that devotes fewer than two paragraphs to the Indian history of the tower. More profound, however, is the visual and conceptual juxtaposition of Indian "mythology" with geological "truth" in the section that describes the tower's formation.

The dominant feature here is "the tower's geological story": three large illustrations depicting the geological processes of volcanic action and erosion that created the formation we see today. Opposite these images a small picture depicting an Indian legend of the tower's formation completes the *Handbook's* visual narrative of creation (see Figure 2). Although the Indian image is appealing, the way it is employed in the context of the scientific narrative codes it in important ways. Much smaller than the scientific illustrations and squeezed into the margin in the least visible, left-hand quadrant of the spread, the Indian image is clearly subordinate to the geological story. In this layout the Indian story does not even compete with the scientific narrative. Rather, it merely confirms the status of Indian narratives in the context of dominant American cultural narratives: not only are native beliefs subordinate, they are not "true." They are merely myths.[9]

This visual message is confirmed by the illustration's caption: "Both the Kiowa and Cheyenne Indians held similar legends on the origin of the Tower. The story goes that tribal members were surprised by a gigantic bear, and their incantations caused a low, flat rock to rise, lifting them above the reach of the bear. The massive beast then gouged huge vertical marks into the rock as it attempted to reach the people. Finally, the Indians were able to kill the bear."[10]

By conflating two distinctive tribal traditions, this caption serves to homogenize the diverse oral traditions of the Cheyenne and Kiowa people and, by extension, those of other tribes as well. And the caption's value-laden language—its substitution of "incantations" for "prayers," for example—both discredits and misrepresents the meaning of the legend. Together the caption and illustration not only mark the legend as superstition but also echo and reiterate the tenacious American mythology of "the vanishing Indian." The illustration depicts a huge, supernatural bear clawing the sides of the tower and a group of Indians on the tower's top. The tiny human figures, gesturing wildly, appear helpless and terrified. More significant, they are doomed by implication: even if they kill the bear, they are marooned on the top of the tower because they lack the climbing technology of modern whites by which to come down.

This final inference, if subtle, is nevertheless salient, because ever since the 1893 ladder stunt, climbing has been one of the park's primary narratives. For more than forty years after the Rogers and Ripley climb, speculation centered on the conviction that the tower was unclimbable without the ladder, but an obsession with the tower as a mighty landscape waiting to be conquered surely underlay this debate. The pioneering climber Fritz Wiessner made the first ascent of the tower using modern rock-climbing techniques in 1937, and since then climbers have considered Devils Tower a world-class destination and the tower's "colorful 100-year climbing history" has been one of the park's central interpretive themes.[11] The 1981 *Handbook* that treated

Indians with such profound negligence devoted five pages of text and a full-color photo spread to climbing. In addition, park interpretive activities have long included climbing demonstrations by rangers.[12]

THE BEAR'S LODGE

Indian people from all over the West refer to the tower by a variety of names, the most common one being Bear's Lodge. To the native peoples of the region Bear's Lodge has always been a profoundly sacred place. Ethnohistorical research indicates that the Arapaho, Cheyenne, Crow, Kiowa, Lakota, and Eastern Shoshone peoples have historical and geographical ties to the area west of the Black Hills, some dating from the fourteenth century. The Park Service reports that as many as twenty distinct tribal groups currently have some form of cultural affiliation with the place.[13]

Bear's Lodge is incorporated to varying degrees and in distinctive forms within the cosmologies, rituals, and cultural traditions of these groups. Narratives, ceremonies, and rituals—including origin legends, annual community ceremonies, vision quests, fasts, and sweats—are associated with the tower in various native traditions, and many of these recognize the tower as a place of spiritual power.[14] Before discussing the cultural narratives associated with the tower, however, we must distinguish between the "Indian legends" collected and retold by whites—charming stories that provide clever explanations of the tower's appearance—and the complex symbolic narratives that these stories more essentially are. The few examples presented here merely illustrate the range and possible symbolism of such stories and ceremonies. They also invite us to reconsider the meaning of the term *sacred land* in historical and contemporary discourses. If these narratives represent the historical and living traditions of many native cultures, they also function in the present as part of a larger public discourse on meaning, authority, and access to the sacredness of place.[15]

According to Cheyenne oral tradition, a band of Cheyenne traveled to Bear's Lodge to worship the Great Spirit there because it was known as a holy place. After a few days one man noticed that his wife was often gone from camp. He finally confronted her and found her back covered with scratches. She explained that a very large bear that lived nearby had charmed her. "The bear had no mate and had become infatuated with her while she was out gathering fruit. Fearing for the safety of the camp, she had submitted to the bear's embraces, which accounted for the scratches on her shoulders." Her husband determined to kill the bear, and the men of the camp prodded the animal out of its cave. But the bear was huge, and they scrambled onto a large rock, frightened, to escape from it. On the rock "they prayed to the Great Spirit to save them. In answer to their prayers, the rock began to grow up out of the ground," and the bear jumped at the sides in an attempt to reach the men. On the fourth jump the bear managed to hook his claws over the rim of the tower, but because the Great Spirit had helped the men, "now they had great courage and they shot the bear and killed him. When the bear fell, he fell backwards and pushed the big rock which made it lean."[16]

This story serves as the basis for the park's interpretive caption, cited earlier. But although the major themes would seem to be accessible to Euro-American readers—faith and prayer, the testing and triumph of courage, divine intervention—these meanings were elided when the legend was summarized for park tourists. By subverting the moral lessons embedded in the story, the park's act of interpretation drained this narrative of its complex significances. Instead, the adulterated story of the *Handbook* serves to buttress a time-honored Euro-American caricature of Indianness. Rather than offer prayers of supplication to a Great Spirit, as in the Cheyenne narrative, the Indians of the *Handbook* chant incantations, implying witchcraft, sorcery, and paganism. And instead of highlighting courage restored in response to the Great Spirit's concern for them, the *Handbook* stresses the stranded Indians' terror, helplessness, and inevitable—indeed supernaturally caused—demise.

Kiowa tradition also associates the origin of the tower with a supernatural bear, but the details of the two stories are quite different, a fact that further demonstrates how the *Handbook* caption adulterates the legend's significance. Although the Kiowa people are considered a Southern Plains tribe, tribal traditions and ethnohistorical evidence indicate that they migrated from an earlier northern homeland through the Black Hills region during the eighteenth century. The Kiowa call the tower *T'sou'a'e*, "aloft-on-a-rock."[17] Kiowa writer N. Scott Momaday recounted the following narrative in *The Way to Rainy Mountain,* a book that considers his people's long journeying:

> Eight children were there at play, seven sisters and their brother. Suddenly the boy was struck dumb; he trembled and began to run upon his hands and feet. His fingers became claws, and his body was covered with fur. Directly there was a bear where the boy had been. The sisters were terrified; they ran, and the bear after them. They came to the stump of a great tree, and the tree spoke to them. It bade them climb upon it, and as they did so it began to rise into the air. The bear came to kill them, but they were just beyond its reach. It reared against the tree and scored the bark all around with its claws. The seven sisters were borne into the sky, and they became the stars of the Big Dipper.[18]

As Momaday observes, this story does far more than explain the supernatural origins of the tower. Through it Kiowa people "related themselves forever to the stars," confirming their own place within the holistic community of the cosmos.[19] Other contemporary native scholars and writers agree that native religious complexes often center on the concept of a comprehensive sense of community that embraces human beings, other-than-human beings, the land, and the cosmos.[20] Here the story works to bind these diverse elements, creating and sustaining that sense of cosmic community through the shared, ritualized repetition of the narrative. The story operates on many symbolic levels, working to ground Kiowas' identity in their southerly migration, to commemorate their historic encounter with the tower, to connect humanity to the great tree, and to reinforce the brotherhood of the great bear. In addition, this narrative recognizes and marks the tower as a holy place, one where supernatural power intervened on behalf of human well-being.[21] The tower's distinctive appearance and awesome presence become tangible symbols of the immediate presence and power of the supernatural.

According to Vine Deloria, Jr., ritual and ceremony function in a similar way, integrating native communities and the land into what is understood to be a larger, cosmic whole. "Indian tribes," he writes, "acquire land as a gift from higher powers, and in turn they assume certain ceremonial duties which must be performed as long as they live on and use the land." Nomadic tribes—like those associated with Bear's Lodge—moved through vast territories in annual migrations, and their "most important ceremonies needed to be conducted at certain sacred places at specific times of the year."[22]

At the center of these place- and time-specific ceremonies lies the Sun Dance. Widely known for its sacrificial components, the Sun Dance is a communal ceremony of world renewal. It is performed at the time of the summer solstice because, explains Ronald Goodman, the disappearance of the Lakota constellation the Hand (Orion) signals "the impending loss of the Earth's fertility." Through the Sun Dance, Lakota men and women "participate in the cosmic renewal of life by shedding their own blood for the sake of all life."[23] The reappearance of the Hand in the autumn skies confirms the successful renewal of the planet and the perpetuation of the seasonal cycle. Anthropologist Joseph Epes Brown elaborates: "The Sun Dance, thus, is not a celebration by man for man; it is an honoring of all life and the source of all life, that life may go on, that the circle may be a cycle, that all the world and man may continue on the path of the cycle of giving, receiving, bearing, being born in suffering, growing, becoming, giving back to earth that which has been given, and so finally to be born again."[24]

One of the many consequences of the reservation era was the virtual and literal exile of migratory Plains peoples from those sacred places and ceremonial sites that did not fall within the boundaries of their reservations.[25] Bear's Lodge was one of these places. As we have seen, places are not external to the traditional native cultures of the Plains but are thoroughly integrated into those human communities through narrative, ceremony, and ritual. Assimilated into culture by these means, places constitute essential components of native spirituality, community, and identity. Thus, as Deloria argues, the loss of access to sacred places disrupts the integrity of these cultural systems, preventing Indian families and communities from functioning fully within the traditional landscape. The disintegrative effects often multiply over time, for "without the group of people sharing a sense of history on the land, there can be nothing more for the individual than a tourist's aesthetic feeling of beauty."[26]

The Sun Dance is celebrated within most Plains traditions, but it is Lakota people who perform this ceremony at the base of Bear's Lodge.[27] Since 1982 Lakota families from Pine Ridge have returned to the tower at the summer solstice to celebrate the Sun Dance at their traditional site. For most of the preceding century, this ceremony was illegal under U.S. law, banned not just at the tower but on the reservations as well. Federal suppression of the Sun Dance began in 1880, and Congress passed a law prohibiting this ceremony in 1884.[28] Four years later prayer bundles were also banned. Although these restrictions were lifted in the 1930s, it wasn't until the 1980s that the Pine Ridge Lakota began coming back to the tower for group ceremonies. But the Lakota had not forgotten about the place. "From the time I was very young," recalls Lakota elder Johnson Holy Rock, "my father used to talk about it. But he didn't talk about Devils Tower. He talked about the Great Spirit."[29] Holy Rock and his community returned to the tower at a time when the number of other visitors was on the rise and the sacredness of this place had begun acquire new connotations.

MODERN MECCA

To rock climbers as well as Indian people, Devils Tower is a place of great significance. In newspaper reporting since at least the mid-1980s Devils Tower has repeatedly been called a mecca by both climbers and reporters, a label that connotes a place of power and of pilgrimage. Climber Sam Davidson observes that "many climbers, in their own way, consider our boulders, crags, and mountains holy places."[30] This assertion is meant to emphasize a basic common ground between climbers and Indians in a shared sense of reverence for place. Indeed, in mainstream climbing literature climbers frequently describe their sport as a spiritual endeavor. In recent years, however, rock climbers have increasingly used the notion of sacred place to articulate their own deeply felt affiliation with Devils Tower and to defend that affiliation politically.

Technical rock climbing involves extremes in height, risk, and exertion that demand both mental and physical precision. It can be the most strenuous, painful, and artful of endeavors, and for climbers, it holds the promise of transcendent experience. By transgressing biophysical, geophysical, and psychological boundaries, climbers can touch a higher dimension, one they often describe in spiritual terms. As Susan Fox Rogers reflects, "Climbing demands a religious devotion, a denial of the flesh for the elevation of the spirit." Professional climber Steph Davis stresses the purity of the experience: "Climbing strips everything away. There's this truthful ideal to climbing." Other climbers find in climbing a quasi-religious path to self-knowledge and self-actualization. As prominent big-wall climber Doug Robinson observes, "Climbing can integrate body, mind, and emotion. . . . That makes it a powerful meditation. A physical meditation." And for Nicholas O'Connell, climbing provides "a glimpse into the essential nature of human life" because it is a "way of experiencing in a short, concentrated time the extremes of human emotion, the extraordinary joy in being fully alive, and the naked fear in facing up to great risk."[31]

In describing the spiritual dimensions of climbing this way, these climbers echo the philosophy of John Muir, who joined the nineteenth-century Transcendentalist notion that nature was the terrestrial manifestation of the divine with the dogged insistence that raw, bodily experience of the wild provided the best means to reach the spirit of God in nature. For Muir, moreover, touching the sacred in wilderness required a properly spiritual interaction with the landscape. He wrote of how, in surrendering one's body to the wilderness, "you lose consciousness of your separate existence: you blend with the landscape, and become part and parcel of nature."[32] This sacralized, experiential notion of wilderness continues to inform both modern environmentalism and environmental aesthetics, and rock climbers represent just one manifestation of this powerful intellectual tradition.[33]

If climbers savor the transcendent experiences that climbing offers them, they relish equally the wilderness experience that complements the act of climbing high peaks, desert crags, or massive geological formations. For many climbers, the personal encounter with wild and distinctive places enfolds the individual climbing experience within a deeply felt sense of the power of the landscape. Writing about the granite formations at Joshua Tree National Monument, Joe Kelsey underscores the rock's sublime indifference to the human struggle upon it. "The hundreds of granite formations scattered across the high desert plain that is Joshua Tree," he writes, "simply stand. They require no climbers, no narratives, not even names. Any significance we try to impose on rock, any grails we quest for, we contrive for ourselves."[34]

This enactment of a personal quest on an untamed and intimidating landscape epitomizes the traditional Western sense of the sublime, with its juxtaposition of awe, terror, transcendence, and individualist experience.[35] In a recent climbing handbook, veteran Yosemite climbing guide John Long expressed the climber's sublime with simple clarity:

> Big walls will always provide the most awesome form of pure rock climbing, because the venues—towering monoliths like El Capitan and Mt. Watkins in Yosemite Valley—are peerless for grandeur and intimidation. Huge sixth class routes are steep, often unnerving trails that terrify and amaze twenty-year veterans. They are sometimes three-quarters of a mile high, and a hammock bivouac at that altitude is an ordeal no climber is fully prepared for—or ever gets completely accustomed to. It's always a game of "keeping the lid on" when most everything around you, as well as your own instincts, tells you that you're a raving loon. Sometimes you are. But the climber who paws over the lip of a big wall, still whole in body and soul, has memories that no other sport can hope to match.[36]

Finally, climbing can be profoundly implicated in the identities of those who love the sport. "It is as a climber that I know myself," Susan Fox Rogers affirms, "and it is through climbing that I learned the most important lessons in life. Hold on, but not too tight; work with the rock, don't fight it; balance is everything; and always remember to breathe."[37] Locals who climb often at Devils Tower have probably developed a strong connection with the place in terms of home and community, perhaps not unlike the sense of place that Indian cultures seek to maintain. But most climbers at the tower are not local. In the sense that they journey long distances to engage with the transcendent experience the tower holds out to them, it may be appropriate to consider them pilgrims, or to recognize that by climbing the rock they experientially incorporate the place into their own identities. At the same time, Devils Tower will likely always be only one of many places they climb—unique perhaps, but always within a broader field of exceptional places and experiences.

In their discourse climbers tend to merge their experience of the wilderness sublime with their sense of sacred place. But the two are nevertheless distinct. The climbers' sublime has been around since at least the 1960s, when the sport started to boom and figures such as Yosemite rockrat Doug Robinson—known as "the Emerson of climbing"—began writing and philosophizing about their sport.[38] But the climbers' discourse of sacred place seems to be a more recent development. Although this rhetoric may indeed be expressive of climbers' own experiences, it should also be recognized as a derivative of a romanticized, New Age mythology of Indian-earth spirituality, as well as an ideological buttress to climbers' own cultural claims to places like Devils Tower.[39] Beyond its origins in American wilderness ideology and New Age thought, the climbers' trope of sacred place has been closely associated with political battles over access, particularly over access to places recently designated Indian sacred sites.

RELIGION, RECREATION, AND BALANCED MANAGEMENT

By 1980 three roughly contiguous developments had set the stage for cultural conflict at Devils Tower. First, tourism at the monument boomed after Steven Spielberg's film *Close Encounters of the Third Kind* was released in 1977.[40] Second, during the mid-1970s climbing at the tower began to accelerate dramatically. Where only 309 climbers had visited the tower in 1973, by 1976 that number had increased to nearly 1,000. In 1979 Devils Tower was ranked among the continent's top climbing destinations in the influential guidebook *Fifty Classic Climbs of North America,* and in 1983 nearly 3,600 climbers took on the tower. By the early 1990s climbing activity at the tower had reached a high of more than 5,000 climbers annually.[41] This boom was accompanied by the establishment of more than one hundred new routes and the installation of six hundred permanent bolts in the rock face.[42]

The third event in this triadic watershed was Congress's passage of the American Indian Religious Freedom Act (AIRFA) in 1978. AIRFA not only extended constitutional protection to practitioners of native religions but also required government agencies to protect Indian sacred sites on public lands as well as Indians' access to those places.[43] The NPS in particular set about implementing policies to accommodate Indian interests at sacred sites under their stewardship. It was after the passage of AIRFA that Indian people began returning to Devils Tower in great numbers for rituals and ceremonies, particularly the Lakota Sun Dance.

Native people who came to the tower to experience a deeply sacred place at the most significant ritual time of the year—knowing that their return to Devils Tower was protected by new laws and that this was a freedom denied previous generations—were deeply offended by recreational rock climbing on the rock they knew as Bear's Lodge. Johnson Holy Rock recalls how seeing climbers on the tower "imparted to me a feeling of violation—a sense of desecration. I thought to myself, 'Why are they doing this? Don't they have any respect for anything?'"[44]

To those who journey to the tower to engage in ritual sweats, fasts, vision quests, and other ceremonies, climbing the tower by any means is, quite simply, profane. Many native spokespeople argue that climbing the tower directly diminishes its spiritual power. And this fundamental act of desecration is worsened by the permanent bolts left in the rock, the strips of colored webbing left hanging at belay stations, and the use of metal chocks and other gear in the cracks. Climbers' behavior has also been offensive: their shouts to their partners are often noisy, profane, and disrespectful of other visitors. Moreover, climbers, able to look down from the rock at those on the ground, invade the privacy needed for ritual purposes.[45] As Elaine Quiver of the Gray Eagle Society stated in 1994, "One of the complaints we have is that climbers are the ones with the eagle view. Some people don't appreciate someone up there looking at them."[46]

These tensions increased during the 1980s until, by the early 1990s, the park's management issues had been utterly transformed. In a few short years climbing had become an acute management problem rather than a colorful historical theme; the NPS had newly committed itself to accommodating Indian interests in the parks; native people were determined to press their interests under the new laws; and the tension between climbers and Indians over access to and treatment of Devils Tower had escalated into open hostility. In 1991 the NPS set out to evaluate the impact of climbing at all relevant parks, including other major climbing destinations such as Grand Teton, Joshua Tree, and Yosemite, with the goal of implementing specific climbing-management policies in these locations.

In 1993 park managers at Devils Tower assembled a task force of representatives from Indian tribes, climber's groups, and environmental organizations to hammer out a climbing management plan.[47] After two years of meetings, public comment, and negotiation the park implemented its final climbing management plan. One cornerstone of the agreement was voluntary compliance with an official policy asking climbers to refrain from climbing the tower in June, the month of the Lakota Sun Dance, "out of respect for American Indian cultural values."[48] Another cornerstone was a commitment by monument administrators at last to begin interpreting the tower's cultural significance to native peoples.[49] Finally, a mandatory ban on commercial climbing during June was to be phased in by 1996, while individual climbers, it was hoped, would continue to comply voluntarily with the June closure.

The final climbing management plan appears to have been a true compromise: all parties were accommodated but none victorious. Some of the

Indian representatives had initially hoped to close the tower to all climbing year round, and many climbing advocates had been opposed to any closure of this traditionally recreational public resource.[50] The NPS's original goals for managing climbing are less clear, but park managers were clearly determined to honor AIRFA along with President Bill Clinton's 1996 executive order requiring federal land managers to "accommodate access to and ceremonial use of Indian sacred sites by Indian religious practitioners and . . . avoid adversely affecting the physical integrity" of these places.[51] The NPS also took into consideration the recommendations of a commissioned ethnographic assessment completed in 1991, and the park consulted more than one hundred government, tribal, recreational, and business organizations as well as the public.[52]

Nevertheless, many of the interested parties saw the plan on which park decision makers finally settled as a betrayal. Climbing representatives strongly opposed the mandatory commercial closure, a clause that the task force had not approved, and they were critical of park staff for inserting this provision at the eleventh hour and outside the sphere of negotiation. For their part, monument staff had been opposed to making the June ban voluntary, and they continued to argue that the voluntary clause could be judged a success only if compliance was total. Indian representatives complained that a closure limited to the month of June failed to address the fundamental sacrilege of climbing the tower at all, as well as the need for privacy for personal rituals throughout the year.[53]

In 1996 local climbing guide Andy Petefish joined with the Bear Lodge Multiple Use Association (BLMUA) to file suit against the mandatory commercial closure. Tensions and rhetoric flared over the next four years as climbers and Indians debated the issue while the court case was repeatedly dismissed and appealed. On 8 June 1996 U.S. district court judge William Downes issued a preliminary injunction that required the NPS to grant commercial permits in June until a final decision could be made on the case. According to Downes, the crux of the suit was the argument that the mandatory closure "coerces the support of some Native American religious practices," amounting to an "impermissible government entanglement in religion."[54]

Duly warned, park managers backed down, issued Petefish his permit, and revised the climbing management plan; in April 1997 Judge Downes dismissed the case. In the final version of the climbing management plan all climbers (recreational and commercial) are *encouraged* to refrain from climbing in June as a gesture of respect for Native American cultures.[55] The issue, however, remained in the news as BLMUA repeatedly appealed Downes's decision. In March 2000 the U.S. Supreme Court refused to hear the case, effectively condoning the cooperative spirit and methodology behind the climbing management plan.[56]

NATURE, IDENTITY, AND THE POLITICS OF PLACE

It was during this extended period of intensely politicized struggle and public debate that Indians began publicly asserting their claims to the tower based on its sacredness and climbers made their counterclaims drawing on the spiritual aspects of their sport. Although the tower has been held sacred by Indian peoples for centuries, in the 1990s its status as a holy place was quickly engaged to provide moral and cultural buttresses to native claims in the face of competition from non-Indians. Devils Tower is only one of many places Indian people have been engaged in such battles, but it is unique because the Indians' primary opponents there are not industries or financial interests but recreationists. In this fundamentally political context the sacredness of place takes on new meanings. Claims of sacred land have become a strategic discourse, wielded by native peoples to position their own identities and interests in opposition to the dominant society.[57]

In recent years native peoples across the United States and Canada have used sacred site arguments to ground their claims for federal protection of sacred sites from the Bighorn Medicine Wheel in Wyoming, to Blue Lake in northern New Mexico, to Kelly's Mountain on Cape Breton Island.[58] Although this strategy has met with varied success, it is crucially limited in many respects. For example, when native activists couch culturally distinctive conceptions of the sacred in the language of the dominant society, they attempt not only to contest and subvert that dominant language but also to identify some mutually defensible common ground.

One of the most frequently used tropes in these discourses is the comparison of Indian sacred sites with churches, cathedrals, and other holy sites within the Judeo-Christian tradition. "It's a place of worship, a church for us," stated Joe Williams, a Dakota spiritual leader and member of the Medicine Wheel Coalition for Sacred Sites of North America (which consulted on the Devils Tower climbing management plan), voicing the moderate version of this rhetoric. But his conciliatory tone is countered by those who express more combative sentiments, such as an elderly woman who argued, "This is my church. I don't go down to you white peoples' church and raise hell." Medicine Wheel Coalition president Francis Brown (Arapaho) agreed, observing that "all hell would break loose if I went to climb the Washington Monument or the National Cathedral."[59]

Frequently, sacred site discourses are effective in providing native peoples with a viable position to contest the industrial development or multiple use of sacred sites—a goal that is often pursued in cooperation with mainstream environmental groups. But the sacred-site-as-church trope has also proved to be a double-edged sword, vulnerable in both public discourse and the courts. Opponents and skeptics often simply refuse to accept the equivalence of places like Devils Tower with the church buildings and Judeo-Christian forms of worship that represent this norm. As legal scholar Charles Wilkinson observes, many judges are powerfully influenced by an inherently Western definition of religion as "something you do in a church. Real religion isn't something you do in nature—the category for that is recreation."[60]

In a similar way the American wilderness tradition and the climber's sublime became overtly politicized in the battle over the climbing management plan. When native activists adopted the church metaphor to contest the recreational rights of climbers, climbing advocates countered on two fronts. As we have seen, both militant and moderate climbing advocates often chose to emphasize the spirituality of climbing. Some—like Sam Davidson, who wrote on behalf of the Access Fund—did so in a diplomatic and conciliatory tone, offering this trope as potential common ground. Even the most radical of climbing advocates repeatedly fell back on the spirituality of climbing in articulating their defenses.[61] But opponents of the climbing ban could also use the trope of sacralized wilderness to their benefit, arguing not only for their own affiliation with Devils Tower as a sublime landscape but also that Indian uses of natural parkland were inconsistent with managed wilderness values. In 1994 Andy Petefish pointed out to a Los Angeles reporter that "the Indians get to build fires in the most beautiful meadow in the park for their sweat lodge and Sun Dance ceremonies . . . [on land that] I own as an American citizen."[62]

Behind the debate, however, the climbing community has taken this issue to heart. The voluntary clause of the climbing management plan was devised by the Access Fund, a nonprofit advocacy group that works to protect access to climbing areas, in part by "developing cooperative, non-regulatory solutions to competing uses of public lands." In its newsletters the Access Fund reminds its members that the closure is not mandatory, but it encourages support of the cooperative agreement and respect for other users: "The Access Fund believes that the vast majority of climbers in the United States are sympathetic to Native American concerns and will sacrifice climbing opportunities for one month per year to support Native American religious practices without the onus of additional regulation."[63] It might be argued that the Access Fund promoted cultural respect merely to avoid formal regulation and limitation on climbing, but the evidence suggests that these ideals are not empty ones among climbers.

After the park implemented the voluntary ban the number of June climbers dropped from a 1994 high of 1,293 to 193 climbers in June 1995. This rate of compliance, about 85 percent, has remained fairly consistent since then, indicating that a significant number of climbers do respect Indian concerns.[64] In fact, most of the climbers whose opinions were published in *Access Notes* and *Climbing* magazine were, like Chris Hendricks, "stunned by the arrogance" of Andy Petefish.[65] Petefish has been the most militant opponent of the climbing management plan as well as the single most-quoted climber in the mainstream press, and his comments are notoriously spiteful. "As far as I'm concerned," he stated in 1994, "prayer bundles are a bunch of trash, and I'm very offended to have them hanging around the monument."[66]

Comments such as these have been coded in mainstream media as being representative of climbers in general. But though Petefish's position reflects the opinions of some climbers, it does not appear to represent the majority. Although their voices made it into the general media less frequently if at all, far more climbers have expressed dismay at Petefish's behavior than the few who have publicly supported him. Todd Perry's troubled letter to the editors of *Climbing* is representative: "I find it sad that in their zeal to climb some climbers do not respect the values and rights of [Native Americans'] culture. Throughout history we have forcibly moved Native Americans from their homes. . . . Each time new promises were made and broken at our convenience. Do we as climbers find it necessary to continue this history of destruction, disrespect, and lies by disregarding Native American religious beliefs . . . [and] climbing at some of their most sacred places?"[67]

In addition to exposing some of the ideological divisions within the climbing community, this issue has raised serious moral questions for climbers who have found their social ideals suddenly running counter to their dedication to climbing and, by extension, to outdoor experiences generally. Unlike the many other cases in which Indian sacred sites have been under threat from commercial, agricultural, or industrial development, the battle at Devils Tower has pitted native people against a recreationally defined group that tends to hold fairly liberal environmental and social views.

In this context the climbers' frequent recourse to tropes of spirituality and sacred place reflects the uncomfortable paradoxes of their position. Many climbers consider themselves to be environmentally conscientious practitioners of a pure, low-impact form of wilderness recreation that provides unparalleled access to and appreciation of the natural world.[68] At Devils Tower their own form of sacralized wilderness experience has suddenly and unexpectedly run head-on into a competing, and morally compelling, native vision of sacred land. Defensive of their motives and aggressive in protecting their interests, climbers, by choosing to highlight the sacredness of their own endeavors at the tower, also betray their discomfort with their status as invasive representatives of a dominating culture.

REFLECTION

If the battle over the tower is just one more instance of identity politics in the New West, it has also been a contest of meanings. The best efforts of climbers, Indian activists, and park decision makers to occupy a middle ground and create a viable compromise notwithstanding, the climber's sublime and sacralized wilderness experience are simply not the same as the native communities' sense of sacred place. The wilderness concept in particular does not provide an appropriate analogue for native concerns, not least because it implies an absence of humans from the landscape—the absolute converse of native conceptions of a holistic cosmic community.[69] The issue is far more complex than a simple conflict between two different ways of appreciating nature; rather, it is a complicated contest of material and cultural interests, pitting native efforts at political assertion and cultural revitalization against longstanding traditions of recreational usage and management of public lands.

Stories overlay the tower thickly, like layers of fallen leaves: the natural wonder, the great bear, the benevolent tree, the geology of erosion, the climber's sublime, the power of place. All these narratives invest the landscape with meaning and in so doing integrate the tower into the identities of those who "own" the stories. The tower is part of the identity of contemporary Indian people, their new access and public claims to this place linking them to homeland and heritage, community and cosmos, and contemporary political discourse. It forms a part of climber identity as well, both as a place of personal endeavor and as an emblem of the interests and commitments of this group.

The battle over climbing here has added still more layers of meaning to the tower: it has become a landscape of contention, of loss, of ambivalence, and of newly politicized identities for both Indians and climbers. For many native people, the tower may well represent the disappointing realization that compromise is often the best possible outcome in disputes over access and protection of sacred sites. If it is a landscape of victory in comparison with similar battles, this victory is a limited one. For climbers as well, questions of victory and loss are perhaps outweighed by other significances. If the tower has become a landscape of defensiveness and arrogance for some, for others it is a landscape of sobering ambivalence.

Both Indians and climbers have asserted and defended their own claims to the tower, but for the last hundred years the real locus of power there has been the federal government. The power to control access to and experience of the tower rests, finally, here. Indeed, the NPS has been exceptional among federal agencies and the judiciary in its efforts to accommodate native concerns regarding public lands, and the Devils Tower climbing management plan is, despite its problems, a case study in the balanced management of competing interests.

Although current park management policy may well be balanced, it is nevertheless an assertion of federal authority. As John Dorst has argued, the accommodation of moderate native and recreational interests by park management is more than an inclusionary multicultural strategy. It also provides a mechanism for containing more subversive discourses that challenge the park's primary orientation toward spectatorial mass tourism.[70]

With that point in mind, it is important to note how the commitments that inform park management have undergone a sea change since the mid-1980s. It wasn't that long ago that monument staff were extolling the spirit of conquest and adventure epitomized by the tower's unique and colorful climbing history while virtually ignoring the tower's Indian history and its significance to native people in the present. Indeed, the turnabout in park managers' attitudes is heavy with an irony that must be painful to climbers, whose own stories have rather suddenly become subordinate, if not villainized. For Indian people, this particular irony may be one to savor. In spite of the atmosphere of bitter contention and hostility, the park is more committed to Indian interests than ever before, climbers are coming to terms with the social complexities of their avocation, and colorful prayer bundles dot the tower's contested landscape.

NOTES

1. N. Scott Momaday, *The Way to Rainy Mountain* (Albuquerque: University of New Mexico Press, 1969), 8.

2. Although the tower was listed as Bear Lodge on maps predating the Newton-Jenney expedition, once it was labeled Devils Tower on the Newton-Jenney map, the name stuck. See Mary Alice Gunderson, *Devils Tower: Stories in Stone* (Glendo, Wyo.: High Plains Press, 1988), 59–71, esp. 71 n. 1.

3. Quoted widely, but Gunderson's treatment in *Devils Tower* is the most complete, 68–69.

4. See Ray H. Mattison, *Devils Tower National Monument: A History* (Devils Tower Natural History Association, 1963; orig. pub. in *Annals of Wyoming,* April 1956), 11; also Gunderson, *Devils Tower,* 75–84.

5. U.S. President, Proclamation, "Devils Tower National Monument," Proclamation 658 (24 September 1906).

6. Alfred Runte, *National Parks: The American Experience,* 2d ed. (Lincoln: University of Nebraska Press, 1987). The National Park Service was established in 1916 and has administered the monument since that time.

7. By 1985 the park's chief interpretive themes—geology, local ecology, first national monument, climbing history, and Indian legends—still reflected these four primary narratives. U.S. Department of the Interior, National Park Service, Devils Tower National Monument, *Environmental Assessment, General Management Plan, Development Concept Plan* (November 1985), 22; and *Final General Management Plan and Development Concept Plan* (February 1986).

8. See Philip J. Deloria, *Playing Indian* (New Haven: Yale University Press, 1998), on how Indianness has been incorporated into American identity.

9. John Dorst argues that this visual deployment of the park's legend image is just one example of the colonial strategy of trivialization in the interpretive management of Devils Tower. Historically, this technique helped park managers contain potentially disruptive narrative claims to the tower within the dominant narratives of Euro-American tourism. John Dorst, "Postcolonial Encounters: Narrative Constructions of Devils Tower National Monument," in *Postcolonial America,* ed. C. Richard King (Urbana: University of Illinois Press, 2000), 303–20.

10. U.S. Department of the Interior, National Park Service, *Devils Tower National Monument, Wyoming, Handbook* 111 (Washington, D.C.: National Park Service Division of Publications, 1981), chap. 1 and pp. 26–27. The illustration of the bear story appears in other park publications as well, including the 1963 publication of Mattison's history.

11. Weissner's was a technical climb, an ascent that did not use any artificial aids. In technical alpine climbing, ropes, chocks, and other types of gear are used only to provide safety in case of a fall and a means for rappelling down. The phrase "colorful 100-year climbing history" is used repeatedly in park literature; see, for example, www.nps.gov/deto/visiting.htm [9 April 2002], under "Climbing," and www.nps.gov/deto/climbing.htm [16 May 2002]. On the climbing history of the tower, also see Gunderson, *Devils Tower,* 73–96; Mattison, *Devils Tower National Monument*; and Steve Roper and Allen Steck, *Fifty Classic Climbs of North America* (San Francisco: Sierra Club Books, 1979). It is worth noting that Roper and Steck begin their chapter on Devils Tower by recounting the "charming" Indian legend of its formation and that Mattison also begins his short history by recounting Kiowa and Cheyenne versions of the legend.

12. National Park Service, *Devils Tower Handbook*; Ann Rovin, "American Album: A Game of King of the Hill at Devils Tower National Monument," *Los Angeles Times,* 13 October 1994, A5.

13. The park currently lists the following tribes as having "potential cultural affiliation" with the tower: Assiniboine and Lakota, Blackfeet, Blood, Crow, Cheyenne River Lakota, Crow Creek Lakota, Devil's Lake Lakota, Eastern Shoshone, Flandreau Santee Dakota, Kiowa, Kootnai and Salish, Lower Brule Lakota, Northern Arapaho, Northern Cheyenne, Oglala Lakota, Piegan, Rosebud Lakota, Sisseton-Wahpeton Dakota, Southern Arapaho, Southern Cheyenne, Standing Rock Lakota, Three Affiliated Tribes, Turtle Mountain Chippewa, and Yankton Dakota. Jeffrey R. Hanson and Sally Chirinos, *Ethnographic Overview and Assessment of Devils Tower National Monument, Wyoming* (Denver: U.S. Department of the Interior, National Park Service, Intermountain Region, 1997), 7.

14. Hanson and Chirinos, *Ethnographic Overview*, 19–30.

15. For a cogent synthesis of the problems and politics surrounding the notion of sacred space, see David Chidester and Edward T. Linenthal, introduction to *American Sacred Space*, ed. David Chidester and Edward T. Linenthal (Bloomington: Indiana University Press, 1995), 1–42.

16. Dick Stone, who recorded many native legends of the tower in the 1930s, transcribed this story as told by Young Bird and translated by Samuel Weasel Bear. I chose to analyze this narrative because it is currently posted on the park's website in a larger section entitled "first stories." The online posting of this legend offers a counterpoint to prior park usage of the narrative in the 1981 *Devils Tower Handbook*. See www.nps.gov/deto/stories.htm [9 January 1999].

17. Hanson and Chirinos, *Ethnographic Overview*, 10.

18. Momaday, *Way to Rainy Mountain*, 8. This version differs in some of its details from another Kiowa legend reported by J. P. Harrington in 1939 ("Kiowa Memories of the Northland," in *So Live the Works of Men*, ed. D. D. Brand and F. E. Harvey [Albuquerque: University of New Mexico Press, 1939], 162–76), but I have chosen to use it because Momaday provided interpretation of this story in another work.

19. Momaday's interpretation is quoted in Gunderson, *Devils Tower*, 35.

20. See, for example, Joseph Epes Brown, "Becoming Part of It," in *I Become Part of It: Sacred Dimensions in Native American Life*, ed. D. M. Dooling and Paul Jordan-Smith (San Francisco: Harper/Parabola, 1992), 9–20; and Leslie Marmon Silko, *Yellow Woman and a Beauty of the Spirit: Essays on Native American Life Today* (New York: Touchstone, 1997), 43.

21. Vine Deloria, Jr., has noted that Bear Butte, near present Sturgis, South Dakota, holds this kind of significance for Lakota people. As in the Judeo-Christian tradition of the burning bush, places where a divine or sacred power once revealed itself to humans are forever holy ground. Vine Deloria, Jr., *For this Land: Writings on Religion in America,* ed. James Treat (New York: Routledge, 1999), 210.

22. Deloria, *For This Land,* 205, 244–46.

23. Ronald Goodman, "On the Necessity of Sacrifice in Lakota Stellar Theology as Seen in 'The Hand' Constellation, and the Story of 'The Chief Who Lost His Arm,'" in *Earth and Sky: Visions of the Cosmos in Native American Folklore,* ed. Ray A.

Williamson and Claire R. Farrer (Albuquerque: University of New Mexico Press, 1992), 215–20.

24. Joseph Epes Brown, "Sun Dance," in *I Become Part of It*, ed. Dooling and Jordan-Smith, 241–45. Deloria offers a parallel description of the significance of these world-renewal ceremonies in *For This Land,* 205.

25. Vine Deloria, Jr., "Out of Chaos," in *I Become Part of It*, ed. Dooling and Jordan-Smith, 259–68.

26. Deloria, *For This Land,* 253.

27. In fact, of the six primary tribal groups with documented affiliations to the tower, the Lakota have the most extensive historical and current ties, and Lakota people engage in most of the contemporary ritual activity that takes place at the tower. Hanson and Chirinos, *Ethnographic Overview*, 13, 21–27.

28. See W. Raymond Wood and Margot Liberty, eds., *Anthropology on the Great Plains* (Lincoln: University of Nebraska Press, 1980), 164–78.

29. Quoted by Karen J. Coates, "Stairway to Heaven," *Sierra* 81 (November/December 1996): 27.

30. Sam Davidson, "The Sacred and the Profane," *Access Notes* 19 (Fall 1997). The Access Fund adopted Davidson's article as its position statement on the Devils Tower issue. For more examples of this type of language, see Penelope Purdy, "Devils Tower Is a Sacred Site to Native Americans," *Denver Post*, 16 June 1996, E3; Charles Hillinger, "Devils Tower Is a Peak Experience for Climbers," *Los Angeles Times,* 2 June 1985, pt. 6, p. 18; "Park Service Crossed Line at Devils Tower," *News Tribune* (Tacoma, Wash.), 17 June 1996, A8; Kevin McCullen, "Devils Tower: Climbers, Indians Forge Agreement on Sacred Site," *Denver Rocky Mountain News*, 19 June 1994, 6A; and George Snyder, "Devils Tower Climbers Suing over Government Ban: They Say Closure for Tribal Events Is Unconst.," *San Francisco Chronicle*, 21 June 1996, A11.

31. Susan Fox Rogers, "Is There Life after Climbing?" *Climbing* 166 (1 February 1997): 152; Candace Horgan, "Life on the Run: The Here, There, and Now and Steph Davis, Adventure Rock Climber," *Climbing* 191 (1 February 2000): 170; Doug Robinson quoted by Brad Rassler in "Running Talus," *Climbing* 165 (15 December 1997): 82; Nicholas O'Connell, *Beyond Risk: Conversations with Climbers* (Seattle: The Mountaineers, 1993), 11.

32. Roderick Nash, *Wilderness and the American Mind,* 3d ed. (New Haven: Yale University Press, 1982), chap. 8, quotation on 126.

33. William Cronon, "The Trouble with Wilderness; or, Getting Back to the Wrong Nature," in *Uncommon Ground: Toward Reinventing Nature*, ed. William Cronon (New York: W. W. Norton, 1995), 69–90. For a thoughtful consideration of the sacramental landscape in Euro-American culture, see Lynn Ross-Bryant, "The Land in American Religious Experience," *Journal of the American Academy of Religion* 58 (Fall 1990): 333–55.

34. Joe Kelsey, "Too Old for 5.12, Too Young for Obituaries," in *Ascent: The Climbing Experience in Word and Image*, ed. Allen Steck, Steve Roper, and David Harris (Golden, Colo.: American Alpine Club Press, 1999), 47.

35. See Nash, *Wilderness,* chap. 3, and Cronon, "Trouble with Wilderness."

36. John Long, *How to Rock Climb!* 2d ed. (Evergreen, Colo.: Chockstone Press, 1993), 183.

37. Rogers, "Is There Life after Climbing?," 152.

38. Rassler, "Running Talus," 82.

39. On appropriations of Indianness since the 1960s, see Philip J. Deloria, *Playing Indian,* chap. 6. David Rich Lewis, "Native Americans and the Environment: A Survey of Twentieth-Century Issues," *American Indian Quarterly* 19 (Summer 1995): 439 nn. 39 and 40, provides a helpful guide to this literature.

40. U.S. Department of the Interior, National Park Service, *Devils Tower National Monument Statement for Management* (July 1986), 15.

41. National Park Service, Devils Tower National Monument, "Climbing Statistics, 1937–2000," fact sheet, n.d.; Roper and Steck, *Fifty Classic Climbs.*

42. In 1995 there were approximately 220 routes on the tower. U.S. Department of the Interior, National Park Service, Devils Tower National Monument, *Final Climbing Management Plan/Finding of No Significant Impact* (February 1995), iii, hereafter FCMP. Bolts are essential safety equipment on routes where there are no cracks or fissures that will accommodate removable protection, and although some bolts can be seen from the ground, most are not visible to visitors. Bolting routes has brought climbers into controversy with wilderness managers and is a contentious issue even within the climbing community. See the Access Fund position statement, "Climbing and Wilderness Areas: Regarding the New Forest Service Rule Prohibiting Use of Essential Safety Devices for Climbing in Wilderness Areas," http://www.accessfund.org/who/wild.htm [10 June 1998]; Joe Kelsey, "Wilderness Should Be More Than Just 'Watchable,'" *Vertical Times* 24 (September 1998); and Gregory Frux's letter to the editor, "Bold but Bolted," *Sierra* 86 (July/August 2001): 15. Frux argues that "while certainly needed in some places for safety and acceptable in many climbing areas, permanent bolts aren't totally in the spirit of the [sport's] 'venturesome minority.' The problem with fixed anchors is that they modify the rock forever, albeit in a small way."

43. Christopher Vecsey, "Prologue," in *Handbook of American Indian Religious Freedom,* ed. Christopher Vecsey (New York: Crossroad, 1991), 7–25.

44. Johnson Holy Rock interview, in *In the Light of Reverence: A Documentary Film,* produced and directed by Christopher McLeod (Sacred Land Film Project, Bullfrog Films, 2001).

45. These and more complaints are documented in the FCMP and in Hanson and Chirinos, *Ethnographic Overview.*

46. Quoted in John Young, "Temporary Climbing Ban Is Sought at Devils Tower," *Houston Chronicle,* 14 August 1994, A7.

47. FCMP, iii, 88.

48. FCMP, 22.

49. That this interpretive theme is wholly new is made clear in language in the FCMP and on the monument's website, which informs climbers that "for the first

time" the tower will be managed as a "cultural resource as well as a natural and recreational resource." See "Devils Tower: Climb," www.nps.gov/deto/climbing.htm [17 April 2000], paragraph 2.

50. "Indians Seek Climbing Ban at Devils Tower," *Salt Lake Tribune*, 10 August 1994, A5; FCMP. One of the five recommendations made in Hanson and Chirinos's ethnographic assessment was a complete closure of the tower to climbing. That document also elaborates on Indian concerns regarding climbing the tower (33).

51. FCMP, 9; U.S. Executive Order 13007, "Indian Sacred Sites" (24 May 1996).

52. FCMP, 85–88.

53. Access Fund, "Access Fund Stand on Devils Tower Lawsuit," *Access Notes* 14 (Summer 1996); and "Why the Access Fund Did Not Support the Devils Tower Lawsuit," *Access Notes* 15 (Fall 1996): 2; also FCMP and addenda.

54. Quoted in "Why the Access Fund," 10.

55. FCM, 22.

56. U.S. Department of the Interior, National Park Service, Devils Tower National Monument, "Supreme Court Refuses to Hear Challenge Against Devils Tower National Monument Climbing Management Plan," news release, 27 March 2000.

57. See Alf Hornborg, "Environmentalism, Ethnicity, and Sacred Places: Reflections on Modernity, Discourse, and Power," *Canadian Review of Sociology and Anthropology* 31, no. 3 (1994): 245–67; and Bruce G. Miller, "Culture as Cultural Defense: An American Indian Sacred Site in Court," *American Indian Quarterly* 22 (Winter/Spring 1998): 83–97.

58. Helpful collections in this growing literature include the anthologies *Handbook of American Indian Religious Freedom*, ed. Vecsey; *American Sacred Space*, ed. Chidester and Linenthal; and *Sacred Sites, Sacred Places*, ed. David L. Carmichael, Jane Hubert, Brian Reeves, and Audhild Schanche (New York: Routledge, 1994). Also see Hornborg, "Environmentalism, Ethnicity, and Sacred Places."

59. Joe Williams quoted in McCullen, "Devils Tower." Unidentified woman interview, in *In the Light of Reverence;* Francis Brown, quoted in Rovin, "American Album." This trope was common in media coverage of the controversy; see, for example, Charles Levendosky, "Lawsuit Threatens Native Americans' Religious Rites at Devils Tower," *Denver Post*, 31 March 1996, F6.

60. On the use of native spokespeople by environmentalists, see Hornborg, "Environmentalism, Ethnicity, and Sacred Sites." Charles Wilkinson interview, in *In the Light of Reverence.*

61. In addition to the newspaper articles cited here, see the climbers' interviews in *In the Light of Reverence.* There Andy Petefish begins by saying, "Climbing lifts my spirits more than any other activity. . . . When I climb the tower . . . I'm fully engaged with nature—I'm actually feeling it and touching it . . . wedging my body into it."

62. Rovin, "American Album."

63. "Access Fund Stand," 13.

64. National Park Service, Devils Tower National Monument, "June Climbers, 1995–2001," fact sheet, n.d.

65. Chris Hendricks, "Letters," *Climbing* 183 (15 March 1999).

66. Rovin, "American Album."

67. Todd Perry, "Letters," *Climbing* 183 (15 March 1999). Also David Roberts, "When Cultures Collide: The Climbers versus Native Americans Conundrum," *Climbing* 181 (15 December 1998): 88–95, 163; Andy Petefish, "Letters," *Climbing* 154 (1 August–15 September 1995) and 160 (1 May–15 June 1996), and responses to Petefish in "Letters," *Climbing* 156 (1 November–15 December 1995), 159 (15 March–1 May 1996), 161 (15 June–1 August 1996), and 162 (1 August–15 September 1996); as well as "Letters," *Access Notes* 16 (Winter 1996): 14; and Purdy, "Devils Tower Is a Sacred Site."

68. See Roberts, "When Cultures Collide," 91, on climbers as conflicted liberals. This perspective has also been expressed by climbers in their ongoing debates about climbing in wilderness areas and the use of permanent bolts. Kelsey, "Wilderness Should Be More," is representative of these views.

69. See Bruce G. Miller, William Cronon, and John A. Grim, "Cultural Identity, Authenticity, and Community Survival: The Politics of Recognition in the Study of Native American Religions," *American Indian Quarterly* 20 (Summer 1996): 353–76, esp. 361–64; quotation from 364.

70. Dorst, "Postcolonial Encounters."

Part Two

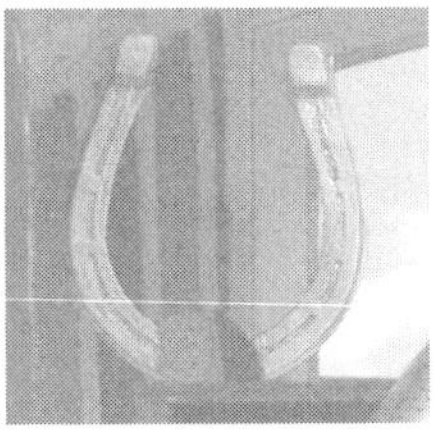

PLAYING IN THE WILD

The three essays in this section address how recreation, the aesthetic value placed on western space, and commodification of nature all intersect in the New West. An REI membership, Patagonia fleece, North Face outerwear, and a Subaru Outback are all vital accoutrements for a New West lifestyle that privileges the recreational value of the western landscape. The understanding that the purchase of a five-hundred-dollar Patagonia jacket somehow brings you closer to nature makes the purchase itself an act of atonement, precisely because it enables its wearer seemingly to access a purer, noncommercial space. Acts of commerce in the New West become almost weirdly purifying because they buy access to nature, to a wilderness that has been defined as purity itself; and the companies that sell access to that nature promote themselves as humane businesses with a cooperative sensibility. But as Gordon Sayre shows in his essay on climbing on Mount Rainier, much of what the consumer is buying access to when purchasing a kayak or crampons is not cooperative at all but rather an individualistic experience in the solitude of the wilderness. The industry built around the New Western lifestyle and the meanings it places on nature ironically have made the western space more commodified than ever, and much of what is sold is an escape from the urban, from humanity itself.

Ken Owens's essay on fly fishing chronicles the dramatic growth of the sport since the 1980s, and Owens notes that "a fresh hatch of pseudo-western fantasy during the closing decades of the twentieth century attracted eager and incautious customers to the sport, willing to be hooked by skilled manipulators of the imagery." Michael Lundblad analyzes what exactly these eager customers are "buying" in his essay on the Patagonia catalog, which, he points out, "trumpet[s] the ideal of 'wilderness' while demonizing consumption." But as Lundblad notes, the meanings attributed to the wilderness in narratives such as the one behind the Patagonia catalog obscure the consumerism that provides its entire reason for being. In turn, the wilderness narrative camouflages much of the consumerism and individualism that is at the heart of the New Western lifestyle. The recreation that all these accoutrements are built around, these acts of play in which people participate in the wilderness, demonstrates a freedom from necessity and the kind of affluence required to engage in acts of play, not work; and it is, after all, a capitalist system itself that affords those playing the privilege of doing so. As the essayists make clear, the narrative of a pure nature untainted by the ugliness and individualism of market forces is an illusion, one that is sustained by the wilderness narrative of corporate entities such as Patagonia.

Michael Lundblad

PATAGONIA, GARY SNYDER, AND THE "MAGIC" OF WILDERNESS

> I am still far from cured. I admit that at times I covet the latest waterproof and breathable fabrics and a lighter sleeping bag. . . . Just remember: owning that gear won't make you happy; using it will.
>
> John Sherman, "Rediscovering the Dirtbag Within"

Finding these words in Patagonia's Fall 2000 catalog might not be very surprising to those customers who receive it in the mail, whether they live in the West or just dream of living there. To be honest, I've had many of the same thoughts living here in Virginia, nostalgic over time spent in Reno and the Sierra Nevada. As I browse through pages displaying the latest fleece vests and windproof shells, superimposed over stunning landscape photography, I find myself pulled in and inspired by pictures of sandstone crack climbing in Utah or backcountry skiing in Montana. I can admit that I covet the right gear for these sports, even if I know how unlikely it is I'll be out there anytime soon. By looking at this catalog I can at least live vicariously through accounts of outdoor adventure written in essay form, published alongside pictures of expedition-worthy garments. The Fall 2000 catalog, for example, offers this account from Gary Snyder: "Ending up on the summit pinnacle of Kaun-dake, 'Changing Cloud' mountain, I push around the boulders and outcroppings a bit, force through the creeping pine, and make a nest, lean back, stretch out my legs, and watch the lifting cloud-mists blowing up on the rock face, watch the world far below."[1] Snyder's travels in Japan evoke my own nostalgia for solitary wanderings in the wilderness, as well as the desire to abandon that "world far below," associated in part with crass consumerism and materialistic impulses. But wait a minute. Gary Snyder in a Patagonia catalog? Isn't his perspective antithetical to the mission of Patagonia—namely, selling products? This juxtaposition makes more sense once I think about the ideologies of both Snyder and Patagonia, but I am left with further questions about the tropes of wilderness experience and anticonsumerism that are embedded both here and in the mainstream environmental movement of today.

As much as I tend to sympathize with these attitudes, I am wary of two dominant discourses that emerge. The first is the idea that "wilderness," by definition, has not been shaped by humans or by social constructions of its meaning. The second discourse on display, particularly in the Patagonia catalog, is an ambivalence toward consumerism that results from a recognition that producing and consuming goods inevitably has an impact on the environment. The irony is that demonizing consumerism is incredibly successful as a way of selling commodities once they become associated with the putative environmental ethic of Patagonia as a company.[2] As much as I might enjoy outdoor experience and share many of Patagonia's ambivalent attitudes, my aim in this essay is to bring more critical awareness to the ways the Patagonia catalog can ignore issues of environmental and social justice and wind up reinforcing the mania of capitalist consumerism it claims to reject.[3]

The most obvious element of the package that Patagonia sells is the glorification of wilderness and the resulting (we assume) desire to protect it. I am fully complicit in idealizing wilderness, and I locate the source of my own environmental awareness in experiences I've had backpacking and climbing in mountain ranges such as the Sierra Nevada, the Rockies, and the North Cascades of Washington. I have taken trips, for instance, designed to bring me near fire lookouts in the Cascades described by Jack Kerouac in *The Dharma Bums*, specifically so that I could emulate my vision of Kerouac's Japhy, modeled after a much younger Gary Snyder.[4] As a result, finding Snyder's work in the Fall 2000 catalog in a celebration of wilderness is, on the one hand, invigorating for me. But on the other hand, I am wary of the unexamined enthusiasm in the catalog, particularly in the context of a company that capitalizes on the way we might fantasize about having the right gear to follow in Snyder's footsteps.

Let me begin by bringing to light some of the words from Snyder's piece. "A Walk in the Great Snowy Mountains" is taken from "hitherto unpublished pages" of Snyder's journal and represents a record of his thoughts on a five-day backpacking expedition in the mountains of northern Japan. We are informed that he is traveling in "probably the largest roadless area in Japan," "about as wild as any place" there, where the Hokkaido brown bear lives and even human-made trails are scarce. In these remote mountains Snyder writes short lines—"the heart sings / by the streams / we feel clean"—while he searches for the "unpredictable sacred." Before reaching the inevitable summit, Snyder desires even closer physical contact with the land, so he literally crawls on his hands and knees, "To see the plants for themselves. . . . Nameless, self-complete, independent, interdependent, fragile, eternal, free." The conclusion he reaches, and confirms in much of his other work, is, "This is the real world," a place that is high enough from the "world far below" that he can find truth:

> On the highest level
> let us not play our usual roles.
> Drop the mask
> show me your shining
> true face.[5]

The privilege of being able to search for truth on a summit like this will be discussed below, but we can first recognize that Snyder's epiphany here, like so many in American nature writing, is constructed as taking place in contact with what's "real," away from the masses, literally or figuratively, down below.

Patrick Murphy makes a distinction between Snyder's thoughts about wilderness and a tradition of American nature writing that represents men (predominantly) seeking to reunite with nature after being alienated from it. Snyder, he writes, "is concerned instead with people conducting practice in place."[6] Although I agree that Snyder is concerned about everyday interactions with nature on the level of the community, I believe he also affirms a romanticized notion of "true" wilderness that corresponds with the general attitude of Patagonia. Max Oelschlaeger has even called Snyder the "Poet Laureate of Deep Ecology,"[7] and I think the label is appropriate for the way it links Snyder with a movement that emphasizes allowing nonhuman nature or wilderness to flourish for its own sake.[8]

Snyder's piece is a good fit for the rest of the Patagonia catalog, then, but for reasons that go beyond the wilderness experience itself. Patagonia celebrates this kind of narrative in the hope that such an experience will lead to an environmental ethic devoted to preserving wilderness areas, biodiversity, and so on. This approach is one actually advocated by Snyder. "The first step," he has said, "is to make us love the world rather than to make us fear for the end of the world. Make us love the world, which means the nonhuman as well as the human, and then begin to take better care of it."[9] On the page following his journal entry in the Patagonia catalog, it is no surprise to find Snyder's notes on the Japanese park system and his views on protecting wilderness. In these notes, after pointing out that Japanese national parks are not actually federally owned, Snyder tells us that there are also "Special Protection Areas," which represent "an effort to actually preserve the original ecosystem, although logging is still not outright banned." These areas make up only 7.3 percent of Japanese national park land.[10] Clearly, the anticipated response is acknowledgment of something called an "original ecosystem," agreement that any logging there is by definition bad, and horror that only 7.3 percent of park land is saved in part by the most stringent restrictions.

As a company, Patagonia works hard for the kind of wilderness protection that Snyder advocates, and other essays in the catalog express this desire. Jil Zilligen, who is identified as Patagonia's director of environmental programs, "works daily to ensure that future generations have the opportunity to learn the lessons of the wild and to thrive in a biologically diverse world."[11] Zilligen's essay is appropriately titled "The Lessons of Wilderness" and appears across the lower third of a two-page spread. The upper two-thirds gives us a tranquil scene from the Great Bear Rainforest in British Columbia, with an apparently uninhabited bend in the broad, calm stream. A mist hangs low over lush green pines and grasses along the water, and no humans or human structures are in sight. Zilligen's visit to this place, we are told, is "with a group of activists and journalists working to protect a biologically rich stretch of the central coast." This wilderness, like Snyder's, is remote (she can reach it only by boat), it's roadless, and it's frequented more often by bears than humans. Away from "traffic, cell phones, horns," she realizes she is "part of the food chain" and, pregnant herself, sympathizes with a mother bear instructing her young cubs. The lesson Zilligen learns is a sort of epiphany: "In discovering the wild, I discover the nature of my self." She quickly extrapolates from her own experience to conclude, "Wilderness allows us to know ourselves" and "the gift of wilderness is always to teach us that we are part of something larger."[12] But who, I want to ask, is included in this "we"? Even as I enjoy thinking about some of my own life-changing experiences in the wilderness, I am uneasy about the putative universality of these statements.

Elsewhere in the catalog we (those of us flipping the pages) can read about other outdoor pursuits that lead to what are called "moments of connection that break down the imaginary divide between ourselves and the rest of nature."[13] We might even find ourselves nodding in agreement when Zilligen writes, "The wilderness itself will tell you why you need it better than anything on these pages."[14] The clear mission for Patagonia is to help ensure that generations to come will be able to experience wilderness in similar ways. As Zilligen points out, Patagonia has pledged 10 percent of its profits or 1 percent of sales, whichever is greater, to support grants to various environmental groups. Since 1985 this commitment has resulted in the donation of more than fifteen million dollars, and several million more in gear, as well as support in the form of art and marketing services and organizing and training sessions. Zilligen summarizes the approach in her essay: "Through our work at Patagonia, we hope to inspire you to get out there and know the wilderness. Touch it, smell it, listen to its lessons. When you feel your soul stir, your mind and feet will follow: You will likely be moved to act, to take a stand on behalf of preservation."[15]

But what are the costs of this kind of preservation and the glorification of something called "wilderness"? The idea remains, in part, that there are "wild" and "untouched" places out there, difficult to reach but ultimately fulfilling because we can come into contact with what Snyder calls the "real world" there. But how "real" are these places? How "untouched"? William Cronon has explored these questions in his provocative article, "The Trouble with Wilderness; or, Getting Back to the Wrong Nature." He points out that most if not all of our federally designated wilderness areas in the United States represent the displacement of indigenous inhabitants. Most tourists to these areas can conveniently forget that American Indians were either killed off or rounded up and forced to move to reservations. As Cronon writes, "The myth of the wilderness as 'virgin,' uninhabited land had always been especially cruel when seen from the perspective of the Indians who had once called that land home." Tourists, though, "could safely enjoy the illusion that they were seeing their nation in its pristine, original state."[16] Recalling Snyder's statement about an "original ecosystem" preserved in the "Special Protection Areas" of Japanese national parks, we can see the irony of Snyder's glorification of "primal peoples": supposedly, we admire their world view even as we deny their contemporary presence. In a discussion of Snyder's "Mother Earth: Her Whales," from *Turtle Island*, Oelschlaeger argues that Snyder "pierces to the heart of the malaise that afflicts the modern age, revealing that even the Japanese, who nurtured Zen in its infancy, torment Mother Earth, having lost touch with their roots."[17] This Orientalist condescension—in Edward Said's sense—to the "malaise" of "even the Japanese" is also implied when Patagonia's catalog constructs notions of "untouched" wilderness: even indigenous people today would apparently "torment" or spoil those areas now reserved for wilderness experience. Breathtaking photographs of landscapes in the catalog sometimes include humans in the form of adventurers but almost never give any indication of a more permanent human presence. Whether the pictures are from Canada, the United States, Argentina, or Japan, most traces of humans and structures they might have built have been either eliminated or avoided to reinforce the notion of "uninhabited" and "pristine" wilderness.[18]

The imperialist nature of the desire for "untouched" wilderness continues to cause problems today in terms of "underdeveloped" countries around the world. As Cronon points out, many countries "face massive environmental problems and deep social conflicts, but these are not likely to be solved by a cultural myth that encourages us to 'preserve' peopleless landscapes." The problem, he argues, is that "exporting American notions of wilderness in this way can become an unthinking and self-defeating form of cultural imperialism."[19] Taking this argument into the specific case of India, Ramachandra Guha has shown that the creation of wildlife parks, for example, ends up transferring the money of European tourists directly into the hands of a declining feudal elite in control of the parks while ignoring the needs of the poor living on or adjacent to the protected areas. Project Tiger, for instance, which was created as a network of parks to protect tiger habitat, "was made possible only by the physical displacement of existing villages and their inhabitants; their management requires the continuing exclusion of peasants and livestock."[20] Even perpetuating these notions in the United States, though, or in countries like Japan, can end up looking like imperialism when the ideal of "pristine" wilderness conflicts with the lives of ranchers, loggers, or others who are prohibited from using land in certain ways by those who fight for things such as wildlife habitat and endangered species.

Self-proclaimed environmentalists would probably cringe at this kind of statement. I include myself in this category and acknowledge, warily, that the same kind of rhetoric is often appropriated to justify all kinds of horrific, large-scale devastation of the environment. But I don't believe the answer to our environmental problems will come from demonizing the small-time rancher, farmer, logger, or even city dweller. Certainly we all need to be much more conscious of potentially harmful activities and seek alternatives, but we also need to examine the tendency to think of "untouched wilderness" as unquestionably good. Cronon identifies the paradox here: "If by definition wilderness leaves no place for human beings, save perhaps as contemplative sojourners enjoying their leisurely reverie in God's natural cathedral—then also by definition it can offer no solution to the environmental and other problems that confront us."[21] We are told that a wilderness experience can bring us closer to nature, but we can never interact with that nature by actually living in it, interacting with it, being a part of it.

The problem is also that valorizing wilderness can result in a tendency to look down on "ordinary" places and people in the cities and suburbs. In terms of what gets labeled an environmental problem, the movements to protect wilderness areas, biological diversity, and endangered species tend to overshadow issues of air and water pollution that affect millions of people, along with health concerns in the workplace and toxic waste dumps, most often located in the poorest parts of town. Andrew Ross has discussed these concerns in much of his work, including a recent interview with Michael Bennett titled "The Social Claim on Urban Ecology." In the eyes of mainstream environmentalists, he writes, "last on the list come the environmental priorities that affect urban residents . . . not to mention the conditions that underpin these hazards, like the slashing of public services and the savage inequities of public housing policy."[22] On an international level Guha reminds us that an emphasis on wildlands preservation ignores "environmental problems that impinge far more directly on the lives of the poor—e.g., fuel, fodder, water shortages, soil erosion, and air and water pollution."[23] But these are not the kinds of problems Patagonia is primarily concerned with. Obviously, we cannot expect Patagonia to solve all our problems, but the company's emphasis on wilderness ends up ignoring environmental justice, a term Joni Adamson and Rachel Stein have defined as "struggles to achieve equity and fairness in the distribution of environmental burdens and environmental benefits, and the understanding that environmental issues are intrinsically connected to social justice issues."[24] The grassroots environmental organizations that Patagonia funds fall rather predictably into such categories as biodiversity, forests, and water/marine concerns, most often in the shape of protecting wilderness, wildlife habitat, and endangered species; only rarely do the organizations appear to be working in the area of environmental justice.[25]

The issues Patagonia fights for are clearly those considered most important by their typical customers, who represent demographic coordinates similar to those of the mainstream environmental movement. Ross points out that this movement "has been a haven, within the landscape of the new social movements, for straight, white, middle-class males who may feel uncomfortable with the obligation to acknowledge their sexuality, race, and gender in other areas of social activism."[26] Indeed, so the argument might go, what does sexuality, race, or gender have to do with wilderness? Doesn't everyone have the same ability to get out there and be like Gary Snyder? Certainly, we must respond, there are millions of people who do not have the privilege, the ability, the time, the luxury, the money, the lack of fear, and so on, to go ice climbing, for example, in a remote national park in the Canadian Rockies or to afford the several hundred dollars required to own a Patagonia jacket. A glance at the individuals pictured in Patagonia's catalog reveals the demographics I'm talking about, beginning with a snapshot of Snyder, the lone white male with hands on hips and valleys below.[27] It's not surprising to find that the vast majority of the figures climbing, skiing, kayaking, or otherwise experiencing the wild in these pages are also white men.[28] Although the representative sample is too small to make definitive conclusions, the ratios at least do not refute my picture of Patagonia's intended audience. Many of the men writing about climbing adventures seem perfectly content to leave the women behind, so to speak, while bonding with their climbing partners. In "Turning Back" Michael Kennedy writes about trying to achieve "that rare, transcendent state where you climb beyond what you know you can do," but even his partner, Greg, cannot ease his worries on this particular trip. Kennedy's comment "I miss my wife and son" informs us that he has a family back home, but they don't enter his thoughts until after he describes other times when he has felt "a certain heaviness in the air."[29] The implication seems to be that the transcendent state cannot be reached until the domestic life is left behind. My point here is not that women are always excluded from Patagonia's wilderness fantasies but that the dominant perspective of the catalog seems to be geared toward the privileged white male.

The typical Patagonia customer would seem to be more interested in wilderness than environmental justice. But there is another primary concern in this catalog that needs to be explored as well: the narrativization of guilt related to consumerism. The central dilemma for Patagonia is presented as trying to avoid the evils of capitalism while living in a capitalist society and running a profitable business. The attempt is to show that greed is not the only motive, that this particular company cares about its environmental impact and actually gives money to organizations fighting to protect the wilderness. For those customers concerned about the impact of their own buying practices, Patagonia advocates what it calls "dirtbag culture," in which people are supposedly self-conscious about consumerism. But as promising as this might sound, there are some rather large questions that need to be asked.

What are we to make, for example, of comments that lament what is called "a conundrum for what has become a medium-sized business," which prefers "the human scale to the corporate, vagabonding to tourism, the quirky and lively to the toned down and flattened out"?[30] Should we overlook the fact that this company grossed over $220 million in 2001 or that it has an estimated one thousand employees?[31] The image of the "dirtbag" takes on new light in this context, but an attempt to address the issue is made by John Sherman in a catalog essay titled, "Rediscovering the Dirtbag Within." Commanding a two-page spread without ads for clothes, two unshaven white male "dirtbags" play chess with bottles of beer, wine, and whiskey as playing pieces, sitting in the middle of a campground identified as being in Yosemite Valley. In the essay Sherman waxes nostalgic about his climbing-bum days in Yosemite when he resisted the materialistic impulses that would plague him later in life. Sustaining himself on saltines, ramen, and Hacky Sack and scrounging the dumpsters for aluminum cans to be exchanged for a nickel apiece, he tells us that this was a time he was in touch with his "Inner Dirtbag," the only thing that can "restore us to sanity."[32] The voluntary nature of Sherman's lifestyle here clearly distinguishes him from negative stereotypes associated with the term *dirtbag*, such as the criminal or villain, but it also indicates how far removed he is from those people whose poverty is not a transcendental choice.

Capitalizing on the associations of climbing-bum culture allows Patagonia to use the idea of the "dirtbag" to recall the legendary history of its founder Yvon Chouinard, renowned for his climbing exploits in Yosemite in the 1950s and 1960s. In 1957 Chouinard first started selling climbing hardware (partly so that he and his buddies could keep climbing), and the company grew to become Great Pacific Iron Works in 1973, as it also added clothes to its product line. The climbing gear production was eventually sold and transformed into what is known as Black Diamond Equipment today, and the clothing line took on the name of Patagonia in 1976.[33] When we are told later in the catalog that "what distinguished Yvon's design approach from the beginning was a bias for simplicity and utility,"[34] the idea seems to be that the company is not a gigantic, evil corporation but rather something along the lines of Thoreau's calls for simplicity in *Walden*: simply a group of people with the desire to make the gear necessary for the rest of us to get out there.

As a company, Patagonia holds up the climbing dirtbag as the model for limited consumerism, for buying only what is truly needed. The catalog tells us, "All products are designed to have long, useful lives that reduce resource consumption,"[35] so we could presumably never need to buy more than one of each item. This idea is confirmed by Karyn Barsa, director of operations, who has said, "If you need a pair of pants, we'd like them to come from Patagonia, and we want them to be the pair you wear all the time. What we don't want is to sell you five pairs of pants in addition to the five pairs you already have in your closet."[36] But can we really accept this as Patagonia's sincere desire? What about Sherman's comment that "nobody wants to be thought of as a Bad American"? He tells us, "You've worked hard for that [Nissan] Pathfinder and damned if you're going to let some flaky climber talk you out of your happiness. Just remember: owning that gear won't make you happy; using it will."[37] Although selling use-value might ease the consciences of some Patagonia customers, I still have some questions about the company's attempt to evade its own capitalist nature. Whether I use its commodities for wilderness travel or not, Patagonia seems awfully concerned about not alienating me if I happen to be able to afford a Pathfinder.

Raymond Williams's essay "Advertising: The Magic System" seems particularly appropriate here for interpreting how Patagonia's products become "validated, if only in fantasy, by association with social and personal meanings."[38] Demand is created not because of actual needs but as a result of what Williams calls "magic": "a highly organized and professional system of magical inducements and satisfactions."[39] Patagonia's attempt to be self-conscious about consumerism in its catalogs winds up being little more than this kind of magic when we consider how many of us actually *need* windproof vests or Capilene long underwear, or how many of us plan to spend a month rock climbing in Yosemite. Do we really need expedition-worthy shells and packs for those not-so-perilous walks from house to car, car to work, and so on? The advertising system works in this case by selling not only dirtbag culture but also the "Patagucci" lifestyle of economic privilege, in which SUVs and conspicuous consumption are par for the course, even if the backcountry is never reached.

The entire Patagonia catalog represents various forms of "magic" advertising, but a quick look at the products themselves and their positioning on the pages is revealing. A typical caption is explicit about how the gear being described would be useful for the desired wilderness experience: "Our stretch Triolet gear was designed to help you move light and fast in the mountains by way of revolutionary waterproof/breathable stretch panels, stormproof detailing, and a clean, clutter-free profile."[40] Often these captions are strategically placed opposite what are called "field reports," such as one by Michele Bianchi, who describes trekking through mountains and icecaps in sleet and snow. Her second-person account addresses us directly: "What you feel: wind, hard rain, cold. A sense of life emptying, and filling in again."[41] While reading about this experience, we can glance over and find prominently displayed ads for the Storm Jacket, Torrentshell Pants, and the Torrentshell Jacket, which tout "basic waterproof/breathable protection so you can stay out when the crowd goes in."[42] This is to be expected, I guess, but in a later section we're told that even fashion can play a part in the design of these clothes, that Patagonia has "ignored the notion that sensible means dull."[43] Flipping to the back of the catalog, we encounter the Men's Polo Shirt and the Men's Techno Crew and then various forms of luggage, such as "expedition-worthy duffels on wheels"[44] that are clearly better suited for airport walking than Himalayan trekking. The caption for the polo shirt is rather amusing in this context: "Most of us here at Patagonia wouldn't know the difference between a polo mallet and a three wood, but it didn't stop us from designing the finest polo shirt available."[45] Oh, yes, for traversing those rugged hills out on the golf course.

But what about the argument that trumpets Patagonia's environmentally friendly business practices? Once the logic of use-value is shown to be vacuous, as in the example of the polo shirt, Patagonia seems to be arguing that even if all the products are not designed for wilderness adventure, we should be inclined to buy just about anything from the company once we discover its low-impact philosophy. In 1991 Chouinard, for example, called for a return to basics (after he had just laid off 120 of his 620 employees) in a catalog essay that criticized his own company's use of harmful materials.[46] Subsequent catalog essays dealt with the use of recycled plastic soda bottles to produce fleece (1993) and the decision to use only organic cotton (1996).[47] In the Fall 2000 catalog we are told that Patagonia is committed to making its products with organic cotton in order to eliminate the use of pesticides in traditional cotton growing. Low-impact dyes and finishes are used when possible, as are recycled fibers, not only in clothes but also in the catalog pages themselves.[48] As much as I might support these practices in general, calling attention to them in the catalog only ends up manufacturing a greater desire for Patagonia's products. It is not the case that Patagonia customers would just be buying these products elsewhere and thus might as well give their money to a good company. Or, as Patagonia might add, that this particular company needs to keep making money in order to give more to environmental organizations. The point is, as Williams explains, that modern advertising is a device "for organizing and ensuring the market . . . [and that] modern capitalism could not function without it."[49] Green marketing is certainly not limited to Patagonia, but if the end result is more "magical inducements" from other companies, then we have bigger problems than the destruction of wilderness areas.

If Patagonia can succeed in persuading other companies to improve their workplaces and to adopt similar eco-friendly practices, it would seem to be a step in the right direction. Patagonia has put pressure on other manufacturers to consider practices such as using organic cotton and has succeeded in getting companies such as Levi-Strauss and Nike to do so on a limited basis.[50] The company conducts an internal environmental assessment of its own production facilities each year and has paid considerable attention to environmental impacts in the construction of, for example, the Reno facility. With recycled building materials, low-maintenance landscaping, and a natural heat-retention system, the facility attempts to minimize its impact on the surrounding environment.[51] But the danger, again, is reinforcing consumerism through the magic of green marketing. The irony is that when Patagonia tries its hardest to explain itself, it is actually most successful in creating new and repeat customers. Even taking a more public position on certain environmental issues over the years, such as running ads to protest the GATT agreement in 1994[52] and agitating for the removal of dams from the Snake River in 1999,[53] can easily become part of an award-winning marketing scheme.[54]

Another way Patagonia attempts to overcome its capitalist guilt is by creating what appears to be fair and equitable working conditions for its workers. It has been awarded a place on such lists as *Fortune* magazine's "100 Best Companies to Work For"[55] and *Working Mother*'s 100 best companies for working mothers,[56] in addition to recognition by *Workforce* magazine[57] and books such as Hal Morgan and Kerry Tucker's *Companies That Care: The Most Family-Friendly Companies in America*.[58] Much of this recognition is based on availability of child care, family leave, vacation plans, product discounts, retirement plans, and profit sharing. But in the case of Patagonia, special acknowledgment is often given to the existence of on-site seminars covering such topics as nonviolent activism. The company will even "spot bail . . . [for] employees who get arrested as the result of their involvement with an environmental cause."[59] The atmosphere is described as having a "distinct air of friendliness and playfulness": the dress code is casual, and the people are mostly "down to earth" or "earthy." A unique internship program gives employees up to two months' paid leave to work for environmental organizations, and "workers are encouraged, if not compelled, to pursue outside activities."[60] At the Reno distribution facility there is even a community vegetable garden, and the cafeteria serves organic food as much as possible.[61]

Sounds like a great place to work, right? But are all these "earthy" people the ones who actually manufacture the products? Not surprisingly, perhaps, information is much harder to find about Patagonia's factories in Thailand and various other countries. As it turns out, Patagonia appears to be highly conscious of rejecting sweatshop labor, and the company is a founding member of the Fair Labor Association (FLA).[62] Most of its good publicity for working conditions, though, is focused on facilities in the United States such as the Reno distribution center. But what about the ethics of who qualifies for the jobs that have been so highly praised? The goal in hiring domestically seems to be to find those folks whose interests match what's represented in the pages of the catalog: wilderness recreation and environmental activism. Jennifer Laabs reports that Patagonia "hires people who fit their culture and mission." They intentionally make it "tough to get into Patagonia because they want to make sure they hire people who are as committed to experiencing and preserving the earth as they are. . . . If it seems like an exclusive club of hard-core outdoorspeople, it is." As a result, there is only 26 percent annual turnover among employees, and Patagonia has the luxury of being as selective as it was in 1999, when it hired only 84 people from a pool of roughly eight thousand applicants.[63] Although these numbers seem to indicate high job satisfaction, they also raise the question of who would be most readily defined as "earthy" enough to land one of these jobs. If the answer is that only certain groups of people (privileged and white, for example) seem to fit in, then we need to dig deeper and find out why greater diversity is not represented in either Patagonia's workforce or the environmental movement in general.

A movement that ignores issues of social and environmental justice clearly faces a challenge when it comes to making its concerns seem relevant to a more diverse constituency. But even if we argue for more dialogue between ecology and social justice, there remains the question of how to evolve toward a more just society. The discourse and practice of a company like Patagonia, some might argue, is admittedly flawed but potentially progressive. This line of thinking is an example of what David Harvey identifies as ecological modernization: "a belief that economic activity systematically produces environmental harm (disruptions of 'nature') and that society should therefore adopt a proactive stance with respect to environmental regulation and ecological controls."[64] Patagonia's rhetoric is even better in this regard, from a conservative standpoint, because it points toward corporate self-regulation rather than government intervention. With its extremely profitable green marketing approach Patagonia has shown that ecological modernization can be a "win-win" situation for both the environment and business. The problem, though, is that ecological issues can be addressed "without necessarily challenging the capitalist economic system head-on. It is reformist in its objectives rather than revolutionary and poses no deeply uncomfortable questions to the perpetuation of capital accumulation."[65] For Harvey, even the environmental justice movement is not the complete answer because its emphasis on local grassroots movements prevents it from linking more fruitfully with broader labor concerns and a fundamental challenge to the capitalist system.

Gary Snyder once asked, "Can capitalism put its own house in order, and not be simply driven by the market and by profits? If it is driven by nothing but the market," he responds, "then the defeat of socialism will not be much of a victory, for capitalism will go on to wreck the whole world and its resources."[66] Snyder's comments here certainly articulate the attitude taken by Patagonia, but they also point out how uncritically notions of capitalism and socialism are being thrown around. Capitalism, by definition, is driven by the market and by profits and sustained by using up the world's resources. Reform or restraint might reduce the speed at which the environment is affected, but reinforcing capitalist consumerism, as Patagonia must inevitably do, only reinforces the systemic problems it claims to be addressing. For Harvey, Marxism/socialism might rest on a similar need for using the world's resources, but it can also offer broader solutions that "deal in the material and institutional issues of how to organize production and distribution in general, how to confront the realities of global power politics, and how to displace the hegemonic powers of capitalism not simply with dispersed, autonomous, localized, and essentially communitarian solutions . . . but with a rather more complex politics that recognizes how environmental and social justice must be sought by a rational ordering of activities at different scales."[67] Harvey wrestles with the question of how to establish social justice, though, particularly when a move toward socialism might call for "transitional political institutions, hierarchies of power relations and systems of governance that could well be anathema to both ecologists and socialists alike."[68]

As readers of Gary Snyder and the Patagonia catalog, we are left with the reality of a $4.7 billion industry in outdoor recreation equipment that is growing at just under 7 percent per year.[69] This industry (and American capitalism in general) will not change according to Marxist ideals overnight without revolution. But whether you believe in that kind of revolution or not, it is clear that Patagonia's anticonsumerism logic doesn't quite make sense. And its emphasis on wilderness experience and preservation seems irresponsible to the extent that it ignores environmental and social justice. But I am unwilling to completely condemn either Patagonia or Gary Snyder. Although my own political commitments lead me further to the left, I believe in embracing opportunities for change within the system as well. Snyder's thoughts in *The Practice of the Wild*, for example, seem to indicate an awareness of both environmental and social problems: "It is proper that the range of the [environmental] movement should run from wildlife to urban health. But there can be no health for humans and cities that bypasses the rest of nature. A properly radical environmentalist position is in no way anti-human. We grasp the pain of the human condition in its full complexity, and add the awareness of how desperately endangered certain key species and habitats have become."[70] Ideal awareness, then, encompasses recognition of both human and environmental suffering and accomplishes what Snyder strives for in his book: "helping people shape the way they want to live and act in the world."[71] Snyder's logic of "bioregionalism," or getting to know and therefore wanting to protect one's own bioregion, along with the human community that lives there, has become a major focus for his life and work in recent years.[72] Even if bioregionalism falls into the category of communitarian solutions that Harvey finds problematic, it at least offers a paradigm for linking environmental and social agendas.

Without Patagonia's financial support Snyder might not have finished *The Practice of the Wild*.[73] Without Snyder's glorification of wilderness I might never have pursued so deeply the joy and exhilaration I feel when I am climbing or mountaineering in less traveled areas. As a white male myself, coming from a fairly privileged background, it is rather easy to see how my experiences are validated by the work of someone like Snyder. But it is also easy for me to see that my desire to share wilderness experiences with others, and the subsequent realization that there are obstacles to that sharing, has led directly to not only my environmental ethic but also my desire to expand environmentalism to include social justice. I am left wondering, then, about how the wilderness discourses of Snyder and the Patagonia catalog have the potential for leading to broader social goals.

We cannot avoid being consumers in this country, but I don't believe we necessarily need to feel guilty about owning Patagonia products. If it gets us outside, even to our own backyards, then there is hope, perhaps, that we can have greater sensitivity about environmental and social problems. But before we all go on Patagonia shopping sprees, we would do well to remember that the injustices of the world will not disappear with offerings given to this company. As I adapt to a new bioregion in the rolling hills of Virginia, far away from Snyder's wilderness experiences in both the Sierra Nevada and the Daisetsu-zan-Hokkaido region of Japan, I think of his poem "For the Children" and his admonition to "stay together / learn the flowers / go light."[74] It is my hope that Patagonia, along with the rest of us, can adapt and learn from these words while paying attention to the impact of the discourses we embrace.

NOTES

1. Gary Snyder, "A Walk in the Great Snowy Mountains," *Patagonia* (Fall 2000): 58.

2. Competitors such as The North Face, REI, and Marmot do not follow Patagonia's practice of publishing nature essays in their catalogs and also do not have the same reputation for being environmentally conscious.

3. Patagonia's website (www.patagonia.com) provides a synthesis of what appears in specific catalogs, including photographs, essays, and incredible amounts of information detailing the company's business practices. For the purposes of this essay, however, I have focused my commentary on the printed catalog.

4. Jack Kerouac, *The Dharma Bums* (1958; New York: Penguin, 1986).

5. Snyder, "Walk," 58. This kind of wilderness experience is often glorified in Snyder's work. For another example in his prose, see Snyder, *The Practice of the Wild*

(1990; New York: North Point, 1998): "To be immersed in ice and rock and cold and upper space is to undergo an eery [*sic*], rigorous initiation and transformation. Being above all the clouds with only a few other high mountains also in the sunshine, the human world still asleep under its gray dawn cloud blanket, is one of the first small steps toward Aldo Leopold's 'think like a mountain'" (117–18).

6. Patrick Murphy, *A Place for Wayfaring: The Poetry and Prose of Gary Snyder* (Corvallis: Oregon State University Press, 2000), 145.

7. Max Oelschlaeger, *The Idea of Wilderness: From Prehistory to the Age of Ecology* (New Haven: Yale University Press, 1991), 261.

8. For the basic tenets of deep ecology, as well as an astute critique, see Ramachandra Guha, "Radical American Environmentalism and Wilderness Preservation: A Third World Critique," *Environmental Ethics* 11, no. 1 (1989): 71–83.

9. Quoted in Murphy, *Place for Wayfaring*, 215.

10. Gary Snyder, "Some Notes on the Japanese Park System," *Patagonia* (Fall 2000): 59.

11. Jil Zilligen, "The Lessons of Wilderness," *Patagonia* (Fall 2000): 43.

12. Zilligen, "Lessons," 42–43.

13. "Committed to the Core," *Patagonia* (Fall 2000): 3.

14. Zilligen, "Lessons," 42.

15. Zilligen, "Lessons," 43.

16. William Cronon, "The Trouble with Wilderness; or, Getting Back to the Wrong Nature," in *Uncommon Ground: Rethinking the Human Place in Nature*, ed. William Cronon (1995; New York: W. W. Norton, 1996), 79.

17. Oelschlaeger, *Idea of Wilderness*, 272.

18. See also Cronon's argument about the sublime in early American landscape painting and frontier mythology ("Trouble with Wilderness," 73–76), which can be applied here to photographs in the catalog.

19. Cronon, "Trouble with Wilderness," 82.

20. Guha, "Radical American Environmentalism," 75.

21. Cronon, "Trouble with Wilderness," 81.

22. Andrew Ross, "The Social Claim on Urban Ecology," in *The Nature of Cities: Ecocriticism and Urban Environments*, ed. Michael Bennett and David W. Teague (Tucson: University of Arizona Press, 1999), 15.

23. Guha, "Radical American Environmentalism," 75.

24. Joni Adamson and Rachel Stein, introduction to "Environmental Justice: A Roundtable Discussion," ed. Joni Adamson and Rachel Stein, *ISLE* 7, no. 2 (2000): 156. Adamson and Stein have also pointed out why so little attention has been paid to literature that addresses issues of environmental justice: "This lack of attention can be attributed, in part, to the fact that these works often redefine the environment as a place where humans live, work, play, and worship, and approach environmental problems as integrally related to problems of social inequality and oppression, while many of those writing in the field of literature and environment focus their study on canonical texts that describe solitary sojourns in wilderness" (156).

25. Organizations that fight for environmental justice have also received grants, but the vast majority of recipients do not seem to address these issues directly. See Patagonia's web pages, which list recipients of grant money by category (http://www.patagonia.com/webapp/commerce/Pgonia/grants).

26. Ross, "Social Claim," 25.

27. Snyder, "Walk," 58.

28. Of 59 adults pictured in the catalog, 37 clearly appear to be men (63%), 8 appear to be women (14%), and 14 are too difficult to distinguish (23%). It is fair to assume, then, that between 60 and 80 percent of these individuals are men. None, to me, appears to be anything but white.

29. Michael Kennedy, "Turning Back," *Patagonia* (Fall 2000): 15.

30. "Committed to the Core," *Patagonia* (Fall 2000): 3.

31. Hoover's Company Profile Database, "Lost Arrow Corporation," 2002, *Lexis-Nexis Academic Universe*, Business: Company Financial, University of Virginia Library, Charlottesville, 26 August 2002, http://web.lexis-nexis.com/universe.

32. John Sherman, "Rediscovering the Dirtbag Within," *Patagonia* (Fall 2000): 76.

33. Patagonia is named after a mountainous region in Argentina. Lost Arrow, the parent company of Patagonia since 1984, is named after a shaft of rock in Yosemite Valley.

34. "Nothing to Take Away," *Patagonia* (Fall 2000): 86.

35. "Sportswear: Function with Style and Responsibility," *Patagonia* (Fall 2000): 64.

36. Quoted in Carol Hildebrand, "Turn Green," *CIO Magazine*, 15 August 1999, 20 November 2000, http://www.cio.com/archive/081599_green_content.html.

37. Sherman, "Rediscovering," 77.

38. Raymond Williams, "Advertising: The Magic System," in *The Cultural Studies Reader*, ed. Simon During (London: Routledge, 1999), 422.

39. Williams, "Advertising," 422.

40. "Men's Stretch Triolet Jacket," *Patagonia* (Fall 2000): 8.

41. Michele Bianchi, "What You See," *Patagonia* (Fall 2000): 24.

42. "Torrentshell Jacket," *Patagonia* (Fall 2000): 25. The field reports are published next to products in the catalog, but in 1999 Patagonia published an entire book of field reports and essays without displaying any products for sale. Through this book Patagonia can make money from publishing environmental writing that ultimately increases brand recognition and associates Patagonia with the work of writers it publishes. The book contains essays from Chouinard, Rick Bass, Kitty Calhoun, Wade Davis, Gretel Ehrlich, and Doug Peacock, among others, all of whom are fascinated with the "wild"; the essays are accompanied by stunning photographs of "wilderness." Customers looking at the Patagonia catalog can find a description of the book (p. 38) and purchase it along with any other mail-order item. See Nora Gallagher, ed., *Patagonia: Notes from the Field* (San Francisco: Chronicle Books, 1999).

43. "Sportswear," 64.

44. "Freightliner & Freightliner Max," *Patagonia* (Fall 2000): 91.

45. "Men's Polo Shirt," *Patagonia* (Fall 2000): 73.

46. Jennifer Laabs, "Mixing Business with Passion," *Workforce* 79, no. 3 (2000): 80, *InfoTrac*, General Business File ASAP, University of Virginia Library, Charlottesville, 20 November 2000, http://web6.infotrac.galegroup.com/itw/session.

47. Larry Armstrong, "Patagonia Sticks to Its Knitting," *Business Week*, 7 December 1998, 68, *InfoTrac*, General Business File ASAP, University of Virginia Library, Charlottesville, 20 November 2000, http://web6.infotrac.galegroup.com/itw/session.

48. See "Sportswear," 64; and Back Cover, 92.

49. Williams, "Advertising," 422.

50. Hildebrand, "Turn Green."

51. Hildebrand, "Turn Green."

52. Janet Ozzard, "Patagonia Anti-GATT Drive Hits Environmental, Health Concerns," *WWD*, 28 October 1994, 11, *InfoTrac*, General Business File ASAP, University of Virginia Library, Charlottesville, 20 November 2000, http://web6.infotrac.galegroup.com/itw/session.

53. Philip Bourjally, "Patagonia's Green Business Practices," *Environmental News Network*, 30 November 1999, 20 November 2000, http://www.enn.com/enn-features-archive/1999/11/113099/patagonia_7263.asp.

54. The marketing strategy has in fact won awards for Patagonia's catalog and has been analyzed for its effectiveness in articles such as Jacquelyn Ottman, "Proven Environmental Commitment Helps Create Committed Customers," *Marketing News*, 2 February 1998, 5–6, *ABI/Inform Global*, ProQuest Direct, University of Virginia Library, Charlottesville, 20 November 2000, http://www.umi.com/proquest/; see also Melissa Dowling, "Patagonia, Winter 1998," *Catalog Age* (September 1999): 123, *ABI/Inform Global*, ProQuest Direct, University of Virginia Library, Charlottesville, 20 November 2000, http://www.umi.com/proquest/>; and Glenda Shasho Jones, "The 10 Best Catalog Covers," *Catalog Age* (June 1999): 151–54, *ABI/Inform Global*, ProQuest Direct, University of Virginia Library, Charlottesville, 20 November 2000, http://www.umi.com/proquest/.

55. Jennifer Laabs, "Mixing Business with Passion," *Workforce* 79, no. 3 (2000): 80, *InfoTrac*, General Business File ASAP, University of Virginia Library, Charlottesville, 20 November 2000, http://web6.infotrac.galegroup.com/itw/session.

56. Hoover's, "Lost Arrow Corporation."

57. Laabs, "Mixing Business with Passion."

58. Hal Morgan and Kerry Tucker, "Lost Arrow Corp./Patagonia, Inc.," *Companies That Care: The Most Family-Friendly Companies in America—What They Offer and How They Got That Way* (New York: Simon and Schuster, 1991), 145–58.

59. Jim Collins, "The Foundation for Doing Good," *Inc.* 19 (December 1997): 41–42, *InfoTrac*, General Business File ASAP, University of Virginia Library, Charlottesville, 20 November 2000, http://web6.infotrac.galegroup.com/itw/session.

60. Laabs, "Mixing Business with Passion."

61. Hildebrand, "Turn Green."

62. Patagonia also funds independent audits of its own facilities abroad. See "Countries of Origin," www.patagonia.com/custserv/product_faqs.shtml.

63. Laabs, "Mixing Business with Passion."

64. David Harvey, "What's Green and Makes the Environment Go Round?" in *The Cultures of Globalization*, ed. Fredric Jameson and Masao Miyoshi (Durham: Duke University Press, 1998), 337.

65. Harvey, "What's Green," 343.

66. Quoted in David Robertson, "Practicing the Wild—Present and Future Plans: An Interview with Gary Snyder," in *Critical Essays on Gary Snyder*, ed. Patrick D. Murphy (Boston: G. K. Hall, 1991), 262.

67. Harvey, "What's Green," 351–52.

68. Harvey, "What's Green," 336.

69. Carlos Alcala, "Outdoor Gear Companies Get Greener," *Knight-Ridder/Tribune Business News*, 2 August 2000, *InfoTrac*, General Business File ASAP, University of Virginia Library, Charlottesville, 17 December 2000, http://web6.infotrac.galegroup.com/itw/session.

70. Snyder, *Practice of the Wild*, 181.

71. Snyder, *Practice of the Wild*, 262.

72. See, for example, *Practice of the Wild*, 37–44 and 94–96.

73. Snyder's acknowledgment to Chouinard in *Practice of the Wild* reads, "I especially want to thank Yvon and Malinda Chouinard and the Patagonia Corporation for generous and swiftly expedited financial help in the final year of writing" (xi–xii).

74. Snyder, "For the Children," in *No Nature: New and Selected Poems* (New York: Pantheon, 1992), 259.

Gordon Sayre

URBAN CLIMBERS IN THE WILDERNESS

Mounts Hood, Rainier, and Shasta and the History of Popular Mountaineering

Mount Rainier, Mount Hood, and Mount Shasta stand tall as icons of the Pacific Northwest. Hood and Rainier are of course the tallest peaks in Oregon and Washington, respectively, and if northern California were separated from its southern half and formed an independent state (a change many in the region would welcome), Mount Shasta would be its highest point. All three peaks are part of the Cascade Range, but as volcanoes they belong in a sense to no range, for they stand apart, far above surrounding mountains. Colorado and California may boast of summits slightly higher than Rainier's 14,410 feet and Shasta's 14,162, yet those peaks, Mount Elbert and Mount Whitney, barely exceed their neighbors in elevation and therefore appear in vistas as just one protuberance on a saw-toothed horizon. And whereas the total elevation gain involved in a climb of those peaks is rarely more than 6,000 feet, a climb of Rainier from Paradise Lodge on its southern slopes involves more than 9,000 vertical feet. Mount Hood, though at 11,239 feet a dwarf by Colorado standards, rises almost directly from the Columbia River barely twenty miles to its north. Moreover, the active glaciers on these three volcanoes ensure a year-round snowy appearance and make climbing them a more serious undertaking than the hikes and scrambles up most of the 14,000 foot summits in Colorado and California.

The social and historic importance of these three volcanoes is measured not in feet, however, but in the visual and visceral pull they exert on the cities that lie at water's edge below. Rainier and Hood loom on the horizon above the Northwest's major cities, Seattle and Portland, respectively. Shasta is visible from much of the Sacramento Valley and is a popular destination from the San Francisco Bay area, a five-hour drive away. The mountains thus tempt and taunt the eyes of residents in three of the most affluent and admired cities in the United States. Although few Americans could identify photos of the remote high peaks of the Sierra Nevada or Colorado's Collegiate range, Hood and Rainier display themselves for millions, and their profiles are as recognizable as those of human celebrities. John Muir, who climbed all three of these Northwest volcanoes, wrote in 1888, "Never shall I forget my first glorious view of Mount Hood one calm evening in July . . . sauntering with a friend across the new Willamette bridge. . . . There stood Mount Hood in all the glory of the alpenglow, looming immensely high, beaming with intelligence, and so impressive that one was overawed as if suddenly brought before some superior being newly arrived from the sky." Yet Muir added, "I had seen it many times before this."[1] It was the unexpected appearance of the mountain amid an urban scene of "gayly dressed people" along the Portland riverfront that so impressed him. Of course, during long, rainy winters in the Northwest a good view of Rainier or Hood is rare, and Muir wrote that Hood was also concealed for most of the summer by smoke and haze from forest fires and lumber mills. But this fact only increases the value of a mountain view. In Seattle's booming real-estate market a Rainier view is an amenity that can command an even higher price for a typical house, already out of reach for most middle-class incomes. Although many residents may choose to live here because of the mountains and wilderness, the contemporary Mountain West is largely urban—86.4 percent of the region's people live in metropolitan areas. The location of Hood and Rainier reconcile this apparent paradox by providing an alpine backdrop to urban life.

And when the prosperous yuppies of Seattle and Portland see their states' highest mountains towering above their skylines, they are presented with an insistent challenge, one perfectly tailored to their ambitious, acquisitive, and self-improving natures. Climb it. The Cascades offer many more challenging and less crowded routes on lower peaks, where more experienced mountaineers might prefer to challenge themselves. But it is Hood, Rainier, and Shasta that attract novice climbers by the thousands, many of whom do not sustain an interest in mountaineering beyond this initial experience. Nearly half those who attempt Rainier (and nearly a third of those on Hood) employ guide services to lead them to the top, a proportion unheard-of in other mountaineering venues in North America. Until 1998 Rainier Mountaineering Incorporated (RMI) held a monopoly concession in Mount Rainier National Park, a lucrative business given that the fee for a three-day ascent was $550 during the 2000 season.

Hence Hood, Rainier, and Shasta are among the most frequently climbed mountains in the world. On a summer weekend day with good weather 300 to 400 people crowd the "Hogback," the base of the steep section a few hundred feet below Mount Hood's summit. Rainier is attempted by close to 10,000 people each year, of whom just under half reach the top. Mount Shasta is even more crowded. Because its Avalanche Gulch route involves no glacier travel and is therefore safer for novice climbers, about 15,000 attempt the peak each year. According to Shasta Forest Service rangers, only a third are successful. Among mountains with permanent snow, only Japan's Mount Fuji, the goal of 300,000 pilgrims each year, hosts more humans on its summit. These staggering populations of climbers have created an outdoor experience quite different from what most visitors to western mountain wilderness areas are seeking. Although even the most popular backpacking locales can offer a relative degree of solitude, such as campsites that are hidden from the view of others, popular high camps on the three volcanoes, namely Camp Muir and Camp Schurman on Rainier and the Lake Helen area on Shasta, are literal tent cities during the summer months. Well-clad, well-shod climbers choose to spend their vacations in conditions that resemble those of a refugee camp. Finding clean snow to melt for drinking water has become a serious problem, and climbers are strongly urged to scoop their own poop, as they might do for their dogs back in the city. Yet still they come.

In a competitive culture preoccupied by lists of firsts and bests, it comes as no surprise that these three mountains attract disproportionate attention from camera-toting tourists and opportunistic advertisers as well as peak-bagging climbers. Mount Rainier's faces appear on beer cans, bottled water, placemats, and other consumer products, as well as on Washington state license plates. Mount Shasta has since the 1970s been a mecca for New Age retreats, and many inns and businesses near its slopes capitalize on notions of the mountain as a navel of the world or site of "harmonic convergence." Commercial enterprises assert symbolic possession of these mountains by appropriating their names or images for packaging (without, of course, paying the peak any royalty fees) and banking on alpine associations of purity, superiority, or even danger. Such marketing invites consumers to rent a small "piece of the rock" by purchasing the product. And it builds up a complex of beliefs in which the only obvious way for the consumer to transcend this commodified relation to the peak, to assert his or her own direct claim of possession, is to climb it. After all, the rhetoric of mountaineering speaks of reaching the summit as "conquering" the mountain and of a series of summits as "bagging" peaks as a hunter does game.[2] As outdoor recreation itself has become more and more commercialized, these three snow peaks risk being cheapened and exploited. Yet although many novice climbers are motivated by a reified relation to the mountains, climbing may also function to restore some respect for their powers. A climber repelled by a storm or challenged by the mere physical effort of the ascent may descend with a heightened appreciation for the mountain he or she hoped to "conquer."

These relationships between the three Northwest volcanoes and the cities near them have fostered a practice of mountaineering quite distinct from the way the sport evolved in Europe and even elsewhere in the United States. Popular climbing clubs, notably the Mazamas and Mountaineers, introduced thousands of people to mountaineering and promoted a democratic vision of the sport as accessible to all, not just to an elite distinguished by class, wealth, commitment, or expertise. During the twentieth century the number of climbers on Hood, Rainier, and Shasta was always high, but attitudes toward mountaineering and toward the mountains as wilderness settings changed profoundly. The intense traffic of climbers culminated in conflicts between federal land managers and recreation interests over issues of conservation, sanitation, safety, and even the legal definitions of wilderness. These issues are best understood, I argue, if we recognize that the wilderness is not necessarily antithetical to urbanity, that the virtues of urban sociability can also be found in wilderness settings, and that mountaineering can be a communal rather than an elitist activity.

The human impact on Hood, Rainier, and Shasta is concentrated around a few popular routes and camps, where climbers, mostly urbanites, crowd together, united by their common goal of making the summit. Away from these crowded camps, other slopes of the three mountains remain lonely, more in keeping with their official designations as wilderness areas. I witnessed this concentration of use in May 1997 when I climbed Mount Hood for the second time. My partner, Jeff, and I drove from Eugene through Portland to Timberline Lodge, the magnificently crafted hotel built as a WPA project in 1935–36. The lodge was still covered by snow, and we entered through a tunnel to a small climbers' kiosk, where we filled out permits, paid a $15 fee, and acquired "blue bags" with enclosed instructions explaining how to collect and pack out our feces. We hiked up the snow next to the Timberline ski runs and stopped to put on warm clothing in a large building at 8,500 feet where the Palmer ski lift machinery hums. An hour later at Illumination Rock we camped among at least eight other tents, some of which were occupied by members of a climbing club from Spokane.[3] We heard them talking with great anticipation of climbing the Mazama Route, a steep but short snow gully that a confident climber might ascend in 90 minutes. But in climbing, larger groups always travel more slowly. These neighbors awoke at one-thirty, and the noise of their preparations kept me awake until four. Jeff and I left at five-thirty for the Sandy Glacier headwall, on the west side of the mountain facing Portland. As soon as we passed over Illumination saddle and down onto the Reid glacier, we left the world of mass mountaineering behind and found solitude. We descended to the base of the Yokum Ridge, Hood's most difficult route, put up by Cascades climbing legend Fred Beckey. We then passed over the Sandy Glacier without seeing a soul and climbed up two thousand feet of steep snow to Cathedral Ridge, just north of the summit. Here we unroped and relaxed in the noonday sun. After hiking a few hundred yards along the ridge, we came to the summit, which was occupied by at least a dozen people. On the way down we passed a nearly continuous line of climbers moving slowly upward, most roped together in teams of three or four. Many had departed Timberline Lodge at midnight, and some were so exhausted thirteen hours later that they collapsed and napped next to the trail.

During our climbing outing in the Mount Hood wilderness we encountered well over a hundred other people, all engaged in the same activity, but none of them on our particular route. By contrast, in May of the previous year, when we climbed Mount Jefferson, Oregon's second highest peak, by a route of comparable difficulty, we saw no one on the mountain at all. Yet the two climbs were equally rewarding, and we bore no hostility toward the throngs we encountered on Mount Hood's south side. Everyone was cheerful and ready to exchange greetings or conversation, and there was no sense among the climbers that they all would rather be alone.

I call attention to the phenomenon of "mass mountaineering" on Mount Hood in part to correct a growing misconception. Mountaineering is perceived by many today to be a sport for daring or foolish rich people, and although untrue, there are abundant reasons for this misconception. Like ocean yachting, climbing requires prodigious outlays of time, effort, and risk in return for rewards so ephemeral as to imply an aristocracy of taste, if not of class, among its practitioners. Moreover, the symbolic analogies between mountaineering and social stratification are so obvious that they act subconsciously, encouraging the notion that the man or woman who climbs a high peak stands above his or her peers and has earned the right to look down on others. Recently, this instinct has manifested itself in a fad for climbing among competitive, educated elites, particularly business executives. The blame for this trend might be laid on Texas oil billionaire Dick Bass, who in 1985 completed his goal of climbing the "Seven Summits," or highest mountains on each of the seven continents. He and Disney executive Frank Wells hired the accomplished mountaineer and filmmaker David Breashears to lead them in two attempts on Mount Everest and spent many tens of thousands of dollars more traveling to Antarctica to climb Vinsson Massif.

Following Bass's feat, and his ego-massaging book about it, *Seven Summits*, other plutocrats sought to prove their mettle in the mountains. Now mountaineering attracts celebrities such as supermodel Christy Turlington, whose guided ascent of another big volcano, Kilimanjaro, was featured in *Women's Sports and Fitness*, one of a rack of new fashion/recreation magazines.[4] Corporate public relations departments have been known to hire climbing guides and production companies to produce slick videos of the corporations' executives engaged in heroic climbs in Yosemite Valley, even if the moves are entirely staged and the ascents fake. As David Brooks writes in his recent work of cultural criticism, *Bobos in Paradise*, "today's educated executives thrill and then eventually bore you with their high-altitude conquests. A quarter of them seem either to be just back from one of those instant-glacier expeditions or to be deep in the midst of training for one."[5]

Much like the royalty of years past, today's corporate executives create spectacles to justify their rule, and mountaineering exploits are among the most effective. A few of the legendary figures from the heroic early years of mountaineering in the late nineteenth and early twentieth centuries really were royalty, such as the duke of Abruzzi, who led the first ascent of Mount Saint Elias in southeast Alaska in 1898. But most climbers of that era were not aristocrats. A survey of the founding members of the British Alpine Club, which organized pioneering expeditions to the Alps in 1857–63, showed a preponderance of upper-middle-class professionals, particularly lawyers. Sociologist Richard G. Mitchell combined this evidence with his own survey of the southern California section of the Sierra Club's Mountaineering Training Committee, where he likewise found a large number of professionals, especially engineers. Mitchell theorized that the alienation of such technical work drove these people to engage in mountaineering, and if he is correct, the Northwest's growing ranks of high-technology professionals may also be a population that breeds aspiring mountaineers, or at least clients for guided ascents.[6]

British Alpine Club members also established the practice of employing climbing guides, a service industry that thrives today on Rainier and Shasta. The first paid guides were men native to the alpine valleys who had learned their way around the mountains while hunting for the chamois, a goat prized for its fine wool. These guides' climbing skills and experience often exceeded that of their clients, but they were not credited with first ascents and generally did not have the means to record or publicize their achievements. Thus a class bias was built into the sport, one that persists, though in new forms. Eric Beck, a Yosemite rock climber of the 1960s, once commented, "At either end of the social spectrum there lies a leisure class."[7] Those who devote their lives to climbing, who live in Yosemite Valley or drive up to Alaska every summer, generally come from the lower end of this spectrum. Many "climbing bums" live off temporary jobs or, if they are lucky, equipment endorsements and guiding fees. These people form the sport's elite. But the throngs who ascend the three major Northwest volcanoes are not from a leisure class; they regard climbing as a recreation, not an avocation, and they are the clients, not the guides. Today's mass mountaineering offers democratic opportunities for elite achievement, commodified services for individual ambitions; anyone can sign up for a guided ascent of Mount Rainier, and if he or she succeeds, the mountain's stature becomes an emblem of the climber's fitness and determination.

In May 1996 the deaths of twelve climbers on Mount Everest brought climbing into the U.S. mass media more than at any other time in the twentieth century, a result of the attempts of bourgeois climbers to extend guide/client mountaineering to the Himalayas, which properly should belong to the sport's elite. Hype surrounding the event, along with Jon Krakauer's best-selling book about the incident, *Into Thin Air*, crystallized the growing cultural perception of mountaineers as rich, self-indulgent risk seekers, the focus of alternating envy and contempt. Yet most of the victims were not wealthy executives but common people like the masses on Rainier; they had worked and saved hard to pay for their trips. Pundits and nonclimbers generally were astonished to learn that the clients had paid as much as $60,000 for the privilege of frostbite, altitude sickness, and for several of them, death in pursuit of the bragging rights of the world's highest mountain. News accounts of major fatal accidents in outdoor recreation, such as tourists drowning in canyon flash floods in Switzerland and in Arizona in 1998 and 1999, now follow a common pattern. The media portray such activities as inherently risky, and therefore exciting and alluring to their readers or viewers, only to then reproach the victims of accidents, as well as the guides who are sometimes held responsible, as selfish or foolish in their desire to seek such thrills. But just as media controversies surrounding an offensive museum exhibit or banned book increase sales and visitors, the 1997 season on Everest drew more clients paying higher fees than ever. In the Pacific Northwest the spring 2002 season saw a fatal accident on Mount Hood which led to a tragic helicopter accident that seriously injured several rescuers and closed the mountain to all climbers for several days. Yet again, interest in climbing Hood is not likely to decline.

All this hype around mountaineering obscures the earlier history of the sport in the Northwest, when most climbers were not self-promoting individualists but more often members of convivial clubs, not headline-grabbing executives employing mercenary guides but middle-class commoners organizing their own expeditions and celebrating their accomplishments within their own circles. Mounts Hood and Rainier were the birthplaces of influential urban mountaineering associations, the Mazamas of Portland and the Mountaineers of Seattle.

The Mazamas Club was founded 19 July 1894 at a meeting held on the summit of Mount Hood. Organizers had placed ads in the Portland *Oregonian* and spread through word of mouth their plans for an association of "Mountain Climbers and Lovers of Nature." More than 300 gathered at a high camp the night before, and according to the club's literature, 193 joined for the summit meeting and became founding members. The founding president was William Steel, who had arrived in Oregon from Kansas in 1870 and, after seeing Crater Lake, campaigned tirelessly for the establishment of that site as a national park. The name *Mazama* comes from the mountain that exploded some 7,700 years ago to form Crater Lake. During the Mazamas' heyday in the 1910s and 1920s, "mass ascents" by hundreds were a yearly ritual. In addition to frequent outings to Hood, the club organized an annual encampment at various sites in the Oregon Cascades, where members gathered to hike, climb, and share meals, stories, and jovial songs around evening campfires. In 1897 they organized a party of 200 to Mount Rainier, which inspired locals around Seattle to establish a similar club, the Mountaineers. Other, smaller cities in the Northwest founded their own clubs, such as the Obsidians of Eugene and the Crag Rats of Hood River. In its early years the Sierra Club also organized much of its activities around climbing outings.

These popular organizations in the Northwest contrasted with the exclusivity and nationalism of the British Alpine Club. The Mazamas did not employ guides and did not observe status hierarchies or military discipline on their outings. Rather than hold a stiff upper lip, they promoted laughter with satiric sketches and comic campfire songs. As historian Eric Weiselberg puts it, "The Mazamas developed an identity as modernizing agents and defenders of civilization, as pragmatic environmentalists and regional boosters, not as environmental radicals, thrill-seeking sport climbers, or even professional recreation managers."[8] There was and is only one requirement for membership: "Any person of good character who has climbed to the summit of a mountain peak on which there is at least one living glacier." The club gives awards to those who "bag" the seven major Oregon Cascades peaks or the sixteen Northwest peaks on club outings. In contrast to popular perceptions of climbing today as a risky endeavor pursued by elite youthful athletes carrying lots of expensive equipment, the Mazamas believed that any able-bodied person might climb Mount Hood or other Oregon Cascades peaks. Those who joined the mass ascents often carried only an alpenstock, shared a few long hemp ropes, and dressed in frock coats or long dresses. So that anyone might feel that his or her climb was historic, the Mazamas installed summit registers on Oregon peaks and maintained these records in their Portland clubroom and library. Historians of climbing are often contemptuous of the Mazamas and Mountaineers because they promoted mass mountaineering rather than training elite climbers to advance the sport with first ascents.[9] Yet consistent with an era of progressive reform, the Mazamas democratized mountaineering, rejecting not only the classist noblesse oblige of the duke of Abruzzi but also the sense of competition that drove other climbers to first ascents and to ever harder routes.

Given the current media craze for mountaineering and the thousands of annual attempts on the three volcanoes, it might seem that the Mazamas have succeeded in their goal of bringing the sport to the masses. However, some aspects of this goal have been self-defeating, and other club values have been lost amid the changing image of climbing. Today the Mazamas number around three thousand, but their median age is fifty-one, and the average member joined sixteen years ago. The club now organizes bus tours, wine tastings, and "rambles" through the streets of Portland and its suburbs, as well as more vigorous hikes and climbs. In an effort to attract younger members, it sponsors an Explorer Scout post and has organized "Adventurous Youthful Mazamas," a subgroup for those under forty, who make up just a fifth of the membership. But these efforts run up against advertising and related spectacles like the X Games which encourage climbers to think of themselves as young rebels who pursue the sport as a means of escaping the social structures organized by their elders. Just as a teenager takes up snowboarding to distinguish himself from his parents who ski, a young Portlander will likely choose to go rock climbing with his buddies rather than join mom and dad on a Mazamas hike, which he regards as hopelessly uncool. In their heyday the Mazamas' ideology held that mountain climbing instilled virtue in its practitioners, but these virtues were much more conformist than the ones popular culture associates with the sport today. In an address delivered to a Mazamas outing on Mount Baker in 1920, member Richard Ward Montague even invoked Puritan leader John Winthrop to assert the communal bonds that climbing could forge: "'And here in the wilderness, of all places in the world, we learn best to know one another's naked souls. . . . Neither good conduct nor bad can be concealed here; every shelter tent and huddle of blankets is a city set on a hill which cannot be hid.'"[10] In contrast to today's image of mountaineers as self-seeking, risk-taking individualists, Montague proposed a quasi-totalitarian vision of the mountain camp as enforcing public order. Those who've experienced the group dynamics of a lengthy wilderness expedition can judge for themselves which is closer to the truth, but there's little doubt that such a communitarian ethic is less appealing today. Beyond the issue of youth versus age, America has seen a decline in the membership of all sorts of clubs and fraternal community organizations in the last three or four decades, a trend that Harvard political scientist Robert Putnam in *Bowling Alone* has diagnosed as a symptom of social anomie and a declining quality of life in middle-class America.[11]

Bruce Barcott's 1997 book *The Measure of a Mountain* sets out to describe "that strange relationship we [that is, fellow Seattle residents] have with the mountain," Mount Rainier, and also reflects how mass mountaineering today contributes to social anomie rather than fosters camaraderie.[12] Barcott admits at the outset to a fear of heights and an ignorance of climbing, yet he doggedly pursues his book project by joining the "REI Army" and buying a full outfit of mountaineering gear. Within the first twenty pages it becomes obvious that the author's summit attempt will be the climax of the book, even if its best chapters are devoted to the scientific study of the mountain and such topics as the danger that volcanic activity could trigger a massive glacial mudslide that will bury Tacoma. Barcott begins his study of mountaineering by interviewing professional guide Scott Fisher, who would die in the tragedy on Everest less than a year later. He then reads books by Joe Tasker, Joe Simpson, and Reinhold Messner, three scarred yet successful climbers, and absorbs an image of climbing as "a challenge . . . to see how much punishment the body can withstand" (131). Barcott finds his "conscience deeply opposed to the macho ethos of climbing" (134) and considers abandoning his ascent in a kind of protest, but because his father wants to climb Rainier, he signs them up for a guided ascent with RMI. On summit day his father tires and turns back, but Bruce goes to the top and returns to hug his father in the book's final line, as if he'd returned from a truly harrowing challenge. Yet his climb doesn't provide a heroic or even sentimental denouement to his book so much as it reveals three major inconsistencies in the image of mountaineering in American culture. Media coverage of accidents, several of which Barcott reviews, and the books of daredevil climbers he reads support the image of Rainier as "the most dangerous mountain in the lower 48" in spite of the fact that several thousand climb it safely each year just as he does. His pact with his father echoes the sordid psychobabble of climber-writers such as Marilyn Mason and the cultural construction of mountaineering as an exercise in personal growth or management training, a commodity peddled by Outward Bound and countless other camps and outfitters. Finally, the fact that Barcott, like so many others who wish to climb Mount Rainier, Hood, or Shasta to valorize their self-esteem, hired the guide company contrasts with the legacy of populist amateur organizations like the Mazamas and Seattle's own Mountaineers. In an earlier age Barcott might have joined the Mountaineers and learned to climb alongside peers who would have joined him in climbing Rainier. He would have undertaken the climb not as a neophyte client roped together with complete strangers just like himself but in the company of new friends who shared his interest and derived real confidence from learning the sport.

The demise of the old democratic, communal pattern of climbing has been hastened by its inherent conflicts with modern wilderness policy and management. Today, even on Mount Hood itself, the bureaucracy of wilderness recreation that the Mazamas helped create—as when William Steel lobbied for the designation of Crater Lake National Park and the Cascade Forest Reserve—has displaced such private clubs and constrains their activities. Where the Mazamas were proud to organize an outing of more than a hundred people to climb Mount Hood, the Forest Service now prohibits any party larger than twelve and places additional restrictions on guided parties, even those of nonprofit clubs led by volunteer instructors. Since the passage of the Wilderness Act in 1964 and the subsequent designation of the higher elevations of Hood, Rainier, and Shasta as wilderness areas, these peaks are no longer considered appropriate settings for social gatherings of mountain climbers. In line with the language of the Wilderness Act, that these areas should provide "outstanding opportunities for solitude or a primitive and unconfined type of recreation," the Forest Service sets "social encounter standards" specifying that on 80 percent of weekend days a hiker should meet no more than ten other groups hiking or climbing in "semi-primitive" zones of a wilderness area and six in "primitive" zones. Yet in spite of the best efforts of forest rangers and bureaucrats, climbing, on Mount Hood at least, continues to follow the patterns established during the glory days of the Mazamas. Mount Hood National Forest documents record an average of 215 persons per day on the South Side route of the mountain on summer weekends, a figure actually no higher than it was in the first half of the twentieth century. The other, more difficult routes on the peak actually see fewer climbers now than they did then, although these numbers have increased in the last twenty years.[13]

In December 1998 the Mount Hood National Forest (MHNF) released an Environmental Assessment plan for the protection of three wilderness areas contained in that forest, the Mount Hood and Salmon-Huckleberry along U.S. highway 26 less than thirty-five miles southeast of Portland, and the Hatfield (formerly Columbia Gorge Wilderness) along Interstate 84 just twenty-five miles east of the city. The professed goals of the plan were to "manage recreation use and protect wilderness values" as laid out in the 1964 Act,[14] in the face of increasing impacts caused by the booming population of the Portland metro area. The report acknowledged that overnight backpacking use in these three wilderness areas, as in most others across the West, had actually declined from historic highs in the late 1970s and early 1980s but that day hiking had increased, leading to severe crowding on some popular trails. Following its usual bureaucratic pattern, the Forest Service laid out alternatives for future policy. Alternative #1 would entail no immediate limits on use whereas #2, the "preferred alternative," called for a permit system to limit the number of parties allowed on major trails and climbing routes. The "primary goal" of Alternative #2 "would be to manage for solitude and primitive wilderness character" of the area. It proposed drastic limits on the most popular routes in the Mount Hood Wilderness. On the Ramona Falls trail, which on summer weekends hosts an average of 190 hikers a day, the proposed permits would limit visitors to 22. On the South Side climbing route the new policy would have reduced weekend traffic from 215 to 25.

Increasing regulation of climbing on Mount Hood is consistent with steps the Forest and Park Services took in the 1990s to deal with traffic on other Northwest volcanoes. Mount Hood climbers, like those attempting Shasta, Rainier, Mount Adams, and Mount St. Helens, must pay a special $15 fee in addition to other park access or trail park fees. Mount St. Helens National Volcanic Monument, established after the 1980 eruption, issues no more than one hundred permits per day during the summer for climbing to the summit, a relatively easy hike with no glacial hazards. A permit system is now in place on Mount Rainier which requires nonguided parties to apply months in advance for reservations at the two crowded high camps, Camp Muir and Camp Schurman. Alternative #2 in the Mount Hood Environmental Assessment differed from the regulations on the other Cascade volcanoes, however, insofar as it was driven primarily not by issues of sanitation or resource impacts but by the "social encounter standards" for wilderness areas. However, on the south side of Hood this standard had been exceeded not only since before the passage of the Wilderness Act in 1964 but for more than a century, since the first of the Mazamas' mass ascents. Alternative #2 extended the values of wilderness backpacking into the world of mass mountaineering, where solitude had never been an important goal. As if aware of this fact, the 1998 Environmental Assessment also included Alternative #3, termed the "South Side Exception," which would have excluded the South Side climbing route from the use limits.

For most of the twentieth century the Sierra Club and Mazamas alike believed that promoting mountain recreation would advance the cause of wilderness preservation. When in 1927 the Cascade Development Company proposed building a tramway from the Cooper Spur to the summit of Mount Hood, prominent Mazama leaders supported the plan. They pointed out that the cables for the tramway would scarcely be visible from a distance, that there was already a fire lookout on the summit, and that a summit lodge could provide overnight accommodation for climbers. It seems that the summit was at that time perceived as less remote and less difficult of access than it is today. Fortunately, a few Mazamas opposed the tramway, and when the Great Depression hit, the project foundered. Similarly, the Sierra Club in the 1930s supported plans for commercial ski areas in the Sierra Nevada of California until David Brower led a change of heart and began to oppose development in the mountains.[15]

In 1998 the Mazamas, the American Alpine Club, and the Access Fund (a nonprofit organization working to preserve access to rock and mountain climbing areas) all reacted sharply to the MHNF proposals. In their newsletters and in press releases the mountaineering organizations argued that to mandate solitude for climbers on Mount Hood was unnecessary and even posed grave risks. The Access Fund argued that "the 1964 Wilderness Act does not guarantee solitude" and that "opportunities for solitude already exist . . . and are largely self-regulated."[16] In the wilderness as in the city, it seems, one must seek out solitude, by hiking away from the most popular trails and routes. Moreover, the groups urged their members to write to the Forest Service, warning of the potential safety issues of such a permit system. If two hundred people were turned away from the South Side route on Mount Hood on a clear May weekend, many would request instead permits for other, more difficult routes, such as the Cooper Spur on the mountain's northeast side or Leuthold's Couloir on the southwest side, which see an average of just two and ten parties, respectively, on weekend days. But whereas a misstep on the South Side route poses little danger, except in a few short steep sections, on those other two routes, like virtually all the others on Hood, a slip can send a climber hurtling down the mountain. The climbers' organizations in effect argued that even if "solitude" is an essential quality of "wilderness," it is a foolish, misplaced goal to set for the management of an alpine climbing area.

To safely cross active glaciers, which are often riven by crevasses, climbers must rope together in teams of two or three and be trained in techniques of self-arrest to catch partners who fall into a crevasse that may be concealed by recent snow. To travel in solitude on a glacier is to invite disaster. The popular routes on Hood and Shasta involve minimal glacier travel and are frequently climbed unroped, but on Mount Rainier the Park Service prohibits solo climbers. Conversely, overcrowding can be dangerous as well. On steep, narrow routes, especially couloirs, climbers face the danger that others above might dislodge rocks, ice, or themselves. On 23 July 1994 two climbers of a group of four on Mount Hood were killed when the party fell one thousand feet from the upper section of the Cooper Spur route onto the Elliot Glacier below. The party had been roped together even though the route was not on a glacier, and when one fell, the others were unable to arrest the force of his fall because the snow was so soft and so steep. I had climbed the same route the previous weekend, also during hot weather and very soft snow. We were the only party on the route that day, and I thank my lucky stars that we faced no danger from falling snow or falling humans, or from a policy that might have encouraged others to be on the route. In mountaineering, as on a darkened city street, one generally sees other people as a source of safety but occasionally regards others as a potential threat.

The public comment period on the MHNF Wilderness Environmental Assessment, and its preferred Alternative #2, elicited more than six hundred responses. The Forest Service convened a Willamette Provincial Advisory Committee to coordinate the response. In April 2000 the MHNF published a follow-up document that summarized and digested the public comment, noting three main issues. The first was that "hikers and climbers said they do not expect solitude in popular areas" and that "encounters with other groups are usually a positive experience."[17] The document also acknowledged that displacing climbers away from the easiest route up the mountain could result in increased search-and-rescue costs (read: more accidents and fatalities) and that reducing use on the most popular trails might have the undesirable effect of increasing the trampling of campsites and lakesides in currently less-used areas. A new proposal, Alternative #4, added a new bureaucratic designation, "Use Management Areas," for the most heavily used destinations, in place of "Semi-Primitive." Within these UMAs, either campsites or popular day-use areas, individual group sites would be designated and "users visiting this destination would be required to camp or picnic at the designated sites to prevent additional sites from becoming established."[18] In effect, the new language sanctioned the "zoning" of a wilderness area for human use, much as cities are zoned for density of residential or commercial use. The number of hikers along "UMA trail corridors," the highways leading to the day-use areas, would not be limited, just as Americans would not think of limiting the use of cars even if they countenance limiting the use of trails and campsites.

For a time it appeared that the interests of climbers had carried the day. In December 2000 the MHNF issued a decision endorsing Alternative #4 and repeating many of the arguments in support of it, including the long history of mass mountaineering on Mount Hood and the danger of forcing inexperienced mountaineers away from the South Side and onto more difficult routes.[19] But then in July 2001 MHNF supervisor Gary Larsen issued a terse one-page letter reversing his decision and apparently returning the issue to the bureaucratic morass of "further study."[20] Whatever the final outcome, the public comments and the resulting documents suggest that the Forest Service recognizes the peculiar dynamic created between Portland (which is home to nearly two million people, two-thirds of Oregon's population) and the fragments of wilderness that are preserved within a ninety-minute drive of the city. The December 2000 decision acknowledged that "many of the existing wilderness social standards (encounters with others for example) do not work well in U.M.A. destinations and trail corridors areas" and declared that "more social research is needed to evaluate what wilderness parameters best reflect a visitor's wilderness experience." It also called for federal recreation managers to "develop and market non-wilderness destinations" as a means of reducing the growing impacts in the Mount Hood Wilderness. Yet since virtually all the remaining acreage in the MHNF is either apportioned to logging or fenced off to protect Portland's water supply, new trails and appealing "non-wilderness destinations" will be hard to find. And in any case, only a few destinations, places such as Eagle Creek in the Columbia Gorge, whose glories are spoken of in Portland cafés and supermarkets, exceed the carrying capacity that Forest Service rangers have determined. There is still ample room for hikers in the wilderness, and in fact, unless people start taking buses to the trailhead, the highways will be clogged before the trails are.

Interestingly, the MHNF studies make no mention of the solution Europeans use for accommodating large numbers of mountaineers without destroying alpine meadows and fouling snow and streams—the problems that plague Paradise and Camp Muir on Mount Rainier and Lake Helen on Shasta. In the Alps, refuges or huts, some of them large stone buildings with kitchens and paid staff members, provide secure lodging at a reasonable price. Many are located at the base of challenging climbing routes, and some are managed by climbers' clubs such as the Club Alpin Français. The small stone hut built by the Sierra Club just below the popular bivouac site at Lake Helen, and the Silcox Hut, a former lift machine house on Mount Hood, hint at the European huts but are too small to accommodate even a fraction of the climbers on those peaks. At Camp Muir a simple plywood bunkhouse has been built for the clients of RMI to catch a couple hours of sleep before their midnight departure. The Mazamas own and operate a lodge at Government Camp, but it is far too low on the slopes of Mount Hood to accommodate climbers on the night before their attempt. Although huts have been established in the Canadian Rockies and in the Adirondacks and White Mountains, they have never caught on in the western United States. To build such a structure within a wilderness area would violate the 1964 law even though it might solve sanitation and impact problems at the high camps. The concentration of climbers in squalid high camps is an urban problem requiring an urban solution, but the politics of wilderness cannot accommodate this solution.

Urban residents often say that they enjoy going hiking to "get away from it all," and they praise the psychological benefits of their brief visits to the wilderness, but they nevertheless frequently carry habits formed by life in cities out onto the trails along with their backpacks. These wilderness users may consider social interaction with friends and family members they hike with to be far more important than the "solitude" that National Forest officials assume is essential to the wilderness experience. Some, particularly women hiking alone or in small groups, may even be fearful of lonely trails and isolated trailheads. Many who have chosen to live in urban settings because they prefer crowded, diverse sidewalks to sterile suburban cul-de-sacs may see a popular mountain trail as another such sidewalk, where they might run into a like-minded friend or be seen while engaged in a fashionable leisure pursuit. And these urban habits are not necessarily bad. Cultural critics from Jane Jacobs to Andrew Ross have pointed out that dense urban settings are actually much more environmentally efficient than the exurban pattern of sprawl that is spreading across much of America, East and West.[21] From this perspective, Forest Service regulations that enforce separation and solitude between people in wilderness areas may appear as short-sighted and self-defeating as zoning laws that require off-street parking and prohibit multifamily residences or small lot sizes. And as the revised Environmental Assessment noted, a public backlash against a new permit system might result in reduced support for the Wilderness Act generally, at a time when roadless areas on public lands desperately need that legal protection.

If the Mazamas and Mountaineers first brought urbanites to the mountains with their mass ascents and progressive agenda, today an even more urbanized West confronts the challenge of balancing wilderness ethics with the continuing popularity of mass mountaineering. In these conflicts the interests of climbers seem to diverge from those of environmentalists. Whereas the Mazamas and other climbers' clubs came out against Alternative #2 for the MHNF, the local Oregon chapter of the Sierra Club took no official position, instead using the occasion to call for designating the entire MHNF a scenic recreation area, a classification that would avoid the high-profile status of a national park but enforce a ban on logging. The contrasting positions of the two groups might be explained by a kind of reverse "not in my backyard" principle: it's okay to restrict use in a distant wilderness area but not in the one I like to play in most. Wilderness supporters have become wary of promoting the attractions of their favorite recreation site for fear of drawing the kind of mobs that crowd the national parks and the easier climbing routes on the three volcanoes. This principle explains the constituency that opposed the idea of designating Mount Shasta a national park or monument because of the worry that even more climbers and hikers would come to it. Likewise, in August 2000 the Oregon Sierra Club announced an alliance with ranchers' groups to oppose plans by the Clinton administration for a national monument at Steens Mountain, a high plateau (with a road to the top) in remote southeastern Oregon (although they later reached a compromise agreement). Only the advent of the Bush administration has changed this dynamic, as recreational interests and environmental lobbyists alike recognize that national monument protection is their best hope.

The urban culture of today's Northwest prizes mountain wilderness more than ever, even if most misinterpret it as something to be seen through the window of a sport-utility vehicle. Those committed to wilderness protection and recreation, those who hike the trails and climb the peaks, inevitably bring some of the social values of the city with them, and this is not necessarily a bad thing. Historian Eric Weiselberg wrote of the Mazamas that they "climbed in a domesticated landscape which reflected their urban origins."[22] The history of the Mazamas suggests that mountaineering on the three volcanoes was once seen as a collective pursuit which promoted not individualist competition or self-esteem but social progress and esprit de corps, and which was meant to be practiced not in solitude but in camaraderie. Today, by contrast, popular attitudes and official policy regard wilderness recreation as antithetical to urban life, even as many of the wild lands' most fervent supporters and frequent visitors are urbanites. In formulating policy for climbing on the three volcanoes and elsewhere in the West, we should avoid this contradiction by recognizing the history of popular mountaineering and the integral sociability of climbing.

NOTES

1. John Muir, *Steep Trails* (Boston: Houghton Mifflin, 1918; reprint, San Francisco: Sierra Club Books, 1994), 210–11.

2. As Bruce Barcott points out, books about the British Mount Everest expeditions of the 1920s were given militaristic titles: *Mount Everest: The Reconnaissance, The Assault on Mount Everest,* and *The Fight for Everest.* Barcott, *The Measure of a Mountain: Beauty and Terror on Mount Rainier* (Seattle: Sasquatch Books, 1997), 127. Among more academic studies of mountaineering literature and its imperialist rhetoric, Simon Schama writes of British explorer William Windham that "the journey to Mont Blanc is, in fact, narrated as a victory of imperial confidence over timorous native superstition." *Landscape and Memory* (New York: Vintage, 1996), 465.

3. Because Mount Hood's South Side route can be done from the Timberline Lodge parking lot in a day, its high camp at Illumination Saddle does not host as many people as the high camps on Rainier and Shasta, but it is still crowded.

4. Christy Turlington, "Kili or Bust," *Womens Sports and Fitness* (September/October 1999): 90–95.

5. David Brooks, *Bobos in Paradise: The New Upper Class and How They Got There* (New York: Simon and Schuster, 2000), 209. Aside from the CEOs who try to use climbing to demonstrate their ambition and superiority, there are many more upper-middle-class Americans who go to the mountains in search of psychological remedies for stress or depression. Marilyn Mason, *Seven Mountains: The Inner Climb to Commitment and Caring* (New York: Dutton, 1997), refers not as Bass did to the highest peaks on the seven continents but to a list of steps for using climbing as self-esteem therapy. It is a typical self-help book made up of case histories drawn from the author's clinical practice and testimonies to the cures effected by outings she organized as a guide-therapist.

6. Richard G. Mitchell, Jr., *Mountain Experience: The Psychology and Sociology of Adventure* (Chicago: University of Chicago Press, 1983), 183. On guides in the Alps, see also Jeremy Bernstein, *Ascent: The Invention of Modern Mountaineering and Its Practice* (1965; reprint, New York: Touchstone, 1989).

7. Quoted in Chris Jones, *Climbing in North America* (Berkeley: University of California Press, 1976), 353.

8. Eric Weiselberg, "The Early Mazamas: Modern Climbers on Top During the Golden Age of Mountaineering the Pacific Northwest," *Mazama* (1999): 20–21.

9. See, for instance, Jones, *Climbing in North America,* 144.

10. Eric Weiselberg, *The Ascendancy of the Mazamas: Environment, Identity, and Mountain Climbing in Oregon, 1870 to 1930* (Ph.D. diss., University of Oregon, 1999), 246.

11. Robert Putnam, *Bowling Alone: The Collapse and Revival of American Community* (New York: Simon and Schuster, 2000).

12. Barcott, *Measure of a Mountain,* 2–3. Subsequent page references are in parentheses in the text.

13. *Wilderness Protection Environmental Assessment for Modification of Standards and Guidelines and Management Actions Relating to the Use of the Mt. Hood, Salmon-Huckleberry, and Hatfield Wildernesses, Mt. Hood Land and Resource Management*

Plan, Amendment #13, April 2000. This lengthy report and title is referred to as the *Environmental Assessment*, or *EA* for short.

14. *Overview on the New Alternative for the Wilderness Protection Plan*, April 2000. This is a summary of the full report cited in note 13.

15. See Michael P. Cohen, *The History of the Sierra Club, 1892–1970* (San Francisco: Sierra Club Books, 1988).

16. "Mount Hood Is Latest Battleground over Social Encounters," *Vertical Times* [Access Fund newletter] (March 1999): 3.

17. *Overview*, 2; *Environmental Assessment*, 22.

18. *Overview*, 4.

19. "Decision Notice and Finding of No Significant Impact," December 2000.

20. "Letter of Withdrawal" from Forest Supervisor Gary L. Larsen, 30 July 2001. All four of these Mount Hood National Forest publications are posted at http://www.fs.fed.us/r6/mthood/pubs.htm.

21. Andrew Ross, *The Chicago Gangster Theory of Life: Nature's Debt to Society* (London: Verso, 1994), and Jane Jacobs, *The Death and Life of Great American Cities* (1961; reprint, New York: Modern Library, 1993).

22. Weiselberg, *Ascendancy of the Mazamas*, 235.

Ken Owens

FISHING THE HATCH

New West Romanticism and Fly-Fishing in the High Country

A prolific hatch of mayflies or stone flies can bring big trout recklessly to a stream's surface, where they may be easily caught by skilled anglers with appropriate concoctions of feathers and fur. In similar fashion, as the fly-fishing industry developed in the American West, a fresh hatch of pseudo-western fantasy attracted eager and incautious customers willing to be hooked by skilled manipulators of the imagery.

At its start, fly-fishing in western America exemplified the practices and social positioning long associated with the British and northeastern origins of the sport. Then, beginning in the 1930s, it gradually assumed a specific regional identity in the West, demonstrating a strong imaginative appeal to both easterners and westerners. This new image of fly-fishing stemmed in part from anglers' experience of fishing on western waters and in part from a re-imagining and re-imaging of western identity through a type of New West romanticism broadly derived from American popular culture. By the late twentieth century, fly-fishing tourism was prospering throughout western America, particularly in the high country of the Rocky Mountain West, as expert entrepreneurs learned to fashion effective lures to match the New Western hatch.

In the United States fly-fishing for trout began during the late colonial era in Pennsylvania, upstate New York, and New England. Imitating the techniques, equipment, and class consciousness of elite Britishers, who had long practiced the sport, a small group of American fly-fishers, for the most part male, pursued their hobby with gusto.[1] By the early 1870s, however, fly-fishing for trout was spreading into the American West, arriving first along the Pacific Coast and then moving into the Rocky Mountain region as a direct cultural transplant. Although trout could be caught by trolling a spinner or a fly behind a rowed boat with a bait rod and reel in western lakes, fly-fishing was really the only alternative to bait fishing in rivers and streams until the advent of monofilament line, fiberglass rods, and open-faced spinning reels after World War II. Certainly it was regarded as the one true sporting way to spend a day, a week, or a lifetime in pursuit of piscatorial achievement.

During the early decades of the twentieth century the British and northeastern influence remained quite apparent in advertisements featuring western fly-fishing. A 1902 advertisement in *Sunset* magazine for a vacation spot in northern California's Siskiyou Mountains, for example, pictures a slender fellow wearing a straw boater and stiff-collared white shirt as he stands at casual ease in a small river. His hip boots and willow creel, along with a fly rod, define him as a fly-fisher. But experienced fishers, knowledgeable about the rough wading and windy conditions usually encountered on northern California trout streams, would have known then as now that this chap was not really outfitted for a day astream. A scene that existed only in the artist's imagination, the advertisement was obviously meant to convey an impression of high-class, refined recreation to potential visitors. Photographs from this era, however, such as a carefully posed shot of three bonneted Montana women in Sunday garb fly-fishing on Lolo Creek while their menfolk stand guard behind them, demonstrate that fly-fishing was also a sport for ordinary westerners and that their streamside wear had not yet become a specialized form of costume.

A few other images dating from the same general period reflect the cultural adaptation that was starting to make fly-fishing in the West different from that in the eastern states. A sporting-goods catalog of 1915, for example, carried a photograph of Mrs. W. S. Phillips, dubbed "Pardner," with an exceptional steelhead trout caught in the Skykomish River of Washington—a fifteen-pound fish that set a size record for fly-caught trout before migratory steelhead were placed in a separate category from resident rainbow trout in the record books. Mrs. Phillips looks altogether like a western gal. She is properly attired for the outdoors in her broad-brimmed, high-crowned canvas hat, a durable short full skirt, and sturdy boots, making her no doubt an extremely suitable "pardner" for Mr. Phillips, the fisherman, who liked to refer to himself as "El Comancho" for reasons now lost to the historical record.[2]

Hats, of course, early became a key element in defining a fisherperson's on-stream image, imparting a quality of costumed playacting to the sport of fly-fishing. The hat worn by Mrs. Phillips was apparently modeled along the lines of a Spanish-American War–World War I army fatigue hat, and this piece of gear soon became an essential part of western fly-fishing iconography. The Kimball-Upson Company, a sporting-goods firm in Sacramento, California, would send you one from the company catalog for a dollar and a quarter in 1916.[3]

The cowboy image became a universal symbol of the West in American popular culture during the 1920s when chambers of commerce and state tourist agencies started marketing the West to outsiders who had perhaps read *The Virginian* or *Riders of the Purple Sage* and who certainly had been thrilled by the film exploits of such early horse opera stars as Broncho Billy Anderson, Tom Mix, and William S. Hart.[4] But this cowboy-izing of the West did not immediately transfer to fly-fishing. In fact, well into the 1930s, California and the Pacific Northwest—not then regarded as cowboy country—remained the focus of fly-fishing promotion in western America, with steelhead angling the best-known form of the sport. The joys of Oregon's fly-rod steelheading were widely broadcast through the writings of Zane Grey, once America's most renowned sports fisherman. Grey publicized the pleasures of fall and winter fishing for steelhead on southern Oregon's Rogue River, where he kept a lodge for some years, and of summer steelheading on the North Umpqua River.[5] Meanwhile, the abundant opportunities for exceptional fly-fishing for wild trout in the Rocky Mountain region were little known and little noticed elsewhere.

This situation began to change slowly by the late 1930s, in large part because of the activities of a few men who became expert promoters of western fly-fishing with a focus on the northern Rockies. The first was Dan Bailey. Born and raised in Kentucky, Bailey was from early adolescence a fly-fishing fanatic in the extreme, a person whose second thought at any time, no matter where he was or what else he was doing, focused on where he would fish next, how soon, and for how long. By the mid-1930s Bailey was living in New York City, a well-known figure in the small world of skilled fly-fishers centered there, close friends with Lee Wulff, Joe Brooks, and others who would also become prominent in this field. But trout angling was not yet Bailey's whole life; he was actually well started on a different professional career, teaching college while working toward a Ph.D. in atomic physics at New York University. Then, in spring 1936, Bailey picked up a Billings newspaper and read a story about Montana's wonderful trout fishing. Using his honeymoon as the opportunity, he drove his old car west and, with the tolerance of his clearly saintly bride Helen, fished the Gallatin and Madison Rivers near Bozeman. By the time they returned the following year, Dan had decided to give up his teaching career, drop out of graduate school, and try to make a living in the fly-fishing business in Montana. Moreover, he persuaded Helen, a charming native New Yorker with a good job as a nurse, to leave work and family behind and move to Montana, though she was reluctant to give up New York and never became too greatly interested in fishing.[6]

Essentially by accident—an automobile breakdown, as he later told the story—Bailey settled in Livingston rather than Bozeman. There he opened a business tying flies and selling them, along with other fly-fishing gear, and guiding tourists to the best fishing on nearby streams. Despite its proximity to the Yellowstone River and other prime waters, Livingston was a small town and would remain a small town. Bailey could not rely on in-store sales to keep his business going. In 1937 he published his first catalog, advertising the flies that he and soon a small part-time crew of local housewives were tying, and advertising as well the attractions of Montana as a fly-fisher's Eden. Sent to everyone he knew in the East and then to a wider and wider clientele, his annual catalogs became Bailey's basic business tool. Through them he effectively publicized the attractions of fly-fishing in Montana. Moreover, his personal ties—and his wife's New York–accented hospitality—drew a good many eastern fishing experts to Livingston, where Bailey's shop and home became their headquarters for exploring the region's exceptional fishing opportunities. Among frequent visitors was his friend Joe Brooks, a talented and popular fishing writer whose stories about Montana trout fishing began appearing in widely circulated outdoors magazines by the late 1940s, drawing even more attention to the Rocky Mountain West. Yet Dan Bailey never went entirely native. He was allergic to horses. And no one ever saw him wearing a wide-brimmed cowboy hat.

Although Bailey's role as a fly-fishing promoter with strong eastern ties was crucial, by no means was he alone as a salesman for Rocky Mountain fly-fishing. His Montana-born counterpart was Bud Lilly, who made a broad-brimmed cowboy-style hat part of his customary fishing regalia. Growing up in Manhattan, Montana, during the 1930s, Lilly began fly-fishing under his dad's tutelage on the Gallatin and Madison Rivers. Home waters for the Lillys, father and son, these streams were not yet famous for their trout. His dad, Bud later said, strongly objected to the invasion of their local fishing territory by the "BBs"—the Butte Bastards. Even when his dad caught a nine-pound brown trout on a small feeder stream, it didn't cause much excitement around town. "Fishing," Lilly explained, "was just something people did; it wasn't news."[7]

Nor did it seem a realistic way to make a living. After eighteen months' service in the navy at the end of the World War II, Lilly finished college at

Montana State University on the GI Bill, married, and started teaching high school science. But the pay was poor, and it was not the sort of life in the outdoors that he had hoped to find. In 1950, after a brief venture in the carwash business, he bought George Grant's small fly-fishing store, the Trout Shop, in West Yellowstone, thinking it looked like "an interesting little business," although it sure "didn't show much financial promise."[8]

Bud and Pat Lilly, later with the help of their three children, ran the Trout Shop as a family enterprise, and they made it fisher-friendly to every tourist who happened to drop by looking for advice and instruction. At the time he and Pat took over the business, according to Lilly, "the crowd of regulars who fished the West Yellowstone area then was pretty highbrow by modern standards. . . . They were few in number, they prided themselves on their fine tackle, and their circle was pretty much closed to newcomers or people who fished differently than they did."[9] With a totally different attitude the Lillys survived the lean times, though for some years Bud continued to teach high school in Bozeman during the off-season.

Then came the fly-fishing boom of the 1970s, a product of growing leisure time for middle-class Americans, increased interest in outdoor recreation, and sweeping innovations in fly-fishing technology and techniques that made the sport more accessible for the beginner. Like the Baileys in Livingston, the Lillys in West Yellowstone found themselves dealing with hundreds and hundreds of eager, anxious, hopeful, novice fly-fishers ready to embrace the sport with all the fervor of new converts. Bud started to make speaking tours, joining other suddenly renowned western fishing authorities. Guiding developed into a major source of income, and Lilly's Trout Shop came to dominate the business in the Yellowstone area. In 1969 the Trout Shop began offering trout-fishing schools, enlisting the services of Lilly's friends among the experts to provide instruction and pleasant company for newcomers to the sport. In addition, Bud and Pat sponsored some of the first conclaves, as they were called, for the Federation of Fly Fishers, a national organization that sought to represent the sport and serve the hundreds of local clubs springing up across the country. "It all fit into my various schemes to promote fly-fishing," Lilly explained in his memoirs, "and do some business at the same time."[10]

The Lillys, the Baileys, and perhaps a half dozen other local fly-shop owners and guides helped set the stage, but no person did more to bring on the 1970s fly-fishing boom in the northern Rockies than Ted Trueblood of Nampa, Idaho. An extremely talented writer and a multifaceted outdoorsman, hunter, and fisher with a college degree in journalism, Trueblood began his career as a newspaper reporter in Boise. There he met and married Ellen

Hinkson, a newspaperwoman and Boise native who shared fully his enthusiasm for wild nature.[11] In 1941, at the age of twenty-four, he persuaded Ellen to move east, where Trueblood served briefly as the fishing editor for the New York–based *Field and Stream*, then the leading outdoors magazine in the United States. A change in management soon cost him the position, but he was reappointed in 1944, only to quit two years later when the heart failure of a recently retired neighbor inspired him to sacrifice security, leave the East Coast, and return to Idaho to hunt and fish and to write about hunting and fishing. His stories sold well, and in 1954 he accepted another offer from *Field and Stream*: an appointment as associate editor with a regular salary in return for one column a month on any subject he chose, which he could mail in from Idaho.

For more than twenty years *Field and Stream* proved to be a perfect medium for Trueblood's messages. Frequently, he wrote accounts of his own adventures but with a lesson to be learned in every story. He was a dedicated advocate for a wilderness ethic long before the environmental movement made this attitude a popular stance. Among other distinctions, he was a pioneer exponent of catch-and-release fly-fishing, arguing for the adoption of this practice in his columns by the mid-1950s, more than twenty years before the movement became generally acceptable to most of his fellow outdoors writers. He also had a leading role in developing and then publicizing the myriad technological advances that revolutionized fly-fishing from the 1950s forward.

One part of that technological revolution with problematic consequences for the fisheries and the embryonic fly-fishing business was the advent of spin fishing. New technologies made monofilament line and fiberglass rods available right after World War II, and a host of companies soon began manufacturing open-faced spinning reels that easily cast bait, spinners, and spoons long distances without the backlashes and tangles so frustrating for all but the most experienced masters of casting reels. With spinning gear it became simple and inexpensive for virtually anyone, no matter how ignorant or clumsy, to catch good-sized fish either on bait or with spinners and spoons. Combined with America's immense rush to the outdoors during the postwar era, spin fishing drastically depleted fisheries stocks in some of the West's best waters.

Moreover, increased exploitation of the western natural environment—virtually unregulated logging, mining, agricultural irrigation, urban growth, and wastewater discharges, as well as major dam-building projects and many other types of assault on streams and fisheries resources—moved Trueblood, Lilly, Bailey, Brooks, and other prominent western fly-fishers to advocacy for the fish and their ecosystems. The results of their leadership remain apparent in many areas, most directly in the adoption by state and federal resource management agencies of special "fly-fishing only" regulations with limited take or zero-take rules and in the catch-and-release ethic that has become all but universal among today's fly-fishers.

Ask any small group of committed western fly-fishers above, say, the age of forty about how they got started in the sport and how they began learning the endless lessons it has to teach. The conversation may start with accounts of personal initiation by family members or other significant elders, but very soon the names Dan Bailey, Bud Lilly, Ted Trueblood, and Joe Brooks inevitably enter. The greater the distance your trout lovers needed to travel to reach the fabled streams of the northern Rockies, the more certain it is that they came in response to the messages these pioneer publicists sent out from the high country to stir the blood of the adventurous young.[12]

A more calculated use of the West as a commercial asset can be found in the extremely successful career of Leigh Perkins. An Ohio native born into a wealthy family, Perkins bought the small Vermont-based Orvis Company in 1965 at age thirty-seven and built it into a multimillion-dollar business. He succeeded in large part by marketing expensive western fly-fishing and hunting experiences—along with the expensive gear required for these experiences—to an upscale clientele mostly in the eastern states.[13] Ahead of Bud Lilly, Leigh Perkins was the first entrepreneur to open fly-fishing schools in the Yellowstone area and to charter exclusive luxury lodge facilities in Montana and Wyoming that would host the financially favored dudes who were attracted west by Orvis promotions. Guided by Perkins's marketing skills, the Orvis Company became a prime beneficiary of the 1970s fly-fishing boom.

The continuation of the boom that began in the 1970s reached a culmination of sorts with the filming of the movie *A River Runs Through It*, a.k.a. Hollywood Discovers Montana Fly-Fishing. Released in 1992, the movie has a place of major importance in this narrative—not, of course, because of Brad Pitt's skills with a fly rod, which remained minimal, and not even because of the beautiful fly-line patterns made by Jason Borger, Pitt's stunt stand-in, who used a modern graphite rod designed to look like an authentic old bamboo fishing stick. Rather, it is significant because *A River Runs Through It* marked the first time fly-fishing fully engaged the attention of American popular culture. It interpreted fly-fishing in essence as a western experience.

With this movie the sport for the first time gained a broad-based validity as an American form of recreation. Still more to the point, it gave western fly-fishing an aura of historical authenticity and credibility that was easy to meld with the emerging images of New Western-ness, the images of our ubiquitous faux-cowboy culture. And the movie's success touched off another sudden boom in the fly-fishing business—predominantly a New West yuppie boom. Thousands of innocents who previously had held only a spinning rod in their hands—if that—came round to the local fly-fishing shops, bought high-end equipment, signed up for casting lessons, and booked their first trips to go fishing in Montana, Colorado, Utah, Wyoming, New Mexico, or Idaho—somewhere away from home, somewhere in the New West of the advertising brochures. Short on stream skills and fishing experience, they hoped that by taking enough gadgets and high-priced gear to the perfect place, they too would become instant FFEs, fly-fishing experts.[14]

The blending of the cowboy concept and fly-fishing in the New West has its quintessential form in an image that has been repeatedly put forward by western promoters and publicists: a cowboy-garbed man with a fly rod in hand sitting astride a horse in a shallow stream or lake and casting for a trout. An imaginative drawing of such a scene appeared in 1965 on the cover of *Field and Stream.* A carefully staged photo of a similar scene headed a story on fly-fishing ranch vacations in 1994 in *Fly Rod and Reel*, a publication prominent among the crop of fly-fishing magazines that sprang up during the 1980s. Still another photo version of this same scene has been used recently by Wyoming's state tourism office to promote its product. Artistically strained and factually bogus, these imaginary scenes are completely hokey. Experienced fishers are certain to doubt that any self-respecting trout, no matter how gullible, has ever really been caught from horseback with a fly rod—except perhaps at the edge of some recently planted trout pond on a dude ranch.

The most perfect of all the New West images to be found in the current fly-fishing literature appears in an ad for the W. L. Gore Company, maker of Gore-Tex waterproof wear. This ad, which recently appeared as a two-page spread in virtually all the fly-fishing magazines, shows three genuine fly-fishing guides posed at what is humorously called the Drive-In Hole on the Bighorn River, located on the Crow Indian Reservation in south-central Montana not far from the Little Bighorn battlefield. In the ad every detail is accurate and authentic. The message is obvious: If these three very western guys (as you can tell by their hats), fishing in this very western spot, wear Gore-Tex, then, by damn, so should you. On the Bighorn. Right now.

The Bighorn River setting for this ad, complete with old cars for riverbank riprap, has become a premier location for fly-fishing in today's West. Stream censuses on this stretch of the Bighorn indicate an astonishing seven thousand good-sized trout per mile. The site is preeminently—and ironically—a New West creation. It was brought into existence for trout fishing, all unwittingly, when the U.S. Bureau of Reclamation constructed Yellowtail Dam in 1966. The blue-ribbon tailwater section of the Bighorn River, in fact, is one of more than three dozen prime tailwater fishing sites in western America created by high-rise, bottom-release dams—irrigation dams and hydropower dams—put into place mainly between 1950 and 1968 on rivers that had previously offered no better than marginal trout fishing.[15] Some of these sites, like the Yellowtail tailwater on the Bighorn, today attract hundreds of fly-fishing enthusiasts from around the world. With catch-and-release regulations in effect, they sustain an incredible number of visitors and still reward them with decent fishing. One astute commentator, the late Montana fly-fishing writer and fly pattern innovator Gary LaFontaine, called them Disneylands with fish.[16]

Not all the New West fly-fishing images have to do with men, their fish, their western hats, and their high-priced fishing toys. The most popular photo ever to appear on the cover of *California Fly Fisher* shows a determined and obviously highly skilled young fisherwoman, blonde hair flying under her well-shaped western felt hat, clad in a heavy buffalo-plaid wool shirt, fishing vest, and chest-high waders, standing tall in the water as she balances her backcast and prepares to send her fly—we naturally assume—toward a rising trout.[17] It emphasizes the fact, obvious to anyone familiar with the current scene on western trout waters, that women in the New West are no longer just the perky smiling "pardners" of fishing men.

In 2001, for the first time, the state of Montana began to limit access to two of its most popular fly-fishing streams, the Beaverhead River (a tailwater) and the Big Hole River, using a permit system that restricts the number of drift boats allowed on the river each day.[18] Because this system mainly affects small guiding outfits with out-of-state clients, the limitation is less controversial among Montanans than issues about landowners' rights and public access to prime fishing sites. But the entire matter gives excellent testimony to the success of the selling campaign that has brought fly-fishing from obscurity to a major income-producing element in the New West's packaging of recreational tourism as a basic industry.[19] As the state of Wyoming tourism office tells us in another recent sham-historical ad, trout aren't stupid; and neither are those entrepreneurs and publicists who "fish the hatch," who catch—but never willingly release—their clients with images of the New West as the natural home for trout, trout that, we are led to believe, possess all the many mythic virtues of a western way of life in the high country's now-legendary rivers and beckoning streams.

NOTES

1. The historical development of fly-fishing in the Northeast is emphasized in Paul Schullery, *American Fly-Fishing: A History* (New York: Lyons and Burford, 1987).

2. Samuel Melner and Hermann Kessler, comps., *Great Fishing Tackle Catalogs of the Golden Age* (New York: Crown, 1972), 68.

3. Kimball-Upson Company Catalog 26, 1916, accession number 82/162/01, Sacramento Archives and Museum Collection Center, Sacramento, California.

4. For this phenomenon, complete with wry commentary, see Robert G. Athearn, *The Mythic West in Twentieth-Century America* (Lawrence: University Press of Kansas, 1986).

5. See the introduction by George Reiger in *Zane Grey, Outdoorsman: Zane Grey's Best Hunting and Fishing Tales* (Englewood Cliffs, N.J.: Prentice-Hall, 1972), and Grey's story "The North Umpqua, Oregon," in the same volume, 269–80.

6. Charles Waterman, *Mist on the River: Remembrances of Dan Bailey* (Livingston, Mont.: Yellowstone Press, 1986), is a fond tribute that serves as the major source on Bailey's life and his contributions to fly-fishing.

7. Bud Lilly and Paul Schullery, *Bud Lilly's Guide to Fly-Fishing the New West* (Portland, Ore.: Frank Amato Publications, 2000), 16.

8. Lilly and Schullery, *Bud Lilly's Guide*, 27. See also Pat Munday, *Montana's Last Best River: The Big Hole and Its People* (Guilford, Conn.: Lyons Press, 2001), 115–16.

9. Lilly and Schullery, *Bud Lilly's Guide*, 23. This group of fly-fishing elitists, Lilly recalled, were typified by the attitudes and the writing in Howard Back's 1938 publication, *The Waters of Yellowstone with Rod and Fly*. Pat Barnes, also renowned as a pioneer Yellowstone-area fishing guide, was well connected with this group when Bud and Pat Lilly took over the Trout Shop.

10. Lilly and Schullery, *Bud Lilly's Guide*, 27.

11. Trueblood has not yet received the biographical attention he merits. An excellent short sketch is Ron Mitchell, "A Gentle Giant," in the Idaho Sporting Congress's *Newsletter* 20 (22 February 1995): 1–6. My account has also benefited from interviews with Mitchell, who learned to fly-fish as a youngster in Nampa aided by Trueblood's gracious tutelage and who is now the director of the Idaho Sporting Congress. Trueblood's work is best seen in the pages of *Field and Stream* and other outdoor sports magazines, but an early sampling is also found in Walter Dower and Ted Trueblood, *Trout Trouble, and Other Trouble* (New York: Crowell, 1948).

12. The importance of these men was emphasized by Gary LaFontaine, for many years Montana's best-known, most innovative fly-fishing authority, who grew up in Connecticut but first learned about fishing in the West in good part by reading stories by Trueblood and Brooks, and who bought flies from Bailey's catalog with his paper-route money to try on Connecticut waters. The Trude, a distinctive Montana fly style named after the Trude Ranch, became young LaFontaine's favorite long

before he got to Montana at the start of his college years. Gary LaFontaine, interview by author, Missoula, Mont., 12 June 2001.

13. Leigh Perkins with Godfrey Norman, *A Sportsman's Life: How I Built Orvis by Mixing Business and Sport* (New York: Atlantic Monthly Press, 1999), is a revealing biography of a superb promoter and businessman who adroitly capitalized on the western enthusiasms of an eastern clientele.

14. I borrow the term *FFE* from Skip Gibson of Bozeman, Montana, a highly skilled and totally addicted fly-fishing devotee who also moved to the West in order to fish the high country and, incidentally, to make his living in the fly-fishing business.

15. The tailwaters phenomenon is the subject of Ken Owens, "Blue Ribbon Tailwaters: The Unplanned Role of the U.S. Bureau of Reclamation in Creating Prime Sites for Recreational Fly-Fishing for Trout in Western America," completed for a history conference sponsored by the Bureau of Reclamation and scheduled for publication in 2002 in the proceedings of that conference. As a special type of angling opportunity, tailwaters first gained detailed attention in Ed Engle, *Fly-Fishing the Tailwaters* (Harrisburg, Pa.: Stackpole Books, 1991).

16. Gary LaFontaine, "The Bighorn River: As You Like It," *Trout* (Spring 1998): 59–61. For a follow-up, see LaFontaine, "Sparring over Fly Lines and Tailwaters," *Trout* (Summer 1999): 57–59.

17. *California Fly Fisher* 2 (November/December 1993), photo by R. Valentine Atkinson.

18. John Randolph, "Riffles and Runs: Limited Entry," *Fly Fisherman* 12 (May 2001): 4–6; Ed Lawrence, "Field Notes: New Montana Restrictions," *American Angler* 12 (July/August 2001): 26–28. As of November 2001, these regulations were listed in full on the website of the Montana Department of Fish, Wildlife, and Parks (www.fwp.state.mt.us) under the category "News."

19. We have partial figures—actually no more than estimates—on the dollar value of fly-fishing and fly-fishing tourism for a few western localities. Recently, a committee of the Colorado state legislature, for example, stated that sports fishing in Colorado—a category in which fly-fishers are prominent—had in 1996 more than one million participants who spent in excess of $972 million. House Joint Resolution 97–1035, Colorado Sixty-first General Assembly, 1st sess., 1996. That figure likely does not count either the catalog purchases of fishing gear or the fly-fishing trips to Colorado sold by out-of-state fly shops and other non-Colorado businesses. More trustworthy, perhaps, are the figures of the American Fly-Fishing Tackle Association, which asserts that there are nationwide seven million active fly-anglers who spend more than $600 million annually on fishing equipment and related gear. News releases posted on www.affta.com, January 2002. Total expenditures for fly-fishing travel and guide services on fish-rich streams are very likely two or three times that amount, judging from estimates by various fly-shop owners.

Part Three

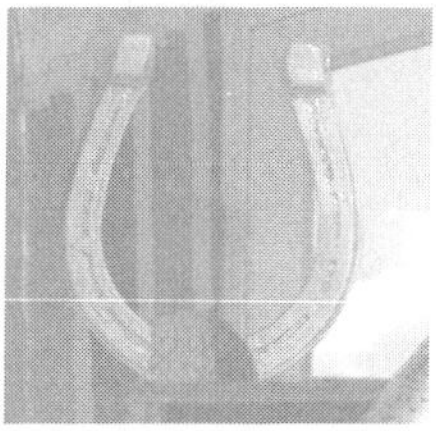

MAKING PLACES

If the West can be characterized by anything, it is continual change. In the twentieth century once-booming mining towns became home to espresso shops while sprawling suburban metropolises transformed cow pastures into strip malls; the West is nothing if not adaptable, and the three essays in this section demonstrate its incredible ability to repeatedly transform itself. Moab, Utah, described here by Michael Amundson, and Red Lodge, Montana, discussed by William Wyckoff and Meredith Wiltsie, once drew people because of the work and wages they could provide and now profit as sites of escape from work. In the mid-twentieth century Moab owed its existence to uranium mining; Red Lodge, to coal mining. The New West imbued both places with new life, and they have been reborn in their value as sites of play.

Wyckoff and Wiltsie note that for Red Lodge, "a landscape of production was gradually transformed into a landscape of leisure." The endurance of these western places reveals the consistency of the West's economic history and the flexibility of these communities to adapt to new realities. Amundson notes that Moab "has been transformed by colonial economies" three times since about 1950. Likewise, Jackson Hole, Wyoming, has a tradition of adapting to current outsider demands, as Lawrence Culver demonstrates. In looking at Jackson Hole's history, Culver shows how "at the end of the [twentieth] century, as at its beginning, Americans beset by the complexities of modern life succumbed to the attraction of wilderness and the romance of the rural past." As places that have shaped themselves to larger cultural expectations, Moab, Red Lodge, and Jackson Hole show that the New West is characterized by the capacity to reinvent itself as a landscape of leisure and aesthetics.

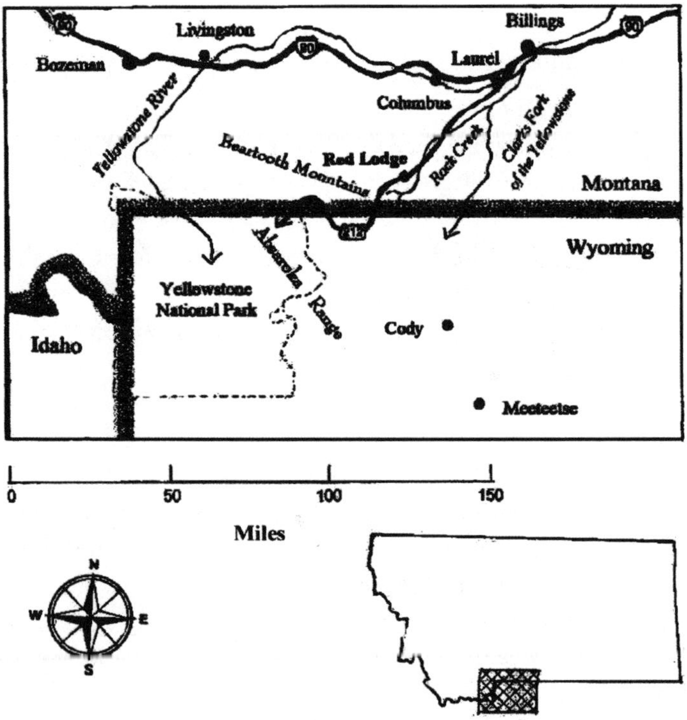

Figure 1. Red Lodge is located just northeast of Yellowstone National Park in south-central Montana.

Meredith Wiltsie

William Wyckoff

REINVENTING RED LODGE

The Making of a New Western Landscape, 1884–2000

Red Lodge, Montana, is a small Rocky Mountain community nestled against the northern slopes of the Beartooth Mountains (Figure 1). Located sixty miles southwest of Billings in south-central Montana, the town epitomizes the dynamic nature of the New American West. Rich in natural resources, spectacular in scenic beauty, and radiating a deep sense of history and community, Red Lodge is the quintessential western mountain town that has seen its economic base and cultural character transformed since the 1920s. The town's brick storefronts and gingerbread-laced Victorian homes speak of another era, one in which coal mining was king (Figure 2). Indeed, tons of the black ore that once powered the settlement and industrialization of the Midwest and northern Rockies were extracted from nearby hillsides between the 1880s and the 1930s.

Over time, however, as technology, economic forces, and cultural values shifted, the community changed.[1] Coal mining withered away, and residents wondered how the community could survive. By the mid-twentieth century Red Lodge had found a new identity as a center for recreational tourism. Today Red Lodge has traded its lost coal dollars for income generated by backcountry outfitting, ski tickets, and affluent second-home construction. Day spas and microbreweries have replaced brothels and union halls. Indeed, this process is not unique to Red Lodge but is the story behind many reinvented communities across the nonmetropolitan West.[2] By tracing the evolution of Red Lodge, we can identify patterns and processes applicable to similar western places.

Figure 2. In downtown Red Lodge the landscape of the commercial district along Broadway has maintained its connections to the past.

THE CONTEXT OF CAPITALISM

The evolution of local land-use patterns and cultural landscape features can be reconstructed to trace the community's transformation from coal town to recreational center. Moreover, such changes in land use and landscape offer invaluable clues to broader cultural and economic shifts.[3] Clues about the landscape come in many forms; for example, the number of motels opened or banks closed during a given year discloses changes in economic activity. Similarly, mapping ethnic neighborhoods or class-differentiated residential districts reveals local social geography. Changes in the visible scene also indicate shifts in cultural values. In Red Lodge the tipples, refuse piles, and headframes of the coal-mining landscape denote competitiveness, material prosperity, and control over nature, a strikingly different picture from the one provided by the motels, backpacking stores, and residential neighborhoods of the subsequent era.

These tangible, visible signatures of the New West suggest how fundamental shifts in the nature of twentieth-century capitalism are reshaping many other localities within the region. Dozens of western mining towns have recently experienced changes parallel to those in Red Lodge. For example, many high-profile ski resorts have emerged from former mining towns: Alta (Utah), Aspen (Colorado), and Telluride (Colorado) illustrate the pattern. Moab (Utah), once a focus of uranium exploration, now hosts thousands of mountain-biking and backpacking enthusiasts, and the former lumber towns of Bend (Oregon) and Coeur d'Alene (Idaho) have been transformed into four-season recreation and retirement centers in the western interior. Larger mining and metals-processing cities such as Butte (Montana) and Pueblo (Colorado) have witnessed similar changes. On a smaller scale, ranching and farming centers such as Dillon (Montana), Bozeman (Montana), Elko (Nevada), and Sheridan (Wyoming) are experiencing the same shifts to more service- and amenity-oriented economies.

In all these centers of change within the New West a similar set of underlying processes is at work. In the case of Red Lodge the development of its coal-mining infrastructure, its subsequent decline, and its rebirth as a center for recreation-based tourism can be seen within the changing context of capitalism.[4] But capitalism is more than an economic system. It also shapes cultural values, landscape perceptions, and community identities.[5] By tracing both economic and cultural change, we achieve a much more complete portrait of any place, and by incorporating the perspective of capitalism, we find that Red Lodge is a case history of larger changes unfolding across the West within the last century.

In many parts of the West industrial capitalism strikingly refashioned land and life, beginning in the nineteenth century. Increasingly after 1850 a distant and rapidly industrializing society forged powerful economic links with selective mineral-rich portions of the West. Growing national and global markets for western resources, improved technologies for resource extraction and refining, and a better transportation system connecting the West to the world beyond facilitated this rapid transformation. This process shaped the cultural geography of the American West in lasting ways, including the establishment of new urban centers with landscapes oriented around the export of raw materials.[6]

The importance of Red Lodge and other isolated urban centers such as Aspen or Butte was defined by their proximity to mineral resources and the availability of investment capital and a labor force to extract them. The value of these new localities was measured by their ability to produce assets, often for the benefit of a distant corporate entity. But even the miners themselves perceived their new environments in economic terms, for the immediate promise of jobs. As one Colorado miner in the early 1870s wrote home, "The chief interest to the world of all this is not the unspeakable grandeur . . . but rather that these are veins of crystalline rock, each one full of wealth."[7] Founded specifically to extract and export ore, such places evolved into landscapes of production shaped by mining companies. They cut timber stands, constructed milling facilities, and diverted creek beds. They built structures to facilitate extraction, including headframes, tipples, powerhouses, railcar tracks, and washing plants. They constructed bridges and processing facilities and often were closely associated with investments in transportation infrastructure. In addition, both mine owners and mine laborers shaped the cultural landscapes of houses, churches, and businesses.[8]

Such outposts of industrial capitalism were never isolated from the larger global economy.[9] As elaborate and seemingly permanent as these urban centers of production became, their continued existence always depended on the value of their extractive assets to a larger society. In time, just as new technology had enabled the initial wave of settlement and extraction, later innovations encouraged cheaper methods of extraction that were less dependent on a large labor force stationed near high-quality ore veins. Often these new technologies, combined with falling mine company profits or simply the depletion of local mineral deposits, led to a mining town's decline. This painful economic transition was common across much of the American West. Some mining centers managed to develop a new economic base and survive while others simply withered away.[10]

Even in the late nineteenth century, however, important changes in American capitalism and society encouraged alternative interpretations of the western landscape.[11] Conservationists such as Theodore Roosevelt and Gifford Pinchot called for more careful stewardship and responsible development of natural resources to preserve them for the benefit of many, not merely for the profit of a few. This school of thought, labeled progressive conservation, was bolstered by scientists George Perkins Marsh, Carl Schurz, and John Wesley Powell, who called for governmental intervention to protect and manage natural resources. The preservation movement also flowered during this period. Inspired by nineteenth-century romantic writers such as Thoreau and Muir as well as artists George Catlin and Frederic Remington, American views of nature and their "natural resources" were gradually being redefined. Some people began to envision nature as a place of transcendental experience, an important escape from urban life, where wild things were valuable not as commodities but in their own right.

By the early twentieth century the country's growing economy provided many Americans with both higher incomes and more leisure time. Passenger trains and the newly introduced automobile facilitated much greater mobility for those with increased free time and spending money, and this combination fueled the growth of mass tourism. Many travelers increasingly explored the West with a fresh awareness of the outdoors. A new kind of appreciation for preserved natural history and wilderness scenery developed, and tourists sought out such places as travel destinations. The preservation movement and the aesthetic appreciation of scenery also revealed their economic potential. The West's major railroads took notice of these new business opportunities and actively promoted national park development and its associated tourist facilities.[12]

Demand for lodging, comfortable transportation, and expanded recreational facilities led to the gradual creation of a new western cultural landscape oriented around the consumption of outdoor amenities.[13] New cottage courts, motels, and resort complexes dotted the landscape along with an abundance of gasoline stations, souvenir shops, and tourist attractions. Indeed, "open space" and "viewsheds" became assets unto themselves. In this context the growth of tourism can be "seen as just one part of the two-century-old shift in the economy from goods to services, which tend to be labor intensive rather than raw material or goods intensive."[14] Such places acquired identity based on the opportunities for pleasurable, leisure-oriented experiences rather than the amount of resources available for extraction.

The recent past has witnessed a continuation of these trends. As both the economy and culture have evolved toward consumption capitalism, and new types of technology such as jet travel, modems, and the Internet became commonplace, many former centers of the extractive economy in the amenity-rich West have seen further economic and demographic growth. The possibility for people to "commute" electronically to work without ever leaving home opened up whole new areas to residential relocation for the newly professionally mobile. When new job descriptions and technologies joined with the interest in amenity-rich locations, scenic areas such as Red Lodge saw an influx of new residents, many of whom had initially visited the area as tourists. These new residents live on dollars from distant jobs, retirement pensions, or other investments. In turn, they bolster the service economies and bring their own changes to isolated areas. New homes and additional commercial businesses sprout and further alter the cultural landscape. Unlike tourists, however, new permanent residents bring a slower, steadier type of growth, often adding an element of stability to the boom-bust cycle common in other western settings.[15] At the same time, the arrival of these new monied residents does not alter the economic inequalities that have existed since the days of mine owners and laborers.[16] Other past patterns persist as well. Even the new amenity economy does not eliminate the possibility of economic fluctuations in such rural western settings.

For Red Lodge, this adjustment from natural-resource capitalism to consumption capitalism was not easy as residents grappled with redefining their economic base. Struggling with deindustrialization, many other western towns have similarly searched for innovative forms of economic activity that would provide a stable future. One solution has been to make the transition from an industrial to a postindustrial world, from places "associated with the past and the old, work, pollution and the world of production" to places associated with the "new, the future, the unpolluted, consumption and exchange, the world of leisure as opposed to work."[17] For Red Lodge, the experience involved a fascinating reworking of local land-use and landscape patterns. Indeed, it demanded a fundamental redefinition of place identity. In the process, a landscape of production was gradually transformed into a landscape of consumption.

CREATING A LANDSCAPE OF PRODUCTION, 1882–1932

Industrial-era Red Lodge was wed to its geological roots. Millions of years ago huge swampy areas developed amid the region's warm, moist climate and abundant vegetation. Over time these settings were transformed into peat, lignite, and one of the region's richest beds of bituminous coal, a resource that saw extensive development between 1882 and 1920.[18]

The earliest records of intermittent human habitation in this landscape date from approximately twelve thousand years ago.[19] The Crow, a hunting and gathering society, settled in the Yellowstone Valley possibly as early as the mid-sixteenth century, having migrated from the Canadian Plains. By the mid-1800s Euro-American trappers, prospectors, and cattle ranchers inhabited the area. But the discovery of rich coal deposits in Red Lodge was the turning point in its settlement history because it coincided with the larger era of industrial expansion in the Intermountain West. Transportation industries, ore smelters, and the growing consumer trade in the northern Rockies and Midwest all demanded coal, and Red Lodge's beds promised particularly hot-burning fuel.

Developments at Red Lodge as a center for natural resource extraction paralleled the pattern in many western mining towns. In its earliest phase, a brief and hectic period between 1882 and 1889, the town was a raucous and disheveled mining camp. Miners dug for coal anywhere and everywhere. Local investors struggled to export the early coal via ox cart on a trail linking Billings, Montana, and Meeteetse, Wyoming. Tradesmen, merchants, and particularly saloon owners moved in to supply the miners. Without benefit of a formal survey or even a proper plat for several years, the town took shape haphazardly.

Gradually, compelled by the growing potential of coal profits from regional industrialization, increased demand from Butte smelters, and voracious new coal-fired steam engines, several of the territory's most powerful

Figure 3. The birth of an industrial landscape: Red Lodge in 1892. *Source: Northwest Magazine, 1892.*

capitalists joined together to invest in the region. Together they formed the Rocky Fork Coal Company (RFCC), and in 1887 they formally commenced large-scale mine excavation at the East Side Mine on the valley's east bench.

Notwithstanding its population growth and industrial foundations, Red Lodge remained isolated until the arrival of the railroad. Annexed from Gallatin County to become part of Park County in May 1887, Red Lodge was tenuously tied to the outside world via a trail to Billings. To conduct any county business, residents had to travel 120 miles to Livingston. Perhaps because of these arduous connections with the outside world, Red Lodge residents developed a strong sense of community, even in the early years. Soon, however, Red Lodge's isolation came to an end. Since the Northern Pacific's Henry Villard was already a part owner of the RFCC, it wasn't long before the railroad built a line between Laurel (on the main line) and Red Lodge. The 1889 arrival of the railroad in Red Lodge opened up its coal resources to much more intensive development and produced dramatic changes in land use and in the local landscape.

At this time a snapshot of Red Lodge would have revealed a wild and rowdy coal camp filled with prospectors, miners, mountain men, and Native Americans (Figure 3). Saloons that never closed were the most prolific and prosperous businesses in town, serving famous visitors like Buffalo Bill and Calamity Jane. A jumble of false-fronted wooden shacks and canvas tents bordered dusty wagon trails that radiated from the town center like spokes on

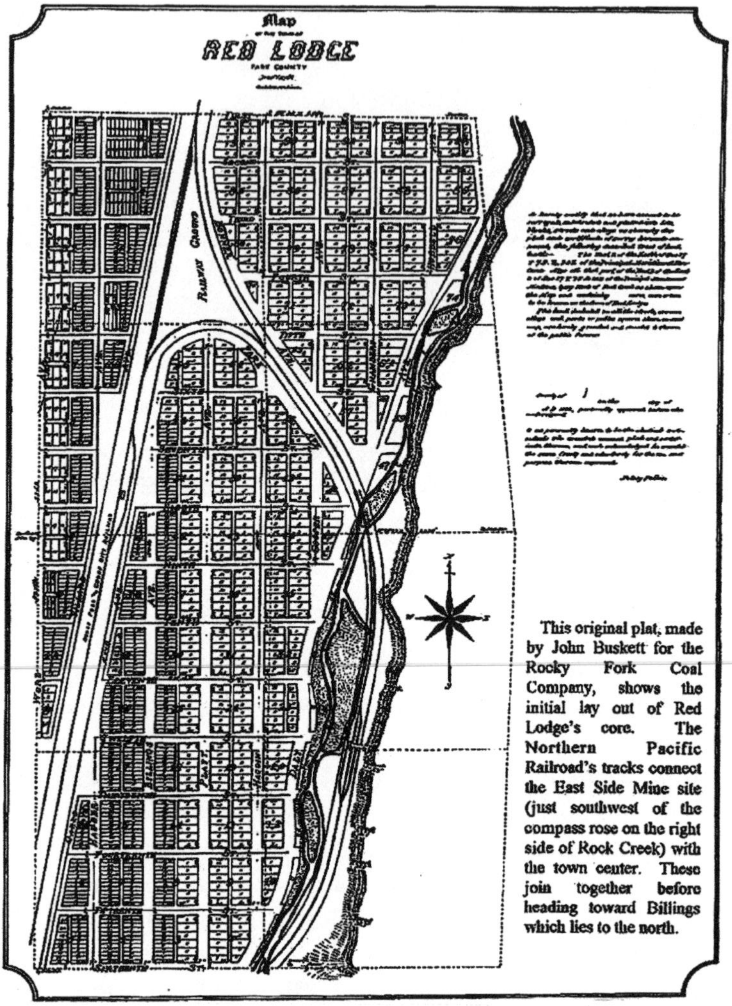

Figure 4. Rocky Ford Coal Company Plat of Red Lodge, 1889. *Courtesy of the Carbon County Historical Society.*

a wagon wheel. This district, generally south of what is now Sixteenth Street, came to be known as Old Town. The Rocky Fork Town & Electric Company (RFTEC), a subsidiary of the coal company, officially platted a grid town north of Old Town, naming streets for investors Villard, Hauser, and Platt (Figure 4). The plans called for an elliptical curve of efficient and rational development within the steep slopes of the Rocky Fork valley. The era of haphazard construction was over. At this point, five short years following its inception, Red Lodge had completed the most chaotic and difficult phase of its evolution toward a fully industrialized landscape of production.

Between 1890 and 1920 Red Lodge matured into a major center of industrial-era coal mining, and its economy and cultural landscape witnessed all the fruits and scars of industrial-era capitalism. The town tightened its connections with Billings, a major rail and livestock center on the Northern Pacific's main transcontinental line. Cattle ranching continued to be an important local economic activity, but Red Lodge's high-grade coal was increasingly in demand. In 1898, in a classic example of corporate expansion, the Northern Pacific seized an opportunity to secure rights to Red Lodge's rich veins.[20] The RFCC was reorganized and gained new management and resources as the Northwestern Improvement Company (NWIC). With this stimulus of outside corporate investment, Red Lodge coal formed the region's financial cornerstone. Local coal supplied company smelters in both Anaconda and Butte. It also fueled many of the Northern Pacific Railroad's locomotives on their continual traverses across the northern Rockies. Amid this growing demand the NWIC greatly increased the scale of the East Side Mine's operations, enlarging the site until it dominated both the local economy and the landscape. Before long, the NWIC built an additional site, the Sunset (or West Side) Mine, on the valley's other bench, effectively sandwiching the town of Red Lodge between twin industrial landscapes.

By the early 1920s Red Lodge's coal economy and population had reached their apogee. The town nearly doubled in size between 1900 and World War I, reaching almost five thousand people, and its infrastructure and services improved with water and sanitation systems, fire departments, and better roads. With a payroll of almost twenty thousand dollars per month from the mines alone, Red Lodge operators extracted more than a million tons of coal annually. Some of the coal came from other newly opened mines nearby, turning Red Lodge into a local center of several connected mining communities. This phase peaked in the years immediately preceding 1920 as wartime demands for coal spurred economic growth, population gains, and more local construction. Improved transportation and communications facilitated the connections between Red Lodge and the world beyond: passenger trains from Billings arrived in 1905, and a telephone exchange was introduced in 1910.

The imprint of maturing industrial-era capitalism was boldly stamped on local patterns of early-twentieth-century land use (Figure 5). One of the most visible clues to Red Lodge's character during this period was its expanding industrial district. By 1920 the gritty sprawl of the East and West Side Mines flanked the town, covering more than fifteen acres with trestles, spiral separators, fuel bins, tipples, wash houses, hoisting engines, and train tracks. Several mine shafts provided access to multiple sloping veins of bituminous coal,

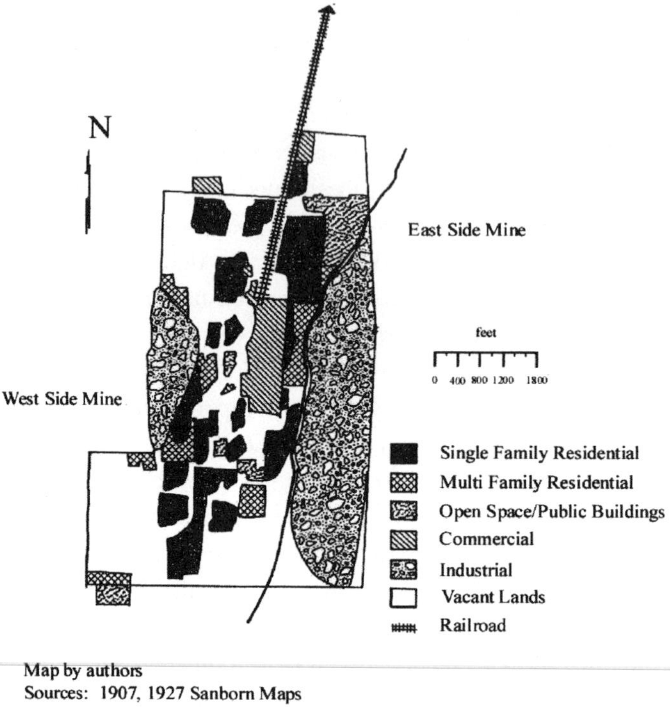

Figure 5. Red Lodge land-use patterns, 1920. *Source: Sanborn Maps, 1907, 1927.*

and nearby, an elaborate collection of covered tramways sheltered carts unloading at the railroad switch. Electric light works, a machine shop, a carpenter's building, and other offices lay near the tracks along with stacks of lumber and refuse.

Other land uses also witnessed dramatic change during this era. Infilling occurred throughout the town, and fewer open lots remained within the city limits. Red Lodge's core commercial district sprawled across Broadway Avenue, spanning an area nearly eight blocks long and three blocks wide. A linear axis of multistoried, tightly bunched brick and masonry buildings gave the town a sophisticated, urban feel, enhanced by ubiquitous arched, leaded-glass windows and elaborately carved sandstone ornamentation. The diversity of stores and businesses reflected the town's draw as a market center for the smaller satellite coal-mining communities of Bearcreek, Belfry, and Washoe. Red Lodge's services included millinery and tailor shops, confectionaries, bathhouses and billiard halls, restaurants, electrical supply stores, and an incongruous mix of livery stables and auto mechanic garages. Citizens from as far away as Wyoming, the Dakotas, and Canada were drawn to the Mount

Maurice Hospital. The local brewery produced an annual thirty-five thousand barrels of beer, amply supplying Red Lodge's many saloons. The zenith of commercial construction during this period was certainly the opening in 1920 of the Theatorium. The one-thousand-seat three-level theater was financed entirely by local investors to house twice-weekly vaudeville shows, and it attracted audiences from miles around.

Residential districts were also a part of the landscape of production.[21] Neighborhoods were defined by both class and ethnic identity, each a crucial element in the social hierarchy of the mining town. Because the mines required much semiskilled manual labor, recent immigrants, including many Finns, Italians, and South Slavs, comprised a large percentage of the population. Differences among these groups became a visible component of the landscape, reflected in architecture, residential patterns, and proximity to the industrial zones.

Several well-defined neighborhoods emerged to serve the local industrial economy. Located farthest from the mines, just to the northwest of downtown, Hi Bug Town was home to the city's English-speaking elite, including mine managers and other professionals. Typical homes in this neighborhood were large, pattern-book houses in the Queen Anne style, standing more than two stories tall with multilayered porches and extensive gardens bound by cast iron fences. These well-manicured properties stood in stark contrast to the gritty mining atmosphere of the working-class districts not far away. At the other end of the residential spectrum lay Davisville, a group of thirty rudimentary rental cabins located farther south in the old part of town. It housed unskilled, immigrant miners, including many Slavs, near the pay scale's low end. Indeed, the Slavs grouped together to create a familiar community, and they effectively transformed Davisville into both an ethnic and economic ghetto.

Between Hi Bug Town and Davisville, both spatially and socially, lay the more prosperous working-class districts, made up of log cabins, clapboard saltboxes, and miscellaneous bunkhouses. Located closest to the mines, these neighborhoods became known as Finn Town and Little Italy and housed many of the mine's semiskilled laborers, merchants, and small business entrepreneurs. The Warila and Suomela Boarding Houses were noteworthy landmarks because they were two of the few privately owned homes in a neighborhood dominated by company-owned labor housing. Over time the impetus for building the nearby local union's Labor Hall, the Co-operative Mercantile, and the social meeting houses arose from these districts.

Even as Red Lodge emerged as a quintessential landscape of production, structural shifts in American capitalism put pressure on the community after

1920, threatening to undermine the importance of an economy traditionally based on the extraction of natural resources. The result was a time of transition in which the old economy faltered and local residents searched for alternatives. Most significant, the economics of coal mining began changing after World War I. As early as 1920 oil began to replace coal as a locomotive fuel as well as in domestic heating (along with natural gas). Also, new technology enabled lower grades of coal to be used in metal smelting. Extended strikes and ongoing labor disputes with Red Lodge miners exacerbated the situation, and by the early 1920s the Northern Pacific began strip mining in Colstrip, Montana. Together all these factors effectively closed down Red Lodge's underground mining industry. In 1924 the Sunset Mine closed, and the East Side Mine operated only until 1932. Because Red Lodge was essentially a one-industry town, the closures devastated the community. With the exception of the operating mines near Bearcreek and Washoe, Red Lodge's highly developed landscape of production ceased to function. Made up of tenacious and deeply rooted residents, however, the community was determined to uncover a fresh economic foundation and way of life.

CREATING A LANDSCAPE OF CONSUMPTION, 1915–1995

Even before the mining era in Red Lodge drew to a close, some community members were actively pursuing alternate sources of income. These efforts, first appearing in Red Lodge in 1915, presaged a major shift in the area's economic base. Building on a strong tradition of local guiding and hunting trips, a few entrepreneurs envisioned expanding visitor numbers by offering accommodations in mountain lodges or ranches. Over time this transition, away from industrial production and toward postindustrial consumption based on service industries and tourist amenities, was tangibly displayed in patterns of land use and fundamental alterations in Red Lodge's appearance. But this metamorphosis was not unique to Red Lodge and in fact mirrored larger-scale social and economic changes in American society.[22]

Tourism in the early-twentieth-century West flourished for many reasons. As the national economy expanded, the population became more affluent than ever before. Particularly after 1915 this affluence gave many Americans the time and financial resources to experience different places and recreational activities. Increasingly, outdoor recreation and scenery became amenity-oriented commodities available to the nation's growing middle class. Technological innovation also played a role in the development of tourism, especially the invention of the automobile. The American public fell in love with the freedom and mobility promised by these newfangled contraptions.

Most broadly, cultural changes in America, propelled by growing urban populations, shaped tourists' perceptions of rural space, nature, and outdoor recreation. The wide-open spaces of the rural West were seen as a national refuge, a place of serenity and relaxation that was far different from an ever more urban America.

The postindustrial transformation of Red Lodge occurred against the backdrop of these larger trends. When faced with deindustrialization, other towns, such as Randsburg (California), Anaconda (Montana), and Jeffrey City (Wyoming), have simply languished or withered away. Most residents in those places chose to move on to find opportunity rather than stay put and create their own. Red Lodge, however, had certain significant advantages: a well-developed rail and road infrastructure, the inherent status and stability of the county seat, and a spectacular setting that drew outdoor enthusiasts. Red Lodge also had the benefit of Dr. J. C. F. Siegfriedt, a visionary leader who conceived and pushed through the construction of the scenic Beartooth Highway, now the town's lifeblood. Finally, the town's vitality was fueled by a strong sense of place among its residents. Firmly rooted, Red Lodge citizens fought a multi-decade struggle to find a new economic niche.

The community's quest for a new economic base had three distinct phases. In the first, 1915–36, initial steps were taken toward developing the town's tourist economy and making a successful campaign to persuade the federal government to invest funds in the Beartooth Highway. The second period, 1937–60, included years of tremendous postwar growth of automobile tourism and the beginnings of winter recreation in the region. The latest phase, after 1961, has seen the area's discovery by footloose entrepreneurs, owners of second homes, ski enthusiasts, and nonlocal retirees, and it has opened an whole new kind of economy in Red Lodge.

Long before there was any hint the mines might close, some area residents took note of visitors' fascination with wilderness scenery, wildlife, and outdoor activities. Early on, a few residents recognized the potential for commercial gain from this kind of appreciation and began promoting the area's tourist potential. Even in 1917 the local landscape began to reflect the growing emphasis on outdoor recreation and tourism.[23] A. H. Croonquist, a prominent store owner in Red Lodge, opened an alpine fishing camp for easterners called Camp Senia sixteen miles up the West Fork of Rock Creek. A second dude ranch, Richel Lodge, was started in 1921 up the Main Fork. Camp Sawtooth and Camp Beartooth, both dedicated to high-country fishing, were built on the Beartooth Plateau, a day's ride from Red Lodge. During the peak of the dude-ranching era eleven outfits operated in the region between Billings, Cooke City, and Columbus.

Additional landscape changes soon echoed the shift to the new western economy. Recognizing that they shared the goal of bringing tourists to the region, the Northern Pacific collaborated with the dude ranchers on marketing efforts.[24] For many years, the railroad published joint promotional materials with the ranchers and hosted the Dude Ranchers Association at its Billings headquarters. During the 1927 season alone, the Northern Pacific and Burlington lines sold 5,500 tickets at an average price of twenty dollars to dude ranch visitors. The rising popularity of automobiles brought other amenity-oriented changes to Red Lodge. The first filling station appeared in 1924, followed by a variety of auto fuel and repair shops. The area's first golf course was introduced by E. M. Adams, a local physician, when he persuaded the Elks Club to convert a meadow up the West Fork into a nine-hole course for the town's enjoyment.

By the 1930s the New Deal brought more extensive tourist-related land-use changes. Of pivotal importance was the passage of legislation that promised a new highway through Red Lodge. The impact of this federal government investment in Red Lodge cannot be overestimated in the success of the town's transition to a tourist economy.[25] Completed in 1936, the Beartooth Highway was the largest and most famous project financed by the public sector in the region. Running between Red Lodge and Cooke City over the Beartooth Plateau, the dramatic sixty-four-mile road was an immediate tourist draw and a new access point for Yellowstone National Park. Even the highway's modern technical construction and its spectacular switchbacks became a tourist attraction.

Dr. J. C. F. Siegfriedt was a critical supporter of the Beartooth Highway project. Siegfriedt initially came to nearby Bearcreek as a coal company physician. He was also elected Red Lodge mayor and state senator, but his most remarkable accomplishment was envisioning the tourist-related benefits of road access into the Beartooth wilderness. A tenacious activist, he lobbied to join private business interests and government agencies in a scheme to diversify Red Lodge's economy. Red Lodge was joined by Cooke City mining interests anxious for alternatives to the Gardiner railhead. Eventually, due in large part to Siegfriedt's efforts, Montana's Second District congressman, Scott Leavitt, introduced an amendment to the Federal Highway Act called the Park Approach Act. This bill permitted the use of New Deal federal funds to construct access roads to national parks, in this case another Montana entrance to Yellowstone. Years of community effort and fundraising paid off in January 1931 when President Hoover signed the legislation. Congress appropriated $2,500,000 for construction of the Beartooth Highway to run between Red Lodge and Cooke City over the Beartooth Plateau.

When the new highway opened in 1936, Red Lodge was transformed from a has-been mining town at the end of the railroad tracks to a gateway city to one of America's crown jewel parks at a time of growing automobile tourism. Instead of focusing on the gritty world of resource extraction and industrial production, Red Lodge's landscape now offered motels, tourist parks, golf courses, and nearby Yellowstone, all growing opportunities for visitors to experience a world of leisure.

By mid-century, Red Lodge boosters came up with other local attractions. As the town's new Civic Center opened in 1950, residents staged a community pageant celebrating the past. A resounding success, the event became the seed from which the annual Festival of Nations celebration was born.[26] Built around the attraction of Red Lodge's history and ethnic diversity, the pageant expanded into a multi-day format with evening programs representing Red Lodge's various cultures. The festival became a huge and widely publicized success. Still nonprofit, today the Festival of Nations is one of Red Lodge's premier annual events, attracting more than fifteen thousand visitors each summer week it is held.

Winter sports also became increasingly important. Skiing, historically a solitary backcountry activity, began to catch on with vacationing Americans in the late 1930s. Ski clubs became prominent in many communities across Montana, and Red Lodge was no exception. The Red Lodge Highroad Ski Club was quite active, and in the winter of 1939 it began a long-term collaboration with the Billings Silver Run Ski Club, including the joint application for a ski-run permit at Willow Creek, three miles southwest of town. By the 1950s investors from Billings and Cody were looking for a new, larger site. In February 1960 they opened the Grizzly Peak Ski Area, complete with three-mile access road, chalet, double chair lift, and poma lift.[27] An immediate success, the resort advertised in Minneapolis to attract midweek skiers. New hotels opened in Red Lodge, including the Alpine Village and Yodeler, and the Bunk House Motor Lodge advertised itself as the "Skiers' Home Away from Home." Even Richel Lodge began advertising "party services for skiing." By the early 1960s the transition to a landscape of consumption was evident, but it had yet to take root and truly dominate the local scene.

The pace of change in Red Lodge accelerated after 1961. The same cultural forces that confronted postwar America also affected Red Lodge. Values changed, landscapes were modified, and land-use patterns adjusted to entirely new sets of postindustrial influences. Changes in Red Lodge's occupational structure illustrate the town's shifting economic base and cultural orientation. At the county level, primary-sector employment declined from 71 percent in 1930 to 54 percent in 1950 and 30 percent in 1970. There was

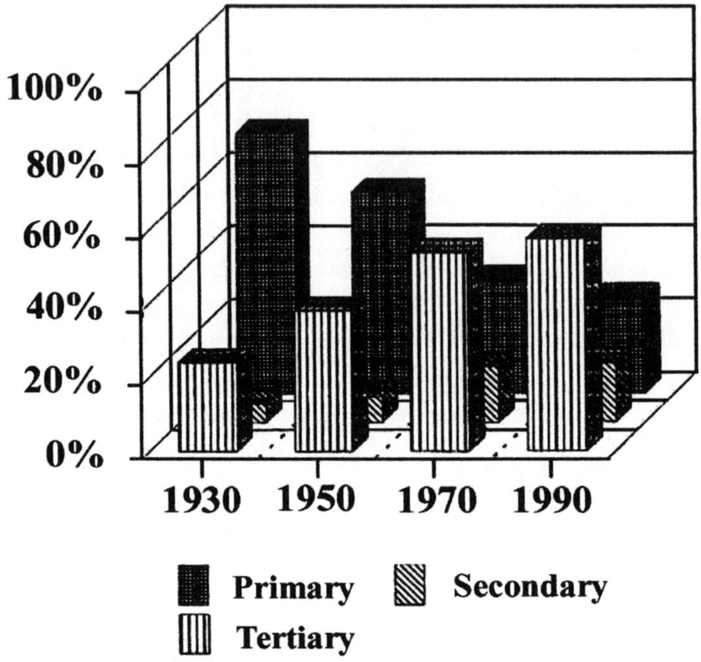

Sources: 1930 Bureau of the Census, Population, Vol III, Part 2
1950 Bureau of the Census, Characteristics of the Population, Volume II, Part 26
1970 Bureau of the Census, Characteristics of the Population, Volume I, Part 28
1990 Bureau of the Census, Census of Population and Housing

Figure 6. Carbon County occupational structure, 1930, 1950, 1970, 1990. *Source: U.S. Bureau of the Census, Census of Population, 1930, 1950, 1970, 1990.*

a slight increase in manufacturing jobs, but the service sector saw the largest gains, increasing from slightly over 24 percent in 1930 to 60 percent in 1970 (Figure 6). City data reflect the same trends. By 1990 outdoor-related tourism and retirement-generated dollars from investment interest or distant pension payments also figured prominently in the community's economy, generating over 40 percent of all Red Lodge income in 1991.[28]

Red Lodge's changing ethnic composition also reflects the community's transformation from the industrial to the postindustrial era. High levels of ethnic diversity are characteristic of extractive-based communities, and Red Lodge was no exception. Carbon County's foreign-born residents peaked at 25 percent in 1920 but declined steadily thereafter, dropping to just over 1 percent by 1990. As the ethnic population declined, its distinctive landscape signatures disappeared as well. Finn Town, Little Italy, and Hi Bug Town still existed, but they were no longer perceived as separate entities. Instead, by

1990 they were integrated neighborhoods with diverse, generally American-born occupants.

Continuing their efforts toward economic revitalization in the 1970s and 1980s, citizens recognized the appeal of downtown Red Lodge with its turn-of-the-century architecture, brick masonry, leaded glass windows, and western feel as a quintessential small-town main street. Business owners began emphasizing Red Lodge's colorful past in their promotions. Soon, however, faced with competition from other regional resort towns, private efforts were not enough. Concerned city officials enlisted help from public agencies to spark Red Lodge's economy, once again illustrating the dynamic and symbiotic relationship of private and public interests in promoting postindustrial economies.[29] In 1984 the Carbon County Historical Society, the Red Lodge Chamber of Commerce, and the Montana Bank formed the Downtown Revitalization Committee and marshaled volunteer efforts to take advantage of government programs aimed at historic preservation. These efforts culminated in the Red Lodge Commercial Historic District Revitalization Master Plan (1986), which enabled the town to participate in programs designed by the National Trust for Historic Preservation as well as claim federal income tax credits that encouraged historic rehabilitation to revitalize the town's physical and cultural heritage.

In addition to bolstering the city's stature and sense of history, revitalization of its historic district had strong marketing advantages. Rowdy tales of Buffalo Bill, Calamity Jane, and Liver Eatin' Johnson bolstered the town's western cachet with visitors. Victorian neighborhoods and quaint downtown shops with tin ceilings attracted others keen to sample the architectural charms of the Old West. Perhaps the best example of such efforts from the private sector was the four-million-dollar renovation of the Pollard Hotel, an important landmark in Red Lodge since 1898. Today it has been restored to its former glamour, albeit with modern conveniences like racquet ball courts and spa facilities. In a further effort toward modernization, the hotel markets outdoor recreational packages for guests who wish to participate in skiing, hiking, and boating excursions. Because of these extensive restoration and preservation efforts, much of downtown Red Lodge and nearby residential areas have been recreated into a charming, nostalgic visual rendition of earlier times.

Indeed, overall land-use patterns have changed significantly since the industrial era of 1920 (Figure 7). Most important, land focused on mining and mining-related industries occupies only a fraction of the space it had in 1920. Much of that land now stands vacant or is in new commercial and residential land use. In addition, most of the high-density residential complexes have disappeared, replaced by single-family residential units. The tourist

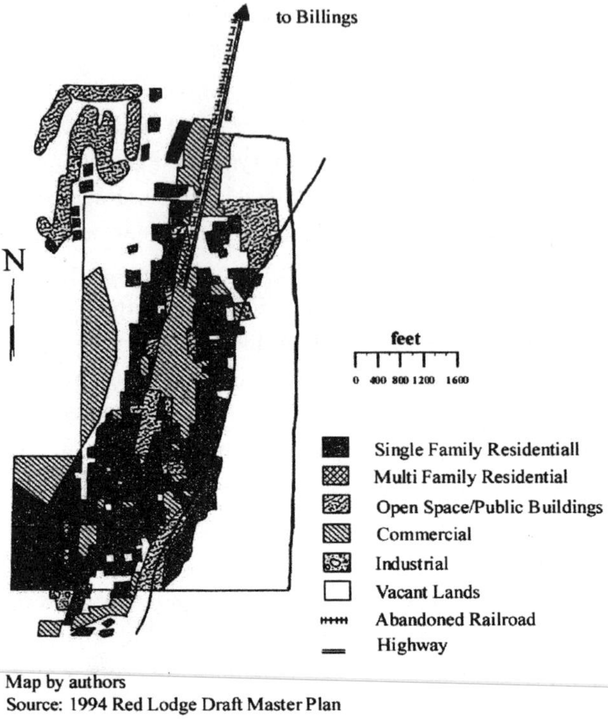

Figure 7. Postindustrial land-use patterns, 1990. *Source: Red Lodge Draft Master Plan, 1994.*

economy is also reflected in a somewhat expanded and elongated commercial district and by dramatic changes in the types of local businesses that dominate the downtown scene. Today there is a strong preponderance of gift shops, sporting-goods stores, quaint cafés, and boutiques in place of the older commercial enterprises that served the everyday needs of the working-class population. The railroad depot was converted to an art center and gallery. The old Finn Opera House became a modern "dry goods and home store" oriented around the idea of "mountain living." Perhaps saloons and real estate agencies tell the story. In 1920 the town supported twenty-six saloons and two real estate offices. By the 1990s only five saloons remained, mostly for the tourists, but the number of real estate offices quadrupled to eight!

The tourist economy has continued to grow and diversify. By the 1990s over one-third of Carbon County workers were employed in tourist-related jobs.[30] The popular new trend toward adventure-oriented recreational experiences inspired outfitters such as Adventure Whitewater, Outdoor Adventures, and Beartooth Wagon & Sleigh Rides. Newly created events for Red Lodge's tourist calendar also demonstrate the continuing interest in outdoor recreation. The Mountain Man Rendezvous, National Ski-Joring Finals, Peaks to Prairie Triathlon, Rocky Mountain Winter Games, and Beartooth Run have all become annual attractions. Traditional events such as the Festival of Nations, the Home of Champions Parade and Rodeo, and the Christmas Stroll continue to bring large numbers of visitors to town as well.

Tourism is not the only driving force behind Red Lodge's New West economy. New residents, seeking the same variety of amenities as visitors, have also had an impact on the area, particularly since the 1970s. Second homeowners, footloose entrepreneurs, and active retirees, drawn by the area's quality of life, have made a significant imprint on many western American communities, Red Lodge included. Recent population growth in rural areas can be traced to the value attached to places with intangible amenities such as beautiful scenery, outdoor recreation opportunities, environmental quality, and a more relaxed pace of life.[31] This description fits Red Lodge, which is close to two national parks, seven national forests, three national wildlife refuges, and a variety of other public lands.[32]

Recent research into the economic and ecological conditions of the Yellowstone region has corroborated this fundamental economic transition. Studies done by both the Wilderness Society and the Greater Yellowstone Coalition demonstrate that the near exclusive reliance on agriculture and extractive industry has been replaced by a diversified service and professional economy.[33] This transformation has been dramatically facilitated by new technology, particularly in the telecommunications field. With fax machines and Internet connections, many professionals and footloose entrepreneurs have flocked to Red Lodge and its rural environs. An increasing array of architects, attorneys, engineers, and independent investors have thus reshaped the area's economic base.

Population growth and growing rural land development have been the inevitable result of these changes. After decades of decline the town began adding population in the late 1970s, but almost all the housing for these new members of the community has been built outside the traditional residential districts. In stark contrast to the high-density in-town residential areas typical of the industrial period, the new homebuilding of the postindustrial era has been concentrated in high-amenity localities within a few miles of town. For example, only 12 new homes were built within Red Lodge between 1990 and 1993, but 130 new residences were constructed just outside Red Lodge in large-lot subdivisions such as "Tipi Village." Driving this shift is the high value placed on amenities such as scenic beauty, viewsheds, access to riparian areas, outdoor recreational opportunities, and proximity to small-town atmosphere.

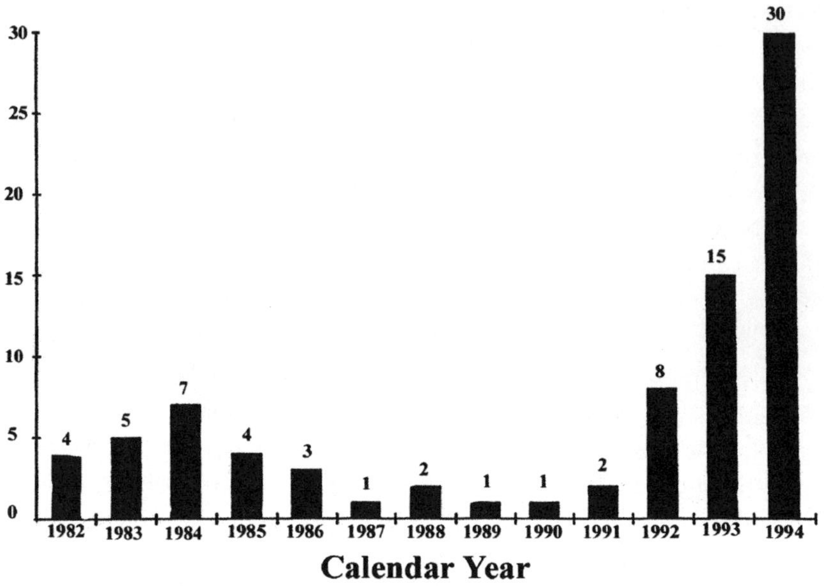

Figure 8. Carbon County subdivision applications, 1982-94. *Source: Carbon County.*

Because of these shifts, more and more blocks of exurban developments are cropping up among the irrigated meadows and rangelands with fragmented riparian corridors that surround Red Lodge. Such development accelerated greatly during the early 1990s. Informal permit application tallies at the county planner's office reveal a doubling of subdivision requests between 1992 and 1993 and again between 1993 and 1994 (Figure 8). Septic system permits, often an indicator of rural development, more than tripled between 1989 and 1994. These residential districts are distinct not only in their spacing and lot size but also in their architecture. Instead of the Queen Anne or even working-class saltbox styles, the new residences are often soaring expanses of cedar and glass, designed to take maximum advantage of the surrounding viewscape (Figure 9).

Recent decades have also seen new types of business develop in Red Lodge and the surrounding area. Some of these are traditional mail-order manufacturing enterprises, but footloose service workers, often in highly skilled and specialized occupations, have also left their mark on the local scene. At first glance, entrepreneurs who export services such as software, filmscripts, or financial market analysis leave a less obvious imprint than coal miners or manufacturing operations. Nevertheless, the growth of home offices and proliferating ranchettes far removed from the urban center reflects this new type of

Figure 9. The postindustrial residential landscape accentuates amenity living and viewsheds in the New West.

business presence on the amenity-rich landscapes surrounding Red Lodge. The impact of these residents is scattered broadly across the local scene in the new homes, yards, satellite dishes, fencing, and driveways that mark each property owner's signature on the rural landscape. Their patronage of local stores and businesses has added stability to the seasonal inflows and outflows of the tourist population and has contributed to the further growth of the service economy.

With these economic shifts and rapid outward spread of development Red Lodge has become a very different place than it was during its coal-mining days. Both land-use patterns and the landscape have changed, and these alterations demonstrate broader changes in the culture. No longer is Red Lodge just the domain of miners and homesteaders. Today it is a place of residence, business, and recreation for a wide spectrum of people with different interests and visions (Figure 10). Red Lodge has become many different things to many different people. Yet in this pluralistic New West landscape, one trend remains clear: the driving force behind Red Lodge's existence is no longer coal but a multifaceted search for environmental amenities and an enhanced quality of life. It is because Red Lodge holds an intrinsic "sense of place" for so many people that it has successfully made the transition into the postindustrial world.

Figure 10. Modern Red Lodge beneath the Beartooths.

PONDERING THE FUTURE

The evolution of capitalism and changing cultural attitudes have radically reconfigured the ways Red Lodge and many other western places are perceived, valued, and used. Red Lodge's story illustrates how both industrial and postindustrial ways of life leave their distinctive marks on the landscape and shape the growth of a community. Particularly in the West, many of these shifts have come quickly. As economic and cultural conditions change, some settlements have weathered the transformation and have redefined themselves. Such localities, with a character molded by the experiences and challenges of the older, extractive economy, have emerged as essentially new places in the consumption-oriented, amenity-based economy of the present. Less certain is how such places will evolve in the future and whether they will be able to define their own identity in the years to come.

In the case of Red Lodge, extensive local fieldwork and discussions with dozens of residents suggest that they share no single definition of their present-day community, nor do they necessarily agree on a proper vision for the future. In such increasingly pluralistic New West settings, that should come as no surprise.[34] Rapid population turnover, the growing importance of seasonal residents, and the always ephemeral tourist populations of the postindustrial setting contribute to a local cultural fabric that is much more fluid and complex than was likely the case in the industrial era of well-defined socioeconomic classes and ethnic neighborhoods. Locals disagree, for example, on the proper amount and character of future growth in the area. On the one hand, many long-time residents are disturbed by the numerous changes in the local landscape that reflect the arrival of new residents and the different attitudes they bring. On the other hand, local business owners are often vocal boosters of growth, and even long-time residents appreciate the fact that the newcomers are attracted to many of the same amenities that keep the natives from migrating elsewhere. The community's newest residents are also a diverse lot, ranging from footloose young people focused on recreation to wealthy retirees or business owners interested in preserving the community's character and integrity once they have arrived on the scene themselves.

Still, there are some shared elements among the local population that help define the cultural character and sense of place of Red Lodge and similar New West communities. First, most Red Lodge residents appreciate the region's natural beauty. Second, nearly everyone, natives and newcomers alike, engages in some form of outdoor recreational activity. Hiking, fishing, camping, skiing, golfing, horseback riding, and mountain biking are very popular. Third, residents also attach special meaning to the tightly clustered downtown area that historically has been the commercial center of the town and more recently has been the focus of preservation efforts. Finally, town residents, both old-timers and newcomers, are known for their involvement in community organizations, ranging from the Chamber of Commerce and local Historical Society to the Beartooth Front Community Forum (BFCF). Recently, for example, the BFCF has called for more comprehensive town planning and preservation, expanding affordable housing and health care in the community, and adding cultural amenities.

Clearly, in such New West settings as Red Lodge there are close ties between the broader evolution of capitalism and local changes in landscape and community. Much of the town's future character will be shaped by the continuing pace of population growth, the changing mix of people attracted to such a setting, and how the community actively responds to and plans for such changes. The cultural geography and economic base of such places probably will continue to diversify. Still, the example of Red Lodge suggests that such localities can also shape a well-articulated sense of place within the New West by searching for common ground in a shared appreciation for local history, a unique physical setting, and a commitment to preserving an amenity-rich, high-quality lifestyle.

NOTES

1. On the changing cultural identity of Red Lodge, see Bonnie Sue Christensen, "Playing with the Past: Heritage and Public Identity in the American West" (Ph.D. diss., University of Washington, 2000).

2. On the broader regional setting and the role of the "New West" in shaping its identity, see Kenneth Johnson, "The Rural Rebound," *Population Reference Bureau, Reports on America* 1, no. 3 (1999): 1–19; Peter B. Nelson, "Quality of Life, Nontraditional Income, and Economic Growth: New Development Opportunities for the Rural West," *Rural Development Perspectives* 14, no. 2 (1999): 32–37; William E. Riebsame, ed., *Atlas of the New West: Portrait of a Changing Region* (New York: W. W. Norton, 1997); and William G. Robbins, "Creating a New West: Big Money Returns to the Hinterland," *Montana: The Magazine of Western History* 46, no. 2 (1996): 66–72.

3. On the value of the cultural landscape concept, see J. B. Jackson, *Landscape* 1 (Spring 1951): 5, and D. W. Meinig, ed., *The Interpretation of Ordinary Landscapes* (New York: Oxford University Press, 1979).

4. On the role of capitalism in the West, see William G. Robbins, *Colony and Empire: The Capitalist Transformation of the American West* (Lawrence: University Press of Kansas, 1994); William G. Robbins, "In Pursuit of Historical Explanation: Capitalism as a Conceptual Tool for Knowing the American West," *Western Historical Quarterly* 30 (1999): 277–93; and William Wyckoff, *Creating Colorado: The Making of a Western Landscape, 1860–1940* (New Haven: Yale University Press, 1999), 1–14, 287-94.

5. Gundars Rudzitis, *Wilderness and the Changing American West* (New York: John Wiley, 1996).

6. See Wyckoff, *Creating Colorado*, and William Wyckoff and Lary M. Dilsaver, eds., *The Mountainous West: Explorations in Historical Geography* (Lincoln: University of Nebraska Press, 1995).

7. Duane A. Smith, ed., *A Taste of the West* (Boulder: Pruett, 1983), 95.

8. On the cultural landscapes of mining, see Richard V. Francaviglia, *Hard Places: Reading the Landscape of America's Historic Mining Districts* (Iowa City: University of Iowa Press, 1991), and Ben Marsh, "Community and Decline in the Anthracite Towns of Pennsylvania," *Annals of the Association of American Geographers* 77 (1987): 337–52.

9. Kevin R. Cox and Andrew Mair, "Locality and Community in the Politics of Local Economic Development," *Annals of the Association of American Geographers* 78 (1988): 307–25.

10. On the varied evolution of mining centers, see Patricia Nelson Limerick, *The Legacy of Conquest: The Unbroken Past of the American West* (New York: W. W. Norton, 1987), 97–133, and Limerick, "Haunted by Rhyolite: Learning from the Landscape of Failure," in *The Big Empty: Essays on Western Landscapes as Narrative*, ed. Leonard Engle (Albuquerque: University of New Mexico Press, 1994), 27–47.

11. On the conservation impulse, see Paul J. Culhane, *Public Lands Politics* (Baltimore: Johns Hopkins University Press, 1981), and Roderick Nash, *Wilderness and the American Mind* (New Haven: Yale University Press, 1982).

12. On railroad promotion of western parks, see Alfred Runte, *Trains of Discovery: Western Railroads and the National Parks* (Niwot, Colo.: Robert Rinehart, 1990); M. S. Shaffer, "'See America First': Re-Envisioning Nation and Region Through Western Tourism," *Pacific Historical Review* 65 (1996): 559–81; and William Wyckoff and Lary M. Dilsaver, "Promotional Imagery of Glacier National Park," *Geographical Review* 87 (1997): 1–26.

13. Alister Mathison and Geoffrey Wall, *Tourism: Economic, Physical, and Social Impacts* (New York: Longman, 1982).

14. Thomas Power, *Lost Landscapes and Failed Economies: The Search for a Value of Place* (Covelo, Calif.: Island Press, 1996), 215.

15. Power, *Lost Landscapes*, 213–16.

16. Robbins, "Creating a New West."

17. J. R. Short, L. M. Benton, W. B. Luce, and J. Walton, "Reconstructing the Image of an Industrial City," *Annals of the Association of American Geographers* 83 (1993): 207–24.

18. Robert A. Chadwick, "Coal: Montana's Prosaic Treasure," *Montana: The Magazine of Western History* 23, no. 4 (1973): 18–31.

19. William Mulloy, "A Prehistoric Campsite near Red Lodge, Montana," *American Antiquity* 9 (1943): 170–79.

20. Michael P. Malone, Richard B. Roeder, and William L. Lang, *Montana: A History of Two Centuries* (Seattle: University of Washington Press, 1991), 338.

21. For extensive local background on Red Lodge's settlement, see Shirley Zupan and Harry Owens, *Red Lodge: Saga of a Western Area* (Billings, Mont.: Frontier Press, 1979).

22. Christensen, "Playing with the Past," and William Wyckoff, "Postindustrial Butte," *Geographical Review* 85 (1995): 478–96.

23. *Red Lodge Picket*, 17 March and 24 August 1917.

24. Lawrence R. Borne, *Dude Ranching: A Complete History* (Albuquerque: University of New Mexico Press, 1983), and Northern Pacific Railroad, *Montana: Vacation Lands* (Minneapolis: Northern Pacific, 1919).

25. *Carbon County News*, 29 January and 11 June 1931, 3 April 1935.

26. Festival of Nations, promotional brochures, 1954, Carbon County Historical Society Archives, Red Lodge, Mont.

27. *Carbon County News*, 17 March 1960.

28. Red Lodge City and Beartooth Front Community Forum, *Red Lodge Master Plan Draft*, April 1995.

29. Short et al., "Reconstructing the Image."

30. Red Lodge City and Beartooth Front Community Forum, *Informing the Process: Factual Information for the Red Lodge Planning Effort*, August 1994.

31. On rural western economic growth, see William B. Beyers and David P.

Lindahl, "Lone Eagles and High Fliers in Rural Producer Services," *Rural Development Perspectives* 11, no. 3 (1996): 2–10; Thomas M. Power and Richard N. Barrett, *Post-Cowboy Economics: Pay and Prosperity in the New American West* (Washington, D.C.: Island Press, 2001); Ray Rasker and Dennis Glick, "Footloose Entrepreneurs: Pioneers of the New West?" *Illahee* 10 (1994): 34–43; and Ray Rasker, Norma Tirrell, and Deanne Kloepfer, *The Wealth of Nature: New Economic Realities in the Yellowstone Region* (Washington, D.C.: Wilderness Society, 1992).

32. Dennis Glick, "Tourism in Greater Yellowstone: Maximizing the Good, Minimizing the Bad, Eliminating the Ugly," in *Nature Tourism: Managing for the Environment*, ed. Tensie Whelan (Covelo, Calif.: Island Press, 1991), 58–74.

33. Albert D. Harting, D. Glick, C. Rawlins, and B. Ekey, *Sustaining Greater Yellowstone: A Blueprint for the Future* (Bozeman, Mont.: Greater Yellowstone Coalition, 1994), and Stewart Mitchell, *County Economic Profiles of the Greater Yellowstone Region* (Bozeman, Mont.: Greater Yellowstone Coalition and the Wilderness Society, 1993).

34. Patrick C. Jobes, "Economic and Quality of Life Decisions in Migration to a High Natural Amenity Area," in *Community, Society, and Migration: Noneconomic Migration in America*, ed. P. Jobes, W. Stinner, and J. Wardwell (Lanham, Md.: University Press of America, 1992), 335–62.

Michael A. Amundson

YELLOWCAKE TO SINGLETRACK

Culture, Community, and Identity in Moab, Utah

In the early fall of 1993 I traveled to Moab, Utah, as part of a research trip for my dissertation on uranium mining towns in the American West. Having already visited three of the communities, I was amazed by what I saw in Moab. Whereas two of the other towns were ghost towns—one was even a Superfund site—Moab was booming. I knew that it had become a tourist town but was shocked to see so many mountain bikers coming to ride the slickrock. All the hotels were packed, there were bike riders all over town, and the annual Fat Tire Festival was about to start. I swore that when I finally finished the dissertation, I would investigate how Moab transformed itself from the "Uranium Capital of the World" to the "Mountain Biking Capital of the World." How did Moab make the change from yellowcake (processed uranium ore) to singletrack (a narrow trail), and how did the transformation affect the community?

The 1950s uranium boom is at the heart of any late-twentieth-century event in Moab. After local prospector Charlie Steen hit it big in 1952, Moab became a boomtown as hopeful prospectors packed into the small agricultural town of twelve hundred residents in southeastern Utah. As national newspapers wrote stories about the country's first "uraniumaire," Steen opened his million-dollar mine and then built a multimillion-dollar processing plant to refine the ore into yellowcake. These efforts stabilized town growth by providing hundreds of well-paying, steady jobs. Along the way, Moab became economically and emotionally dependent on uranium. Uranium served as a multiplier in the community: the mines and mills paid high wages, and locals spent their money on houses, groceries, and recreation. Townspeople also adopted uranium into their landscape, erecting an "Atomic Motel," a "Uranium Building," and a "Uranium Street."[1] Local newspaper editor Sam

Taylor remarked in 1957: "Let there be no mistake. Moab has grown to five times its size in 1950—and this growth has been brought about by the uranium industry and nothing else. A good percentage of the local population is now directly associated with the industry, and another large portion is dependent upon uranium associated people for a livelihood through service industries. There is hardly a person in the entire community that is not touched by the uranium economy in one way or another."[2] Through two ups and downs, uranium remained at Moab's center until 1982.

For mountain biking, uranium provided several important contributions. First, it put Moab on the national map. It brought thousands of people to the area and publicized the nearby red-rock country to hundreds of thousands more across the country. For those who stayed, it meant high-paying jobs and the means to explore the area. Second, it helped open up the backcountry. Not only did backcountry prospectors mark new trails into the slickrock country, but the Atomic Energy Commission helped build roads from the mines to the larger roads connecting to the Moab mill. Third, uranium modernized Moab's infrastructure. Because of the mill, Moab straightened the highway through town, built motels and trailer courts and housing developments, created a new hospital, started new businesses, built a new bridge across the Colorado River, created the need for better communications, and made other such civic improvements that would later benefit biking and tourism. Fourth, the production of yellowcake helped create Moab's 1950s and 1960s image as a hardworking, extractive-industry community. This image, combined with the discovery of large potash deposits nearby, brought the community another boom in the early 1960s that repeated many of uranium's impacts for the town. Finally, uranium went bust in the early 1980s and left a void that was taken over by mountain biking. More on that later.

Mountain biking's second cornerstone in Moab is the tourist industry. With its spectacular slickrock, nearby arches, the La Sal Mountains, and the Colorado and Green Rivers, it would seem that Moab had always been a tourist mecca. But that is not the case. Although Arches National Monument had been established in the late 1920s and a number of movie productions had come to the town in the 1940s and 1950s, Moab's tourist industry hinged on guided Jeep tours into the backcountry and boating trips up and down the river. Beyond that, Moab's ruggedness kept it isolated until the uranium rush of the 1950s. As boomtown conditions led to better infrastructure, Moab's town fathers began to promote tourism as a buffer against uranium dependency. When yellowcake sales dimmed during the 1960s, it seemed a good move. A spectacular new entrance to Arches National Monument, a movement to beautify the city, the creation of Canyonlands National

Park around the nearby confluence of the Colorado and Green Rivers in 1964, increased promotion in Salt Lake City, the construction of a visitor's center, the doubling of Arches' land base in 1969 and its change from national monument to national park two years later, and the completion of Interstate 70 north of the town all helped reorganize Moab into a tourist center.[3] During this period the local chamber of commerce even changed the town's motto from "Uranium Capital of the World" to "Heart of the Canyonlands." By the close of the decade Moab stood atop two major enterprises: mining and tourism. Local editor Sam Taylor commented on the need for both industries amid competing land values:

> All efforts should be made to bring about the progressive development of all segments of the economy in the future, with maximum utilization and protection of the public domain.
>
> Minerals resource people should be thankful for the broadened tax base brought about by the construction of motels, restaurants, service stations, and other facilities which serve primarily the tourist industry. They should be in the front ranks of those who would promote the scenic attractions of Southeastern Utah.
>
> On the other hand, those who view the aesthetic values of Canyon Country as the *only* real values of the land should be realistic enough to know that the above-mentioned industries gave us the standard of living which included sufficient leisure to enjoy the aesthetics; and that people who have carved out an existence here for three-quarters of a century have a certain right to remain in that self-sufficient existence.
>
> Whether or not we like it minerals are going to be developed in Southeastern Utah in the future as they have been in the past. And whether or not we like it, hordes of people are going to continue to come to this area to view the scenic wonders that have made residents of so many of us in the past.[4]

In the following decade tourism surged ahead as Moab became a gateway to two national parks. Visitation increased, the number of motel rooms grew, and the town rebounded from the effects of the slowing uranium industry.[5] With its mild climate and low rents, Moab attracted a growing number of retirees and a small arts community. Like extractive industries, the service industry created a demand for workers, and more people moved to the town. Although wages in this sector were certainly lower than in mining, tourism buffered the town against the ups and downs of mining.[6]

As with uranium, Moab's burgeoning tourist industry helped set the stage for the later popularity of mountain biking in several ways. First, it created an infrastructure of motels, restaurants, Jeep tours, and river tours that provided jobs and kept the town alive during downturns in the uranium industry. Second, the early tourist industry allowed Moab to reevaluate its civic identity and then promote itself not as the center of extractive industry but as a gateway to natural beauty. Finally, the growth of local tourism provided valuable experience in how to cater to visitors.

The third leg of Moab's transformation from yellowcake to singletrack, the invention and explosive popularity of the mountain bike, occurred outside the community. Although the technical evolution of what came to be called mountain bikes is central to the story, the context includes a new cult of strenuosity, a back-to-nature movement, and the baby boomers. Among the growing bibliography on the history of the mountain bike,[7] there is little dispute about how what is now called mountain biking began. To start off, a definition of exactly what constitutes a mountain bike is in order. According to former *Bicycling* magazine engineering editor Frank J. Berto, a mountain bike must have fat tires (26 by 2 inches), flat handlebars that produce an upright riding position, derailleur gearing for multiple "speeds" and easy hill climbing, good brakes (for going down those same hills), and a design suitable for off-road use. According to most sources, this type of bike first made its appearance around 1973 in Marin County, California, when local riders took "clunkers"—old one-speed, coaster-brake, newsboy-type Schwinn bicycles found at garage sales and dump yards; fitted them with better brakes, new cranksets, and multiple gears; and raced them down the Pine Mountain Fire Road on nearby Mount Tamalpais.[8]

By the end of the decade the supply of "clunkers" was diminishing, so frame builders such as Charlie Kelly, Tom Ritchey, Gary Fisher, and Joe Breeze began designing and constructing their own frames. The new "mountain bikes" often were made from aluminum and so were stronger and lighter than the fifty-pound Schwinns. The new designs quickly caught on, and mountain biking spread to such places as Crested Butte, Colorado. By 1981 builders were constructing two to three hundred custom frames per year. The following year, Specialized Bikes began importing a mass-produced design called the "Stumpjumper" that was based on the custom frames of Tom Ritchey. Five hundred of these bikes were sold at $750 each. Univega followed suit with its Alpine Sport model, selling three thousand models at only $500. The following year, mountain bikes went mainstream as fifteen bicycle companies began supplying bicycle shops across the country with mass-produced bikes. Additionally, three more companies sold inexpensive mountain bikes to department stores.

The introduction of mass-produced mountain bikes brought a revolution to the bicycle industry. In 1983 mountain bikes accounted for 5 percent of all bicycles sold in the United States, with ten-speed "road bikes" accounting for the rest. Ten years later the numbers were reversed as mountain bikes accounted for 95 percent of all sales. Along with roller blading, participation in mountain biking grew almost 500 percent between 1987 and 1998.[9] Although simple factors such as a more upright comfortable ride contributed to this growth, a more basic influence was the baby boomers.

The reasons baby boomers took to mountain bikes in the 1980s as they took to SUVs a decade later are embedded in the concepts of strenuosity and primitivism.[10] With dual incomes and smaller families providing discretionary spending money, suburban baby-boomer couples had the time, money, and location to take up the new sport. In addition, more and more of them participated in an active lifestyle to gratify ideas of self-presentation and to overcome inadequate satisfaction in work, consumption, and personal relationships. Sports historian Benjamin Rader called this phenomenon the "new strenuosity," harking back to the strenuous life of Teddy Roosevelt's era that championed exercise to improve middle-class health and to build stronger women so they could bear larger families of white, Anglo-Saxon children.[11] Followers of the new strenuosity, like their Progressive predecessors, followed a type of primitivism by adopting "back to nature" activities such as cross-country running, hiking, and backpacking to escape from the increasing urbanization and bureaucratization of overcivilized modern life.[12] In the 1980s physical fitness proponents added to the equation prolonged life, personal satisfaction, and improved physical appearance.[13]

The mountain biking craze offered baby boomers a number of outlets for self-expression. First, the new sport was elitist, requiring the money to purchase a specialized bicycle and the clothing and gear needed to both succeed and look good as well as the time to learn to ride and the ability to reach the countryside.[14] Second, because the bikes stationed their riders in a more upright position, cushioned on fat tires and, especially by the early 1990s, on motorcycle-like shock-absorbing forks, seatposts, and even frames, aging baby-boomer riders could enjoy their forays for longer periods with less discomfort.[15] Third, as a new type of cyclist that rejected the skinny tires and seemingly always-serious attitude of road racers, mountain bikers were often seen as different, a sort of marginalized "other" among wheel enthusiasts.[16] In short, mountain-biking baby boomers could reaffirm their yuppie status while exhibiting a form of exoticism, emphasize their new bodies, get back to nature, and feel little pain all by showing up at remote trailheads on Saturday mornings dressed in skin-tight Lycra and specialized riding shoes and gloves and toting two-thousand-dollar bikes sporting lightweight aluminum or composite frames and shock-absorbing front forks.[17]

Before we examine how these factors came together in Moab, one more piece of the puzzle needs to be addressed: the establishment of Moab's famous Slickrock Trail—for motorcycles! In 1969, just as the uranium industry and the tourist industry were vying for dominance, a group of local motorbike enthusiasts, with cooperation from the Bureau of Land Management, laid out the famous Slickrock Trail two miles north of the Moab city dump—later proclaimed "America's Most Scenic Dump" in a 1970s publicity stunt.[18] According to the local paper, the trail was located on "knobs of bald navajo sandstone whose undulating slopes and rounded surfaces provide a great deal of sport to riders of light [motor] bikes." It was within sight of Arches National Monument, the Colorado River, and the La Sal Mountains and provided access to a "pure, unspoiled wilderness seldom visited."[19] Although the trail enjoyed limited success over the next dozen years, it never achieved the popularity for motorbikes that it later had for mountain bikes.[20]

Ironically, it was not the growth of mountain biking or the baby boomers that finally brought the sport to Moab. Instead, the decline of extractive industries, first uranium in 1982 and then potash four years later, forced locals to turn to tourism and outdoor recreation. At the center of this change was Bill Groff.[21] Bill had come to Moab with his parents in 1963 after his father took a job in the uranium industry. He and his brother, Robin, followed suit. Bill worked as a pilot for uranium companies and ran the Moab airport, and Robin was a mining engineer. Then came Three Mile Island in 1979, and the domestic uranium industry collapsed. By 1982 Moab faced 25 percent unemployment and increasing outmigration.[22] Wanting to stay in red-rock country, Bill, a avid road cyclist, persuaded the family to open a bike repair and sales shop. They scraped $4,500 together and on 1 July 1983 opened Rim Cyclery, the only Utah bike shop south of the Wasatch. They sold kids' bikes, road bikes, and innertubes and did a lot of repair work. The following year they added climbing gear, but in 1985 a fire destroyed their building. They reopened in two weeks and later that year brought in their first mountain bikes. The business and the town have never been the same.[23]

Although the timing for getting into mountain biking was perfect, Bill worked hard to promote his shop and Moab. After looking through the nationally distributed *Bicycling* magazine and seeing nothing about Utah, Robin and Bill placed an ad that read "Finest Bike Shop in Southeast Utah." Bill jokes today that it was the *only* bike shop in southeast Utah. This move helped put Moab on the bicycling map. Rim Cyclery then established a local bike club and started inviting members of out-of-town clubs to join them. Although most of this early activity involved road racing and touring, Bill also started mountain biking and riding the Slickrock Trail. One of the industry friends to come to Moab was Hank Barlow, an early mountain bike enthusiast from Crested Butte, Colorado. He fell in love with the place. In late 1985 Barlow began publishing *Mountain Bike* magazine. The inside cover of the first issue featured a two-page, full-color spread of Moab's Slickrock Trail. The following year, business boomed as mountain bikers around the country discovered Moab.[24] In the fall Robin and Bill—known in their ads as "Rob'em and Bill'em"—invited friends from other bike clubs and mountain bike industry representatives to Moab for a group ride. About fifty people showed up for the road races, the Slickrock ride, and a Halloween party. The next year Barlow put a blurb about it in *Mountain Bike* magazine, six hundred people showed up, and the Fat Tire Festival became an annual event.[25]

At first, local businesses in Moab did not know what to make of the Fat Tire Festival or the people it brought to town. Although the city of Moab allowed the festival to use the city park for bike polo, there were few volunteers, and motel owners didn't show much support. Many locals saw mountain bikers, with their skin-tight Lycra, as unwanted outsiders.[26] With the extractive industries dead and the service industry offering only one-third the wages, some wanted to build a nuclear waste repository or incinerator nearby. But as mountain biking grew and extended the tourist season by four months, the locals caught on.[27] *California Bicyclist* columnist Art Read offered this view of Moab during the 1988 Fat Tire Festival:

> The Moabites we encountered seemed to have a positive attitude about being a tourism-dependent town. They were gracious enough to put up with the half-a-thousand or more fat[tire]heads and their kin that kept rolling into town the last week of October. . . .
>
> Moab also hosts a major four-wheeler convocation at Easter, offers raft and jet-boat tours on the Green and Colorado Rivers all summer, and offers a number of guide services to tour the canyonlands by bus, microbus, foot, hoof and fat tire, so folks there are used to welcoming tourists.
>
> I'm sure they wouldn't mind if more of those bucks kept rolling in year-round, and the locals have told me that the riding is good most any time. . . . The air is so dry you can wash your Lycra, wring it out and hang it up indoors with the window open on an overcast night and it will be dry by morning!
>
> Moab didn't feel like a classic Mormon Utah town where the locals give you the evil eye and little kids hurl invectives for coming out of the State Liquor Store with a package. It might have something to do with all those tourists or its history as a former mining boom town.[28]

In 1989 visitors were already looking for alternatives to the Slickrock Trail, and Moab was known nationwide as the Mountain Biking World Capital, Nirvana for Mountain Bikers, Slickrock Heaven, the Aspen of Mountain Biking, and the Mountain Bike Mecca of the Western World.[29]

Mountain biking also was transforming Moab. One issue was waste. The increasing number of bicyclists camping along the Colorado contributed tons of human waste that fouled the river and its banks. Garbage accumulated along the Slickrock Trail, becoming so bad that it detracted from the wilderness experience of other tourists. Eventually, the city began charging bikers impact fees, prohibited riding on city sidewalks, and located portable toilets along the trail.[30] Another issue was Aspenization, as mountain bikers began to take advantage of Moab's depressed real estate market. Compared with homes on either coast or in Colorado ski towns, Moab's $50,000, five-bedroom houses seemed a steal. Arches Realty reported that 90 percent of its business came from cyclists and recreation-oriented buyers who either moved to town or, more likely, bought second homes. Although there were complaints about Utah's unusual liquor laws, the higher costs of goods, and the difficulty of finding a job outside the service industry, the mild climate, grand scenery, cheap housing, and miles and miles of riding trails made living in Moab worthwhile for its five thousand residents.[31]

Three times during the last fifty years Moab has been transformed by colonial economies. In the 1950s uranium boomed the town as thousands of prospectors arrived. Bound to Uncle Sam and an extractive economy, the town met this onrush of neo-natives and reinvented itself as the "Uranium Capital of the World." When that went sour, the town turned to tourism, one of the most colonial economies in the West. Rather than simply having their pursestrings controlled by outsiders, Moabites in the 1960s and 1970s had to learn to live while tied to an impactive economy. Although the federal government was once again in the shadows with the creation of Canyonlands National Park and the expansion of Arches, Moabites again reinvented themselves for tourists who came to the "Heart of the Canyonlands." Then with mountain biking's rise in the early 1990s, Moab became part of the New West as now three generations of neo-natives battled for the identity.[32]

The decade of the 1990s found another cultural group, the members of Generation X, traveling to Moab to mountain bike. Defined as the generation born between 1960 (or 1965) and 1980, X'ers have made outdoor sports such as river rafting, rock climbing, and mountain biking mainstream activities.[33] For Moab, this has meant increasing popularity, visitation, and Aspenization.[34] By 2001 glimpses of the newly emerging Moab showed up in an article by *Mountain Bike*'s John Thompson, "Dirtopolis Dream Towns: The 10 Best U.S. Cities for Mountain Biking":

> Every mountain biker dreams of killer trails close to home, of jobs that provide the time and dough to ride more, of wide-open spaces, singletrack—in other words, the good life. Here, we'll help you find it. This story is a snapshot of what the U.S. is like for mountain bikers in 2001. Our criteria for making the list was twofold: First, there had to be great trails within or very close to the chosen city; second, and perhaps most important, the city had to be a place where people could actually live—with good jobs, decent schools, affordable housing, arts and sports, a sense of community—all the things that Americans require. *That's why places like Durango [Colorado] and Moab didn't make the cut.* Though the riding in those places is perhaps the best in the world, unless you're a pro rider, a trustafarian, or like living in the back of a Ford Econoline van, those meccas offer few incentives—unlike the 10 cities we share with you here. (Emphasis added)[35]

Mountain biking is driving Moab into its third variation of the devil's bargain theme of successful economic development leading to growing loss of control. During the uranium boom local leaders pushed atomic ore and tied the town's future to the federal government via cold-war fears followed by the energy crisis. When this failed, tourism took the lead and local boosters reinvented the community as a gateway to the nearby grandeur of Arches and Canyonlands National Parks. This move replaced the failing but lucrative extractive economy with a more vibrant but lower-paying service economy. Soon the growing tourism business brought bigger chain hotels and restaurants that replaced the local mom-and-pop places. The spinoff into mountain biking reinforced these trends by bringing affluent baby boomers and later their Generation X children to Moab in search of authentic experiences. Liking what they saw, these neo-natives bought real estate in the area, thereby driving up prices beyond the means of many of the locals in a classic case of Aspenization. As John Thompson's article implies, by 2001 most mountain bikers could experience Moab only as tourists as the New West's combination of a low-paying service economy and rising housing costs limited migration to a select few. As this trend continues, three generations of neo-natives—one shaped by uranium, one by tourism, and one by mountain biking—will struggle for Moab's identity.

NOTES

1. Moab's uranium history is covered in Michael A. Amundson, *Yellowcake Towns: Uranium Mining Communities in the American West* (Boulder: University Press of

Colorado, 2002). A general history of Moab and Grand County is Richard A. Firmage, *A History of Grand County* (Salt Lake City: Utah State Historical Society, 1996).

2. Samuel J. Taylor, "Bright Future or No Future," *Moab Times-Independent*, 24 October 1957.

3. On the development of Moab's tourist industry in the 1960s, see Arthur R. Gomez, *Quest for the Golden Circle: The Four Corners and the Metropolitan West, 1945–1970* (Albuquerque: University of New Mexico Press, 1994), esp. 119–48. On local attitude, see "Valuable if We Want It," *Moab Times-Independent*, 19 March 1970.

4. Samuel L. Taylor, "Needed: A Diversified Base," *Moab Times-Independent*, 22 May 1969.

5. Douglas Palmer, "Moab's a Boom Town Again—With Tourists Instead of Uranium Fever," *Deseret News*, 26 August 1972, A3.

6. Nick Allen, "Uranium's Gone, but Tourism's Booming in Moab," *Deseret News*, 21 January 1974, B1, B13.

7. Frank J. Berto, *The Birth of Dirt: Origins of Mountain Biking* (San Francisco: Van der Plas, 1999); Hal K. Rothman, "The War for the Future: Mountain Bikes and Golden Gate National Recreation Area," *George Wright Forum* 18, no. 1 (2001): 34–47; Kevin Patrick, "Mountain Bikes and the Baby Boomers," *Journal of American Culture* 11, no. 2 (1988): 17–24.

8. Berto, *Birth of Dirt*, 19–21.

9. Romuald A. Stone and John E. Gamble, "Cannondale Corporation," in *Strategic Management: Concepts and Cases*, ed. Arthur A. Thompson, Jr., and A. J. Strickland III (Boston: McGraw-Hill, 2001), C196–C224. "Riding High," *Southwest Airlines Spirit* (July 1987): 51–52, 72.

10. "Summer Joy Riding: More and More People Find That Biking Is Both Fun and Healthful," *Time*, 8 August 1988, 60. This article quoted a shop owner in Houston who called mountain bikes a new "kind of urban assault vehicle."

11. Benjamin G. Rader, "The Quest for Self-Sufficiency and the New Strenuosity," *Journal of Sport History* 18, no. 2 (1991): 255–66.

12. On primitivism, see Leah Dilworth, *Imagining Indians of the Southwest: Persistent Visions of a Primitive Past* (Washington, D.C.: Smithsonian Institution Press, 1996), 5. On the later back-to-nature movement, see Hal K. Rothman, *The Greening of a Nation? Environmentalism in the United States since 1945* (Fort Worth: Harcourt Brace, 1998), 128–29.

13. Patrick, "Mountain Bikes and the Baby Boomers"; Rader, "Quest for Self-Sufficiency."

14. Hank Barlow, "In Praise of Elitists," *Mountain Bike* 5 (March/April 1989): 6. Although Barlow takes exception to the idea of mountain bikers as elitists, his examples of baby boomers and their families who had driven "half-way across the continent" to bike in Moab seem to counter his argument.

15. "It's Just Like Being a Kid Again," *Adventure Bike* 1, no. 1 (1987): 1. As the title suggests, this article touted the mountain bike as a chance for renewed youth.

16. The concept of new sporting communities as cultural others is guided by Benjamin G. Rader, *American Sports: From the Age of Folk Games to the Age of Televised Sports* (Upper Saddle River, N.J.: Prentice Hall, 1999). A compelling analogy in the sport of snowboarding can be found in Duncan Humphreys, "Snowboarders: Bodies out of Control and in Conflict," *Sporting Traditions* 13 (November 1996): 3–23. Humphreys argues that snowboarding was not accepted by the mainstream skiing industry until record sales left no choice. An insight into mountain bikers as bicycling "others" can be found in David M. Abramson, "Spokes Person," in *Image: The Magazine of Northern California*, in the *San Francisco Examiner*, 23 November 1986, 30–33, 51–52. The article's subject, Jacquie Phelan, described the fathers of mountain biking: "the core of adrenalated Marin boys who had started the whole fad had grown into a tribe of fat-tire flyers who thought of themselves as an intentional community on wheels." In his study of competing resource management plans at Golden Gate National Recreation Area, Rothman maintains that a more complex mountain biking community exists, including "radical riders who flouted the system, mainstream riders who sought to work within the system, and bikers who engaged in other activities and sought to bridge gaps between different groups." See Rothman, "War for the Future," 45.

17. Charles Kelly, "Gray Power," *Mountain Bike* 6 (April 1990): 2. This article lamented the loss of anarchy among aging mountain bikers as the sport went mainstream.

18. The "most scenic dump" contest is detailed in Conrad Walters, "City Puts Worst Foot Forward: Moab Says Rubbish to Any Town Thinking It Has a Prettier Dump," *Salt Lake Tribune*, 12 October 1986, B1, B3; "Scenic Dumps Bond Moab and Its Sister City," *Deseret News*, 10 March 1987, B1.

19. Dick Wilson, "Proposed New Slickrock Trail Would Provide Thrills for Trail Bikers," *Moab Times-Independent*, 27 March 1969.

20. Bill Groff, interview with the author, Moab, Utah, 9 September 2001.

21. Malcolm Fearon, "Hot Rockin' in Moab," *Mountain Biker* (January 1991): 38–41.

22. On the commercial uranium bust of the late 1970s and early 1980s, see Amundson, *Yellowcake Towns*, chaps. 8–9.

23. Information on Bill Groff and Rim Cyclery comes from Rose Gilchrist, "Rim Cyclery: Moab Mining Family Creates New Business," *Utah Business* (July 1991): 57–59; Diane French, "The Rimsters," *Rocky Mountain Sports* (July 1992): 13–18; and Groff, interview with the author.

24. An example of how the national media caught on to mountain biking and Moab is Bob Devine, "Baptism by Fat Tire," *America: The Nissan Student Travel Guide* (Fall 1986): 10–14.

25. Gilchrist, "Rim Cyclery," and French, "Rimsters."

26. Groff, interview with the author.

27. Robert H. Woody, "Moab: Big Boom Now Long Gone, But a Revival Bid Is On," *Salt Lake Tribune*, 16 October 1988. Ed Blankman, "Slickrock: Biking the

Rock, Skiing the La Sals: A Different Kind of Spring Touring," *Powder: The Skier's Magazine* (February 1988): 74–79. Blankman points out that Moab rhymes with "snow slab."

28. Art Read, "Fatheads, Moabites, and Real Rocks in Utah's Off-Road Disneyland," *California Bicyclist*, Northern Edition, 6 (September 1988): 21, 23.

29. T. R. Reid, "Pedaling the Paths of the High Desert: Mountain Biking in Utah," *Washington Post*, 29 April 1991, E1; Brian Hemsworth, "The Other Moab," *Mountain Biking* (September 1988): 25–32; Morten Lund, "Gone to Slick-Rock Heaven," *Snow Country* (June 1989): 21–22; "Rock of Ages: Becoming Nirvana for Mountain Bikers," *Spokane Chronicle*, 4 June 1989, D10; "Boom Town, '80s-Style," *Los Angeles Times*, 12 May 1989.

30. Jerry Spangler, "Moab Dislikes Smell of Success: Human Waste Turning River Areas into Cesspools," *Deseret News*, 20 May 1989, B1.

31. John Kukoda, "Own a Piece of the Rock: Exceptional Mountain Biking, Great Weather, and Cheap Real Estate. That's Moab," *Mountain Bike* (April 1990): 8–11.

32. Neo-nativity is discussed in Hal Rothman, *Devil's Bargains: Tourism in the Twentieth-Century American West* (Lawrence: University Press of Kansas, 1999).

33. Generation X's contribution to mountain biking in Moab and the New West is worthy of its own work. On Generation X, see Geoffrey T. Holtz, *Welcome to the Jungle: The Why Behind "Generation X"* (New York: St. Martin's Griffin, 1995), and the website http://www.youth.co.za/genxthesis/ch3.htm [17 October 2001].

34. Although hard numbers of mountain bikers to the area are difficult to obtain, one member of the Bureau of Land Management office in Moab told me that trail use grew steadily from the late 1980s to 1997 and since then has reached a plateau. Katie Stevens, phone interview, 17 October 2001.

35. John Thompson, "Dirtopolis Dream Towns: The 10 Best U.S. Cities for Mountain Biking," *Mountain Bike* online, June 2001 [2 October 2001].

Lawrence Culver

FROM "LAST OF THE OLD WEST" TO FIRST OF THE NEW WEST

Tourism and Transformation in Jackson Hole, Wyoming

By the late twentieth century Jackson Hole emerged as one of the most desirable destinations in the "New West." Images of the Teton Range appeared everywhere, from commercials for sport utility vehicles to the plastic surface of credit cards. This valley in northwestern Wyoming, bordered on the west by the Tetons and on the north by Yellowstone National Park, has come to embody both the promise and problems of the tourist West. Grand Teton National Park facilitates tourist visitation but protects the Tetons and the glacial moraine lakes at their base from development. The National Elk Refuge preserves grassland on the valley floor and provides a winter haven for the elk population of the Greater Yellowstone ecosystem. Retail and property taxes from ski resorts, boutiques, and vacation homes have made Teton County prosper, and tourism has become a primary industry for Wyoming and other western states.[1]

Yet tourism has also led to unsightly urban sprawl around the community of Jackson, and automotive traffic contributes to congestion and air pollution. The region's popularity as an exclusive vacation home market has led to exorbitant real estate prices, forcing service industry employees to commute from as far away as Idaho Falls. With the middle class increasingly absent, some employers rely on undocumented immigrants for labor.[2]

The same ambiguities were part of the earlier history of Jackson Hole, a story of the transformation of a marginal agricultural region into a landscape of leisure that became a global tourist destination. Tourist development and wilderness preservation in Jackson Hole raised difficult questions and occasionally produced bitter debates. It pitted locals against outsiders and against one another. Residents first had to accept tourism as a viable basis for a regional economy and then determine how best to attract visitors. No less important were questions concerning the essential qualities of wilderness and "westernness": What were they, what should they look like, and how should they be preserved? These questions remain for the tourist West in the twenty-first century.

For much of the twentieth century, Jackson Hole promoted itself as the "Last of the Old West." In reality, it was the vanguard of a new West. This valley would serve as a focal point for a distinct sort of regional recreation. Travel and tourism, however, predate the "New West" of the late twentieth century. Spectacular scenery early drew tourists to the Rockies and Sierra Nevada, and affluent vacationers flocked to European-style resorts at places such as Colorado Springs and Monterey. Other visitors came west as well, drawn by promises of a healthier climate or by the exotic allure of the Spanish missions of California or the Pueblo villages of New Mexico.

What drew tourists to Jackson Hole, and what remains a potent attraction at the beginning of another century, was a different kind of tourist West. Although Jackson Hole offered spectacular scenery, it did not possess luxurious resorts or exotic cultures. Instead, it claimed to contain a preserved remnant of the archetypal Anglo-American West—a rural world of cattle, ranches, and cowboys. Ranching, which in Jackson Hole survived as a major economic enterprise for only a few decades before being eclipsed by tourism, would nevertheless be intricately associated with the valley, the state of Wyoming, and much of the rural West. Yet this "Old West" Shangri-La, advertised as an unchanging relic, underwent wrenching economic, political, and cultural transformations from the late nineteenth century to the end of the twentieth. More than just a tourist destination, Jackson Hole offers an encapsulation of the complex interplay of preservation and promotion essential to the tourist West and serves as a touchstone for the value and function of the scenic West in modern America.

The first Anglo-American settlers of the valley hardly imagined such a future. Not arriving until the mid 1880s—only a few years before the U.S. Census Bureau would declare the frontier closed—they tried to fulfill long-standing American ideals of an agricultural frontier. Although Jackson Hole offered ample alpine grazing land and reliable streams and rivers, its geology and climate hampered agriculture. The primary route of access to the valley was a daunting trail over 8,400-foot Teton Pass. The valley floor was composed of stony, alluvial soil that did not retain moisture. Growing seasons were exceptionally short. The last major frost of spring could come as late as July and the first frost of autumn arrive by August. Agricultural production was largely limited to the growth of hay for winter livestock feed. Cattle raising became the major economic activity, and 14,000 head of cattle grazed in

Jackson Hole by 1917. Yet the population of Teton County remained small—barely 2,000 in 1930 and just over 2,500 in 1940—with Jackson, the only sizable town in the valley, serving as county seat.[3]

Even as locals tried their luck at ranching, they also curried another source of income—tourists. By the 1890s wealthy hunters from the East and Europe were frequenting the valley, and some enterprising inhabitants began offering their services as hunting guides. The region had already received national attention in 1883, when President Chester A. Arthur and his entourage spent several days in Jackson Hole on their way to Yellowstone. Hunters, most notably author Owen Wister, also built cabins in the valley.

Hunting revenue led locals to adopt a proprietary sense of ownership of game animals. It also precipitated conflict with the Bannock Indians, who had traditionally hunted in the valley. Settlers demanded that the Bannocks be confined to the Fort Hall reservation in Idaho, regardless of treaty agreements guaranteeing their right to hunt. In 1896 the Supreme Court agreed, abrogating treaties that preserved Native American hunting rights.[4]

Soon, however, the appeal of a hunting vacation was surpassed by a new tourist experience: the dude ranch. For Americans of the Progressive era, a stay at a dude ranch seemed the perfect cure for a nation purportedly effeminized by Victorian social mores and enervated by urban life and the loss of the frontier. Instead of lounging on the veranda of a resort hotel, tourists could ride horses, rope cattle, and get a satisfying taste of the strenuous life espoused by figures such as Theodore Roosevelt. Some existing ranches began accepting paying guests to supplement their revenues, but new ranches, far more dependent on tourists than cattle, quickly appeared.

The publication of Owen Wister's *The Virginian* in 1902 only heightened the appeal of dude ranch vacations. Wister had fled his native Philadelphia after a physical and emotional collapse and found rejuvenation living on a ranch in central Wyoming. His novel associated the rural, ranching West with adventure, romance, and virility. The novel denigrated nonwhites, as well as women who attempted to transcend their social position. To Anglo-American men, however, *The Virginian* offered the tantalizing possibility of becoming a "real" man—tough, independent, and attractive—without losing any of the status accorded members of the eastern elite. The new dude ranches of Jackson Hole offered similar lures. For example, pamphlets for the Bar BC Ranch, owned by Philadelphian author Struthers Burt, promised a rugged western adventure while highlighting its owner's Ivy League pedigree and providing personal references from the highest strata of eastern society.[5]

Despite dude ranches and hunting parties, Jackson Hole remained relatively isolated. By the early 1920s, however, economic, technological, and political developments would force residents to engage the outer world. A new technology—the automobile—would bring many more tourists to the secluded valley. The advent of the automobile transformed the United States and remade American recreation. Nowhere was change more marked than in the West, where cars made a region once reserved for affluent train travelers far more accessible. In 1910 Americans owned fewer than five hundred thousand cars. By 1920 they would own eight million, and by 1930, twenty-three million. A rudimentary network of roads had spread across the continent by the end of World War I. Auto tourism boomed during the 1920s and continued through the Great Depression.[6]

Almost simultaneously, a conflict erupted over plans to include the Tetons and some portion of Jackson Hole within Yellowstone National Park. The park controversy, which began in 1918, would last more than three decades. In a valley that benefited from tourism, national park status would seem a positive development that could aid publicity and increase visitation. Locals had already demonstrated their support of conservation. They urged federal action after the disastrous winter of 1908-9, when approximately ten thousand elk, cut off from grazing areas by fences and development, starved to death in Jackson Hole. The National Elk Refuge, created in 1912, represented one of the first efforts to protect not only scenery but wildlife and habitat.[7]

Although residents of Jackson Hole were willing to support wildlife preservation, they were unwilling to support what they saw as the negative aspects of national parks. Cattle ranchers, not surprisingly, worried about the loss of grazing land. Other park opposition, however, came from less expected quarters. The Park Service promised that the expansion of Yellowstone would mean more roads for the area. Yet dude ranchers depended on the valley's reputation as a remnant of the unspoiled West and feared that road construction would endanger that image. Hunting guides likewise knew that national park status could terminate their livelihoods. Hotel and restaurant owners, instead of anticipating increased business, feared that park concession companies would monopolize the valley.[8]

Subsequent events forced residents to reconsider their opposition. The global collapse of the beef market after World War I spawned an agricultural depression that proved devastating in Jackson Hole, where ranching was already a marginal enterprise. The valley's rustic western image also faced new threats. Dam construction was one such danger, for Jackson Lake, the largest of the moraine lakes, had been converted into a reservoir in 1906, leaving it surrounded by dead, inundated trees. Plans for more dams, as well as sawmills, also worried locals.[9]

These concerns, along with continued hard times, made national park status more acceptable. Political compromise yielded a plan for a small park separate from Yellowstone, encompassing only the central peaks of the range, with continued grazing rights and the prohibition of any hotels or even permanent camps in the park. These provisions allayed local fears. In 1929 Congress passed an act creating Grand Teton National Park.[10]

Presiding at the dedication ceremony was Horace Albright, director of the Park Service. Unbeknown to most of the assembled crowd, Albright had already instigated a land-purchasing plan to expand the new park. The financier for this secret project, whom Albright had courted earlier in the decade while superintendent of Yellowstone, was none other than philanthropist John D. Rockefeller, Jr. Rockefeller had bankrolled the restoration of Colonial Willamsburg and aided in the creation of Acadia, Smoky Mountains, and Shenandoah National Parks. The Snake River Land Company, headed by Salt Lake City attorney Harold Fabian, was created in 1927 to obscure Rockefeller's involvement and to preclude land speculation. Over the next few years the company bought thirty-five thousand acres in Jackson Hole.[11]

The mutual goal of Rockefeller and Albright was the protection of the valley floor, especially the moraine lakes at the base of the Tetons. More specifically, they aimed to combat the construction of lodging, dining, and retail facilities for an increasingly common type of visitor, the auto tourist. This growing tourist sprawl understandably upset preservationists, but it also threatened tourist businesses in Jackson, located in a low-lying portion of the valley several miles away from the most spectacular peaks in the range.[12]

Although visitors might still stop in town for gasoline, they now often sought accommodations at more scenic spots closer to the Tetons. Dude ranchers also feared the automotive influx, which impinged on the rustic, remote atmosphere they sought to preserve. Auto tourists were often western urbanites on shorter, less expensive vacations than those taken by the predominantly eastern clientele of the most exclusive dude ranches. Moreover, increasing numbers of auto campers, who slept in tents beside their cars, had no need for dude ranch accommodations.

The Snake River Land Company paid fair prices and found most landowners willing—and often eager—to sell. Nevertheless, the 1930 admission that Rockefeller had been behind the purchases caused an uproar in Jackson Hole and many parts of the West. Even though some residents agreed with Rockefeller's goals, many were angered by the plan's secrecy and by the perception that Rockefeller's project had benefited from local economic hardships. As a result, lawmakers from western states repeatedly blocked legislation adding the Snake River Land Company's properties to Grand Teton. Ultimately, President Franklin Delano Roosevelt resorted to the Antiquities Act, designating the company's holdings as Jackson Hole National Monument in 1943.[13]

Roosevelt's executive order sparked nationwide debate. Congress passed a bill to abolish the monument, which Roosevelt vetoed. In Jackson Hole some apoplectic locals accused the Park Service of harboring plans to absorb the entire county and urged a boycott of war bonds. Yet local anger proved less remarkable for its vitriol than its brevity. Money would silence the monument controversy. As World War II ended, local resentments disappeared under a deluge of tourists. On 14 September 1950 President Harry Truman signed an act creating an enlarged Grand Teton National Park. He stated his hope that the new park would allow residents "to go forward with the recreational development of the area on a sound and enduring basis."[14]

Locals were in fact already doing exactly that. Despite the controversies spawned by the creation of the park, Rockefeller's purchases, and the national monument, efforts to lure more tourists only accelerated. Particularly important were projects aimed at extending the valley's tourist season beyond the summer months. Depression-era mayor Harold Clissold succinctly summed up Jackson's predicament: "We're too much alone here in winter. We need new blood, fresh faces, friendship, neighborliness with our neighbors, a spirit of cooperation, a mixing up of people. Also, we need more money."[15]

While the park controversy dragged on through the depression, something more subtle occurred. The new Grand Teton National Park began drawing substantial numbers of tourists. Though national park visitation faltered during the depression, this decline meant little in isolated Jackson Hole. By the end of July 1930 attendance already stood at 10,162, up from a total of 2,140 for 1929. Almost all visitors came in summer, for travel the rest of the year remained treacherous. By the end of the 1935 summer season approximately 100,000 had visited Grand Teton. Perhaps even more significant, the number of tourists passing through the southern entrance of Yellowstone once rarely used—increased as more tourists combined tours of both parks. In 1933 approximately 15,000 entered Yellowstone via the south gate. By 1940 more than 75,000 did. Yet that same year Yellowstone had a total visitation of 526,437, with most travelers still arriving from other park entrances.[16]

Tourism grew during the 1930s across Wyoming. What had often been dismissed as a secondary activity, not a "serious" economic enterprise such as agriculture or mining, became increasingly prominent. In 1935 the University of Wyoming's College of Agriculture inaugurated a four-year degree program in "Recreational Ranching." By 1940 there were more than a hundred dude ranches in the state. In Jackson Hole lingering hopes for large-scale agriculture, industry, or urban growth gave way to a realization that plans for development had to be weighed against the atmosphere and imagery of the "Old West" that tourists came to see.[17]

Thus the town of Jackson had to avoid reminders of modern life that might project an overly urbane image. The *Jackson's Hole Courier*, for example, editorialized against electric signs and even the installation of streetlights: "It might be well to consider that Jackson represents the last of the Old West to many, many people and while there were no signs in the Old West, neither were there any street lights." The town's plank boardwalks, instead of being replaced by cement sidewalks, were likewise preserved.[18]

To further promote their western image, Jackson and the neighboring community of Wilson hosted summer rodeos and fairs beginning in the 1930s. Staged shootouts became regular summer events. Jackson also inaugurated a Dude Ranch Rodeo for employees and guests of dude ranches. In later years this popular event included a parade, with a prize awarded to the float "best depicting the 'Old West.'"[19]

Perhaps the most visible manifestation of "Old West" design was the development of Jackson's town square. Long a vacant lot, it was developed in 1934, when the town council allocated two thousand dollars for the project—no small sum in a municipal budget totaling less than five thousand dollars. The Forest Service donated trees and shrubs, and the town laid out paths and benches. Later the community added the small park's most distinctive features: large arches built of elk antlers, gathered from those shed annually on the Elk Refuge. Perceptive visitors realized that the square's appearance, like that of the town, was to some degree an affectation. When writer Thomas Wolfe traversed Teton Pass and drove into Jackson in 1938, his stream-of-consciousness diary recorded his impressions: "down below the miracle of Jackson Hole—the milky winding of Cottonwood Creek and the Hole (and wild west enchantments and the bad-men legendries) terrific—and so down to it—and into Jackson—the Square of Old West now beduded—the western hands by the filling station."[20]

Whether contrived or merely rediscovered, the "Old West" revival proved popular well beyond Jackson Hole. The entire state of Wyoming claimed this heritage, adding a bucking bronco to vehicle license plates in 1935. State boosters who had long tried to convince outsiders that Wyoming was sophisticated and progressive now instead promised the lure of the remote and rustic in a remnant of the Old West. Like rural westerners elsewhere, Wyoming residents participated in the "wilding up" of the West. Towns that had never witnessed shootouts or roundups now reenacted them for outsiders. Communities that had once hidden the fact that they lay far from railroads or major highways now trumpeted their inaccessibility as a virtue. Native Americans, who had been subjected to forced assimilation, were encouraged to return to older ways, donning traditional attire to appear suitably picturesque for tourists. Wyoming newspapers reacted with alarm to news that Shoshoni Indians had endangered their photogenic potential by constructing a cannery on their reservation to make money.

Yet this romantic imagery also served as a rebuke of the heady ambitions of Wyoming's earlier politicians and boosters, who had extolled the state's natural resources, climate, and cosmopolitanism. For them, industrialization always lay just around the corner, and Cheyenne or Casper or Sheridan would soon inevitably emerge as the next Denver. Instead, Wyoming would remain sparsely populated, a resource and recreation hinterland for other regions. The state adopted the imagery of the ranching frontier and the cowboy because they resonated powerfully with many Americans. Yet it was also true that the state adopted this iconography because it was the only viable option. The citizens of Wyoming might well congratulate themselves on their open spaces and lack of urban ills, but the state they now promoted would have been a bitter disappointment to the boosters of an earlier era.[21]

Although posing as the "Last of the Old West" proved a useful strategy, it was a new form of recreation that would ultimately emerge as the dominant force of economic development in Jackson Hole. Despite humble beginnings, skiing would reshape the real estate market, social structure, and international image of the valley. Unlike some other western skiing destinations, created seemingly overnight by corporations, skiing in Jackson Hole developed slowly, through years of local effort. Early in the century, skiing resorts that cultivated a European atmosphere and an elite clientele had been constructed in the Northeast. Touring ski stunt shows, Ivy League university ski teams, city ski clubs, and even gypsum-coated miniature ski runs in department stores popularized the new sport. This popularity, however, produced an influx of new, less affluent skiers at formerly exclusive resorts. Resort developers looked to the West, hoping to find longer ski runs, better alpine scenery, and a shortage of undesirable skiers.[22]

Averell Harriman, chairman of the Union Pacific Railroad, hoped to profit from America's skiing infatuation. In the fall of 1935 he hired Austrian count Felix Schaffgotsch to survey possible sites near Union Pacific lines. Schaffgotsch dismissed Colorado as too cold, Oregon's Mount Hood as too rainy, and eastern Idaho's scenery as too plain. He felt that the Wasatch of Utah and Sierra Nevada of California were already too crowded with locals. On seeing the Tetons, however, Schaffgotsch thought he had found the ideal location. Yet in the secret negotiations that followed, the state of Wyoming refused Harriman's demand to keep Teton Pass plowed and open year round. This refusal would have infuriated Jackson Hole residents, who regularly berated state officials about their lackluster efforts to keep the pass open in winter.

The count moved on, ultimately selecting Ketchum, Idaho, the future home of Sun Valley. Harriman arrived in February 1936, bought land, and returned east to plan the resort. Constructed with amazing speed, Sun Valley opened just before Christmas. With a skillful advertising campaign and endorsements by Hollywood celebrities, the resort proved a stunning success.[23]

In Jackson Hole, residents enviously monitored the growth of Sun Valley. Jackson Hole's harsh winters had always hindered development. Even boosters admitted that "discussions of the joys of winter have been conspicuous by their scarcity." Jack Huyler, a longtime resident, was more blunt: "This was a totally depressed area in the winter. All people had to do was go into the bars and drink." Hopes of breaking this seasonal cycle had led to the formation of the Jackson Hole Winter Sports Association in 1931. However, efforts to foment winter sports activity did not intensify until after the success of Sun Valley. Skiing promoter Paul Petzoldt, writing in the *Courier* in January 1937, explained the stakes: "Last year the inhabitants of Ketchum, Idaho, hibernated for the winter. This year there will be no hibernation. In one year Ketchum has changed from an isolated mountain village to a winter playground, comparable to the best resorts of Europe. . . . There is a possibility that Jackson Hole will be next."[24]

In 1937 locals organized the Jackson's Hole Ski Club, affiliated with the National Ski Association. The club hosted tournaments and regional competitions. Most of the organization's efforts aimed at developing the small mountain that rose up just south of Jackson. "Town Hill" had become popular in the 1920s as a skiing site for local daredevils. Members of the ski club suggested renaming Town Hill the more impressive "Snow King," the name the hill has borne ever since. In 1935 and 1936 Civilian Conservation Corps workers cleared a hiking trail to the summit, creating the first unofficial ski "run." The next major development came during the winter of 1939-40, when a tow mechanism commenced operation. Local businesses and merchants donated funds, and the town leased the necessary land. Modeled after a device local skier Neil Rafferty had seen at a Salt Lake resort, the tow carried six people at a time. Skiers clamped onto the cable with wrenches fitted with rope and were haltingly pulled to the summit. A cantankerous Ford tractor engine powered the entire operation. The popularity of the ski area grew further with the installation of a chairlift in 1947, which also served as a sightseeing attraction in summer. Though hardly equal to Sun Valley, the development of Snow King laid the foundation for future growth.[25]

For the present, the two national parks remained the primary attraction. By the late 1940s attendance at Yellowstone surpassed a million, and more than two hundred thousand of those visitors entered the park from Jackson Hole. That number only increased as federal and state projects improved the highways leading to the valley. Crucial to improved automobile access was the Snake River Canyon road, which entered Jackson from the south and was constructed by the CCC from 1935 to 1939. Though winding and narrow, the road offered a lower-altitude route into the valley and remained accessible when blizzards closed Teton Pass. The Park Service also completed an improved road from the southern entrance of Yellowstone to Grand Teton in 1953. By the late 1950s the south entrance had become the most popular gateway to the park.[26]

No less important was an airport. Although the valley possessed an airfield, it remained nothing more than a cleared pasture. In 1946, after a landing strip had been graded, Western Airlines announced regular flights to Jackson Hole from Salt Lake City and Billings, Montana. Overjoyed locals welcomed the first flight while mounted on horseback and decked out in their best "Old West" attire. The greeting reportedly proved so raucous that the intimidated passengers initially refused to get off the plane. Drawn by the promise of the "Wild West," they had stumbled into a West that was too wild for them.[27]

Construction of an actual airport would not occur until the 1950s. Unlike other properties purchased by the Snake River Land Company, the JY Ranch—the first dude ranch built in Jackson Hole—had been retained by the Rockefellers as a family retreat. They grew tired of the days of train travel and the bone-jarring, five-hour ride north from the Union Pacific Railroad at Rock Springs which were required to reach Jackson Hole. John D. Rockefeller hoped the Park Service would pay for transportation improvements, and the airfield was annexed to the park for that purpose. As no Park Service funds materialized, however, the Rockefellers and others donated money for the cause. By the close of the decade the family could fly from New York to Jackson Hole in five hours. A useful convenience for the Rockefellers, the new airport portended greatly heightened visitation in the future.[28]

Another portent was the arrival of Hollywood. Even as World War II ended, Harold Fabian, writing a letter to Rockefeller, noted that the town of Jackson was changing: "Jackson is no longer the pioneer cow town where I first spent an October night. . . . It has gone western in true Hollywood style." Indeed, Hollywood would soon arrive. Filmmakers had used the spectacular scenery of the valley as early as the 1920s. A watershed, however, came in 1951, when three films—*The Big Sky*, *The North Country*, and *Shane*—were filmed during the summer tourist season. The *Jackson's Hole Courier* noted that the "Last of the Old West" had become "a Mecca for tourists who prowl the streets looking for celebrities, or go about the valley staring at movie sets and pictures in the making." *Shane* alone injected $400,000 into the local economy. The film, which took full advantage of the scenic potential of the valley, was far more valuable as a cinematic advertisement for Jackson Hole. Movie audiences worldwide now associated the Tetons and Jackson Hole with the mythic West but also increasingly recognized them as an alluring tourist destination.[29]

By the end of the decade a report prepared for the Jackson Hole Chamber of Commerce bluntly stated the new economic reality: "The future of Teton County is so intimately connected with the growth in the American vacation trade, that it is generally thought hardly worth while to consider anything else." One sardonic resident suggested that the community should change its longstanding motto to fit the times. No longer "The Last of the Old West," Jackson Hole could now greet tourists with a new slogan: "The Last of the Old West Happened Here."[30]

Of course, the burgeoning tourist visitation of the 1950s would be rendered small, even quaint, by subsequent events. The remarkable story of Jackson Hole in the last decades of the twentieth century—the metamorphosis of a national park gateway and minor ski resort into an exclusive international travel destination—would seem a tale of utter transformation. Yet, like its earlier history, the more recent story of Jackson Hole was the product of an interplay between the local and the national, and even the international. Moreover, little of what happened in Jackson Hole was truly new.

The national story is perhaps best conveyed by two words that had once described places but by the 1990s instead designated processes: Californication and Aspenization. Californication was simply suburbanization writ large, with mostly white, middle-class urbanites searching for more affordable housing, better jobs, and, in some cases, escape from a state that they felt contained too much racial, cultural, and linguistic heterogeneity. Most of these migrants settled in other western cities, such as Phoenix, Seattle, and Las Vegas. Jackson Hole, which was remote, with expensive real estate and long winters, did not attract a large number of the Californians in exile.

The other term, Aspenization, was more relevant. Like Jackson, Aspen had struggled for decades after mining, its original economic basis, had faltered. Unlike Jackson, however, Aspen earlier emerged as a skiing destination. With skiing came affluence, and culture in the form of arts and music festivals. The wealthy increasingly flocked to Aspen not because of the scenery, or even really for the skiing, but instead for the scene—to see and be seen by the crowd that mattered. In this respect the late-twentieth-century resort culture of the New West looked much like the elite tourism of an earlier era, when rich easterners had traveled to enclaves reserved for others of their class. Film celebrities supplanted the Astors and Vanderbilts, but the underlying similarities remained. If Californication made all the West a suburb of Los Angeles, then Aspenization rendered scenic portions of it a new version of Newport or the Adirondacks, where the rich built retreats to escape common society. The effect this process would have on local real estate prices was hardly surprising.[31]

In Aspen, and in other affluent vacation home enclaves from Santa Fe to Park City, locals and service workers complained of outsiders who transformed their communities and priced them out of the real estate market. The characteristically understated Hunter S. Thompson, for example, described his adopted hometown as a place where "absentee greedheads are taking over the town like a pack of wild dogs. . . . Aspen is a big-time tourist town, and only two kinds of people live here—the Users and the Used—and the gap between them gets wider every day." Though not groundless, such rhetoric obscured the fact that much of the West, rural and urban, had long benefited from tourism without being devoured by it. In the 1970s, 1980s, and 1990s Jackson Hole attempted to maintain this equilibrium, with mixed success.[32]

From the end of World War II through the 1960s, Jackson Hole had prospered primarily as a summer gateway community for Grand Teton and Yellowstone. Snow King remained a secondary attraction, though it drew some skiing enthusiasts. One of these, Californian Paul McCollister, spearheaded the creation of a much larger resort, Teton Village, which opened in 1965 and made the valley a more popular winter destination.

In the 1970s, however, changes came with greater rapidity. Beef prices fell again, and new environmental regulations restricted grazing. The remaining ranches began to sell out—not to a philanthropist like Rockefeller but instead to real estate developers. At the Jackson Hole Airport, runway expansion and the construction of private airplane hangars increased traffic. Regular service by commercial 737 jetliners commenced in 1981.[33]

A different sort of tourist and homebuyer began to frequent Jackson Hole. The relatively modest vacation home construction of the 1970s was followed in the 1980s and 1990s by extravagant gated complexes with golf courses and athletic clubs. Film celebrities, and other members of an affluent elite from America and abroad, began to frequent the valley, and an increasing number purchased homes. A Teton County master plan, completed in 1978, had attempted to ensure a rural atmosphere by limiting residential density to one house for every three acres. Instead, that rule threatened to carpet all private land in the valley with three-acre ranchettes.

The county, which contained fewer than five thousand residents in 1970, had more than eighteen thousand by 2000. Yet this figure did not reflect the housing constructed for nonresidents, who by the 1990s owned more than half of all new homes. By 1993 the median home price in Teton County had risen to 635 percent of the median annual income for county residents.[34]

In 1994 the town of Jackson and Teton County adopted new planning guidelines, aiming to preserve the rural appearance of the landscape and local communities. The new plan allotted some tracts for denser residential development while using conservation easements to preserve open space. Significantly, rural residential development was rezoned from one house per three acres to one house per thirty-five acres. Regulations guaranteeing public access to new roads and a maximum house size of eight thousand square feet aimed to curtail the construction of gated communities and behemoth vacation homes. Development soon spread westward to Idaho's Teton Valley, where land was less expensive and regulations more lax. In Jackson Hole, however, the new regulations prevented the wholesale development of all rural areas not under federal control. New conservation organizations such as the Jackson Hole Land Trust also helped preserve open space. Home affordability, unfortunately, proved more elusive.[35]

Story Clark, one of the founders of the Jackson Hole Land Trust, stated what her group was trying to save: "What we're trying to do here is preserve the myth . . . and what the myth really involves is the landscape and the beauty of the area. What we want to get away from is industry, even tourist industries, that aren't related to the land." Certainly, the society scene of ski resorts and gargantuan vacation homes was disconnected from the local landscape. The re-created ranch and cowboy atmosphere that tourists saw in Jackson Hole was likewise less a historic reality than a mythic overlay that only occasionally intersected with the place from which it had sprung. Now a prime destination for the global tourist industry, Jackson Hole had ceased to be simply a place and had become a commodity.

Yet tourism, no matter how problematic, remained inextricably connected to the land. The pastoral atmosphere, the wilderness vistas, even the snowy ski slopes—it was the land that tourists had come to see and that most still hoped to experience. A new museum for wildlife art, as well as a proliferation of galleries, demonstrated that tourists were now less interested in hunting trophy animals than in collecting representations of wildlife in the form of art. Jackson Hole had changed in profound ways since its settlement a century before, but what it offered to outsiders remained remarkably constant. At the end of the century, as at its beginning, Americans beset by the complexities of modern life succumbed to the attraction of wilderness and the romance of the rural past. Though sport utility vehicles had supplanted Pullmans, and motels and gated communities had replaced auto camps and dude ranches, the lure remained as potent as ever.[36]

NOTES

1. The Tetons proved so visible in the 1990s that members of the Jackson Hole Chamber of Commerce, irritated by the repeated appearance of "their" mountains in advertisements for tourist destinations in Montana, Colorado, and elsewhere, threatened to have the mountain range trademarked. Patricia Nelson Limerick, "Seeing and Being Seen: Tourism in the American West," in *Seeing and Being Seen: Tourism in the American West,* ed. David M. Wrobel and Patrick T. Long (Lawrence: University Press of Kansas, 2001), 51–52.

2. On the deleterious effects of tourism in Jackson Hole and other parts of the West, see Hal Rothman, *Devil's Bargains: Tourism in the Twentieth-Century American West* (Lawrence: University Press of Kansas, 1998).

3. Elizabeth Weid Hayden, *From Trapper to Tourist in Jackson Hole,* 2d ed. (Jackson, Wyo.: By the author, 1963), 31; Tim W. Clark, *Ecology of Jackson Hole, Wyoming: A Primer* (Jackson, Wyo.: By the author, 1981), 11; A. C. McCain, "Economic Survey, Jackson Hole Region" (1932) [typescript], 1, Horace Albright Papers, National Archives, College Park, Md.; Department of Commerce, Bureau of the Census, *Sixteenth Census of the United States, 1940: Population, Volume 1, Number of Inhabitants* (Washington, D.C.: Government Printing Office, 1942), 1184.

4. Louis S. Warren, *The Hunter's Game: Poachers and Conservationists in Twentieth-Century America* (New Haven: Yale University Press, 1997), 1–5.

5. David J. Saylor, *Jackson Hole, Wyoming: In the Shadow of the Tetons* (Norman: University of Oklahoma Press, 1971), 150–51; "The Bar BC Ranches: Bar BC Ranch, White Grass Ranch, Lower Bar BC Ranch," pamphlet, 1927, Research Center, Autry Museum of Western Heritage, Los Angeles. On the development of dude ranching, see Lawrence Borne, *Dude Ranching: A Complete History* (Albuquerque: University of New Mexico Press, 1983). Jane Tompkins discusses the problematic elements of Wister's novel in *West of Everything: The Inner Life of Westerns* (New York: Oxford University Press, 1992).

6. Studies of the history of automotive tourism include Warren James Belasco,

Americans on the Road: From Autocamp to Motel, 1910–1945 (Cambridge: MIT Press, 1979); James J. Flink, *The Automobile Age* (Cambridge: MIT Press, 1988); and John Jakle, *The Tourist: Travel in Twentieth-Century North America* (Lincoln: University of Nebraska Press, 1985). The automobile ownership figures are quoted from John Daugherty, *A Place Called Jackson Hole: The Historic Resource Study of Grand Teton National Park* (Moose, Wyo.: Grand Teton National Park, National Park Service, 1999), 258.

7. Raye C. Ringholz, *Paradise Paved: The Challenge of Growth in the New West* (Salt Lake City: University of Utah Press, 1996), 65–66; Margaret and Olaus Murie, *Wapiti Wilderness* (New York: Alfred A. Knopf, 1966; reprint, Boulder: Colorado Associated University Press, 1985), 7–8; McCain, "Economic Survey," 2. See also relevant portions of Dennis H. Knight, *Mountains and Plains: The Ecology of Wyoming Landscapes* (New Haven: Yale University Press, 1994). Robert Righter, *Crucible for Conservation: The Struggle for Grand Teton National Park* (Boulder: Colorado Associated University Press, 1982), analyzes the complex political wrangling that accompanied the creation and expansion of the park.

8. Righter, *Crucible for Conservation*, 28; *Jackson's Hole Courier*, 28 August 1919; Horace Albright and Robert Cahn, *The Birth of the National Park Service: The Founding Years, 1913–1933* (Salt Lake City: Howe Brothers, 1985), 99.

9. Horace Albright, Washington, D.C., to Wilford Neilson, Jackson, Wyo., 5 April 1933, reprinted in *Mr. John D. Rockefeller Jr's Proposed Gift of Land for the National Park System in Wyoming: History of the Snake River Land Company and of the Efforts to Preserve the Jackson Hole Country for the Nation*, ed. Vanderbilt Webb (New York: Snake River Land Company, 1933), Grand Teton National Park Library, Moose, Wyo.; Richard Winger to Margaret Murie, 5 January 1965, Grand Teton National Park Library, Moose, Wyo.; *Jackson's Hole Courier*, 27 January 1921; Saylor, *Jackson Hole*, 159.

10. Righter, *Crucible for Conservation*, 46–47.

11. *Jackson's Hole Courier*, 28 February 1929; Sam T. Woodring, "Dedication of the Grand Teton National Park" (Moose, Wyo.: National Park Service, 1929), 1–6. Horace Albright Papers, National Archives, College Park, Md.; Horace Albright, interview by John Stewart, 13 September 1974, audioreel, Rocky Mountain Voice Library, Special Collections, Merrill Library, Utah State University, Logan; "Jackson Hole Agreement" (1927) [typescript], Horace Albright Papers, National Archives, College Park, Md.; "Remarks of Harold P. Fabian before the Community Builders Council of the Urban Land Institute" [typescript], 22 September 1974, Harold Fabian Papers, Special Collections, Marriott Library, University of Utah, Salt Lake City; Mrs. Harold (Josephine) Fabian, interview by John Stewart, 29 July 1973, audioreel, Rocky Mountain Voice Library, Special Collections, Merrill Library, Utah State University, Logan.

12. Horace Albright interview, Rocky Mountain Voice Library, 1974.

13. Righter, *Crucible for Conservation*, 85–110 passim. Despite the controversy Rockefeller's actions engendered, many locals remained eager to sell. Newcomers to

the valley in the 1930s, such as Del Jenkins, sometimes found themselves overwhelmed by offers to sell land. Del Jenkins, interview by John Stewart, 26 August 1974, audioreel, Rocky Mountain Voice Library, Special Collections, Merrill Library, Utah State University, Logan. See also *Jackson's Hole Courier*, 22 March 1934, for a petition from residents of the community of Mormon Row urging Rockefeller to buy their properties.

14. *Jackson's Hole Courier*, 22 December 1949; Dyan Zaslowsky and T. H. Watkins, *These American Lands: Parks, Wilderness, and the Public Lands* (Washington, D.C.: Wilderness Society and Island Press, 1993), 31–32; *Jackson's Hole Courier*, 21 September 1950.

15. Donald Hough, *The Cocktail Hour in Jackson Hole* (W. W. Norton, 1956; reprint, Worland, Wyo.: High Plains Publishing Co., 1993), 182.

16. *Jackson's Hole Courier*, 31 July 1930, 22 August 1935, 22 October 1936, 24 June 1937, 5 October 1933, 17 October 1940.

17. *Jackson's Hole Courier*, 5 September 1935, 17 September 1936; Writers' Program of the Works Project Administration, *Wyoming: A Guide to Its History, Highways, and People*, American Guide Series (New York: Oxford University Press, 1941), 118–19.

18. *Jackson's Hole Courier*, 14 July 1938. The community later formalized zoning goals. See, for example, "Design Guidelines: Jackson, Wyoming," n.d., Planning Library, Teton County Planning Office, Jackson.

19. *Jackson's Hole Courier*, 30 July 1936, 14 July 1949, 17 June 1952.

20. Jackson Town Council Meeting Minutes, 7 May 1934; *Jackson's Hole Courier*, 28 September 1933, 30 May 1935, 14 March 1938; Thomas Wolfe, *A Western Journal: A Daily Log of the Great Parks Trip, June 20–July 2, 1938* (Pittsburgh: University of Pittsburgh Press, 1951), 44.

21. On the "wilding up" of the West, see Robert G. Athearn, *The Mythic West in Twentieth-Century America* (Lawrence: University Press of Kansas, 1986), 150–59. Frieda Knobloch analyzes this phenomenon as a cultural and economic process within Wyoming in "Creating the Cowboy State: Culture and Underdevelopment in Wyoming since 1867," *Western Historical Quarterly* 32 (Summer 2001): 201–21.

22. On American skiing before World War II, see E. John B. Allen, *From Skisport to Skiing: One Hundred Years of an American Sport, 1840–1940* (Amherst: University of Massachusetts Press, 1993).

23. Rothman, *Devil's Bargains*, 186–201; Peter J. Ognibene, "At the First Ski Spa, Stars Outshone the Sun and Snow," *Smithsonian* (December 1984): 111–16; Allen, *From Skisport to Skiing*, 143. On one occasion a crowd of two hundred irate Jackson residents stole two Wyoming Highway Department snowplows and cleared Teton Pass themselves. See *Jackson's Hole Courier*, 4 and 11 January 1940.

24. *Jackson's Hole Courier*, 10 December 1931, 31 December 1936, 7 January 1937; Raye C. Ringholz, *Little Town Blues: Voices from the Changing West* (Salt Lake City: Peregrine Smith, 1992), 94.

25. "The Town Hill," *Teton Magazine* (June 1973): 23–57; Thomas Turiano,

Teton Skiing: A History and Guide to the Teton Range (Moose, Wyo.: Homestead Publishing, 1995), 35; *Jackson's Hole Courier*, 5 October 1939; Jackson Town Council Meeting Minutes, 3 and 10 March 1941, 7 April 1941.

26. *Jackson's Hole Courier*, 27 June 1935, 2 July 1936, 27 August 1936, 13 October 1949, 9 July 1953, 4 September 1958; *Kemmerer (Wyoming) Gazette*, 8 December 1938.

27. *Jackson's Hole Courier*, 11 July 1946.

28. Dennis Turner, interview by John Stewart, 17 September 1974, audioreel, Rocky Mountain Voice Library, Special Collections, Merrill Library, Utah State University, Logan; Jackson Town Council Meeting Minutes, 11 July 1951, 27 September 1954, 5 April 1955, 7 May 1956, 7 August 1957.

29. Harold Fabian quoted in Daugherty, *Place Called Jackson Hole*, 264; *Jackson's Hole Courier*, 26 July 1951, 23 August 1951.

30. Floyd K. Harmston, Richard E. Lund, and J. Richard Williams, *A Study of the Resources, People, and Economy of Teton County, Wyoming* (Cheyenne: Wyoming Natural Resource Board, 1959), 75; Hough, *Cocktail Hour in Jackson Hole*, 242.

31. Annie Gilbert Coleman discusses Aspen's earlier history in "A hell of a time all of the time": Farmers, Ranchers, and the Roaring Fork Valley During 'the Quiet Years'" *Montana: The Magazine of Western History* 47 (Spring 1997): 32–45, and offers a critical analysis of the skiing industry in "The Unbearable Whiteness of Skiing," *Pacific Historical Review* 65 (November 1996): 583–614.

32. Hunter S. Thompson, *Songs of the Doomed: More Notes on the Death of the American Dream, Gonzo Papers Number Three* (New York: Summit Books, 1990), 271–72. Thompson apparently does not consider the possibility that earlier Aspen residents may have been no less enamored by the arrival of the counterculture set to which he belonged. For more perspectives on "Aspenization" and "Californication," see Editors of *High Country News*, *Living in the Runaway West: Partisan Views from Writers on the Range* (Golden, Colo.: *High Country News* and Fulcrum Publishing, 2000).

33. National Park Service, "Statement for Management: Grand Teton National Park," Department of the Interior, 1985, 1–21. See Ringholz, *Little Town Blues*, for more on the history of Jackson Hole in the late twentieth century.

34. U.S. 2000 census figures quoted from FedStats website, http://www.fedstats.gov/qf/states/56/56039.html. Housing information is found in Jackson Town Council Ordinance 517, an amendment to Town of Jackson Land Development Regulations, adopted 27 December 1995, http://ci.jackson.wy.us/ordinances/517.pdf. Other relevant ordinances can also be accessed through the town's website.

35. By 2001, even with the inclusion of special affordable housing units as well as homes built by Habitat for Humanity, less than 5 percent of Teton County households could afford to purchase nearly 80 percent of homes sold between July 2000 and July 2001. Teton County Housing Authority, Housing Needs Assessment 2001 Executive Summary. Teton County website, http://www.tetonwyo.org/housing/docs/NeedsAssessmentSummary.pdf.

36. Ringholz, *Paradise Paved*, 79. Carl Abbott discusses the continuing allure of the rural in "The American West and the Three Urban Revolutions," in *Old West/New West: Quo Vadis?* ed. Gene M. Gressley (Worland, Wyo.: High Plains Publishing Co., 1994).

Part Four

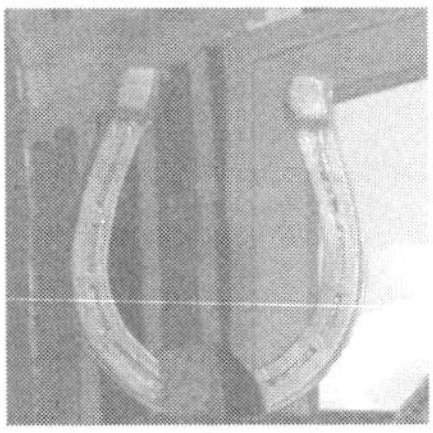

CHOOSING HISTORIES

The three essays in this section illustrate how in the New West the stories about a place's past directly influence its present and future. These essays remind us of the continuing centrality of history in understanding regional challenges and inequities and show how westerners make selective use of particular views of regional or local history for economic or even political ends. In "Buffalo Chips or Computer Chips?" Amanda Rees examines how a region's fate is tied to the stories told about it. A national narrative that promoted settlement and production drew the first white residents to the Great Plains, but the Plains' traditional narrative of place has increasingly fallen out of favor in a New West that privileges leisure and technology over agricultural production. Rees shows us how in its struggle to ensure its relevance in the New West, the Plains region is caught between two competing narratives. As Rees puts it, "Control of the Plains image defines the difference between continued Plains decline versus continued economic progress."

In "Reno's Silver Legacy" Alicia Barber notes that "one of the most prominent characteristics of the New Western service economy is its use of the Old West as amenity." Barber describes how one Reno casino pragmatically adjusted Nevada's silver mining legacy to regenerate a downtown identity, and she analyzes both the benefits and problematics of how the city's gambling industry puts its mining past to work to carry its gaming past forward. Robert Dykstra and Jo Ann Manfra demonstrate how Dodge City chose the mythic version of its violent past to remake itself into a commodity for consumption by tourists. "In the end," write the authors, "the symbolic battle over Boot Hill was won by those locals who collaborated with, rather than resisted, metropolitan America's increasingly weighty cultural investment in a mythological West." All these essays reflect how the past of the Old West is ever present in the unfolding future of the New West.

Amanda Rees

BUFFALO CHIPS OR COMPUTER CHIPS?

The Battle over the Future of the Great Plains

In the last quarter of the twentieth century many parts of the West became play areas of moneyed baby boomers and hip Gen-Xers. Buffalo and elk take pride of place on menus that once boasted only beef and chicken, and REI stockholders play in the fields of a new western aesthetic. However, not all areas in the West have been touched by this newfound wealth and high "cool" quotient. Lying to the east of the Rocky Mountains is an enormous subregion of the West, covering half of ten states, that has traditionally received little attention since the dust-bowl days of the 1930s. It is the American Great Plains.

The Great Plains has lost one-third of its population since its heyday in the 1920s. Vast parts of this region, which encompasses a fifth of the lower forty-eight states, have been left with fewer than six people per square mile. The Plains has suffered an economic cycle of boom and bust that emphasizes the bust. Induced by federal homesteading policies, small farmers settled the region after the Civil War. But the Plains' climatic extremes conjoined with farm subsidies that disproportionately compensate large-scale agriculture mean that small farm enterprises often end in failure. Much of the region's post–World War II agriculturally dominated economy has been established on the back of an aquifer whose water is not replenished. At current rates of use the aquifer may last only until the first quarter of the twenty-first century. But even this region was not immune to the dramatic re-envisioning of the New West. Indeed, the sparser the environment, economy, and population, the more dramatic the visions for this region have become. The future of the Plains is and will continue to be shaped by those who write and speak about it. This is the story about the battle between two of the most visible and competing visions of this region, proposed by Frank and Deborah Popper and by the Center for the New West.

In 1987 Frank and Deborah Popper, two New Jersey academics, laid out a scenario of the Great Plains economic, environmental, and population decline. To address this decline they presented the Buffalo Commons proposal, arguing that the 110 most distressed counties, located primarily in the Northern Plains, be returned to the buffalo. The other major voice speaking about the Plains came from the Center for the New West. The Center argued that the Poppers misinterpreted change as decline and believed that the region's future would be ensured by new computerized communications technology linking population centers.

From its image as the Great American Desert in the early part of the nineteenth century to the promotion of the region as the nation's breadbasket, the portrait of the Plains has changed over time. Since the 1970s the story of the West as a whole has undergone a dramatic transformation. Gone is the celebratory tale of western conquest. Instead, historians have offered more nuanced and inclusive regional stories that introduce class, race, ethnicity, and gender to complicate the tale of the rugged frontier. Led by New West Historians such as William Cronon, Richard White, Patricia Limerick, and Donald Worster, yet another category of analysis was added to understand the New West: the environment. Similarly, the environment became a central player in the public policy battles of the New West. Environmental preservation has often been placed in dramatic opposition to economic progress, especially on the stage of large, western federal landholdings. This conflict is exemplified in the battle between the preservationist requirement to reserve federally owned, old-growth forest as habitat for the endangered spotted owl versus the economic benefits to the logging industry of cutting down that same forest.

Two issues distinguish the Plains buffalo chip–computer chip debate from issues in the rest of the West: the role of the federal government and the focus on the region's image. The Plains is a predominantly privately owned landscape. For example, in Wyoming, a Rocky Mountain state, 54 percent of the state is in private ownership, whereas next door in Kansas, a Plains state, 98.7 percent of the state is privately owned. In terms of resource management, unlike in the West the federal government has little role in the Plains. What gives the Plains debate a western feel was the Poppers' proposal to federalize much of the privately held land in order to apply their Buffalo Commons idea.

In addition, this tension over preservation versus economic progress fails to resemble other western environmental resource disputes because there is no particular resource such as wood, water, or oil in contention. Instead, it is the image of the Plains and how that image shapes public policy decisions that is at stake. Control of the Plains image defines the difference between continued Plains decline versus continued economic progress. In striving to claim control of the regional image, these two visions contrasted primarily in two ways: their definitions of Plains boundaries (what areas are included and excluded) and the measures used to indicate Plains economic health.

Arguing that the Plains faced extreme economic, ecological, and population decline, the Poppers maintained that the answer to regional decline was to deprivatize the most severely affected parts of the region, take them out of cultivation, and depopulate them with assistance from the federal government.[1] The aim was to allow the most depressed areas to become an enormous national park for buffalo.[2]

The Poppers made use of an environmentally determined definition of the Great Plains region, ending their data at the 98th meridian (see Figure 1). In doing so they draw on the work of the Plains historian Walter Prescott Webb, who used a variety of environmental variables to conclude that the eastern edge of the Plains was the 98th meridian (see Figure 2).

The Poppers' proposal was given weight by the statistical analysis Deborah Popper prepared for her dissertation. Her analysis of census data revealed that the Plains population was shrinking and aging and that the region was in economic decline. In making the Buffalo Commons proposal, the Poppers addressed the limitations of the contemporary agricultural economy and discussed the possibilities of a new buffalo-based economic and environmental strategy.

Funded by a modest departmental grant and speakers' fees, the Poppers wrote jargonless essays on the future of the Plains and made numerous speeches in the region. With occasional police protection the Poppers gave talks to groups as varied as the Oklahoma Academy for State Goals, the Mobridge Industrial Development Committee, and the North and South Dakota Farm and Ranch Realtors. Their vision of the region's future gained the attention of local, regional, national, and international print and television media and stimulated discussion of a multitude of political, social, environmental, and commercial concerns.[3]

The Buffalo Commons concept converged with several independent environmental and political factors that drew large media coverage. During the winter of 1988 there was a major drought in the Plains. Four senators, the secretary of agriculture, and all the regional governors made statements criticizing the Poppers. North Dakota governor George Sinner, concerned that

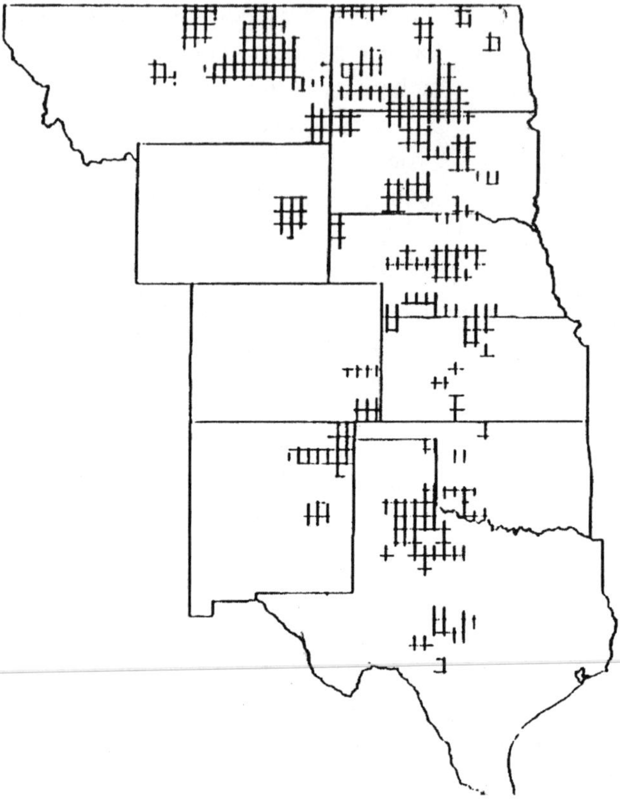

Figure 1. The Poppers' Great Plains and the 110 counties in greatest land–use distress. *Source: Deborah Epstein Popper, "Holding Steady on the Great Plains: An Exploration of the Characteristics of the Region's Population–Stable Counties" (Ph.D. dissertation, Rutgers University, 1992).*

the federal government would fail to support Plains farmers, referred to the work of an unnamed "eastern graduate student" (Deborah Popper) as an example of the incomprehension of nonagrarian easterners of the plight of Plains folk.[4] Thus, the Poppers' vision was swept up by the media as an example of eastern ignorance of western concerns.

The Buffalo Commons challenged commonly shared ways of making sense of Plains life, and some Plains people simply dismissed the Poppers as crackpots. The Poppers argued that the region must go back to its "prewhite" condition. Agriculture dominates the regional economy, and to already struggling farmers and ranchers, the Poppers' idea was a threat to their livelihoods, their vision of the region's history, and its contemporary meaning. Indeed, to propose to Plains dwellers that their region should revert to its prewhite state suggested more than an erasure of its economy and its non-Indian racial

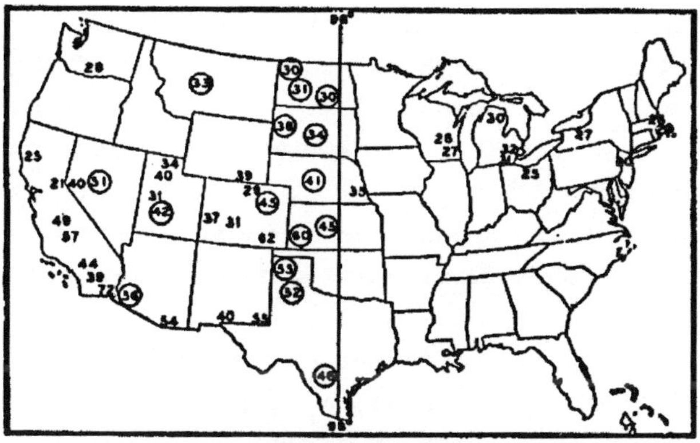

Chart showing evaporation in inches during summer, April to September, inclusive

Note the relatively higher figures in the South. Circles show official experiment stations where measurements are taken in the same way and can be compared

Lines of equal and equivalent rainfall in the Great Plains region

The solid lines marked 15 and 20 pass through points of equal rainfall; the corresponding dotted lines pass though points having a rainfall which is equivalent to 15 and 20 inches, respectively, on the Canadian boundary

Figure 2. Walter Prescott Webb's definition of the eastern edge of the Great Plains at the 98th meridian. *Source: Walter Prescott Webb,* The Great Plains *(reprint; Lincoln: University of Nebraska Press, 1981), 20–21.*

experience.[5] Others were irritated and frustrated that the Poppers had not consulted Plains people before proposing their ideas. Farmers, heavily invested in contemporary agricultural practices, dismissed the proposal, though they acknowledged that the lack of water might change the situation.[6]

Environmental critics of the Poppers' proposal argued that though it called for a varied Plains economy and ecology, the single-minded focus on buffalo ignored diversity. They criticized the Poppers for failing to explore other self-sustaining alternatives or even to investigate whether a buffalo economy would be an environmentally and economically sustainable activity. In addition, critics questioned whether federal intervention contradicts the commons concept, which suggests that Plains people require a share in the future.[7] In contrast, other environmentalists saw the debate as an opportunity to introduce and discuss other less agriculturally intensive ways of living in the region.[8]

Some Plains residents were more sympathetic to the Buffalo Commons, seeing the Poppers as a lightning rod that would save the barn from burning. However, there was still concern that people from outside the region were in control of the Plains image.[9] The Buffalo Commons proposal captured, at least for a few, a rather romantic longing for a somewhat mythical and simpler past, echoed in part by the great popularity of Kevin Costner's film *Dances with Wolves*, released in 1990. Though they were not directly addressed in the proposal, a number of Native Americans recognized in the Buffalo Commons the ghost dancers' prophecy of the buffalo's return and the disappearance of the white man.[10]

The Poppers' work created a rich set of responses. It was seen at once as a proposal in which some found themselves ignored, threatened, and disenfranchised; as a half-baked idea without rigor; as a useful political symbol; as a romantic ideal; and as a tool to challenge regional complacency. However, without doubt the Plains population was engaged in the debate.

One of the most powerful aspects of the Poppers' work, and something that has contributed to its longevity, is the chemistry the Poppers had with the region's population.[11] As Frank Popper pointed out ten years after the initial proposal, he and Deborah preferred to spend their time traveling and talking in the region rather than follow the traditional route of rigorous academic publishing. The result was a muting of the initial, harsh proposition of federalizing this very private landscape.

It is difficult to measure the chemistry between individuals and an audience, but Frank and Deborah made a powerful team. Frank's pronouncements were loud, brash, provoking, and exciting. He followed his ideas up hill and down dale, delighting in the sheer momentum of thinking and speaking. He was indeed an entertainer and raconteur. Deborah was a more soft-spoken and focused thinker who gave root to Frank's high-flying ideas. Deborah was interested in the particulars, feeling vulnerable in generalities, a place where Frank soared. Frank and Deborah both referred to their talks as a double act.[12] He began by warming if not heating up the audience with an animated prediction of the Plains future, and then she offered a cooler, directed, and detail-oriented analysis. Whether people were irritated, angry, or interested, the Poppers' Buffalo Commons proposal became a regional phenomenon that engaged the public's imagination.

Fifteen years later the Poppers' work is still a powerful influence in regional discussions. In evaluating the longevity of their own work, the Poppers argued that the Buffalo Commons has evolved into a regional metaphor.[13] There is little doubt about the power of their vision. It is almost impossible to find a discussion of Plains issues in national and regional papers or in regional texts without mention of the Poppers and buffalo.[14] Nevertheless, the Poppers were not without organized and well-funded detractors.

Appalled by the negative image of a region in decline, a business-oriented conservative think tank, the Center for the New West, arose to challenge the Poppers' vision. The Center recognized the power of words in regional debates: "Words matter. And words can create a self-fulfilling prophecy. Indeed, the region is in danger of becoming what its detractors say it is. Feelings of hopelessness or retrenchment strategies at the community or state level—encouraged by a doom and gloom perspective—do not inspire grassroots leadership to move the region towards economic health. What is needed is an openness to change, new ideas, innovative solutions, models of success, guidance from people and institutions who can help. What is needed is possibility thinking and bootstraps action."[15] Decline was understood to be a direct threat to a positive business climate, so the Center stepped in to present a more optimistic upbeat regional vision.[16] But who was this knight in shining armor for the business community, the Center for the New West?

Established in 1989, directed by Philip Burgess, and underwritten primarily by the regional phone company USWest (one of the former Baby Bells), the Center for the New West was also generously funded by five large corporate sponsors.[17] The Center's paid membership was made up of regional and local businesses, state and local departments of economic development, chambers of commerce, and university business research organizations. To wrestle control away from the "doom and gloom" mongers, the Center developed a three-pronged strategy: research, media exposure, and roundtable meetings to shape regional public policy.[18]

In establishing its Great Plains research project, which would cost almost a third of a million dollars and was funded primarily by outside sources, the Center created an advisory group of people concerned about the region's future to give rigor to its research methodology and findings.[19] In the invitation letter to potential advisers it was made clear that although research would focus on community possibilities and opportunities, the Center would not repudiate "the serious problems of poverty and disintegration" in the Plains.[20]

Nevertheless, poverty, disintegration, the plight of the farmer, and the Plains environment would play no part in the Center's regional vision.

On the morning of 15 April 1991 twenty-one men and women attended the Center's first advisory group meeting.[21] This mix of academics, research consultants, federal and state agency representatives, funders of the research, and consultants shared at least one trait: they disliked the Poppers' story of Plains decline.[22] To combat this negative narrative, the advisory group recommended two fundamental and interrelated concepts to frame the Center's research: a remapping of the region to add economically healthy areas not normally included in the regional definition and an identification of new measures of economic health to challenge the Poppers' statistics.

In deciding to redraw the Poppers' map, Louis Higgs stated the need for redefinition most succinctly: "[If] we want to define the question, [we must] redefine the map."[23] Like the Poppers, the Center claimed Walter Prescott Webb as its guide in defining the Plains. However, though the Center clearly located Webb's 98th meridian on its maps, it did not use this boundary in its regional definition (see Figure 3). Indeed, the Center claimed that "noted historian Walter Prescott Webb bounds the area much further east,"[24] thus drawing the mantle of Webb on its shoulders while gutting his definition of the region. Why did the Center create this radical regional interpretation?

The Center argued that the disappearing Plains population was relocating. Declaring that 70 percent of the Plains population now lives at its fringes, the Center bent its boundaries to include large, economically healthy metropolitan areas. In the process the environmental definition of the region was compromised as areas east of the 98th meridian and west of the Rocky Mountains were included.

Not only did the Center reject Webb's boundary, it also created a number of inconsistent regional definitions. In one of the Center's documents the boundaries of the region follow the transportation corridors Interstate 25 in the west and Interstate 35 in the east, and the international boundaries between Canada and Mexico define the northern and southern limits.[25] This definition encompasses twelve states and the large metropolitan regions of Denver, San Antonio, Kansas City, and Minneapolis. In a second study the Plains is stretched west well beyond the I-25/Rocky Mountain barrier to include the state of Utah and contracted to exclude the two southern Plains states of Texas and Oklahoma.[26] The Center's malleable remapping introduced confusion and inconsistency and seemed to question the need for regional boundaries, as if they were unimportant to the Center's vision of the future. The internal contradictions also suggested a carelessness that raised doubts about the validity of the Center's results.

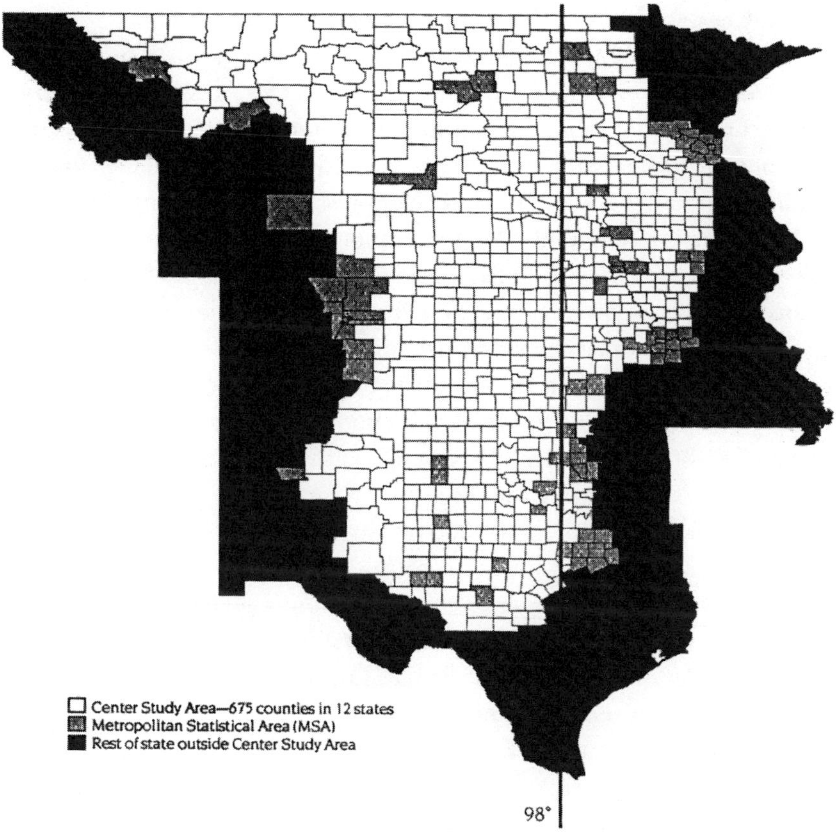

Figure 3. The Center for the New West's Plains boundary. *Source: Louis D. Higgs and Philip Burgess,* Overview of Change in America's New Economy *(Denver: Center for the New West, 1992), 3.*

Having created several reconfigurations of the region's boundaries, the advisers then looked to establish new criteria for measuring Plains health. The advisory group rejected quantitative data analysis in favor of a qualitative case-study approach to tell the story of "successful exceptions." Labeling number crunching old-fashioned and unresponsive, the advisers agreed that traditional quantitative methods could not capture the Plains "New Economy."[27] The New Economy, they argued, called for new measures such as communications technology to link population centers. Agreeing that such technology would dissolve traditional geographic constraints (suggesting again that boundaries and the environment are immaterial), the advisory group saw it as the key to making wealth unlimited. It must be remembered that communications technology was USWest's primary product.

The result of the advisory group's call for new measures came to fruition in the Center's *Survey of Successful Communities*, which contained thirteen brief narratives of small communities.[28] These stories revealed much about the way the Center viewed the region's future. The successful communities were defined as those with a population of ten thousand or under, sharing at least one of three characteristics. They were close to interstate highways, or within commuting distance of larger cities (such as Amarillo and Lubbock), or had recently received new communications technology. A number of the towns identified in the study fell outside the Center's own definition of the Plains (see Figure 4). The Center described the Plains as an archipelago society in the New Economy, a society of "urban islands surrounded by sparsely populated areas connected to each other by transportation and information (telecommunications) networks. Archipelago societies prosper primarily by the quality of the relationships amongst urban islands."[29] In using this metaphor the Center left unaddressed the vast seas of grass between the cities, in which there is no viable economic activity, places unconducive to regional tales of optimism.

Over half the information used in the community profiles came from state economic development agencies often hundreds of miles away from the communities under discussion.[30] Less than a third of interviewees were community members. Of those community members interviewed, over half were members of local chambers of commerce, and others included city managers and administrators. There were no interviews with social service agency personnel, and no other social institutions such as the church or community groups were consulted. Indeed, the business-focused representatives the Center chose to interview bore a remarkable resemblance to the membership of the Center itself.

These community profiles also shared certain narrative characteristics. Each profile began with the community in a state of decline, usually a few years back in the community's history. Then the reader was brought up-to-date with a short narrative of success that left the impression that more prosperity will come in the future.[31] These profiles focused only on business and its diversity.

In one of the few instances in which the Center addressed regional economic and social distress, it referred obliquely to the Poppers as applying city values to measure rural communities: "Like the parable of the city mouse and the country mouse, the values do not always translate." The Center claimed that "many people accept lower wages in rural areas in exchange for higher quality of life, and personal choice on the relative value of different types of work and leisure affect the way people value monetary income."[32] In this sole

Figure 4. Location of the thirteen successful communities surveyed by the Center for the New West.

reference to issues of poverty and economic decline in the report, the Center firmly placed the responsibility for lower wages on the shoulders of the individual as a simple matter of personal choice and regional values.

The community profiles featured communications technology prominently, and the Center chose one Plains community—Brush, Colorado—for an in-depth community profile. In this Plains story none other than USWest replaced Brush's old electromechanical telephone office with fiber optics that provided digital switching. In doing so the company linked Brush with other small towns in Morgan County to Denver. In blunt promotion the Center claimed that "by the end of the year USWest will also complete another upgrade which will make one-party service available to any subscriber who wants it."[33] Thus, the Center's vision unfolded as a technologically linked archipelago society facilitated by its prime sponsor.

In its final Great Plains report the Center carefully characterized its findings as descriptive rather than analytical, and heuristic rather than strictly evidential, with conclusions that indicated implications rather than made recommendations. It would be difficult to find a more hesitant introduction. Not to be undone by its tentatively described research, the Center then boldly claimed that the research's "insights" would be translated into "new tools for policy driven by new paradigms, new indicators and a new contextual interpretation of important traditional indicators—in short, a new understanding."[34] However, these claims and tools were to come under the severe scrutiny of the Center's own advisory group.

Having completed its research, the Center sent a draft of the final report to its advisers. Though they were generally pleased with its tone and narrative style, the content and conclusions were less well accepted.[35] One commentator was happy to see that the Center represented the business constituency, contrasting it with the Poppers' work, which focused only on agriculture. Several of the group liked the nontraditional perspective and did not miss the quantitative data.[36] But most of the academic faction of the advisory group was bluntly critical of the Center's work.

Several of the academic advisers were surprised at the lack of discussion of important regional problems such as the environment, energy, health care, education, and the problems of a persistent rural underclass. In conclusion, one wondered why the Center ignored the "dark side of the Plains."[37] Another characterized the research as extremely soft and anecdotal, producing data that could not stand up to scrutiny. "For that reason, I feel it would be extremely difficult to draw any conclusions from the research other than the obvious one that this is what we saw given what we chose to look at."[38] Yet another stated that although he was favorably disposed to the need for unconventional economic measures, the Center still didn't beat the Poppers at their own game: "Most of 'us' (for what that may be worth) get skeptical quite quickly when an analysis has to rely on backstopping a point with anecdotes and assorted local color."[39] Thus the qualitative methodology used to established the Center's conclusions was labeled insubstantial and lacked rigor in the eyes of a number of the project's advisers.

The way the Center devised its new measures also came under scrutiny. Several advisers criticized the naive manner in which communications technology was defined as liberating communities. Yet another critic argued that the case studies were not contextualized with the region and thus were not useful as examples for the way to solve regional problems: "Many of the successes will come only at the expense of other Great Plains communities. Where is the region-wide evidence to support your generalizations?"[40] Still another adviser stated flatly that "the numbers don't convince me. It's boosterism."[41] These criticisms concisely revealed the limitations in the anecdotal and generalized nature of the research, the simplistic definition of its new measures, and the problem with using these measures in understanding the Plains at a regional level.

Not to be deterred by criticism, the Center had its network of senior associates prepare weekly op-ed columns on the future of the Plains for regional news outlets. Philip Burgess, the Center's director, made it clear that the media were central in shaping thought: "You can't tell people what to think but you can have some influence on what people think about."[42] The Center was very effective in obtaining media coverage for its views and attitudes. Three of its senior fellows were syndicated columnists, including Burgess, and the Center's primary media outlets were located in southern California and the Denver–Colorado Springs conurbation. However, research conducted in name recognition of the Poppers and the Center for the New West in one Plains town revealed that most people had heard of the Poppers but few were aware of the Center. Indeed, of those who did find the name familiar, most confused it with a right-wing paramilitary group.[43] Though some thought that communications technology would greatly assist business, most remained convinced that it was the agricultural economy that shaped the Plains and their lives.[44]

Once published in western newspapers, these op-ed columns were then reprinted and sent off to the Center's mailing list of eight thousand names, including its own members and federal and regional political leaders. Indeed, it would seem that the media exposure was less important than the air of authority it conferred on the reprinted text subsequently circulated to its membership.

Having established research and a media presence, the Center quickly moved to shape regional attitudes in a more focused manner by sponsoring three invitation-only roundtable meetings on the region's future (1992, 1997, and 1999).[45] These meetings drew the leaders the Center saw as essential in influencing regional policy: local and economic state planners, locally elected and appointed officials, local and state economic development specialists, tribal representatives, and directors of university research and technical-assistance centers.

The first roundtable focused specifically on envisioning future regional prosperity and how to realize that vision. The participants were asked to rank the top ten Plains issues/problems/opportunities. The environment was placed fifth, agriculture ninth, and personal-income level tenth. These are surprisingly low marks for major Plains concerns until one realizes that these issues do not neatly fit into an upbeat, future-oriented notion of the Plains. The roundtable concluded that Plains communities should focus first on getting local leadership to share a consensus of vision, second on creating a partnership of business, local government, and education, and finally on implementing "changes in public attitudes."[46] Not only did the Center effectively orient the Plains dialogue to a bright, economically focused future, it minimized the environment, agriculture (still the region's economic mainstay), and income levels. In addition, the Center positioned itself as the obvious organization to address these concerns through its work as the region's think tank.

It is stories that imbue regions with meaning, and the reiteration of those stories is paramount to obtaining and maintaining control of regional discourse and thus regional image. The Poppers' and the Center's agendas directly focused on control of the Plains image in order to influence regional public policy. The Poppers envisioned an environmentally sustainable region, the Buffalo Commons, whereas the Center imagined an archipelago society threaded together by communications technology.

The competing visions of buffalo chips versus computer chips reveal the perennial ideological tension between environmental preservation and economic progress. The tension did not revolve around one particular publicly owned environmental resource. Instead, it was a battle for the metaphorical control of the region played out in a privately held landscape.

In articulating their vision of the future, the Poppers used a conservatively mapped, environmentally defined region to tell the story of small and dying towns, population decline, a degrading environment, and regional distress. This image focused on the vast, sparsely populated agricultural Plains—the counties that did not feel the influence of interstate highways, of large, economically buoyant population centers, or of the new technology that the Center promoted.

The Poppers addressed the Plains population, but even the Poppers recognized that their vision was not embraced by a majority of the Plains public.[47] Indeed, many Plains residents felt that in the Buffalo Commons proposal their lives were ignored and disenfranchised and their experiences wiped out. Others felt that the proposal was too narrow in that it did not encompass those not participating in a buffalo economy. Interestingly, Frank Popper pointed out that reaction to the proposal had some regional variation. According to Popper, it was most accepted in the Northern Plains, where the consequences of regional decline had been felt first. By modifying their vision in response to their audience, the Poppers attracted a variety of groups that interpreted the Buffalo Commons for their own needs, from environmentalists to farmers to Indian nations.

The Center defined the Plains in more expansive and contradictory ways and did not confine itself to an environmental definition of the region. Instead, it stretched the region in all directions at various times to include adjacent metropolitan areas and small islands of population that present "successful exceptions."

The Center addressed two audiences, the Plains nonagricultural business community and national business and political leaders, in order to promote an upbeat regional vision. In describing a scattering of urban, archipelago communities, some at the edge of the region and others linked by chains of interstates and communications technology, the Center left the vast rural spaces between these urban islands unrepresented. Unlike the Poppers, the Center did not revisit its research and did not respond to the changing economic demands of the region or the shifting needs of its inhabitants.

In the years since the Poppers made their Buffalo Commons proposal, it has remained a lively contemporary vision of the Plains future. Though the herds were decimated more than a century ago, there are now approximately three hundred thousand buffalo in the region that live under a mix of public and private initiatives such as the Nature Conservancy and the InterTribal Bison Cooperative, as well as Ted Turner's and other Plains ranches. Recently, this varied collection of buffalo owners was joined by a new project to create a million-acre Buffalo Commons core. The Denver-based Great Plains Restoration Council sought to make the Buffalo Commons a reality, as its founder and director Jarid Manos stated: "We want to give the buffalo and other native wild animals of the Plains back their homelands . . . so they can flow like salmon across the ocean of grass."[48] The Buffalo Commons proposal indeed became a powerful, flexible, and enduring regional metaphor.

If the aim of the Center was to present an effective alternative regional vision, or at least limit the power of the Buffalo Commons idea, it failed. The Center's own advisory group realized the serious limitations of the Center's vision, and media coverage of this vision remained comparatively limited. Nevertheless, having established its credentials as a research and policy think tank, the Center created a mantle of authority. Using the roundtable forum, the Center articulated its pro-business and boosterish vision of the Plains, situated itself to continue this work, and promoted the products of its major sponsor, USWest.

As for the Center's influence on regional leaders and public policy, that is more difficult to measure. The comments by one Plains governor, John Hoeven (Republican, North Dakota), in 2001 offer a small but useful window into one of the Center's primary targets, regional leadership. In 1988 Hoeven's predecessor, George Sinner, had characterized Deborah Popper's work as yet another example of the opinions of an easterner who didn't understand the Plains. However, in a dramatic turnaround Hoeven commented, "There is a lot of that Buffalo Commons idea that's probably true. . . . It's never going to look like it did before, when all the farms and ranches were healthy."[49] Moreover, the roundtables to which regional political and economic leaders were invited did not continue after the merger of USWest with Qwest in 1999. The Center lost its first director, Philip Burgess, and suffered a large reduction and turnover of staff.

It is the story of the Buffalo Commons that dominates the narrative of the Great Plains and its future. This flexible regional metaphor has been embraced by the region, though not by all its inhabitants. Its multiple reiterations since the mid-1980s have maintained control of regional discourse and regional image. The Center's well-financed efforts to recapture that narrative have not been realized in the general media, and the results are at best mixed within the political community. The Poppers' Buffalo Commons has become an overarching metaphor for the region, but the Plains technological archipelago community promoted by the Center for the New West has, at least at the turn of the twenty-first century, been submerged in a sea of grass.

NOTES

1. The following works form the backbone of the Poppers' writing about the Great Plains: Frank J. Popper, "The Surviving American Frontier," *American Land Forum* (Summer 1983): 5–8; Frank J. Popper, "The Strange Case of the Contemporary American Frontier," *Yale Review* 76, no. 1 (1986): 100–121; Deborah Epstein Popper and Frank J. Popper, "The Great Plains: From Dust to Dust: A Daring Proposal for Dealing with an Inevitable Disaster," *Planning* 53, no. 12 (1987): 12–18; Deborah Epstein Popper, "Holding Steady on the Great Plains: An Exploration of the Characteristics of the Region's Population-Stable Counties" (Ph.D. diss., Rutgers University, 1992); Frank J. Popper and Deborah E. Popper, "Great Plains: Checkered Past, Hopeful Future," *Forum for Applied Research and Public Policy* 9, no. 4 (1994): 88–100; Frank Popper and Deborah Popper, "The New Significance of the Frontier in American History" (paper presented at the annual meeting of the Association of American Geographers, 1995, Chicago); Frank Popper and Deborah Popper, "The Buffalo Commons: Metaphor as Method," *Geographical Review* 89, no. 4 (1999): 491–511. A highly readable account of one turbulent year when the Poppers visited and spoke with a number of Plains communities is Anne Matthews's best-selling

book *Where the Buffalo Roam: The Storm over the Revolutionary Plan to Restore America's Great Plains* (New York: Grove Press, 1992).

2. Popper, "Strange Case," 119–20.

3. Matthews, *Where the Buffalo Roam.*

4. Matthews, *Where the Buffalo Roam,* 26.

5. Amanda Rees, "Envisioning the Great Plains: Contemporary Narratives of the Landscape" (Ph.D. diss., University of Kansas, 1998).

6. Rees, "Envisioning the Great Plains," 149.

7. Dave Egan and Bill Whitney, "Buffalo Commons: Model or Metaphor?" *Forum for Applied Research and Public Policy* (Winter 1994): 113.

8. David A. Gauthier, "The Buffalo Commons on Canada's Plains," *Forum for Applied Research and Public Policy* (Winter 1994): 118–20.

9. Rees, "Envisioning the Great Plains."

10. Matthews, *Where the Buffalo Roam,* and Florence Williams, "Plains Sense," *High Country News,* 15 January 2001.

11. Their speaking engagement costs are borne by the inviting organizations, including such diverse groups as universities, real estate agents, newspaper editors, state humanities councils, the Harvard Club of Montana, and the International Buffalo Producers Convention and Trade Show.

12. Frank Popper, interview by author, tape recording, September 1996.

13. Popper and Popper, "Buffalo Commons."

14. A web search using Lexis-Nexis for all Great Plains regional discussion in newspapers during 2001 reveals that they all make mention of the Poppers. See Timothy Egan, "As Others Abandon Plains, Indians and Bison Come Back," *New York Times,* 27 May 2001, 1; Glen Martin, "Humans Are Disappearing from Great Plains as Bison and Other Wildlife Return," *San Francisco Chronicle,* 22 April 2001; and Jeff Glasser, "A Broken Heartland," *U.S. News and World Report,* 7 May 2001. Works that discuss the Buffalo Commons idea include James Dickerson, *Home on the Range: A Century on the High Plains* (Lawrence: University Press of Kansas, 1995); John Opie, *Ogallala: Water for a Dry Land* (Lincoln: University of Nebraska Press, 1993); Richard Manning, *Grassland* (New York: Penguin, 1995); and Ernest Callenbach, *Bring Back the Buffalo* (Covelo, Calif.: Island Press, 1996).

15. Louis D. Higgs and Philip Burgess, *Overview of Change in America's New Economy: A Report to the Ford Foundation and Aspen Institute* (Denver: Center for the New West, 1992), 4.

16. Philip Burgess, interview by author, tape recording, May 1996.

17. The Center's five main corporate sponsors were GTE, a telecommunications firm; Coopers and Lybrand, accountants; Goldman Sachs, investment bankers; Arthur Andersen, accountants and business consultants; and Mortenson Construction, the builders of Coors Stadium, which played an important role in the redevelopment of Denver's downtown. It must be noted that Philip Burgess was also employed as a special adviser to USWest's chief executive officer.

18. The following documents were produced as part of the Great Plains in

Transition project and made available for sale (all published in Denver by the Center for the New West): Colleen Murphy, *Survey of Successful Communities* (January 1991); Cathy Quantic, *The Great Plains, Canada, and Mexico: Policy Issues in Rural Development and the Free Trade Agreement* (August 1991); John C. Shepard, *Leadership Through Partnerships: The National Trust's Main Street Program as a Community Economic Development Tool* (November 1991); Heartland Center for Leadership Development, *A Case Study of Superior, Nebraska* (November 1991); Claudia Giannetti, *The New Role of Librarians and Libraries in Economic Development* (December 1991); Colleen Murphy, Louis D. Higgs, and John C. Shepard, *Roundtable on the Future of the Great Plains* (December 1991); Colleen Murphy, *Survey of the Future of the Plains* (January 1992); Colleen Murphy, Louis D. Higgs, and John C. Shepard, *A Case Study of Brush, Colorado* (1992); Mark Drabenstott and Tim R. Smith, *The Changing Great Plains Economy: New Directions for Economic Policy* (1992); Louis D. Higgs and Philip Burgess, *Overview of Change in America's New Economy: A Report to the Ford Foundation and Aspen Institute* (1992); Louis D. Higgs and Claudia Giannetti, *The Economic Development Strategies of the Great Plains States* (1992); John C. Shepard, *Redefining "Place": Community and Vitality in the New Economy* (1992); John C. Shepard, Matthew Muehlbauer, and Louis D. Higgs, *Measuring Distress: Economic Indicators and the Great Plains: A Report to the Economic Development Administration of the U.S. Department of Commerce* (1992).

19. This project cost approximately $325,000, which came from the following sources: Ford Foundation, $50,000; Economic Development Agency (EDA), $25,000; Center for the New West, $176,000; and corporate sponsorship, $175,000 (Center for the New West archives).

20. The Great Plains in Transition advisory group letter of invitation, Center for the New West archives.

21. The Center's archives contain a collection of rough, penciled notes taken at the 15 April 1991 meeting. The notes outlined the main speakers and what they said, occasionally quoting directly from the advisory group members.

22. The following list of twenty-six advisers includes nineteen who were able to attend the first meeting and those who were asked to comment on the draft report. Those marked with an asterisk did not attend the initial meeting. *Academics*: Tom Anding (Center for Urban and Regional Affairs, University of Minnesota), Robert Einsweiler (Department of Planning and Public Affairs, University of Minnesota), Donald Hicks (Bruton Center for Development Studies, University of Dallas), Larry Leistritz* (Department of Agricultural Economics, North Dakota State University), William J. Waelti (Department of Economics and Business, Colorado College), William Weida (Department of Agricultural Economics and Agricultural Business, New Mexico State University), and Marvin Kaiser* (Department of Sociology, Anthropology, and Social Work, Kansas State University); *consultants from research organizations*: Jeffrey Bauer (Bauer Group [health care]), John Niles (Global Telematics), John Whisman (community development in rural high schools), Milan Wall (Heartland Institute), Joseph Luther* (Heartland Institute), Vicki Luther* (Heartland Insti-

tute), and Marty Strange* (program director, Center for Rural Affairs); *federal and state representatives*: Sara Mills Mazie, (assistant director, Agriculture and Rural Economy Division in the Economic Research Service, USDA), Joe Tritehen (because of handwritten notes, spelling is not clear) (EDA [Center for the New West's research funding source]), Robert Turner (EDA), and Lucy Creighton (Board of Land Commissioners, Colorado Department of Natural Resources); *others*: Mark Drabenstott (vice president, Federal Bank of Kansas City), William Hornby (editor, *Denver Post*), Schnittker, (full name not given and affiliation unknown), and DeWitt John* (Aspen Institute [funding source affiliated with the Ford Foundation]); *Center for the New West personnel*: Philip Burgess, Bob Wurmstedt, Colleen Murphy, and Louis Higgs. Meeting minutes, Center for the New West archives.

23. Louis Higgs, notes from 15 April 1991 advisory group meeting (Center for the New West archives).

24. Higgs, notes from 15 April 1991 meeting.

25. Murphy, *Survey of Successful Communities.*

26. Murphy, *Survey of the Future.*

27. The New Economy is defined by the Center for the New West "by global competition in global markets, the fragmentation of mass markets into niche markets, intensive use of information and technology, entrepreneurship and innovation, rapid turnover in products and markets, and the growing economic importance of leisure and tourism activities." Shepard, *Redefining "Place,"* 63.

28. Murphy, *Survey of Successful Communities*. The thirteen towns were Brush (Colorado); Deming and Raton (New Mexico); Dimmitt, Post, Roaring Springs, and Tulia (Texas); and Jackson, Powell, Worland, Buffalo, Wheatland, and Cody (Wyoming).

29. Higgs and Burgess, *Overview of Change*, 49.

30. For example, the information gathered for the six Wyoming towns came from the Wyoming State Department of Economy, Planning, and Development in Cheyenne.

31. A useful example of the style of community profiles can be found in the portrayal of Deming, New Mexico, characterized as a once-thriving, stable community that lost its military training base and then lost population. The profile focused only on positive things: the growing retirement community, a newly converted industrial park (the old base), and a *maquiladora* (an American-owned company manufacturing furniture in Mexico and warehousing the products in the town).

32. Higgs and Burgess, *Overview of Change*, 10.

33. Murphy, Higgs, and Shepard, *Case Study of Brush*, 4.

34. Higgs and Burgess, *Overview of Change*, iv.

35. Responses were drawn from letters and notes from telephone conversations about the advisory panel's work (Center for the New West archives).

36. Telephone calls on 2 March 1992, notes taken from the conversations (Center for the New West archives).

37. Letter from Professor Thomas Anding, 3 March 1992 (Center for the New West archives).

38. Letter from Professor William Weida, 26 February 1992 (Center for the New West archives).

39. Memo from Donald Hicks, 27 February 1992 (Center for the New West archives).

40. Letter from Mark Drabenstott, 5 March 1992 (Center for the New West archives).

41. Dewitt John, notes from telephone conversation, 2 March 1992 (Center for the New West archives).

42. Burgess, taped interview, April 1996.

43. In interviews I conducted with residents of one small Plains town in 1996, most had not heard of the Center for the New West. Several people wondered if it was a right-wing extremist group similar to the Posse Comitatus, a right-wing organization in the region. Another respondent asked, "Is the FBI after them?" Rees, "Envisioning the Great Plains," 164.

44. Rees, "Envisioning the Great Plains," 164.

45. Murphy, *Survey of the Future.*

46. Murphy, *Survey of the Future*, 7.

47. David Hendee, "Group Seeks Core of Buffalo Commons," *Omaha World-Herald*, 25 August 2001, 1.

48. Hendee, "Group Seeks Core," 1.

49. Egan, "Others Abandon Plains."

Alicia Barber

RENO'S SILVER LEGACY

Gambling on the Past in the Urban New West

Nestled amid the neon lights of downtown Reno, Nevada, just one block north of the famous arch that spans Virginia Street and gives the "Biggest Little City in the World" its nickname, stands a grand hotel entrance. Its elegant arched stone edifice, three stories high, graces the center of an uninterrupted block of brick and stone Victorian storefronts. Large display windows on ground level face Virginia Street, and those of the upper floors are shaded by brightly colored canopies. Iron lampposts, benches, and slender trees line the sidewalk. The entire hotel block contrasts sharply with its surroundings. On either side stretch the windowless, modern facades of the Eldorado and Circus Circus casinos, both built in the 1970s. Directly across the street, jewelry and loan, liquor, and T-shirt stores, a taco shop, and a dilapidated bar share the block with a dusty empty lot and a cheap motel. With its historic architecture and careful landscaping, the elegant hotel, dated 1895, is unique, picturesque, charming.

It is also a complete fabrication. As closer inspection reveals, the doors of the block's Victorian storefronts are sealed shut, and their windows offer no glimpses into the buildings' interiors, just shallow displays fronting opaque backdrops. A single step through the working doors at the block's center or at any of its four corners reveals the buzzers, bells, slot machines, and blackjack tables of an expansive 85,000-square-foot gaming floor. This is the Silver Legacy, a "resort casino" that opened to great fanfare on 28 July 1995. A joint venture between the Mandalay Bay Resort Group and the Eldorado Hotel Casino, the $310 million project was touted proudly as the first "Las Vegas–style," or completely themed resort casino, in Reno.

The facade is just one component of an elaborate Old West silver mining theme, complete with a founding myth that begins "when a young man named Sam Fairchild traveled west in search of a dream." Fairchild, the story continues, found his fortune in the mines of Nevada in the late nineteenth century, ultimately became "the wealthiest of all the Silver Barons," and built this hotel as a showcase for his accumulated riches.[1] Inside, the casino's centerpiece and main attraction is a giant, 120-foot-high "mining rig," said to mark the site of Fairchild's original silver mine. This rig, an oversize headframe, stands underneath an 180-foot diameter composite dome, advertised as the world's largest. Its curved surface depicts a lightly clouded sky and serves as an enormous screen for occasional light and laser shows.[2] Far larger than any working gallows frame and hoist pulley, the rig is constructed of massive steel girders connected to an array of wheels and bellows that periodically spring into motion, complete with projected clanking industrial sound effects. Signs posted on the rig and its attached "claims office" advertise the Nevada Central Railroad, the Gold Bullion Theatre, and other western-flavored sites and attractions.

Although its configuration—set up to look as if it is mining and then minting silver coins that empty into a bank of slot machines—is an obvious fiction, its sheer size and intriguing design are built to thrill. As one traveler's guide reported, "It doesn't have to be historically accurate to be appreciated. From an engineering standpoint alone, it's fascinating to see all the parts working together."[3] This is precisely the reaction the casino is looking for. Its owners are not trying to fool anyone into thinking that they are actually mining silver from below the surface of Virginia Street; the goal is simply to entertain. The purveyance of the obvious fake is by now standard in Nevada's casinos. This activity has, of course, been raised to an art form in Las Vegas, where increasingly elaborate resort casinos such as the Venetian, Paris Las Vegas, the Aladdin, and New York–New York revel in false edifices and doors that lead nowhere—the gaming floor as stage set. To criticize such creations for their inauthenticity would be to reveal oneself as an intellectual snob or, at the very least, a cynical spoilsport. As suggested in a recent article about the meticulously designed Venetian, "The new meaning of authentic is simply something that looks as you imagine it might, based on movies and television."[4] It is unlikely that the majority of casino visitors have seen an actual mining headframe, but they can clearly recognize the reference and marvel at the grand effect.

Offering suggestion over accuracy, the Silver Legacy presents a modified turn-of-the-century West, with its founding narrative complementing the architecture and decor. According to an official press release, the twenty detailed storefront facades on the Silver Legacy's exterior reflect "the timeless appeal of Nevada's silver mining heritage." In simulating the look of a bustling Victorian downtown retail district, they invite onlookers to "take a legendary trip back in time," drawing them into the casino for more "totally themed" turn-of-the-century atmosphere.[5] The display windows fronting Virginia Street contain period props: faux breads and sausages, an icebox, and antique tin cans at the "Legacy Saloon & Deli Exchange"; period maps and luggage at the "Sierra Pacific Railroad, Reno, Nevada Branch Office." In the gleaming, marble-filled hotel lobby, tucked away on the second floor at the rear end of the building, employees gamely sport Victorian-style garb in all its glorious high-necked discomfort (with cocktail waitresses in low-cut black velvet minidresses demonstrating the degree of tolerated deviance from Victorian mores). Mining carts filled with glittery golden nuggets, a bright red Wells Fargo stagecoach, stained-glass ceilings, and murals depicting turn-of-the-century western scenes continue the theme throughout the casino.

One of the most prominent characteristics of the New Western service economy is its use of the Old West as amenity.[6] The trend is readily apparent in Robert Redford's Sundance empire; in the Million Dollar Cowboy Bar in Jackson, Wyoming; and at the ubiquitous "Pony Espressos" that dot the western landscape. The heritage and imagery of the Old West are invoked constantly in the marketing of contemporary goods and services. Similar cultural references occur throughout the urban West, where the Old West pops up in events, attractions, restaurants, and museums, from Cheyenne's Frontier Days to Denver's Buckhorn Exchange to Oklahoma City's Cowboy Hall of Fame. All these are sites of consumption and recreation as much as any attraction in the more commonly understood "New Western" towns of Vail and Moab.

And yet western cities have largely been left out of conversations about the New West, apparently because they do not fit the image of the more picturesque resort towns.[7] Continuing their historic roles as centers for growing and often transient populations, western cities are particularly vulnerable to the disintegration of public memory and shared experience. With their more diversified economies and less coherent identities, they resist easy classification and consumption. But only by bringing these cities into the conversation can we create a more complete picture of the New West and the dynamics of economics, myth, and power at play in the entire region. Reno's Silver Legacy Resort Casino may not seem to be a typical attraction, but in its updated incorporation of Old West iconography it demonstrates an unmistakable link to processes occurring throughout the recreational playgrounds of the New West. Its story may help us understand the means by which western cities attempt to combat increasing homogenization and loss of place through the manipulation and presentation of local heritage.

NOT JUST ANOTHER CASINO

The decision to adopt an Old Western theme for the Silver Legacy was to many a surprising one, coming at a time when the newest casinos in trend-setting Las Vegas were incorporating European and even more exotic influences in such resorts as the Venetian and the Egyptian-themed Luxor. Paeans to the Old West are not often found in contemporary gaming establishments, where western images tend to seem provincial and dated. Many of those that remain, such as Vegas Vic, the forty-foot-high neon cowboy that has graced the top of the Pioneer Club on Fremont Street in Las Vegas since 1951, are quietly decaying, remnants of a bygone era.

The Silver Legacy, in contrast, was built from the ground up in the mid-1990s on a prime piece of real estate in the center of Reno's downtown strip. Long before construction began, the structure was charged with meaning as a symbol both of and for the community. According to Arthur Valdes, a conceptual consultant for the project, the casino's Old West silver mining theme was specifically intended to provide a connection both to local history and to the greater culture of the American West.[8] As one of the city's redevelopment officers maintained, the casino "takes us back to the roots of our community, founded in mining, gaming and cattle country."[9] This mining of the city's roots was intended to be more than figurative. In employing this pseudohistoric narrative of the Old West, the casino's owners were attempting something of a boom-by-association, essentially invoking a historic economic bonanza in the hopes of securing a contemporary one.

Reno was in the market for a new bonanza. Whereas much of the West had relatively recently turned its attention to the postindustrial economy, Reno had recognized the value of its service economy as early as 1931, the year Nevada both legalized gambling and decreased the residency requirement for divorce seekers to six weeks. In subsequent decades, long before Las Vegas emerged as a potential competitor, Reno attracted national attention and patronage as a bustling divorce, gaming, and entertainment center. However, Reno's casinos have been increasingly threatened in recent decades by the exponential growth of Las Vegas gaming and the spread of casinos nationwide, particularly on Indian reservations near Reno's traditional California feeder markets. It is difficult for many Reno residents to accept their city's change in fortune over the last half-century, since the transformation of formerly provincial Las Vegas into Nevada's largest city and an international destination.

In response, Reno city officials have recognized the need to reestablish an attractive civic identity by providing something that other gaming destinations cannot offer. Struggling for years to achieve this goal, Reno embarked on a new revitalization program in 1983. Like many cities nationwide, its downtown had been visibly deteriorating, characterized in Reno's case by spiritless rows of pawnshops, souvenir stores, and boarded-up casinos. The $6 million Raymond I. Smith Truckee River Walk, a spacious pavilion and performance area, was constructed in 1991 in an attempt to beautify the section of downtown abutting the river.[10] But urban problems persisted. As a gas station employee working one block away from the Silver Legacy's future site noted in 1993, "This part of town is dead. We've got all the transients and the hookers downtown." Of the projected casino, he suggested, "Not only will it have a financial impact . . . but I think it will help class up this part of town."[11] The building's architects shared his hope, designing the Silver Legacy to literally transform the streets, capturing not just the appearance but the vitality of a Victorian retail district. Its old-fashioned lampposts, storefronts, landscaping, and "people areas," developers predicted, would help create not just a "pedestrian atmosphere" but a "world-class walking city," returning Reno to its earlier glory.[12]

Perhaps most important, property taxes from the massive Silver Legacy project could contribute to the financing of Reno's continued downtown redevelopment.[13] While the casino was still under construction, Reno councilman Jim Pilzner admitted that if the casino did not "jumpstart" downtown, "we're going to have terrible problems."[14] The Silver Legacy's owners enthusiastically embraced this enormous economic and social challenge. At a highbrow ceremony in December 1994, when the casino's name was first revealed to the public, an actor playing the ghost of Sam Fairchild exclaimed, "This marks the rebirth of Reno. It's the renewal of the silver age . . . a Reno-vation of Reno."[15]

Despite the appearance of lengthy thematic deliberation, silver mines and Victorian storefronts did not dance through the original plans of the casino's developers. The mining theme was introduced belatedly, in summer 1994, with the new casino already in mid-construction. Until that point the chosen theme was that of a sixteenth-century Spanish Lost City of Gold, with a fantastical castle rising on the site of the existing giant mining rig. The surprise midstream change in design was prompted by a reevaluation of community needs and marketing concerns. One of the partners was quoted as saying that the Lost City was an exciting theme but that he "couldn't get his arms around a castle," reflecting the rather remarkable conclusion that a casino should inspire not only admiration but also a degree of familiarity and even affection. It seems unlikely that such a discussion would ever occur regarding new attractions on the Las Vegas strip.[16]

As the executive had hoped, the decision to connect Reno's newest casino to Nevada's mining heritage met with widespread community approval. Bob Jones, executive director of the Builders Association of Northern Nevada, agreed that "keying into our own history is great. We cannot out–Las Vegas Las Vegas. It's silly to try."[17] Recognizing the potential of emphasizing heritage over exoticism, Circus Circus president and CEO Clyde Turner expressed his satisfaction that "we have finally got something that is really Reno." Eldorado CEO Don Carano agreed that the Silver Legacy's theme was "uniquely Nevada, uniquely Reno," an assertion that no one appeared to dispute.[18]

But to what extent is the Silver Legacy "really Reno"? What endows its Old Western mining theme with any degree of currency, by which I mean both economic value and contemporary relevance, within the city's and the region's cultural landscape? In their comments regarding the Silver Legacy, planners and observers alike seem to take for granted that the casino's silver mining theme provides a direct and meaningful link to Reno's historic past. But is this purported link just another "invention of tradition," a deliberate fiction adopted in the service of tourism and promotion of civic identity?[19]

If so, Reno would certainly not be the first to embark on such a course. Cities, communities, and organizations have long deployed the past for practical ends. In the history of the urban West the most notorious case may be that of Santa Fe, which established mandatory citywide architectural standards in 1912 in order to create a coherent appearance ostensibly reflecting the city's Spanish and Mexican heritage. In establishing the critical difference between history and heritage, I adopt David Lowenthal's definition of heritage: "not a testable or even a reasonably plausible account of some past, but a declaration of faith in the past."[20] For cities deploying heritage, the strategy is a declaration of faith that the references to the past will reverse the relentless course of community fragmentation and homogeneity. Nationally, this trend, memorably described by Lowenthal as a "heritage crusade," advanced with increasing frequency toward the end of the twentieth century. And indeed, manufactured narratives and faux heritage have become popular components of neotraditional developments and new urban villages across the country.[21]

The Silver Legacy likewise represents a declaration of faith in the power of the silver mining heritage to help overcome Reno's turbulent economic state by inspiring tourists and locals alike to come in and play. The power of heritage stems from the associations it prompts and the nostalgia it summons for a chosen period in the past. In the case of the Silver Legacy, that power resides in the imaginative strength of Reno's mining heritage, a heritage that, although perhaps not readily apparent on the contemporary landscape, is no mere flight of fancy.

RENO'S SILVER LEGACY

Although not located directly at the site of mining activity, Reno has a long history as a supply town and center of commerce for Nevada's scattered mining districts. The best known of these, and the specific historical reference on which the Silver Legacy bases its theme, was the immensely profitable Comstock Lode, discovered in 1859. Located at Virginia City, just twenty-three miles southeast of Reno, the Comstock ultimately produced approximately $400 million in silver and gold.[22] Sam Fairchild, the fictional proprietor of the Silver Legacy, was clearly modeled after the four so-called Comstock Bonanza Kings: James G. Fair, John Mackay, James Flood, and William O'Brien. Befitting the hotel narrative's mythic proportions, of course, Fairchild became "the wealthiest of all the Silver Barons," ambitiously surpassing them all.

The casino reinforced this purported link to the Comstock barons by displaying in its hotel lobby several pieces of an impressive thirteen-hundred-piece silver service, manufactured for John Mackay in 1876 by Tiffany's New York from a half ton of Comstock silver. A plaque accompanying the display staked out the casino's historical claim, asserting that "just as the Mackay silver collection evolved from the great history and heritage of Nevada, so too did the Silver Legacy, Reno's first themed Resort Casino." In relating the Silver Legacy to Nevada's legacy of silver, the hotel goes beyond recognizing the inspiration for its theme to asserting its own place in that historic lineage.

In the tradition of the Mackay silver service, the Tiffany-inspired lamps, crystal chandeliers, and sumptuous armchairs of the hotel lobby are clearly meant to evoke the lavish establishments built from the fortunes of the era's true mining magnates. Many of these structures remain, including the opulent Italian Renaissance–style Fairmont Hotel on San Francisco's tony Nob Hill and Denver's Brown Palace, with its nine-story atrium lobby filled with imported onyx. These and a handful of other luxury historic hotels such as Aspen's Hotel Jerome are the true architectural legacies of the mining barons and, frequented by today's barons of commerce, directly link the Old West to the New.

Reno was simply too small to attract the attention, or the capital, of the Comstock millionaires as they sought out sound investment opportunities. Despite its closer proximity to Virginia City, Reno did not profit in the same way as San Francisco and other Bay Area cities from the accumulated wealth of the new mining magnates. Virginia City itself was far more cosmopolitan than Reno during the Comstock's peak years, boasting the ornate Piper's Opera House and an elegant hotel, the renowned International. Rebuilt after an 1875 fire to a splendid six-story height, the International was famed as one of the "grandest structures west of the Mississippi," complete with a gourmet restaurant and the first hydraulic elevator in Nevada.[23]

Reno, in contrast, served primarily as a shipping and distribution center throughout most of the nineteenth century. The city's townsite was not formally platted until 1868, with the extension of the Central Pacific Railroad to the fledgling settlement, then known as "Lake's Crossing," on the banks of the Truckee River. Beginning in 1869, the Virginia and Truckee Railroad connected Reno to Virginia City, enabling the transfer of critical supplies to the isolated mining town. These supplies included fresh produce from an increasing number of farms established throughout the Truckee Meadows south of Reno. By 1895, the fictional founding date of the Silver Legacy, Reno boasted a population of approximately four thousand and a small but thriving commercial area alongside the railroad tracks, four blocks south of the current casino site.

Reno's connection to the mining industry was strengthened in the first decade of the twentieth century with the discovery of massive veins of gold and silver in the southern Nevada districts of Tonopah, in 1900, and Goldfield, in 1902. Although farther than Virginia City from Reno, these districts inspired further immigration to Nevada, resulting in the doubling of Reno's population from 4,500 in 1900 to 10,867 a decade later.[24] The new discoveries together produced more wealth than the Comstock, as well as multimillionaires such as capitalist George Wingfield, who, unlike the Comstock barons, invested his considerable fortune in Reno in the form of banks, hotels, and a degree of political influence unsurpassed before or since.[25] Wingfield's impact on Reno's landscape is still visible, from the Reno National Bank, to the elegant Riverside Hotel, to the namesake park he donated to the city in 1920.[26]

By this point the city featured another strong connection to the mining industry in the form of the Mackay School of Mines, founded at the University of Nevada's Reno campus in 1888. In 1906 the family of silver baron John Mackay donated the funds to construct the mining school's main building, providing the Comstock connection that had eluded Reno decades before. In addition, the family tapped sculptor Gutzon Borglum, who would later achieve fame as the designer of Mount Rushmore, to produce a statue of John Mackay that would be placed in front of the building. The stone figure still stands at the top of the university's Jeffersonian quadrangle, overlooking downtown Reno with pick and piece of ore in hand, a romanticized image of the multimillionaire as solitary prospector.

The Tonopah and Goldfield mines went into decline by the depression years, but Reno continued to reap the rewards of the short-lived but lucrative boom. In 1931 Nevada's legalization of gaming and establishment of a six-week residency requirement, the shortest in the country, for divorce seekers, set off a new service-oriented boom that would change the face of Nevada. The gaming legislation, and the subsequent growth of the industry, single-handedly transformed Nevada from a rural, mining-based economy to an urban, service-oriented one. And yet mining remained tied to the Silver State's economy and outward identity, so much so that a writer for the Work Projects Administration's Writers' Program included in its 1940 Nevada edition of the American Guide Series a glossary of mining terms such as "make a stake" and "kiss it goodbye," in order to provide a key to understanding Nevadan speech, "a language often bewildering to outsiders."[27] In the second half of the century the role of mining in Reno's identity was further eclipsed by that of the gaming and tourism industry, which grew to dominate the city's economic and cultural landscape. Casino operators soon realized that the perceived exoticism of the American West, evident in the breathless fascination of the WPA guide, could be used to their advantage.

FROM INDUSTRY TO ENTERTAINMENT: MINING AS THEME

The use of Old Western themes in casinos in Reno, as in Las Vegas, reflected the widespread popularity of and nostalgia for the American West from the 1930s through the 1960s. Stereotypical images of prospectors, cowboys, and the wild frontier appeared throughout many of the city's earlier gaming establishments. Perhaps the most famous of these, Harolds Club, opened on Virginia Street in 1936 and eventually became a global destination, with the help of billboards announcing "Harolds Club or Bust" throughout the country and as far away as the North Pole. The casino's Roaring Camp room overflowed with Old West memorabilia, and in 1950 the club's owners commemorated Nevada pioneers and settlers in a sixty-thousand-dollar mural installed above the casino's main entrance. Local schoolchildren were regularly taken to visit Harolds' extensive collections of western artifacts, including an enormous gun collection, in order to gain an understanding of their region's history.[28]

Nevada's great appeal to tourists of the 1940s and 1950s owed much to the popularity of western film and television shows of the era, resulting in the construction of what historian Earl Pomeroy has called "the most patently commercial Western charades."[29] In recent decades, however, the Old West has lost its currency in the gaming industry, replaced in tourist dreams by the exotic appeal of the Luxor, Bellagio, Venetian, and Monte Carlo. The majority of Nevada's western-themed casinos have not survived, although their colorful names punctuate Reno's history. The Frontier Club, with its bucking bronco logo, operated on Virginia Street from 1946 to 1956, and the Silver Spur, founded just across the street in 1968 with a lavish Old West interior and plush "Virginia City Parlor," survived until 1981. In a dramatic move that signified to many the end of an era, Harolds Club itself, Reno's venerable gaming pioneer, was demolished on 15 December 1999.[30]

In their names and decor these casinos primarily celebrated the stock western images of the pioneer and the cowboy. Perhaps predictably, the world of mining has proved less inspiring for the gaming industry. On the surface this preference seems largely aesthetic. The cowboy captured the national imagination in a way the miner never could. Cowboys work outside, under the wide-open sky; the hats and boots of their everyday uniform have been assimilated into contemporary fashion; they sing catchy tunes and, in these modern times, even recite poetry. Miners, in contrast, toil underground in large numbers in conditions that are usually cold and wet. It is difficult to imagine a crew of miners bursting into song as they enter the dark tunnels for a day of mucking.[31]

Like mining towns themselves, miners could not become valued until they were romanticized. This is perhaps less of a challenge for the physical settings, which are often breathtaking, located in remote, mountainous, scenic spots such as Park City, Utah, and Cripple Creek, Colorado. As Richard Francaviglia notes in his excellent study of America's mining landscapes, nostalgia following World War II transformed mining districts in such places from industrial sites to tourist destinations and cultural symbols of American risk taking and ingenuity. It was then a short step to the creation of fully fabricated mining districts, such as Disneyland's Big Thunder Mountain, as themed sites of recreation.[32]

As the epitome of risk taking, mining seems perfectly suited as a theme for gaming operations. The two industries are often linked in tales of the frontier. Both perpetuate the myth of the rare exception, the individual who defies the odds to make of the West a true land of opportunity, his own Big Rock Candy Mountain. If Fairchild found his fortune, the Silver Legacy implies, why not the urban prospector of the New West, mining for Megabucks®? If one slot machine doesn't produce, there's always another vein to tap, another chance to strike it rich at the dealer's next hand. Every gambler wants to consider himself or herself the exception; this is the guiding American Dream that fueled the gold rush and other western booms that brought riches to a few and disappointment to most.

Until the advent of the Silver Legacy the venue with the most elaborate mining theme in Reno was the aptly named Comstock Hotel-Casino. The Comstock opened for business on West Second Street in 1978 with a prospector-pick logo and an interior evoking a rollicking mining boomtown. Life-sized mannequins, including "Lulubelle and Slim," a burlesque singer and piano player, and the "Pick and Shovel Gang," a ragtag band of musical miners, sprang to life above the casino floor every fifteen minutes. Continuing the theme were restaurants and shops, including the Miner's Café, Silver King Saloon, General Mercantile Emporium, and Prospector Club, as well as a change counter labeled the "Cashier and Assay Office." The overall effect was that of a raucous Wild West.[33]

Although the Silver Legacy features some similar thematic components, it aspires to a higher degree of cultivation than the Comstock. The Wild West does appear in unexpected places, such as the hotel's beauty and barber salon, where a showgirl mannequin bearing a close resemblance to the Comstock's Lulubelle, complete with red feather boa, poses alluringly on an antique piano. And of course, the gaming floor, despite the rich carpeting and stained glass, could never be considered subdued, with the raucous din of the slot and video poker machines, all spouting electronic musical riffs, and alarms that ring relentlessly with every new jackpot. But the furnishings suggest more rarified ambitions. In the words of the casino's own press, the goal is to portray "the fun and excitement of Nevada's silver mining era with European touches."[34] The casino's eating and drinking establishments are titled accordingly, with the Silver Baron Bar and Lounge taking the place of the Comstock's Silver King Saloon. The elegance of Sterling's Seafood & Steakhouse and Fairchild's Oyster Bar further demonstrates the Silver Legacy's attempt to create a more sophisticated atmosphere within the boundaries of the sometimes-cacophonous modern casino.

The most surprising and perhaps most significant aspect of this attempt is reflected in the depictions of mining and miners in the Silver Legacy, or, more precisely, the lack thereof. Whereas the Comstock Hotel-Casino, which closed unexpectedly in November 2000, featured many representations of miners themselves, from the prospector's pick to murals of the boomtown, the Silver Legacy depicts no miners. The mining rig itself is simply an enormous mechanical prop, divorced from any human interaction, evoking the industrial source of Fairchild's wealth without dirtying it with any suggestions of physical labor.

The casino's mining references are, with the exception of the rig, disconnected from the entire process of industrial production. By locating its thematic setting at a time—1895—and a place—a more cosmopolitan turn-of-the-century Reno—removed from the actual site of mining activity, the Silver Legacy transfers the focus from the mining itself to the hotel ostensibly funded by the mine's bonanza. In essence, it is romancing not the miner but the capitalist, honoring John Mackay's silver collection rather than his role as a prospector, as captured by the Borglum statue at the School of Mines.

The difference seems entirely in keeping with New Western consumerist sensibilities. By literally banking on the romantic image of the silver barons, the Silver Legacy relies on our attraction to that image and the positive associations it generates in our collective memory. In its separation of production from consumption, past from present, the casino seems to provide a metaphor for many recreational sites throughout the American West, where activities from skiing to climbing are often pursued without reference to or consideration of the industrial activities, past and present, that shaped the very landscapes on which they take place. Indeed, in today's cultural and political climate the Silver Legacy's thematic choice is rather surprising in its unapologetic romanticization of a solitary white ("Fair-child") male protagonist who achieved extraordinary wealth through what is perhaps the most demonized of extractive industries. However, the casino manages to evade any negative associations through its careful selection and presentation of images, a strategy that, ironically, bears a striking resemblance to that of the mining industry itself.

THE DEMONIZATION OF PRODUCTION

By locating him a full century ago in time, the Silver Legacy places its mining magnate, Sam Fairchild, on a pedestal where he can remain untouched by modern industrial debates over cyanide-heap leach processing, the EPA's Toxic Release Inventory, and mercury pollution. The success of the theme relies on the ability of myth to quarantine entertainment from the potentially fatal contagion of politics. Mining enterprises past and present are not linked in the Silver Legacy just as they are not linked in the national imagination. As Patricia Limerick points out, this perceived disjunction, seen in commemorative events such as the 150th anniversary of the California gold rush, allows us to romanticize the past as an era of honest, individualistic enterprise. Once created, Limerick argues, this romanticized image of the small individualistic prospector is commonly invoked to justify the industrial practices of large international mining corporations.[35]

Nevertheless, in Nevada today's miners seem much less inclined to romanticize the prospector or glorify the industry's history. Some nostalgia for the mining past does occur, of course, as evidenced by the School of Mines' statue of Mackay-as-prospector and an intriguing annual Intercollegiate Mining Competition in which University of Nevada students compete against other universities in events such as hand mucking, track standing, hand steel drilling, and Swede sawing, all skills practiced by Comstock-era miners.[36]

But the industry itself seems more inclined to disconnect from its past, emphasizing recent improvements in environmentally sensitive extraction technology over outdated images of picks and prospectors. As one prominent industry figure stated in February 2000, "To compare today's mining industry to the industry of the first half of the 1900's is like trying to compare a 747 to the Wright Brothers plane first flown at Kitty Hawk. There is virtually no comparison."[37] The past can seem more of a liability to an industry that has undergone some rocky times since the heady days of the Comstock, Tonopah, and Goldfield.

Mining remains the second largest industry in Nevada, which continues to lead the nation in gold and silver production. But since the discovery of the Carlin Trend, a gold bonanza of unprecedented size in eastern Nevada that set off a boom in the mid-1990s, the industry has fallen victim to the diminishing value of precious metals. The subsequent industry-wide loss of jobs led one reporter to conclude recently that "Nevada miners have little to cheer about."[38] Companies have closed statewide, with the number of mining firms in Nevada decreasing from 267 in March 1999 to 239 in March 2001, a drop of 10.5 percent.[39] In the same two-year period, the number of mining firms in Washoe County, where Reno is located, fell from 66 to 50, a decrease of 24.2 percent.[40]

The industry has been battered not just by economic but by cultural shifts that have turned a more critical eye toward traditional western industries, in one case labeling mining a central component of the "ugly West."[41] When mining appears in the headlines of Reno's newspapers, it is frequently in reference to concerns over environmental damage, the dangers of abandoned mines, or the declining value of gold. Groups such as the Great Basin Mine Watch, founded in Reno in 1995, regularly monitor the environmental practices of the state's mining companies. The emergence of such groups complements revisionist interpretations of mining history spearheaded by Limerick and the other seminal figures of the so-called New Western History. In her myth-busting *Legacy of Conquest*, Limerick pointed out the poor working conditions for western miners, describing many mine owners and operators as powerful capitalists whose valuation of property over workers kept laborers wage-dependent and without the protection of unions.[42] While acknowledging the industry's contributions to the state, Nevada historian Russell Elliott echoed Limerick's assessment in describing the true legacy of the state's mining as a pernicious one of corruption, criminal speculation, and industrial control of the government.[43]

In tacit recognition of the mining industry's precarious public image, the Nevada Mining Association, founded in 1913 by the state's leading mineral producers, has begun to promote Nevada mining through a myth-busting publicity campaign emphasizing the practical over the romantic, the future over the past, and public service over private profit. The NMA even went so far as to co-host a booth with the Division of Minerals and the Nevada Bureau of Mines and Geology at the 1999 Earth Day celebration in Wingfield Park. Asking, "How can one think of the Earth's riches without thinking of mining?" the booth provided information on reclamation projects and uses of minerals and allowed children to create cakes made of concrete.

The association's promotional slogan, "Everything Begins with Mining," draws attention to our universal dependence on mined products, touting the use of silver as a key medical bactericide, silicon in computer chips, and industrial minerals such as limestone in consumer goods ranging from automobile tires to toothpaste. In a running campaign that includes regular television advertisements, coloring books for children, and an annual Nevada Mining Week, the NMA attempts to generate local awareness of the positive contributions of mining to everyday life.[44] Limestone may not quite carry the glamour of Comstock silver, but that is precisely the point. The silver candelabras and embossed ashtrays of John Mackay's thirteen-hundred-piece silver service may be expendable luxuries, but who can live without toothpaste? In the same way, the Silver Legacy maintains its focus not on the controversial process of mining but on the desirability of the products it enables: today, thanks to mining, computer companies can manufacture computer chips; in 1895 Fairchild built a hotel.

In their abandonment of the romantic prospector image, both the Nevada Mining Association and the Silver Legacy Hotel Casino demonstrate their recognition of the changing currency of traditional western images. With so much at stake, neither the mining nor the gaming industry can afford to misread public sentiment toward the Old West. To one, mining's nineteenth-century heritage is a dangerous quagmire; to the other, it is a bonanza of images that can be mined, or undermined, to produce the most desirable and marketable effect. The result, for the Silver Legacy, is an adapted post-industrial mining heritage that, while reflective of the region's past, is even more attuned to the needs of the present and future.

≈

Nevada is no stranger to the bucking of trends. So the fact that one Nevada casino has recently chosen to incorporate a western theme others might consider passé, drawing on a heritage some might consider politically incorrect, is perhaps not surprising. And yet in its reinvention of that heritage to correspond with the marketing demands of the New West, the Silver Legacy reflects a timely appreciation of changing consumer tastes and the contemporary cultural and political climate. Appropriately for a western city, the casino depicts an urbanized Old West, selectively taking what it wants from local and regional heritage and reinterpreting a traditional extractive economy in the service of the new postindustrial economy, recreational tourism. In the process, the Silver Legacy has successfully created an Old West for the New Western era, a recreational playground in keeping with its region and its times.

NOTES

1. *Silver Legacy*, promotional brochure, Silver Legacy Hotel Casino, Reno, c. 1995.

2. Silver Legacy Hotel Casino, official website, http://www.silverlegacyreno.com/generalinfo2.php?id=4 [10 December 2000].

3. Insider's Guide to Reno & Lake Tahoe, www.insiders.com/reno-tahoe/index.htm [2 December 2000].

4. Wayne Curtis, "Belle Epoxy," *Preservation* (May/June 2000): 39. Regina Bendix offers a useful overview of the modern hunger for authenticity in *In Search of Authenticity: The Formation of Folklore Studies* (Madison: University of Wisconsin Press, 1997).

5. "1890s Facades Featured at the Silver Legacy Resort Casino in Reno, Nevada," press release, Silver Legacy Hotel Casino Website, www.silverlegacyreno.com/1890_facades.html [2 December 2000].

6. William Riebsame, gen. ed., *Atlas of the New West: Portrait of a Changing Region* (New York: W. W. Norton, 1997), 120.

7. For example, Hal Rothman addresses surprisingly few cities besides Las Vegas in *Devil's Bargains: Tourism in the Twentieth-Century American West* (Lawrence: University Press of Kansas, 1998).

8. Susan Skorups, "Previous Themes Didn't Fit Reno's Western Image," *Reno Gazette-Journal*, 3 June 1994, 7A.

9. Susan Voyles, "Victorian Look Sparks Debate on Reno's Tone," *Reno Gazette-Journal*, 3 June 1994, 7A.

10. Barbara Land and Myrick Land, *A Short History of Reno* (Reno: University of Nevada Press, 1995), 123.

11. Mike Henderson, "Callers Mostly Favor Project, But Many Have Concerns," *Reno Gazette-Journal*, 20 May 1993, 4A.

12. Voyles, "Victorian Look," 7A.

13. Susan Voyles, "Mega Resort Means Major Revenue Boost," *Reno Gazette-Journal*, 20 May 1993, 4A.

14. Voyles, "Victorian Look," 7A.

15. James Robbins, "Ghostly Host Announces Name for Project C," *Reno Gazette-Journal*, 16 December 1994, 1B.

16. Skorups, "Previous Themes," 7A.

17. Gaye Delaplane, "Movers, Shakers Like Changes," *Reno Gazette-Journal*, 3 June 1994, 6A.

18. Susan Skorups, "Project C Trading 16th-Century Spain for Old West Look," *Reno Gazette-Journal*, 3 June 1994, 1A.

19. See Eric Hobsbawn and Terence Ranger, eds., *The Invention of Tradition* (Cambridge: Cambridge University Press, 1983), and M. Christine Boyer, *The City of Collective Memory: Its Historical Imagery and Architectural Entertainments* (Cambridge: MIT Press, 1996).

20. David Lowenthal, *Possessed by the Past: The Heritage Crusade and the Spoils of History* (New York: Free Press, 1996), 121.

21. For a description of such fictionalized heritage at play in a suburban California development, see Karen Till, "Neotraditional Towns and Urban Villages: The Cultural Production of a Geography of 'Otherness,'" *Environment and Planning D: Society and Space* 11 (1993): 709–32. See also Steven D. Hoelscher, *Heritage on Stage: The Invention of Ethnic Place in America's Little Switzerland* (Madison: University of Wisconsin Press, 1998).

22. Grant H. Smith, *The History of the Comstock Lode* (Reno: Nevada Bureau of Mines and Geology and University of Nevada Press, 1998), 313.

23. Ronald M. James, *The Roar and the Silence: A History of Virginia City and the Comstock Lode* (Reno: University of Nevada Press, 1998), 117, 232.

24. Land and Land, *Short History of Reno*, 35.

25. Work Projects Administration, *Nevada: A Guide to the Silver State*, American Guide Series (Portland, Ore.: Binfords & Mort, 1940), 149; Russell R. Elliott, "Nevada's Mining Heritage: Blessing and Burden," in *East of Eden, West of Zion: Essays on Nevada*, ed. Wilbur S. Shepperson (Reno: University of Nevada Press, 1989), 50.

26. The Reno National Bank is currently living a new life as the Planet Hollywood themed restaurant, part of the Harrah's complex. The Riverside Hotel reopened in 2000 as partially subsidized housing for working artists.

27. Work Projects Administration, *Nevada*, 58–60.

28. Dwayne Kling, *The Rise of the Biggest Little City: An Encyclopedic History of Reno Gaming, 1931–1981* (Reno: University of Nevada Press, 2000), 61–65.

29. Earl Pomeroy, *In Search of the Golden West: The Tourist in Western America* (Lincoln: University of Nebraska Press, 1957), 185.

30. Kling, *Biggest Little City*, 52–53, 152–53. A similar process has occurred in the small gambling towns of eastern Colorado, where a number of family-owned mining-themed casinos, often in historic buildings, have been put out of business by expansive corporate casinos brandishing Las Vegas names and connections. See Katherine Jensen and Audie L. Blevins, *The Last Gamble: Betting on the Future in Four Rocky Mountain Mining Towns* (Tucson: University of Arizona Press, 1998), 177.

31. Limerick humorously attributes the greater popularity of the cowboy over the miner to the greater aesthetic appeal of the horse over the lowly burro. Patricia Nelson Limerick, *Something in the Soil: Legacies and Reckonings in the New West* (New York: W. W. Norton, 2000), 218.

32. Richard V. Francaviglia, *Hard Places: Reading the Landscape of America's Historic Mining Districts* (Iowa City: University of Iowa Press, 1991), 172, 198.

33. Kling, *Biggest Little City*, 31.

34. "Silver Legacy Resort Casino Fact Sheet," Silver Legacy Hotel Casino official website, http://www.silverlegacyreno.com/fact_sheet.html [15 October 2001].

35. Limerick, *Something in the Soil*, 226.

36. Jeff DeLong, "Teams Battle in Mining Event," *Reno Gazette-Journal*, 14 April 2001, 1C.

37. Russ Fields, "President's Message," *Nevada Miner*, February 2000, Nevada Mining Association website, www.nevadamining.org/news/pres/pres_949392000.html [20 December 2000].

38. Don Cox, "Nevada Miners Have Little to Cheer About," *Reno Gazette-Journal*, 6 October 2000, 5A.

39. "Nevada Statewide, Firm Data Report for 1st Quarter 2001/Jan–Mar," Nevada Research & Analysis Bureau, http://detr.state.nv.us/lmi/data/empprofiles/siz_018.htm [10 October 2001].

40. "Washoe County, Nevada, Firm Data Report for 1st Quarter 2001/Jan–Mar," Nevada Research & Analysis Bureau, http://detr.state.nv.us/lmi/data/empprofiles/siz_031.htm [10 October 2001].

41. Riebsame, *Atlas of the New West*, 135.

42. Limerick, *Something in the Soil*, 117, 124.

43. Elliott, "Nevada's Mining Heritage," 53–54.

44. Melissa Reed, "Minerals Are Used for More Than You Think," *Celebrate Nevada's Mining Week*, special advertising section (Reno: RGJ Custom Publishing Group, 29 September 2000), 2.

Robert R. Dykstra

Jo Ann Manfra

CONTESTING BOOT HILL

The Saga of Metaphorical Dodge City

For 130 years no western venue has proved more enduringly fascinating to readers, viewers, and tourists than Dodge City, Kansas. Yet its pioneer settlers and their successors divided sharply over the iconographic identity of frontier Dodge. In the end, the symbolic battle over Boot Hill was won by those locals who collaborated with, rather than resisted, metropolitan America's increasingly weighty cultural investment in a mythological West. The modern Dodge City of metaphor and theme park uniquely exemplifies the quintessential Old West that never was.

In the summer of 1872 two liquor dealers pitched a store-tent along the right-of-way of the Atchison, Topeka & Santa Fe Railroad in southwest Kansas, forming the entrepreneurial nucleus of what within a few years would become the nationally famous Dodge City. In its first ten months of formal existence Dodge and the county of which it was a part were without civil organization. Thus the town lacked law officers, courts, and prosecutors, resulting in frequent gun violence. Between September 1872 and July 1873 eighteen adult male fatalities certifiably occurred at Dodge.[1]

Once its business elite assumed political control of the town in 1873, however, violent deaths abruptly ceased. Not until 1876, so far as is known, would another adult homicide take place there. By that date Dodge was a full-fledged cattle-trading center protected by a formidable array of peace officers: a county sheriff, an undersheriff, as many deputy sheriffs as needed, a city marshal, an assistant marshal, as many policemen as needed, two township constables, and a deputy U.S. marshal. This deployment and strict enforcement of gun-control laws help explain the relatively modest body count of Dodge's cowboy era. During that celebrated decade only seventeen adult residents or sojourners died violently, an average of about one and a half victims per cattle-trading season.[2] Efforts by a few historians to inflate these figures by transforming them into the criminologists' "per 100,000 population" ratio are—for such a numerically tiny place—without statistical validity.[3]

From the very beginning two themes defined Dodge City's image: gun violence and a certain wry humor about it. During Dodge's *annus horribilis* of 1872-73 a visiting news correspondent remarked that "the town, which is scarcely four months old, . . . has in that time attained considerable notoriety for liveliness, especially in the lively extinguishment of disputes and disputers at point of arms." A joke made the rounds of the Kansas press: "A gentleman wishing to go from Wichita to Dodge City, applied to a friend for a letter of introduction. He was handed a double-barreled shot-gun and a Colt's revolver." Quipped an editor: "Only two men killed at Dodge City last week."[4]

At Dodge itself, meanwhile, despite the business community's insistence that law and order reigned supreme, local yarn-spinners merrily retailed "the number, accomplishments and glorious ends of those who rest[ed] on 'Boot hill,'" as a local editor complained. Even before the town's first anniversary the pioneer cemetery had become a tourist attraction. "After we had dinner," reported a traveler of early 1873, "we went around to view the stores, saloons [and] dance houses, and then . . . the western hill, where lie six men that have 'died in their boots,' killed in some affray about the town." A few years later a visiting Pennsylvanian, interviewed while gathering souvenir pebbles, remarked that where he came from, Boot Hill was "considered almost as great a curiosity as the grave of Shakespeare." In 1879, when the old cemetery was finally moved to make way for a school, it was found to contain twenty-five or thirty burials, not all of them shooting victims and at least one a woman.[5]

Victorian definitions of sin and debauchery flavored Dodge's violent image. Although few tourists could testify to having witnessed a gun battle on Front Street, anyone could see that the town's all-night bars and dance halls, its licensed gambling and sanctioned prostitution, flourished seven nights a week. Visitors' reactions ranged from fascination to righteous fury. Some mixed moral condemnation with amusement. In 1884, for instance, an excursion train carrying a party of wealthy New Englanders paused at Dodge on its way west. "One lady," testified a witness, "jumped off saying she wanted to set foot on the soil where stood the worst town in America."[6]

≈

The epiphany of the settlement's bad press came with the so-called Dodge City War of 1883.[7] This bloodless but potentially lethal conflict grew out of a business rivalry and extended over several weeks. Eventually, the Kansas adjutant general negotiated a peace settlement, but not before the news out of Dodge had earned headlines from St. Louis to New York. "ANARCHY IN DODGE CITY, KANSAS" was one of the pithier—this on the front page of the *New York Tribune*, arguably America's favorite family newspaper. Other big-city editorialists joined in, often commenting with cutting levity. One speculated that Dodge "must be a delightful place of residence, cowboys and six-shooters being as thick as huckle-berries in fly time." Yet another hoped "that the inhabitants of that noted center of wickedness, Dodge City, will endeavor to reform it altogether. If they succeed, then there is every chance of a man dying a natural death there once in a while."[8]

Coming in the waning days of the town's prosperity as a cattle market, the Dodge City War sparked a taste within the local business elite for national exposure, whether praise or criticism, whether serious or tongue-in-cheek. Until then the town's entrepreneurs had shunned notoriety, considering it economically counterproductive. Now, to the discomfort of a growing number of local evangelical reformers, they embraced the modern dictum that any publicity is good publicity.

The new consensus prompted a scheme to sponsor the first "genuine Spanish bullfight" held on United States soil. The planned entertainment provoked much criticism and, consequently, press coverage in St. Louis, Chicago, and New York papers. Although the bulls proved to have little fight in them, not so the festive onlookers. A shouting match in a saloon became a shooting affray, resulting in the death of a prominent young cattleman at the hands of a professional gambler.[9]

Time, however, was running out on frontier Dodge. Rural settlement enclosed it in 1885, ending both its Texas cattle trade and its illegal amenities. In 1886 a local editor politely asked that the *Kansas City Daily News* cease referring to Dodge City as the "devils own." "We have reformed," he rather wistfully announced.[10]

For many years Dodge City's evangelicals relaxed in the knowledge that gone were the days when their hometown was all too frequently dubbed "the Sodom of the West." Those who supervised the community consensus relegated Dodge's frontier experience to oblivion. A headline over a news dispatch of 1910 disclosed, "Staid Dodge City Regrets Its Past." Six years later a similar piece assured readers of "The Tameness of Dodge City," asserting that the town "has forgotten its past."[11]

But the nation's journalists and popular writers had not forgotten. At the turn of the twentieth century the history of frontier Dodge attracted the attention of the new mass-circulation magazines and their middle-class readers, initiating a national discourse on its character. Virtually without exception, writings focused on the old cattle town's law officers, two of whom—Wyatt Earp and W. B. ("Bat") Masterson—were already national celebrities.[12] As would be true of western fiction and cinema as they evolved in these same years, the confrontation of lawmen and desperadoes was the primary theme. Although this "true West" literature lent a historical gloss to early western movies, the most important flow was probably in the other direction. With so many Americans learning their frontier history in darkened theaters, such fantasies as the fast-draw gunfight came to be recycled back into popular nonfiction and fiction.[13]

Dodge City's first important appearance in this genre came in a 1902 article by a Kansas writer, E. C. Little. Published in *Everybody's Magazine*, "The Round Table of Dodge City" literally mythologized the town's frontier officers as "KNIGHTS-ERRANT WHO SURPASSED THE ACHIEVEMENTS OF HEROES OF ROMANCE." Ironic testament to the success of Little and later writers is that today many Americans believe that Dodge, like Camelot, was and is a wholly imaginary place.[14]

E. C. Little offered biographies of three lawmen who had served at one time or another at Dodge: Bat Masterson, David A. ("Mysterious Dave") Mather, and Patrick Sughrue. The last evidently still lived in Dodge and was the author's main informant. Pat Sughrue's cooperation with Little helped define an issue of the next thirty years: the extent to which Dodge would cooperate in the formation of its historic image.

Most spectacularly featured by Little was Dave Mather, said to be a direct descendant of the renowned Puritan clergyman Cotton Mather. The article's main illustration, rendered by the famous Frederic Remington, depicted Dave, in action, as mysterious indeed—a ghostly, smoke-obscured background figure, his several victims sprawling front and center. In a recurrence of the rhetorical marriage of violence with humor the picture's caption described Dave as "THE ONLY DESCENDANT OF COTTON MATHER WHO HAS DISTINGUISHED HIMSELF."[15]

The following year a novelized but masterfully true-to-life cowboy's view of Dodge appeared in the first "adult Western" novel written by an actual ex-trailhand. Andy Adams's *The Log of a Cowboy* is still praised by scholars for its verisimilitude, and the chapter in which his Circle Dot crew visits Dodge is no exception. Its other attributes aside, the Dodge City episode was unusual for its use of the local gun-control law as a plot device. But Adams, too, took a paragraph to extol the virtues of the town's frontier lawmen. And, like E. C. Little, Adams concluded that "the puppets of no romance ever written can compare with these officers in fearlessness."[16]

In 1904 popular magazines printed four Dodge City short stories written by Alfred Henry Lewis, editor of *Human Life*, a Hearst magazine published in New York. Much less wedded to historical veracity than Adams, Lewis offered heavily fictionalized accounts of real events and personalities based on information provided by Bat Masterson, now a sportswriter at the *New York Morning Telegram*. In one story, for example, a factually unrecognizable account of Masterson's election as Ford County sheriff, remarks were put into the mouths, and thoughts into the heads, of real Dodge City pioneers, nearly all of whom were made to speak the type of "western" patois popularized by Bret Harte.[17] In 1905 these stories reappeared in Lewis's full-length novelization of Masterson's frontier adventures, *The Sunset Trail*. Of its sixteen chapters, ten were fanciful versions of actual events that had occurred at Dodge. Although the novel was remarkable for its minimalist gun violence, it elevated the former sheriff's lifetime shooting victims from two, his true total, to five.[18]

Masterson himself, at A. H. Lewis's urging, wrote a series of articles for *Human Life* called "Famous Gunfighters of the Western Frontier." These 1907 essays on Luke Short, Ben Thompson, J. H. ("Doc") Holliday, Bill Tilghman, and Wyatt Earp remain valuable for their insider's account of the famous Dodge City War. An additional article on Masterson was contributed by editor Lewis.[19]

Six years later, in part to counter his hometown's old reputation, in part to capitalize on it, pioneer merchant Robert M. Wright brought out a memoir, *Dodge City: The Cowboy Capital*. Wright's estimate of homicides in Dodge during its first year of existence as "twenty-five, and perhaps more than double that number wounded," turned out to be the work's most quoted passage. Published by a Kansas press, the book did not sell well, but it proved a gold mine for later writers, especially those who sensed readers' credulous fascination with the body count at early Boot Hill.[20]

As the century wore on, national and regional journalists writing in a wide variety of publications created ever more lurid portraits of Dodge that would stick tenaciously to the American consciousness. "It was in Dodge City . . . that the practice of 'setting a killer to kill a killer,' was brought to perfection . . . when the revolver was the only sign of law and order that could command respect" (*Outing*, 1904). "The reign of law at Dodge was enforced by the 6-shooter and . . . the court of last resort there was presided over by Judge Lynch" (*Kansas City Star*, 1918). "They were buried literally with their boots on . . . these victims of saloon, dance-hall, and gambling fights. When one was 'bumped off,' the authorities just hustled the body out to Boot Hill and speculated upon what else the day would bring forth in bloodshed" (*Literary Digest*, 1925). "Bat Masterson, as peace officer at Dodge City when it was the most lawless and disorderly town in America, added thirty-seven to the graves on Boot Hill" (*Saturday Evening Post*, 1926). "Dodge . . . the Old Hell-Raising Trail's End Where Colt was King" (*Liberty*, 1928).[21]

And always there were old-timers ready to tell a tall story or offer a picturesque overview to an eager writer. Although ex-lawmen Pat Sughrue and H. B. ("Ham") Bell readily admitted that they never had to kill anybody during their terms of office at Dodge, less restrained pioneer survivors offered wild exaggerations. "I suppose I would be safe in saying that from first to last more than 200 men died with boots on at Dodge," reminisced "Colonel" T. S. Jones, an elderly lawyer, in 1910.[22]

By the end of the 1920s national notoriety produced by professional writers began to appear with more regularity. And Dodge itself, astride both a transcontinental railroad and the now heavily traveled U.S. Highway 50, played host—not always comfortably—to increasing numbers of inquisitive passers-by. As a dispatch to the *New York Times* described the situation: "'Wild Dodge,' famous for Boot Hill, where early-day bad actors were buried unceremoniously and with their boots on, is a black spot in its history that present-day Dodge City is trying to erase. Try as its citizens may to think of Dodge [as other than] the proving ground for the straight shots of 1872, horse thieves, cattle rustlers and the other hard-boiled gentry, visitors still insist on seeing Boot Hill . . . and the bullet holes in what is left of French Annie's redlight apartment instead of the $300,000 high school and athletic field and Wright Memorial Park."[23]

Ham Bell, the evident patriarch of Dodge's surviving pioneers, now conceived of transforming an upcoming city hall cornerstone-laying on Boot Hill into a "Last Round-Up" of the old settlers of southwest Kansas and the Texas Panhandle. Bell and several cronies mailed two hundred invitations to those who, as Bell's letter phrased it, "knew Boot Hill when there was some purpose in its name," urging them to "come back and we'll make the old camp live again." Wire services picked up the story and gave it national circulation. More than six hundred old-timers pledged attendance.[24]

The prospect did not please all. The Last Round-Up was "an idea that aroused no particular enthusiasm with the Dodge City generation that never knew the cow town," reported the *Saturday Evening Post*. Those "citizens who believe Dodge City's unsavory past should not be capitalized [on]," said the *New York Times*, forced a compromise: the Boot Hill commemoration would also include a religious revival at which the celebrated evangelist Billy Sunday agreed to preside. The Last Round-Up's opponents, concluded the *Times*, "see in the revival services a means of giving Boot Hill at least a semblance of decency. They hope it will be remembered as the place where Billy Sunday spoke rather than as a picturesque spot of the seamy West when Dodge City was the toughest town on the frontier."[25]

So it was that a certain cultural ambiguity surrounded the 1929 rendezvous. Some twenty thousand turned up for the affair. The Rev. Mr. Sunday kicked off the festivities, holding forth from an enormous wooden podium erected on Boot Hill. He "shouted against sin," reported *Time* magazine; his final words, said the *Kansas City Star*, were that he had "come to dig one more grave on Boot Hill—to bury the devil in!"[26]

The secular ceremonies that followed the next day featured a parade to the now famous promontory. There, in "a re-dedication" of the long-gone cemetery, dignitaries unveiled a life-sized statue of a cowboy-as-gunfighter caught in the instant of yanking his six-shooter. Finally, everyone adjourned to Billy Sunday's podium for a keynote address by a Kansas City journalist, A. B. Macdonald. Macdonald, who had recently helped produce a commercially published book of dubious and sometimes laughably implausible frontier memoirs, reminded hearers that they stood or sat on almost sacred ground, perhaps the most historic spot in Kansas, if not the entire region. It was, he said, a site that uniquely reflected the great change from Old West barbarism to modern civilization. But it was clearly the notorious past, not the progressive present, that preoccupied both speaker and audience. Boot Hill would forever remind Americans, concluded Macdonald, that "Dodge was once the wildest, wickedest and woolliest town in the whole country."[27]

On hand that week composing the *Saturday Evening Post*'s dispatch was a California writer, Stuart N. Lake. Lake offered a history of Boot Hill as an index to the old cattle town's allegedly unrestrained gun violence. A few newspaper citations from the 1870s lent the article a fraudulent authenticity, but most of it simply reflected the tall tales or badly eroded memories of a few elderly conventioneers. An "Old Cowman" supposedly told Lake that "more than a hundred" shooting victims had been interred on Boot Hill; a moment later he lowered his estimate to a "conservative" figure of ninety-two.[28]

Three other *Saturday Evening Post* articles by Lake followed in 1930 as a run-up to publication of the author's biography of Wyatt Earp. The final piece summarized Lake's version of his hero's law-enforcement career in Wichita and Dodge. "Trouble was Dodge's synonym," wrote Lake. "By the time Wyatt Earp reached the camp [in 1876] some seventy or eighty argumentative visitors had been buried with their footgear in place—Dodge had lost accurate count."[29]

The subsequent appearance of Lake's book was perhaps the most important event since the Dodge City War in the evolution of the town's image. *Wyatt Earp: Frontier Marshal*, which included Lake's exaggerated body count at frontier Dodge, became an instant best seller. Reprinted as recently as 1994 and available on audiocassette, the book has provoked some forty years of controversy over its factual merits.[30] Flaws and all, the widely acclaimed biography elevated Earp into a major American historical figure and definitively established old Dodge City as a cultural icon.

The national spotlight and the Great Depression's effect on southwest Kansas collaborated in wiping out any remaining local resistance to capitalizing on Dodge City's past. Citizens busily reshaped their town into a marketable commodity. In 1932, as preparation for a state Rotary Club convention, Dodge Citians dug fifteen or twenty make-believe graves in the city hall lawn on Boot Hill, erected comic headboards supposedly identifying their inhabitants, and planted cacti and sunflowers. Later amplified with a "hanging tree" and proudly tended by city employees, this bizarre exhibit—"half-shrine, half-stunt," as one journalist aptly described it—became a permanent display for tourists' mystified contemplation. In 1937 a transcontinental bus line added Boot Hill to its list of stops at points of historic interest, and in July of that year some 250 persons per day paused to view Boot Hill's odd attractions. "It doesn't make a bit of difference if Boot Hill is a lot of baloney," a Dodge businessman told a visiting reporter. "People are going to keep right on coming anyway."[31]

By the 1930s western cinema had assumed its role as a staple of mass entertainment. References to frontier Dodge occurred on film from time to time, and a movie called *The Dodge City Trail* had appeared in 1914. Now, coinciding with the old cattle town's refurbished importance to popular culture, a remake of that movie came out in 1936. It was forgettable.[32] But the next film, *Dodge City* (1939), proved more than memorable. When Warner Brothers announced plans to produce it, the Dodge City Chamber of Commerce sent off a delegation led by Ham Bell and the lieutenant governor of Kansas to beg that the film be premiered at the real Dodge City. The studio readily agreed and happily turned the premiere into a major media event.

The presence of the film's principal actors—the motion-picture luminaries Errol Flynn, Olivia de Havilland, and Ann Sheridan—lent glamour to the occasion, while the governors of Kansas, New Mexico, and Colorado provided suitable gravitas. (The studio also invited the U.S. secretaries of war and agriculture, but apparently they had more important matters at hand.)

Special railroad sleeping cars, routed to Dodge, sat on sidings to help house overflow crowds. Some twelve thousand visitors signed the register at Boot Hill. The movie itself, filmed in mellow Technicolor, is considered by motion-picture historians to be a classic, "the first of the big town-taming Westerns," as one phrases it.[33]

Dodge City relocated its namesake backward in time, portraying it as a flourishing cattle market four years prematurely. An on-screen text, titled "Dodge City, Kansas—1872," summarizing the town's civic infancy, read like a parody of popular clichés:

> Longhorn cattle center of
> the world and wide-open
> Babylon of the American
> frontier . . . packed with settlers,
> thieves and gunmen.
> Dodge City . . . . rolling in
> wealth from the great Texas
> trail-herds . . . . . . the town that
> knew no ethics but cash and
> killing.[34]

Surprisingly, the movie's intrepid lawman/hero had to kill only two villains in pacifying Hollywood's Dodge.

Several other westerns followed the 1939 blockbuster, but they did little more than capitalize on historic Dodge City's now very recognizable name.[35] A great deal more influential were three enormously popular television serials that featured Dodge: *The Life and Legend of Wyatt Earp* (1955-61), *Bat Masterson* (1958-61), and especially *Gunsmoke* (1955-75), the longest-running prime-time series in television history.[36] Indeed, *Gunsmoke*'s television tenure exceeded the real Dodge City's frontier era by six years. The adventures of Matt Dillon, Kitty, Doc, and the successive Dillon sidekicks Chester and Festus constituted a kind of western soap opera. Ironically, far from intrinsically violent and anarchic, *Gunsmoke*'s Dodge was an island of civic stability amid weekly onslaughts of outsiders—drunken cowpokes, pugnacious owlhoots, crazed nesters. Many times more homicidal than its real-life counterpart, the television Dodge did resemble the old cattle town in the sense that it was a dangerous place only because of those who did not live there.

From 1937 to 1947 more than a million tourists visited Boot Hill. Some five hundred typically arrived on Sundays, two hundred on weekdays. When the Dodge City Chamber of Commerce assumed control of the site after World War II, a new Boot Hill Museum rose on its summit. In 1950 local Jaycees revamped the fake gravesites, and members of the fire department contributed new inscriptions for the mock headboards. By 1957 Boot Hill was reckoned to be one of Kansas's most important attractions; in that year alone more than three hundred thousand tourists pushed through the turnstiles at the Boot Hill Museum.[37]

Early the next year Hugh O'Brien, television's Wyatt Earp, arrived in Dodge to unveil the cornerstone of the "Front Street Replica," an elaborate stage-set reconstruction built on the street below Boot Hill. And that summer the wildly popular cast of *Gunsmoke* came to Dodge for the dedication ceremonies.[38]

Even today, when neither Hollywood nor television regularly produces westerns, Dodge's museum welcomes more than one hundred thousand visitors annually. In summer at the Front Street Replica they watch actors fight gun battles with blanks or dance the can-can in a reconstructed Long Branch Saloon. A Dodge City Convention and Visitors Bureau inhabits a period-style building just off Boot Hill on what is now Wyatt Earp Boulevard, the modern town's main east-west thoroughfare.[39]

The imaginary Dodge City entered American speech as a fully shaped metaphor during the Vietnam War. Young service personnel, nurtured on television portrayals, deployed its name to designate any fearsomely defended hostile or friendly locale, such as Hanoi or Tan Son Nhut. To "get out of Dodge" meant to evacuate speedily any dangerous area, and the phrase continues to be used by military professionals who served in Vietnam.[40]

The cultural metaphor also flourishes among Americans at large. In the two decades between 1980 and 2000, for instance, the *Boston Globe* published 120 articles that referred to Dodge City. Of these, 62 cited the Dodge of myth and legend rather than the modern town. The metaphor appeared an average of three or four times per year in the *Globe*, experiencing over the decades a modest increase in use—twenty-five times in the eighties, thirty-four thereafter.[41]

Its most common employment at large has been as a pejorative for some allegedly deadly locale, from the Mexican border at Eagle Pass, Texas, to Thirty-Eighth Street in Indianapolis, to U.S. Highway 20 outside Springfield, Massachusetts.[42] Those who spoke for the nation's famously high-homicide metropolitan areas frequently felt called on to deny the metaphor's applicability. "Miami is not Dodge City, U.S.A.," insisted the president of the Miami Beach Crime Watch. "It is not a shooting gallery." "Washington is not Dodge City," asserted the beleaguered mayor of the nation's capital, "and I would hope the media would not depict our great city as Dodge City." "There is law and order [here]," growled New York's angry chief executive. "Things are not out of control, and this is not Dodge City."[43]

Politicians proved especially fond of the metaphor. "No one knows who's going to be here next year and who's going to leave," remarked a Reagan aide worried about White House layoffs. "It's like Dodge City: Everyone's looking over his shoulder." A Long Island county executive characterized a contentious local legislature as the "Dodge City of politics." A Virginia gubernatorial candidate facing a crucial caucus vote declared, "If I lose Fairfax County it's lights out in Dodge City." An Oregon congressman compared intense competition among fertility clinics to "Dodge City before the marshals show up." A Bush administration functionary planned his future after Bill Clinton's victory. "I'm getting out of Dodge two days before the inaugural," he said. Later, ex-president Bush himself refused to debate critics of his White House legacy. "They of course are free to do their thing," he said. "Mine is to stay the hell out of Dodge."[44]

Although metaphorical Dodge is mainly violent, it also accrues other negatives. San Diego sophisticates visiting a suburb for the first time expressed surprise. "They just couldn't get over how civilized El Cajon was," a resident observed. "They thought [it would be] little more than Dodge City with fast-food joints." A writer described a "squalid, swelling market town" in India as "a subcontinental Dodge City." Another international dispatch reported that in one war-ravaged Serbian community the most flourishing business was prostitution. "Dodge City," muttered a citizen. The African-American owner of a failed business could not wait to leave Boston. "It's full of hidden racism," he said. "It's like the old Dodge City." In nearby Brockton the owner of a new strip joint denied that his bar attracted trouble: "It's not a den of sin. There are no drugs. It's not Dodge City."[45]

The public discourse on handgun control sometimes features the metaphor. A letter to the *Boston Globe* offered a caricature of the famous cattle town that seemed to accommodate both sides in the debate. "In the Old West," asserted its writer, "Dodge City was not a safer place because everyone carried a firearm. Quite the contrary: It was a paradigm of the kind of dystopia that the English philosopher, Thomas Hobbes, warned us about, one in which there was a war of 'everyman against everyman,' and where the life of each was 'poor, nasty, brutish and short.'"[46] As if in reply, two Second Amendment fundamentalists, writing in *Guns & Ammo* under the title "Goodbye Dodge City," exulted that recent criminological research "amounts to nothing short of the death-knell for the anti-gun lobby's fear-mongering 'Dodge City' prophecy."[47]

The important subtext here is that the metaphorical configuration of Dodge City was not contested terrain. The *Globe* and the *Guns & Ammo* writers agreed: violent, anarchic Dodge was a historical reality. Thus the metaphor works, politically speaking, for both the left and the right.

At one level Dodge City is a commodity. Since 1872 its association with gun violence has made it a consumer product retailed to a primary market of tourists and wholesaled to media managers for resale to readers and viewers. But at another level imaginary Dodge is also a cultural production, a text revealing some of the nation's core values.[48] Whether as symbol or metaphor, frontier Dodge is hard at work helping the United States define its virtue by furnishing the archetypal bad civic example. It argues that things can never be as dreadful as they were in the Old West, thereby proving (in yet another idiom) that Americans have evolved into a uniquely civilized people.[49]

But if the Dodge of myth and make-believe reassures the American psyche, it also incites it to relish and celebrate a frontier past brimming with aggression and murderous self-defense. These lethal imaginings offer a spurious validation of Americans' love affair with handguns and assault rifles: the West wasn't won with a registered gun; unrestricted ownership is in our genes, never mind the U.S. Constitution. Scholars intent on condemning historical violence have sometimes unwittingly supported such nonsense.[50]

Perhaps this multilayered complexity of early Dodge City's meaning is why references to it—even in Dodge itself—have been as often comic as earnest. We seem to be of more than one mind about that long-ago Kansas settlement. Or more properly, we divide into two persuasions: those who believe the received visualization of civic anarchy (the earnest ones) and those who simply find it hard to swallow (the smilers).

Thoughtful scholars may consider this something of an intellectual dilemma demanding resolution. If so, the "historical truth" depends on which Dodge City one measures the contested image against: the violent Dodge of 1872-73, the nonviolent Dodge of 1874-75, or the occasionally violent Dodge of 1876-85. But popular culture demands no consensus on such matters, helping clarify how historic Dodge City lends itself to so many uses and why it endures to the present day.

NOTES

1. This figure, the result of new research, is slightly higher than that reported in Robert R. Dykstra, *The Cattle Towns* (New York: Knopf, 1968), 113.

2. Nyle H. Miller and Joseph W. Snell, *Why the West Was Wild* (Topeka: Kansas State Historical Society, 1963), 642–45; Dykstra *Cattle Towns*, 119. Here, too, the original figure for adult homicide has been slightly revised.

3. Dykstra, *Cattle Towns*, 144. This and related themes are discussed in the following articles by Robert R. Dykstra: "Overdosing on Dodge City," *Western Historical Quarterly* 27 (Winter 1996): 505–14; "Dodge City, Kansas," in *Encyclopedia of the American West*, 4 vols., ed. Charles Phillips and Alan Axelrod (New York: Macmillan, 1996), 1:454–55; "Violence, Gender, and Methodology in the 'New' Western History," *Reviews in American History* 27 (March 1999): 79–83; "Dodge City, Kansas: Omicidi, Discorso Morale e Identità Culturale," *Storia Urbana*, no. 87 (April/June 1999): 83–95; "To Live and Die in Dodge City: Body Counts, Law and Order, and the Case of *Kansas* v. *Gill*," in *Lethal Imagination: Violence and Brutality in American History*, ed. Michael A. Bellesiles (New York: New York University Press, 1999), 210–26; "Imaginary Dodge City: A Political Statement," *Western Historical Quarterly* 31 (Autumn 2000): 278–84; "Dodge City," in *Violence in America: An Encyclopedia*, ed. Ronald Gottesman (New York: Scribner, 2000), 417–19.

4. *Kansas Daily Commonwealth*, 14 January, 18 March 1873; *Ellsworth Reporter*, 27 March 1873.

5. *Ford County Globe* (Dodge City), 18 March 1879; J. H. C. in *Kansas Daily Commonwealth*, 6 April 1873; *Ford County Globe*, 10 February 1880. The female corpse was Alice Chambers. *Ford County Globe*, 28 January 1879. The contemporary sources are not clear as to whether Dora Hand, killed in 1878, was buried at Boot Hill. Miller and Snell, *Why the West Was Wild*, 351–52, 361–63.

6. *Ford County Globe*, 25 November 1884.

7. Accounts of the Dodge City War appear in several books. For a concise treatment, see Dykstra, *Cattle Towns*, 273–74. For many of the original sources, see Miller and Snell, *Why the West Was Wild*, 520–64.

8. *New York Tribune*, 6 June 1883; *New York Commercial* in *Ford County Globe*, 24 July 1883; *Chicago Press* in *Dodge City Times*, 20 September 1883.

9. Kirke Mechem, "The Bull Fight at Dodge," *Kansas Historical Quarterly* 2 (August 1933): 294–308; Dykstra, *Cattle Towns*, 173–75.

10. Dykstra, *Cattle Towns*, 328–42; *Ford County Globe*, 23 March 1886.

11. *Topeka Capital*, 6 August 1910; *Kansas City Star*, 2 April 1916.

12. The two ex-lawmen were featured in the aftermath of the Dodge City War, the term *celebrity* actually being applied to Earp. See Harry E. Gryden, "Dodge City's Sensation," *National Police Gazette*, 21 July 1883, 5. For a remarkably early example of the war expressed in a storytelling vernacular, see "When 'Dodge' Was in Its Glory," *Kansas Magazine* 7 (June 1887): 58–60.

13. No such Hollywood-type street duel ever occurred at frontier Dodge. Invented by novelist Owen Wister in his classic *The Virginian* (1902), the climactic fast-draw contest made its film debut just four years later. William K. Everson, *The Hollywood Western* (New York: Citadel Press, 1992), 26–27.

14. E. C. Little, "The Round Table of Dodge City," *Everybody's Magazine* 7 (No-

vember 1902): 432–39; Shirley Christian, "Where Wyatt Earp Stood Tall," *New York Times*, 17 January 1999, sec. 5, p. 18.

15. Little, "Round Table of Dodge City," 436. Actually, Mysterious Dave was only a collateral descendant of Cotton Mather. Horace E. Mather, *Lineage of Rev. Richard Mather* (Hartford: Case, Lockwood and Brainard, 1890), 391.

16. Andy Adams, *The Log of a Cowboy: A Narrative of the Old Trail Days* (Boston: Houghton Mifflin, 1903), 177–209; Robert R. Dykstra and Jo Ann Manfra, "The Circle Dot Cowboys at Dodge City: History and Imagination in Andy Adams's *The Log of a Cowboy*," *Western Historical Quarterly* 33 (Spring 2002): 19–40.

17. Alfred Henry Lewis, "The Deep Strategy of Mr. Masterson: The Story of a Stampeded Election," *Saturday Evening Post*, 17 December 1904, 8–9, 23–24; compare with the actual election as documented in Miller and Snell, *Why the West Was Wild*, 327–28. The other three stories were "Diplomacy in Dodge," *Metropolitan Magazine* 20 (April 1904): 90–102; "An Invasion of Dodge: The Story of a Craven Desperado," *Collier's Weekly*, 16 April 1904, 19–20; and "The Fatal Gratitude of Mr. Kelly," *Collier's Weekly*, 17 September 1904, 16–17. For Lewis's friendship with Masterson, see Robert K. DeArment, *Bat Masterson: The Man and the Legend* (Norman: University of Oklahoma Press, 1979), 371–72, 380, 389.

18. Alfred Henry Lewis, *The Sunset Trail* (New York: A. S. Barnes, 1905). It seems worthy of note that Wyatt Earp, Masterson's close friend at frontier Dodge, is missing from the Dodge City chapters of the book. The fictional "Cimarron Bill" may be an Earp stand-in.

19. W. B. Masterson, "Famous Gunfighters of the Western Frontier," *Human Life* 4 (January 1907): 4–5, 8–9, 12–13; (February 1907): 9–10, 22; (April 1907): 9–10, 20; (May 1907): 5–6; (July 1907): 11–12; Alfred Henry Lewis, "The King of the Gun-Players: William Barclay Masterson," *Human Life* 4 (November 1907): 7–9. All but Lewis's contribution are reprinted in Masterson, *Famous Gunfighters of the Western Frontier*, ed. Ed Bartholomew (Fort Davis, Tex.: Frontier Book Co., 1968).

20. Robert M. Wright, *Dodge City: The Cowboy Capital and the Great Southwest* (Wichita: Eagle Press, 1913), 171; C. Robert Haywood, *The Merchant Prince of Dodge City: The Life and Times of Robert M. Wright* (Norman: University of Oklahoma Press, 1998), 177–78. The original printing of Wright's book was five thousand copies; by the end of the 1920s they had all been disposed of. In 1930 a second edition of five hundred copies, with slightly different pagination, appeared. As a Boston book collector recorded: "I was told in Dodge City [that] the second edition was printed simply to supply the 'home folks' in and around the old 'cowboy capital.'" George T. Watkins, note on the flyleaf of a second edition, at the American Antiquarian Society, Worcester, Mass.

21. Arthur Chapman, "The Men Who Tamed the Cow-Towns," *Outing* 45 (November 1904): 138; "The Seven Able Gun Fighters from Kansas City," *Kansas City Star*, 13 January 1918; "The Man Who Put Goodness into the 'Wickedest Town,'" *Literary Digest*, 22 August 1925, 46; Fred E. Sutton, as told to A. B. Macdonald,

"Fill Your Hand," *Saturday Evening Post*, 10 April 1926, 15; William MacLeod Raine, "Dodge," *Liberty*, 19 May 1928, 12.

22. Little, "Round Table of Dodge City," 438; "Man Who Put Goodness," 46; *Topeka Capital*, 6 August 1910.

23. *New York Times*, 18 August 1929, sec. 3, p. E6.

24. Stuart N. Lake, "Straight-Shooting Dodge," *Saturday Evening Post*, 8 March 1930, 25.

25. Lake, "Straight-Shooting Dodge," 25; *New York Times*, 18 August 1929, sec. 3, p. E6. As confirmation of a strong moralistic element in Dodge City, a newspaper story a year earlier reported considerable local sentiment against repeal of national Prohibition. At a community meeting the loudest applause was reserved for a speaker who said that "not in a thousand years would the prohibitory law, either state or national be repealed, or the Eighteenth amendment be stricken from our fundamental law." *Topeka Capital*, 27 May 1928.

26. Lake, "Straight-Shooting Dodge," 148; "Boot Hill," *Time*, 11 November 1929, 66; *Kansas City Star*, 4 and 17 November 1929. In the days following the celebration Billy Sunday continued to preach from Boot Hill, turning his Dodge City appearance into a protracted revival.

27. *Kansas City Star*, 4 November 1929. For the memoirs, see Fred E. Sutton and A. B. Macdonald, *Hands Up! Stories of the Six-Gun Fighters of the Old Wild West* (Indianapolis: Macmillan, 1927). This work, an extension of the coauthored article cited in note 21, discussed the supposed fighting techniques of various outlaws and lawmen, many of whom Sutton claimed to have known well. Among other self-referential exaggerations, he maintained that he, Bat Masterson, and J. B. ("Wild Bill") Hickok were the best of friends and that, for example, the three got together at Dodge after a fatal encounter at Hays City forced Hickok to flee that place. The Hays incident, however, occurred in 1870, almost a year before Masterson arrived in Kansas from Illinois, and two years before Dodge City's founding. Sutton and Macdonald, *Hands Up!* 84; Miller and Snell, *Why the West Was Wild*, 198–99; DeArment, *Bat Masterson*, 10.

28. Lake, "Straight-Shooting Dodge," 24. Lake's citations of the *Ford County Globe* for 1878 and 1879 contained both half-truths and outright fabrications. He correctly cited the issue of 30 April 1878 as stating that at nearby Hays City the cemetery contained sixty-four bodies. But then Lake added a supposed quip by the *Globe*'s editor—"Hays will soon be giving us a run"—that is nowhere to be found in the newspaper. The 7 May issue, said Lake, reported two more graves discovered on Boot Hill; there is no such report. The 14 May issue supposedly chronicled new burials resulting from "a half-dozen shootings"; it didn't. And a quote from that same issue referring, philosophically, to the planned Prairie Grove Cemetery—"Hurry up with that cemetery, for 'we know not the day nor the hour'"—is misleadingly made to seem like evidence that space was running out at Boot Hill. "Additional Boot Hill burials were noted frequently during the fall of '78," said Lake, but this was false. The 4 February 1879 issue, he said, reported that thirty-three bodies had been removed

from Boot Hill to Prairie Grove; no figures of any kind were given. As for the credibility of Lake's informants, it can be judged by the story one of them told about how the Dodge City Cowboy Band was formed to lure the Texas cattle trade to Dodge. Actually, the first herds arrived in Dodge in 1875 whereas the Cowboy Band was not organized until 1882. Dykstra, *Cattle Towns*, 60–61; Clifford P. Westermier, "The Dodge City Cowboy Band," *Kansas Historical Quarterly* 19 (February 1951): 1–11. For Lake's background, see Casey Tefertiller, *Wyatt Earp: The Life Behind the Legend* (New York: J. Wiley, 1997), 325–26.

29. Stuart N. Lake, "The Frontier Marshal," *Saturday Evening Post*, 15 November 1930, 104.

30. Stuart N. Lake, *Wyatt Earp: Frontier Marshal* (Boston: Houghton Mifflin, 1931). The two most recent Earp biographers disagree sharply in their evaluations of this work. Compare Tefertiller, *Wyatt Earp*, 342 ("Lake was more right than wrong"), with Allen Barra, *Inventing Wyatt Earp: His Life and Many Legends* (New York: Carroll and Graf, 1998), 10 ("Lake wrote a terrific novel").

31. *Topeka Journal*, 18 August 1937; *Dodge City Globe*, 27 February 1947; *Wichita Morning Eagle*, 23 October 1949.

32. Everson, *Hollywood Western*, 54; "The Internet Movie Database," at www.imdb.com.

33. Barra, *Inventing Wyatt Earp*, 344–45; *Topeka Capital*, 2 April 1939; *Topeka Journal*, 3 April 1939; *Dodge City Globe*, 27 February 1947; Rudy Behlmer, ed., *Inside Warner Bros. (1935–1951)* (New York: Simon and Schuster, 1985), 80–81.

34. The suspension periods are in the original.

35. These were *King of Dodge City* (1941), *Vigilantes of Dodge City* (1944), *West of Dodge City* (1947), *Desperadoes of Dodge City* (1948), and *The Gunfight at Dodge City* (1959). All were no more than stock western yarns. See "Dodge City, Kansas" website at www.americanwest.com/pages/dodge.htm. This inventory does not include several movies devoted more exclusively to Earp or Masterson, which often featured Tombstone, Arizona, rather than Dodge. For a definitive discussion of Earp films, see Barra, *Inventing Wyatt Earp*, 342–74. Much more distinguished were two unusual cinematic treatments of the sixties. The first was the Dodge City interlude in John Ford's *Cheyenne Autumn* (1964); providing comic relief in an otherwise tragic story were a mean-spirited Earp and a drunken Doc Holliday. The second film was *A Big Hand for the Little Lady* (1966), retitled *Big Deal at Dodge City* for British release. This unpretentious western told the story of a homesteader and his wife suddenly drawn into a high-stakes poker game. Despite its all-star cast—Henry Fonda, Joanne Woodward, Jason Robards, and Burgess Meredith—the film is almost unknown today. Barra, *Inventing Wyatt Earp*, 356; Ron Castell, ed., *Blockbuster Video Guide to Movies and Videos* (New York: Blockbuster Entertainment, 1994), 93, 178; "Internet Movie Database."

36. David T. Courtwright, *Violent Land: Single Men and Social Disorder from the Frontier to the Inner City* (Cambridge: Harvard University Press, 1996), 104–5. The televised *Gunsmoke* was preceded by a radio version that ran from 1952 to 1961.

Detailed information on both programs is widely available on the Internet; one of the most useful sites is "Tamara's Gunsmoke Web Page," at comp.uark.edu/~tsnyder/gunsmoke/index.html. For the other two shows, see the "Life and Legend of Wyatt Earp" website, at www.mnc.net/we.htm, and the "Gene Barry Fan Page" (Barry having played Masterson), at www.xmission.com/~emailbox/barry.htm.

37. *Wichita Morning Eagle*, 23 October 1949; *Dodge City Globe*, 24 February 1947, 7 June 1950, 13 February 1956; *Topeka Capital*, 1 June 1958.

38. *Topeka Capital*, 1 June 1958; *Kansas City Star*, 30 July 1958; *Wichita Evening Eagle*, 25 September 1958; "Dodge City, Kansas" website.

39. "Dodge City, Kansas" website; Christian, "Where Wyatt Earp Stood Tall," sec. 5, pp. 18, 28. But all is not fluff. The town's Kansas Heritage Center, built in the early 1960s, houses a serious research library, whose staff members have a respect for historical scholarship. Much of their time is spent fielding inquiries, some coming from as far away as Great Britain, Germany, and Japan.

40. Courtwright, *Violent Land*, 107. For apparently typical post-Vietnam military usages, see Charlie A. Beckwith and Donald Knox, *Delta Force: The Army's Elite Counterterrorist Unit*, rev. ed. (New York: Harcourt Brace Jovanovich, 2000), 153; Tom Clancy and John Gresham, *Special Forces: A Guided Tour* (New York: Berkley Books, 2001), 43.

41. "Boston Globe Indexes & Databases" website, at www.mlin.lib.ma.us/databases/globe.shtml. "Lexis-Nexis Academic Universe" was the source for articles in newspapers other than the *Boston Globe* cited in notes 43–45.

42. Steve Fainaru, "A Line in the Sand," *Boston Globe*, 4 January 1998, Sunday Magazine, 25; Brian McGrory, "GOP Sets Tone in City Halls," *Boston Globe*, 8 July 1995, Metro Sec., 1; Sean P. Murphy, "Springfield Roadway Is Called Killing Site for Drunk Drivers," *Boston Globe*, 2 March 1993, Metro Sec., 21.

43. "Crime-Victim Travel Fund Sought," *Boston Globe*, 8 May 1981, no page listed; Jeffrey Goldberg, "Dodge City Agrees: D.C. Is No Dodge," *Washington Post*, 16 February 1989, A14; "3 Charged with Killing Boy in N.Y. Apartment," *Boston Globe*, 1 August 1990, National/Foreign Sec., 69.

44. Steven R. Weisman, "With Election Day Looming, 'Jitters' Fill the Halls," *New York Times*, 21 September 1982, A24; Lindsey Gruson, "Lawmakers in Suffolk are Thinking Big," *New York Times*, 4 November 1984, sec. 4, p. 10; Molly Moore, "Tonight's Vote Is Key Test for Parris," *Washington Post*, 2 April 1985, C1; Geoffrey Cowley, Andrew Murr, and Karen Springen, "Ethics and Embryos," *Newsweek*, 12 June 1995, 67; John W. Mashek, "GOP Elite Sets Plans for Exile after Shift," *Boston Globe*, 13 January 1993, National/Foreign Sec., 17; George Bush, *All the Best: My Life in Letters and Other Writings* (New York: Scribner, 1999), 610.

45. Teri Sforza, "25 to Study the Image of El Cajon," *San Diego Union-Tribune*, 13 September 1989, B1; Michael Kenney, "Raising the Curtain on South Asia," *Boston Globe*, 14 February 1994, Living Sec., 38; Lawrence Weschler, "Letter from the Republika Srpska: High Noon at Twin Peaks," *New Yorker*, 18 August 1997, 29; Joseph P. Kahn, "Still Climbing the Mountain," *Boston Globe*, 18 January 1999, C1;

Alexander Reid, "Passions Rise Anew over Brockton's Nude Club," *Boston Globe*, 26 December 1999, South Weekly Sec., 1.

46. Paul Nevins, "Guns Are Everywhere, but I Don't Feel Safer," *Boston Globe*, 22 June 1998, A18. The slightly misworded Thomas Hobbes quotation is from *Leviathan* (1651): "such a Warre as is of every man against every man . . . and the life of man [is] solitary, poore, nasty, brutish, and short." See Hobbes, *Leviathan*, ed. C. B. Macpherson (London: Penguin Books, 1985), 186.

47. Paul Gallant and Joanne Eisen, "Goodbye Dodge City: How the Antis Torpedoed Their Own Movement," *Guns & Ammo* 42 (December 1998): 12–16.

48. Theorists of nationalism such as Benedict Anderson and E. J. Hobsbawm have stressed the cultural authority of a nation's media and literature in defining its values. Anderson, *Imagined Communities: Reflections on the Origin and Spread of Nationalism* (London: Verso, 1983), 61–79; Hobsbawm, *Nations and Nationalism since 1780: Programme, Myth, Reality* (Cambridge: Cambridge University Press, 1990), 90, 94.

49. We are not sure how frontier Dodge relates to Michael Kammen's interesting distinction between "popular culture" and "mass culture." Perhaps the community's historical image moved from the former to the latter in the 1930s when the locals began self-consciously collaborating with media presentations. Kammen, *American Culture, American Tastes: Social Change and the Twentieth Century* (New York: Knopf, 1999), 18, 21.

50. Dykstra, "Imaginary Dodge City," 278–79.

Part Five

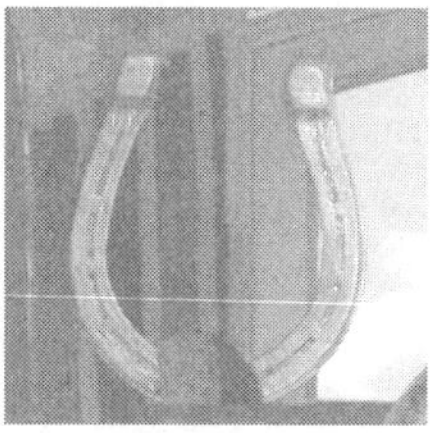

DECONSTRUCTING SUNDANCE

Robert Redford has built a repertoire as an actor, director, environmental activist, and entrepreneur around representations of the West. The role of Sundance in the 1969 film *Butch Cassidy and the Sundance Kid* transformed Redford into a western icon. The famous film character with which Redford would become universally associated provided him with a western identity—a sobriquet for his future empire, which would include a Utah resort, a film festival, and a catalog. Redford has represented the West in a series of films throughout his career, including *The Horse Whisperer* (1998), *A River Runs Through It* (1992), *The Milagro Beanfield War* (1988), *The Electric Horseman* (1979), and *Jeremiah Johnson* (1972). Two interconnected themes run through Redford's movies, environmentalism, and retail operations: a profound longing for the past and a disenchantment with the contemporary urban space, especially Los Angeles, where he was raised. Redford's views of the present, of course, have determined how he values and deploys the past, and for some time he has used it to decry the modern condition. For Redford, both the past and its primitive ideal become ways to transcend the disappointment and degeneracy of his own American culture. Redford's quest to preserve a western past encouraged his involvement in environmental politics, where his celebrity status ensured attention for his positions.

In her essay "Scripting the West: Robert Redford's Persona and Film," Elaine Bapis examines how Redford's Sundance Kid persona and his romantic view of the West have given him a powerful say in the circulation of knowledge about the people and places of the region. The value Redford attaches to "escaping" from the urban to the "primitive wilderness," represented in his films *Jeremiah Johnson, The Electric Horseman*, and *The Horse*

Whisperer, voices a dominant narrative of the New West, in which places once used by local residents for making a living are now valued by outsiders for recreation and aesthetic enjoyment. In her essay "1-800-SUNDANCE: Identity, Nature, and Play in the West," Liza Nicholas shows how Redford offers up relics from the "rejuvenating" West via the Sundance catalog and the U.S. Postal Service. Not only does the catalog commodify such objects; it seemingly reconciles the numerous conflicting meanings of the region. Finally, in "The Sundance Kid and Sundance: The West as Nature," Thomas Harvey looks at how Redford's environmental activism and view of nature intersect with the narrative of the Sundance resort near Provo, Utah. In many ways the Sundance Kid sits at the heart of how western spaces have been produced, consumed, and ultimately understood, and Redford's West in turn typifies the New West and its myriad contradictions.

Elaine M. Bapis

SCRIPTING THE WEST

Robert Redford's Persona and Film

I don't want to be no story. I just retired from public life.
Sonny Steele, *Electric Horseman*

The only biography that I would ever want is the work. And the rest is my business.
Robert Redford

The view of the West is . . . important to me, the truth of what the West is.
Robert Redford

B*utch Cassidy and the Sundance Kid* (1969) ends with a medium shot of the two outlaws attempting a final getaway. Ready to shoot their way out of an ambush, guns in each hand, they leap from a doorway, daring and confident. The action then stops, and the Yankee bandidos are frozen in a still life of their valiant pose of escape from their Bolivian hideout. Superimposed on this freeze-frame is the sound of three rounds of countless rifles from Bolivian soldiers awaiting the outlaws' exit. The frame fades from a Technicolor medium shot to a sepia-toned long shot of the two caught with their backs against the wall in a larger-than-life image, inviting the audience to confuse the historical "Butch" and "Sundance" with the cinematic Newman and Redford. The viewer hears the gunshots but never sees the characters die. The final image fills in the legend with the sepia tone of old photographs and adds its historical perspective to the stories of the real western outlaws, whose history was little known in Utah before the film. This last image of courage and daring, however, did more than end a story.

Together the Sundance Kid and Robert Redford stepped off the screen into a lively future, leaving Butch and Newman behind. The Sundance Kid would see new life through the cultivation of a western persona so closely associated with Redford that to hear of the latter as an actor whose roles include an aspiring attorney, the Great Gatsby, a Washington newspaper reporter, a prisoner, the Great Waldo Pepper, or a downhill racer—to name a few—would be rare. A stunning blond Kid in leather vest and hip hat connected viewers to a mythic West reproduced in the popular marketplace by the late 1960s. With the Kid in hand, Redford cultivated Sundance iconography over the years and drew audiences to the glamour of a popular cowboy West.

When Redford appropriated the name *Sundance* for his resort (a "reference to a native American ritual and the way the sun dances on the ridges of the canyon") and marketed the Sundance Resort as "the last outpost"[1] while bringing the independent film industry to Utah in the 1980s, he inextricably tied his enterprise to the cinema and both to the West. One result of this tie was to celebritize two western states, Utah and Montana, for their lustrous landscapes while ignoring much local identity, culture, and history. Redford's films offered new ways of seeing Utah and later Montana through perceptions of desire for open spaces in contrast to the everyday use of land as a resource and a place of work. Redford's films became a kind of Disneyland of western identity and authenticity, largely through the way they visualized spaciousness and positioned the main character in relation to that space. Add to that the cultivation of a persona associated with the popular American West along with Redford's environmental activism, and the result is a new dynamic of influence.

Redford's films that celebritized western states for their lustrous landscapes and promoted his western persona raise issues of claims and usage. Three films, in particular, stand as forums for debate about the use of the West as places of desire (if pristine). *Jeremiah Johnson* (1972), *The Electric Horseman* (1979), and *The Horse Whisperer* (1996) frame Redford's vision of the West as a location to be desired yet preserved. Through strong visuals, these films connect to an argument of preservation and accentuate a shift in the meaning and use of the West. Moreover, the timing of *Jeremiah Johnson* and *Electric Horseman* in the 1970s places them inside a turbulent environmental debate when land became a site of contention and film became a means of legitimizing new attitudes and beliefs. In addition, Redford's Sundance Kid persona became a new kind of national commodity attached to popular assumptions about what the West should be and how it should be used.

The public cultivation of the western persona that would dominate Redford's identity began in a 1970 *Life* magazine feature article titled "New Star

Robert Redford, a Real Sundance Kid," by Richard Schickel, Redford's then New York neighbor. "For years I've been telling him," Schickel explained, "that someday someone would put *him* [author's italics] down on paper; not an image." A photograph of Redford as the Sundance Kid—longish hair and mustache—appeared on the cover. Inside, photographs and text told the story of Redford and his family in their Utah home. "The Redford family manages to spend at least three months of the year in Utah," read the caption below a photograph of Mr. and Mrs. Redford. Redford posed in "western" attire as if playing a part in a script. With cowboy hat, bandana, casual jacket, and his Sundance Kid mustache, Redford offered a slice of western life, suggestive of a kind of western casualness—all in his rough-hewn wood kitchen. "Lola and Redford wait for the punch line as an actor friend spins a yarn in their kitchen," the caption continued. Other photographs featured him on his Ski-Doo, riding one of his eight horses at the base of the Wasatch Mountains near Provo, and casually conducting business in "western" attire—hat, boots, and jeans—while vacationing in his Utah A-frame. Schickel officially declared him "the star everyone has been predicting he would be for a decade."[2]

With the "Kid" on the cover and Redford inside, the feature offered a seamless, if intertextual, westerner, one who attracted a local and national audience to horses, snowmobiles, and cowboys. Redford's western imagery and the persona of the Sundance Kid sealed themselves in the naming and promotion of the Sundance resort, and through the years headlines of one kind or another substantiated the image: "Sundance Kid Gets Little Respect Around Sundance" (1989), "High Noon at Sundance Kid's Utah Resort" (1997), "The Eclectic Horseman" (1998); "The Existential Cowboy" (1998), "The Star, the System and that Thing Called Sundance (1998)."[3] Redford's iconic value would accrue interest, though, through one more connection—the way his assumptions about the West fed into the shape of his enterprises, making the Sundance phenomenon as much about cultural invention as economics. Other film stars have appropriated star status to support various causes. Marlon Brando, Paul Newman, and Clint Eastwood are among them. Bruce Willis and John Denver have celebritized the Rocky Mountains, but Redford is unique in the way he has so self-consciously intertwined his film persona, social causes, and economic empire building into a complex whole, all rooted in a traditional western image that has more to do with popular representations of western history than life as people lived it.

Since 1962 Redford has acted or starred in some forty films. Of those, he also directed four, produced three, and produced, directed, and starred in one. He received the Golden Globe in 1966 for "Most Promising Newcomer" male and in 1975, 1977, and 1978 for "World Film Favorite" male.

In 1981 he received an Academy Award for best director, and he was nominated three other times for directing and acting. At the seventy-fourth Oscars the Board of Governors of the Academy conferred an honorary award for Redford's "dedication to independent filmmaking" and his "positive impact on the motion picture industry since . . . Sundance."[4] In addition to popular film, Redford has either narrated or authored nine documentaries on subjects ranging from Shoshoni Indians to the California Condor. Of all his projects, none of the personae took hold like the Sundance Kid. Redford felt himself better suited to Sundance than to the role of the young eastern attorney he played a year earlier in *Barefoot in the Park*. "I had a strange identification with Sundance that I can't quite put my finger on," he recalled in *The Outlaw Trail*.[5] Reflecting his own image as a renegade individualist, an activist running against an established system, he donned a cowboy chic mustache, longish hair, cowboy boots, jeans, and lots of western casual. "At Robert Redford's place, even the senators wear blue jeans," noted one writer.[6]

Redford's identification with the Sundance Kid brought a glamorized western history to the Utah landscape and a celebrity who could also be imagined as a westerner with some clout. Redford often appeared at charities and bankers' meetings and asked Utah locals to serve as board members for his enterprises.[7] Much to his dismay, however, his audience was usually more interested in his star image than what he had to say about various causes. At an appearance before Utah bankers in 1970, for example, Redford hoped to encourage a dialogue between local business people and national environmentalists. But he was vexed when the first question asked after his speech was about his film: "The guy got up and said, 'Did you really jump off that cliff in "Butch Cassidy," or was that a stand-in?'"[8]

To be sure, celebrities constantly fight being commodified, as Redford complained to an *Omni* writer in 1982: "I've seen too many accounts of what kind of shoes I was wearing, what color my boots were, whether my clothes were hand-tailored or not, and how tall I was and how big I was or whether my hair was sandy-colored or my teeth were white rather than what the hell I was talking about."[9] Of course, Redford cannot be reduced to teeth, hair, and boots, but by surrounding himself with western icons in interviews and gluing his businesses together with the Sundance image, he early-on crossed boundaries between fact and fiction, product and producer.[10] In the words of one writer, "He'[s] become his own story."[11] Redford's desire to de-romanticize and de-commodify himself before the public, to get people to listen to his activism instead of just seeing his image, is part of that story. The power of his celebrity status may have trapped him inside a paradox as indicated in the bankers' incident, but negotiating his role as an activist depends on that trap.

Protesting commodification relocates his voice as an activist outside the celebrity image and justifies his resentment of the public's objectifying him.

Referring to this trap makes Redford's power as an activist even more disproportionate than just celebrity status would allow. As shown at the bankers' meeting, Utahns enjoyed Redford's celebrity strength but many people soon found his wielding of power suspect. Utah reporter Rod Decker explained as early as 1978 that "Redford acts as if the Utah issues he cares about should be decided by glamorous people outside the state. . . . He sits on the boards of directors of national organizations which use the courts to impose strict and unpopular regulations on the state." Redford's celebrity status gave "his views and opinions a disproportionate prominence, pushing them on public attention. And Utahns have a right not to like it."[12] By the 1980s the Sundance Kid persona was well associated with Robert Redford and Utah as more than a fictional reference. Sundance and its correlation with the boots, the jeans, the hat, the horse, and the Kid raise questions about who commodifies and consumes.

In 1981 Redford opened the Sundance Institute and by 1985 had renamed the United States Film Festival the Sundance Film Festival. Redford's commitment to independent film materialized from a desire to provide support and instruction for emerging screenwriters and filmmakers by bringing together "professionals across the country with diverse backgrounds in many areas such as writing, directing, producing, casting, production design, and marketing" in a laboratory environment.[13] The Sundance Institute provided a way for a beginning artist or filmmaker to develop the art of cinema under the tutelage of the experienced. Redford said of his newly formed institute, "I would much rather use this as a cultural place than as a business."[14] The institute offered chances for diverse screenplays, and diversity gave it a prominent social value in the 1980s as it provided women, Native Americans, and other marginalized groups a way out of the blockbuster channel that separated the institute from Hollywood. Independents' work would not just stop with the institute but would have a new means of distribution through the film festival. The institute and the film festival have become well publicized throughout the world, drawing film professionals and vacationers to Utah. Through the successful marketing of a popular concept about the West, all tied to Redford's persona as Sundance's representative, Redford in turn commodifies places and identities. His intent to "use this as a cultural place" intimates a paradox that places him in the role of both consumer and producer.

Redford's cultural appeal in film, of course, had little to do with Utah at first. Rather, his appeal came from his attractive fit with the beloved western, yet Redford never starred in a classic western, nor did his signature role promote the prototypical persona in the style of John Wayne, Gary Cooper, or his contemporary, Clint Eastwood. *Butch Cassidy* echoed classic western elements, but the film also subverted the image of the gunslinger in favor of a kinder, gentler male character, an updated 1960s outlaw.[15] Butch and Sundance lamented lost frontier space, imagined for years in most westerns as the site of regeneration and self-transformation.[16] However, *Butch Cassidy and the Sundance Kid* parted ways with classic western narrative tradition by undercutting the representation of western masculinity with humor and music, producing a "soft" violence. Butch and Sundance were the good-natured outlaws, the clever robbers, and the quick wits but not the silent, violent, tough-guy types. Butch's brains complemented Sundance's quick-draw heroism. "Boy, I got vision, and the rest of the world wears bifocals," he tells the Kid. Cassidy performed a circus-like ride on a modern invention, the bicycle, in sync with the hit song "Raindrops Keep Falling on My Head." Finally, when bandits ambushed them on their journey through Bolivia, Cassidy admitted he was no killer: "Kid, there's somethin' I think I oughta tell ya. I never shot anybody before."

This film's softened violence critiques the western hero as the champion of justice. Butch and Sundance, a couple of carefree spirits, liberated masculinity from the burden of toughing it out as protector, responsible for the town's future. Their heroism cultivated a western persona that revised the John Wayne–type masculinity in classic westerns because heroism was not attached to the town any longer. To be sure, by the 1960s the town's future had little relevance in the western genre. This revisionist strain favored the renegade, individualist, outlaw hero (or anti-hero), who just does "what comes naturally, as much for the fun of it as anything else."[17] Like Redford himself, the Sundance Kid exemplified a common American mythology. This film commented on "the men of the mythic American West who have outlived their day."[18] "It's over," the Carbon County sheriff tells them in the film; "don't you get that your times is over and you're going to die bloody and all you can do is choose where." But *it* was not really over. Butch and Sundance were physically graced like classic Western heroes. These roles unleashed masculinity from its protector role but restored individualist strength as male authority reflected in romantic notions of banditry and measured by the cleverness of their run for freedom across wide-open spaces. Unlike traditional western films that iconized the redemptive power of violence through the sheriff, cowboy, or the good outlaw, *Butch Cassidy and the Sundance Kid* iconized the two men. The two gentle outlaws reconfigured the western hero from a redemptive soul to a carefree, natural man. Yet even if an era was over, as this film suggested, the life of the Redford persona had just begun.

The popular desire for western subjects found more life three years after *Butch Cassidy*, when Redford collaborated with long-time friend Sydney Pollack to produce *Jeremiah Johnson*, with Redford as the lead and Utah mountains in the supporting role. Johnson, the western version of the natural man, was not an outlaw, just a social resister who left industrialized America during the mid-1800s and traveled to the Rocky Mountains. Here men could test their masculinity in the outdoors by living the code of the land and learning from those who knew its "secrets." Johnson builds shelter, catches fish in subzero streams, and survives harsh winters in the mountains.

This film is important for its placement of the mountain man in the specific setting of the Rocky Mountains. The location was essential to Redford. He and Pollack spent several years persuading Hollywood to film on Utah landscape instead of behind studio walls.[19] Redford would use Utah not just as backdrop for the film's story but for establishing authenticity. The valleys and rivers of the Wasatch helped define the central character, Jeremiah, as the nineteenth-century rugged individualist whose search for a natural way of life took him to the untrammeled West. Filming on location meant selectively representing the landscape as pristine, seen from Jeremiah's point of view. *Jeremiah Johnson* expresses desire and sorrow for an unspoiled time and place. Like Redford's later lamentation films that grieve the end of eras, this film remained true to the sensibility of his vision of the West as a site in need of recovering and western identity in need of preserving.[20] Like the fixed setting of a Bierstadt painting, *Johnson* produces Utah as a scenic spectacle, valued because of its alleged naturalness and its lost, simple past, as opposed to contemporary Utah landscapes accessible with modern technology.

Popularizing the notion of the West as best if preserved, while taking the film crew into the Wasatch Mountains so audiences everywhere could glimpse "authentic" landscape, marks the point of convergence in Redford's film projects and marketing strategies. Location is particularly cultural because places accentuate identity. Visualization is a kind of language on screen that influences how people understand the use of places and see themselves. Audiences respond out of familiarity (imagined and experienced) with the location visualized. Filming the Wasatch Mountains as pristine helps market the West as the last outpost and influences popular expectations about the use of the land.

The vision of loss and the request for lamentation recur in another medium, Redford's book *The Outlaw Trail*, in which he proclaimed that westerners were losing "a life steeped in tradition and custom" since "much tangible evidence of [their] heritage: monuments, graves, hideouts, homesteads" were being bulldozed out of sight and erased.[21] Redford stepped out of his role as actor and into the role of historian when he trekked across Wyoming and Montana in search of outlaw history, but by this time Redford would forever be the star, the famous Sundance Kid appearing on talk shows, in magazines, and other forms of media. Like other stars, his news would be about new releases, making a film, and in effect, what the film represents.[22]

Indeed, stars can rarely step out of their celebrity status. It is their mass appeal, after all, that makes them assets in the film industry. Stars become valued because they connect psychologically and culturally in specific ways to audiences. Stars appearing as individuals (outside the film itself) help audiences separate the person from the persona.[23] Ironically, since celebrity status has already determined the reason for a media appearance, promotionals add more to the cultivation of the persona than to the person. The construction of Redford's persona also depends to a certain degree on its own transparency. Accordingly, *The Outlaw Trail* offered a seamless crossing from western persona to western person.

By the late 1970s, a decade after *Butch Cassidy and the Sundance Kid*, Redford found the star dynamic troubling. He collaborated with Sidney Pollack to produce *The Electric Horseman* (1979), the story of a sympathetic western maverick who succeeds in "de-commodifying" both himself and a show horse. Shot on location in Utah and Las Vegas, this film dramatized the problem of star status and its reductive rendering of complex individuals. The picture begins with a long shot of a horse in the wilds running toward the camera and segues into a close-up of the horse's face. The sequence juxtaposes Redford's character, Sonny Steele, and his rise to fame through a montage of rodeo competitions and the accumulation of belt-buckle trophies, with the last one being won at the rodeo finals in Madison Square Gardens. The final shots of the sequence display Sonny Steele, five-time world champion, on the cover of *Rodeo* magazine as the new "advertising symbol for Ampco Corporation." The newspaper headline reads, "Ampco Corporation Signs Champion to Pitch Ranch Breakfast Cereal." Sonny markets cereal and makes appearances at coliseum events ranging from boxing matches to roller derbies, all with his new marketing symbols—the neon-lighted glittery shirt, white hat, and a Sundance Kid–like mustache. The opening sequence establishes the film's critical stance by revealing the commodification process that takes Sonny from honest competitor to the object and subject of popular consumption and the horse from a natural setting to the glittery world of celebrity glamour. The film's narrative begins with Sonny too drunk to put on his boots for his appearance at the next event, a publicity ride inside a Las Vegas arena.

Like Redford, who has often positioned himself as a maverick resisting the system, Sonny, the neon cowboy, takes a stand against his employer, the corporate giant Ampco. He notices Ampco's show horse, Rising Star, in the Caesar's Palace rehearsal room and discovers that the horse has been drugged for the performance. After a few run-ins with both Ampco's CEO and the news media, Sonny plugs in his neon cowboy outfit and rides Rising Star off the Caesar's Palace runway, through the casino floor, and into the lighted Las Vegas strip. Overcoming one obstacle after another in an attempt to decommodify both the cowboy/star and the horse, he finally gets Rising Star to an unencumbered landscape, Silver Reef, Utah. Redford's character battled the "New West" of image makers and eventually broke through the consumer world to a purer, more natural environment by freeing the twelve-million-dollar thoroughbred to roam the wilds of southern Utah.

In the course of his flight he defies the quintessential image maker, eastern news reporter Hallie Martin, played by Jane Fonda. Here the narrative shifts focus from Sonny the maverick to Sonny the tutor. Fonda's character, "con artist and truth teller," debuts onto the Utah wilderness in spike-heeled fashion boots, tripping along rocks and weeds, and carrying her tripod and camera.[24] Sonny begins her western education by throwing the camera, tripod, and other electronics into the river. Fonda's character is now ready to be inspired by the natural setting and Sonny's knowledge. But after she cons her way into Sonny's cause, she eventually must go back East, taking technology with her, leaving the West alone. At the same time as Sonny liberates the horse and himself by equating freedom with an unencumbered land, he excludes the modern female from the landscape. She remains outside the representable West because she is overeducated and underexperienced for western landscapes. By sending Hallie Martin back to the East, enlightened by the instruction, Sonny centers his role as redeemer and spotlights his identity as the authentic westerner.

Sonny has already been centralized by the fans portrayed in the film as the subjects of commodification and the corroborators of Sonny's heroism: they love the cowboy. They eat the cereal, buy tickets to see the cowboy, and dress in his image—like patrons of American popular culture who buy and manufacture the look of the West.[25] Unaware at first that the Electric Horseman they are cheering is really a double for Sonny because Sonny is too drunk to stay on the horse, the public responds accordingly—they applaud for the outfit riding the horse. "It's not me," Sonny argues when he shows up late for his performance and sees a substitute "Sonny" riding in his neon outfit. "They don't know the difference," the Ampco executive claims. Later in the film when the fans learn that the corporation has hurt the horse by giving it steroids, they rally around the Electric Cowboy gone authentic. They identify with the redeemer Cowboy who exits from the Las Vegas runway and turns the horse loose in Silver Reef, Utah. They, too, can claim heroic identity.

At the same time, a less noticeable identification occurs. The fans in this film become advocates for both horse and cowboy because they believe in the ethical nature of Sonny's actions and the wilds as the natural place for the show horse. "Maybe they bought him, maybe they own him, but there's some rights you can't buy, even from an animal," Sonny tells Hallie's news camera. "The horse earned a better life and I'm gonna try to see he gets it." He explains, "I'm gonna turn him loose. . . . I'm gonna get him back to where he was, what he was. It's in his blood. He knows what to do. It's just half forgotten's all."

Silver Reef becomes a reference point for the ethical act because the land is the site on which to display and perform heroism.[26] Silver Reef represents the unencumbered and natural, in contrast to the constructed Las Vegas, a symbol of corporations (where people work) that exploit western regions. The contrast recalls Redford's project, *The Outlaw Trail*, in which he declared some of these same areas under siege and argued that his trek would release the western past from historical amnesia. Yet remembrance can also objectify. This film, if juxtaposed with the *Outlaw* project, raises just that issue. Silver Reef, regenerative, is also timeless space, a kind of utopia for the liberation of a commodified horse, to be redeemed by purveyors such as those imagined in Sonny Steele. Representing Utah wilderness once more as a place to be saved because it saves, defines it as a last outpost of hope, unencumbered by human societies but privileged as an object of preservation.[27]

Of course, Sonny Steele de-commodifies himself in the narrative and becomes an individualist redeemer, but *Electric Horseman* functions as an active construction, if not re-commodification, rather than a simple reflection of Silver Reef. When he rides Rising Star off the Strip, sheds his neon-lighted shirt, sets the horse free, and eventually hitchhikes out of the wilderness at the end of the film, Sonny's simple story of a commodified horse and popular star becomes a polemic on saving things in uncontaminated places. The various panoramas and close-ups of the Utah wilderness with Sonny and the horse posed in front of them do not simply reflect visually attractive landscapes. These prominent visuals transfer landscape desire to the viewer at a time particularly appropriate for the 1970s, when environmental awareness advocated saving rather than developing western areas. Certainly, this impression continues the duality between urban and wild landscapes and connects the viewer to the narrative's critical stance against development. Yet *Electric Horseman* also functions as a form of its own commodification by transforming Utah landscape into a material image, a commodity, without calling attention to the process of consumption or Silver Reef's new role as a "utopian fantasy." In this role it is a place to be consumed not merely on the screen—as a reflection of what's out there—but also as a new aesthetic of the West, as a spot of regeneration.[28]

Naming Utah wilderness on screen has important consequences for the materialization of the West through visualization. The visuals help dissolve the film's polemic of saving things because the film compiles frame after frame of beautiful landscapes and juxtaposes them with the iconic cowboy corrupted by consumer society. The film's "utopian dimension"—the purified cowboy, the naturalized horse, the regenerative wilderness—resolves commodification anxiety by valuing "natural" spaces over populated ones and by making the world a better place through Sonny's actions of de-commodification. *Electric Horseman* offers to reinvent the myth of the West as a last outpost but conceals that myth's dependence on popular consumption of both the abstract and the material. Sonny's de-commodification, like the land's, is already impossible to salvage because it is the iconic value in both that creates public interest.

Electric Horseman strategically displaces commodification anxiety by offering a solution that ultimately consists of taking the horse to the wild; trading glittery clothes for a cowboy hat, a denim jacket, and jeans; and exposing corporate greed. On a general level the film sustains popular approval in the late 1970s, when the public was already suspicious of consumer culture and corporate greed. Moreover, *Electric Horseman* envisions a simple relationship between saving things and people at a time when debates over the environment came to be as much about local and national power as about the land. The film reverts to valorization of the landscape, contributing to an aesthetic gaining ground in the local and national argument of the 1970s. Redford's activist voice, strengthened through the western persona, may not have directly influenced land policy, but it helped promote an environmental aesthetic that valorizes western regions as the unchanged icon of the past. In that dynamic of influence it is difficult to ignore film as part of the process constructing the material use of Utah landscape.

Certainly, *Electric Horseman* can be understood as sheer entertainment that brilliantly connects to audience taste with its anticonsumer stance, not to mention its use of Willie Nelson's popular western music. Indeed, it is this film's entertainment nature that makes it a cultural producer. Its utopian visuals give the viewer a sense of what Utah landscape would be like in its material reality, but what the viewer experiences is Utah landscape seen through the eye of a camera. The seamlessness between the camera and the land collapses the filming of the landscape into the viewing of an aesthetic value acquired in a movie theater. The significance of such a viewing is that the visuals are not simply an aspect of the narrative but representational in themselves.[29]

The wider application of this film's visual potential can be seen twenty years later when Redford took his persona as protector of things lost to Montana by directing, producing, and acting in *The Horse Whisperer*, a film about a New York mother who goes West seeking Tom Booker, a New Age horse healer, to rejuvenate a traumatized horse. *The Horse Whisperer* takes place in Montana during the 1990s but parallels *The Electric Horseman* of the 1970s in its assumptions about western regions and in Redford's polemic on western issues. A high-powered eastern magazine editor, Annie (Kristen Scott Thomas), travels West to repair her damaged daughter and horse, but in Montana's wide open spaces, like Fonda's character in Utah, Annie also regains what the city had depleted. She sheds "city" signifiers, dropping eastern sleek for a little-flower print dress, and replaces her designing talents with attempts to cook. Annie lets go of the last obstacle, her computer, and under Tom Booker's tutelage and his sister-in-law's stories, she repairs her damaged soul. By the time Annie leaves Montana, she has learned to love and is renewed as a mother and wife. Booker's traditional family, whose members sit down together to eat dinner prepared from scratch, holds a mirror up to Annie's mixed-up life and reinforces the image of the West as rejuvenating and the city as lacking proper tools for building healthy family relations.

Annie's tough business acumen contrasts with the new methods of horse training that this film popularizes. The trainer is a gentle, American male character and the rural family exemplary of Montana's pristine world. The sensitive Booker, who tamed violent nature by training horses through whispering and gently touching, evokes a compassion for people desensitized by a city environment. Redford's Tom Booker, a renewed westerner, represents the better traces of American society and culture, in contrast with Kristen Scott Thomas's ambitious and misguided role as corporate executive. Like Hallie in *Electric Horseman*, Annie is an intelligent producer and tough negotiator. Both films critique those traits but ironically so, because ambition and success are overlaid onto a female character, and that is what makes those traits undesirable.

The Horse Whisperer follows a similar plot line for the male and female as *Electric Horseman*, but it updates the visuals for a contemporary audience. The film fills the screen with high-angle shots of wide-open landscapes, more domesticated than southern Utah wilderness. Mountains descend into rolling, green hills and well-groomed crops. The ranch houses sit on prime real estate at the bottom of the mountain next to the river. Booker and Annie ride through hayfields and quaking aspen, silhouetted against the blue sky and shimmering sunlight, to a promontory point. Love scenes and deep conversations take place near the calm and flowing river in moonlight or under the warming sun. Campfires glow while the cowboy sings, and "locals" all wear snap-pocket cowboy shirts and lots of denim. Extreme close-ups detail hands preparing ropes, cedar log fences, stirrups, chaps, the fringe on chaps, and lots of cowboy hats—seven men and seven white cowboy hats.

Annie's exit scene consists of a pan around the inside of the ranch house for one last disclosure of Booker's identity. The camera details pictures of Booker as a young boy wearing the oversized cowboy hat and of his horses and his rock-solid family. The pan invites us to compare Annie's instability with Booker's Montana-defined self, located in the peaceful and simple life of wide-open spaces. Annie consumes one last moment in this idyllic setting. Her gaze takes us outside the doorway, to the porch, across the handmade pillows sitting on the loveseat, to the river once more, and eventually to Creek House, where she stayed during her journey toward reconciliation. Pictures are worth a thousand words in this film. In these landscapes, imagining oneself on vacation or even living in Montana without the annoyance of flies, the bothersome ranch work (even branding seems like a vacation activity one might sign up for), the choking dust, or the inconvenience of dirt roads would be easy. *The Horse Whisperer* sells eternal spring, pastoral Montana, and the escape vacation of now.

All three of Redford's films tell a story about western areas through visualizing and naming specific places, Utah and Montana, and placing them in western narratives. It is a strategy difficult to resist, considering Redford's celebrity status and the success of his projects, but by representing the landscape as a repository for lost things, these films also tend to construct borders around everyday people and western regions, as if they should remain the objects of popularized images of the West. Redford's unique blend of celebrity, activist, and entrepreneur helps reconstruct and reinvent westernness to "save it." But his films, like his documentary text *The Outlaw Trail*, carry in them an essentializing tendency, often reducing western identity to popular images of horses and hats and western history to popular narratives of the individualist running against the system or finding regeneration in the West. In 1978, at the beginning of his activist career, Redford explained to a civic group that the portrayals of the Sundance Kid and Jeremiah Johnson influenced him beyond his role as just an actor. In addition, he noted, the *National Geographic* project inspired him to speak out. Riding into the past for the project was rejuvenating for him and also disconcerting because of what he saw as the traces of mining. Mining on this trail ride seemed to Redford "an anomaly that's hard for the mind to face." The same photographs from this book were used as slides to advocate environmental awareness and to explain his vision of who represents the "real" West.[30] In 1998 Redford sold *The Horse Whisperer*, in one critic's words, as "an ode to a disappearing West," as a warning to anyone not committed to saving it, and in his own words as an "homage" to something "that was about to go away."[31] The films that cultivate and perpetuate the romantic notion of westernness also give him the most cultural power because they make the persona and the man seem so transparent.

Redford's vision of westernness still circulates through the Sundance Film Institute, where film-industry visitors expect an isolated world apart, a rustic getaway, simple and regenerative. At the Sundance Institute's famous workshop in 1992, for example, a Ute Indian performed a cleansing ritual as the lab's opening ceremonial rite. She "banged on a drum and chanted, offering prayers to cleanse the Earth and connect the newcomers with the spirit of this place, an isolated spot blessed by the beauty of the Rocky Mountains. She burned an eagle feather, smeared it on the faces of those standing in a circle on the grass." After the ceremony she explained that she would be available for "acupuncture, body work or shamanic counseling."[32] The brochure advertising the 1998 Sundance Independent Producers Conference showed the Wasatch Mountains looming large behind a single writer sitting relaxed on a stone wall in front of a path leading to Sundance. These marketing tools brought together Redford's vision of a West dominated by the imagery of unencumbered land as at the heart of what identifies westerners. This expectation of what one will find there extends to assumptions about what can be built in the Wasatch Mountains. "You don't treat this place like an enclosed theater. You celebrate its simplicity, the naturalness of this environment," explained Jayne Luke, artistic director of Sundance Theater. Hoyt Cousins, Boston-architect-moved-West, agreed that "every effort has been made to have the theater blend into the environment. The mountain remains the dominant attraction."[33]

Sundance, the resort, can make Hollywood stars seem ordinary and make ordinary people seem important since they may be skiing next to, or having their script read by, or dining in the same room as celebrities. It is a place used by travelers, named by Redford—a kind of guarantee of his version of the West. Redford's ownership of that land can be understood as the vehicle through which his persona as the Sundance Kid could be reproduced, born again in the offspring of the Sundance Institute, the film festival, and the feature film.[34] Whether or not one agrees with Redford's social and political activism, his public persona cannot be separated from his public projects. He promotes westernness as synecdoche in persona and by filming the unencumbered landscape as a place of authenticity, a place for preservation. As late as 1999, when *People* magazine ran an article on Redford and *The Horse Whisperer*, it was hard to tell the man from the lead role. A full-page photograph showed Redford as a denim-clad Tom Booker walking out of the barn on the set for *The Horse Whisperer*. On the cover Redford appears as himself, an older Sundance Kid, without mustache but complete with boots, jeans, and Levi-casual.

Marketing films as statements about the West circulates knowledge about western regions, but privileged representations understood as western converge at the point of paradox. Redford's ability to wield power, both economic and political, depends on promulgating a romantic notion of the West and limiting its narrative. All this, in the economy of the New West of entertainment, depends on popularizing western regions as static, privileging western cultures as artifact, and valuing their ability to remain so.

Yet the romance itself is part of the process, the person, and the thing they call Sundance. Cultures and commodities are always contingent, not fixed like the frames in film, or frozen like the West of mythic men. And whatever the meaning, Redford, with the help of the Kid, framed the West in his own image and made sure it would never again be the same.

NOTES

1. The explanation written on the museum hall at the resort in 1998 explained that the name *Sundance* is a "reference to a native American ritual and the way the sun dances on the ridges of the canyon." Thus the timely link between Redford's film character the Sundance Kid and the purchasing of land and building the resort is a conscious association, not only a marketing tool but a subject in the public imagination. The "last outpost" are his words written on the wall in the museum hall.

2. Richard Schickel, "Robert Redford Riding High," *Life*, 6 February 1970, 49.

3. Schickel, "Redford Riding High"; Robert Tomsho, "Sundance Kid Gets Little Respect Around Sundance," *Wall Street Journal*, 28 September 1989, 1; Ken Baker, Cathy Free, Todd Gold, Larry Hackett, and Danelle Morton, "The Eclectic Horseman," *People*, 8 June 1998, 86; Richard Rayner, "The Existential Cowboy," *New Yorker*, 18 May 1998, 60; Jillian Lloyd, "High Noon at Sundance Kid's Utah Resort," *Christian Science Monitor*, 19 February 1997; Sean P. Means, "The Star, the System, and That Thing Called Sundance," *Salt Lake Tribune*, 11 January 1998, J1. Even as late as the Salt Lake City 2002 Olympics, Tom Brokaw referred to Redford in a CNBC interview as the Sundance Kid.

4. http://www.oscar.com/oscarnight/winners/winner_redford.html.

5. Robert Redford, *The Outlaw Trail: A Journey Through Time* (New York: Grossett and Dunlap, 1976, 1978), 13.

6. David Foster, "Redford Is Real-Life Star of an Environmental Epic," *Deseret News*, 7 January 1990.

7. In 1976, for example, he appeared at a ribbon cutting for a friend's Wasatch Shadows Nursery; he and Lola were honorary chairs of Primary Children's Hospital and appeared at the 1976 fundraiser; Salt Lake City locals such as real estate developer John Price sat on boards in the early years.

8. Christopher Hicks, *Deseret News*, "An Interview with Robert Redford," 7 December 1990.

9. Gordon F. Sander, "Sundance to a Different Drummer," *Omni* 4 (April 1982): 78.

10. Redford's unique appropriation of a particular vision of westernness and the perception of that vision he cultivated as inextricable from himself suggests discursive practice in three ways: performing, representing, and politicizing. I've based my assumptions on Stuart Hall's theory of representation, Michel Foucault's argument of knowledge as power, and current theory about acts of discovery through naming and classifying as "generative power." Annie McClintock's *Imperial Leather: Race, Gender, and Sexuality in the Colonial Contest* (New York: Routledge Press, 1995) and Mary Louise Pratt's *Imperial Eyes: Travel and Writing and Transculturation* (New York: Routledge, 1991) have illuminated the concept "imperializing contest." As Redford becomes "his own story," he circulates discourse that implicates both western and gendered identities. This leads to objectification of the subject, which "immobilizes" and "alienates subjectivity" while constructing western regions as "exceptional spaces." The "normalizing" power Redford brought to western regions through cultural images simultaneously reproduced uneven gender and regional relationships. Very helpful has been Della Pollock's "Making History Go," in *Exceptional Spaces: Essays in Performance and History* (Chapel Hill: University of North Carolina Press, 1998).

11. Richard Rayner, "The Existential Cowboy," *New Yorker*, 18 May 1998, 68.

12. "Robert Redford as Utah Politician," *Deseret News*, 4 April 1978.

13. Redford's Welcome Letter, in David Terr Petrie, "The Sundance Institute: The First Four Years" (Ph.D. diss., Brigham Young University, 1987), appendix.

14. Nancy Funk, "A Place for New Plays in the West," *Salt Lake Tribune*, 28 September 1980, E3.

15. See David Savran, *Taking It Like a Man: White Masculinity, Masochism, and Contemporary American Culture* (Princeton: Princeton University Press, 1998), 126–27.

16. See Lee Clarke Mitchell, *Westerns: Making the Man in Fiction and Film* (Chicago: University of Chicago Press, 1996).

17. Tom Milne, "Butch Cassidy and the Sundance Kid and Tell Them Willie Boy Is Here," *Sight and Sound* 39 (Winter 1970): 101–2.

18. Vincent Canby, "Slapstick and Drama Cross Paths in 'Butch Cassidy,'" *New York Times*, 25 September 1969, 54.

19. Petrie, "Sundance Institute," 41.

20. This lamentation repeats itself in *A River Runs Through It* (1992), a film of the "handmade" era, "the era of faith." Redford framed Montana in this film as a vestige. "Rural outposts like Missoula," he explained, "were paving their streets and installing electricity. The expanding population was pushing back the wilderness." Judith Thurman, "Portrait: Robert Redford: The Politics and Pleasures of Managing a Western Landscape," *Architectural Digest* (June 1993): 36. *The Horse Whisperer* (1998) illustrates yet another example of the same assumptions.

21. Redford, *Outlaw Trail*, foreword.

22. See Toby Miller, "Stars and Performance," in *Film and Theory: An Anthology*, ed. Robert Stam and Toby Miller (Malden, Mass.: Blackwell, 2000), 596–97.

23. See Richard Dyer, "Heavenly Bodies: Film Stars and Society," in *Film and Theory*, ed. Stam and Miller, 607.

24. Transparency, Movie and TV Criticism, http://www.transparency now.com/horse2.htm>, "More on The Electric Horseman . . . The Players."

25. See Ann Fabian, "History for the Masses: Commercializing the Western Past," in *Under an Open Sky: Rethinking America's Western Past*, ed. William Cronon, George Miles, and Jay Gitlin (New York: W. W. Norton, 1992). The last part of the article ("Dressing for the West") is particularly helpful for understanding how Ralph Lauren "has made a fashion empire out of a magnificent pastiche, out of materials culled from British imperialism, native American aesthetics, and working westerners' rugged wear" (235). *Electric Horseman*'s critique of commodifying the West depends on an exaggeration of outerwear, the kind that belongs on stage, but the film reinforces a version of "dressing for the West" through Redford's appropriation of western signifiers. Although Redford would most likely object to the Ralph Lauren–type of commercializing, he is part of the process that has naturalized the West in terms of outerwear and cultural identity.

26. On bringing back the ethical past in regions and regionalism as a "quest for . . . a place of freedom" and "an original past," see Roberto Maria Dainotto, "'All the Regions Do Smilingly Revolt': The Literature of Place and Region," *Critical Inquiry* 22 (Spring 1999): 486–505. Redford continued the ethical act by taking Rising Star to join other horses that were available for trail riding at his Double R Ranch, where Rising Star "was bred to Double R mares prior to being gelded." Rising Star became part of the process with an invented past, albeit one that may contradict an observable present. Quotation is from "Lifestyle Section," *The Salt Lake Tribune*, 3 August 1981. Again, the importance of the film's narrative is the power to promote the value of saving things and places without calling attention to its role in creating an uneven power relationship based on an assumption that change in western regions is unnatural.

27. See homi k. bhabha, *the location of culture* (London: Routledge, 1994). Redford's representation of the landscape tends to collapse categories and erase geographical, cultural, and historical processes. This kind of representation spills over into his environmental advocacy. As Richard White argues, attitudes toward the land create rifts between people who work in the extractive resource industry and people who see

the land as a site of preservation, whether for play or for regeneration. See White, "'Are You an Environmentalist or Do You Work for a Living?' Work and Nature," in *Uncommon Ground: Toward Reinventing Nature*, ed. William Cronon (New York: W. W. Norton, 1995), 178.

28. References to utopian fantasy and the utopian dimension are taken from Fredric Jameson, "Reification and Utopia in Mass Culture," in *Signatures of the Visible* (New York: Routledge, 1992), 27.

29. Mitchell, *Westerns*, 4–6, for instance, claims that the western has provided "ideological terrain" because it abstracts the landscape. It is the abstract quality of land that has provided the western with its powerful iconography. Western iconography has signified regional space in relation to a national country, but by appropriating named places such as Rim Rock and Silver Reef for both narrative and advocacy, Redford's films tend to make specific places (instead of specific landscapes) ahistorical and static. In that sense *Electric Horseman* and *Horse Whisperer* perform a kind of othering of both land and people, specifically the eastern female and the ranch family along with Utah and Montana.

30. Ralph Wakley, "Redford Takes to Trail in Defense of Heritage," *Deseret News*, 13 October 1978. Getting a Utah audience to see mining as an anomaly would be a challenge. Moreover, removing labor from a preferred history of the West would be similar to removing people from the landscape in his films. If Redford's choosing Utah at first felt empowering, as a way to update westernness, identifying with the western iconography he brought with him challenged Utahns' identification with traditional industry and desires for urban environments.

31. First quotation is from Baker et al., "Eclectic Horseman," 89. Second quotation is from Betsy Pickle, *Scripps Howard News Service*, 1998, Nando.net.

32. Caryn James, "Sundance Lab: Is There More to It than Making Movies in the Mountains?" *Salt Lake Tribune*, 19 July 1992.

33. "Sundance Shows Off Its New Theater," *The Salt Lake Tribune*, 21 June 1992.

34. McClintock argues in *Imperial Leather* that "the desire to name expresses a desire for a single origin alongside the desire to control the issue of that origin" (28). At a cursory glance the name *Sundance* appears to be honoring a legacy, a history, and a mythology that have defined western cultures in general and Utah history in particular. On closer inspection, however, the Sundance story gained notice in Utah only after the film. Since then, eleven histories have been written, most of them intending to "correct" the historical record that the film's narrative distorted. Before the film the Butch and Sundance episodes rarely appeared as part of Utah heritage. Moreover, pioneer history usually eclipses outlaw history in the way the state has defined itself. Redford's act of naming expresses a desire to control the narrative of origin, focusing on outlaw history instead of the more popular pioneer history. In doing so, Redford's persona not only legitimized Redford's claim but bolstered a traditional, masculine West.

Liza Nicholas

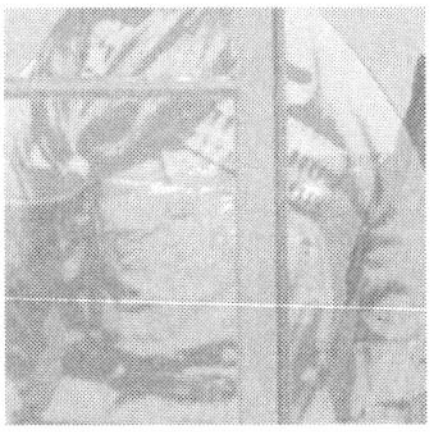

1-800-SUNDANCE

Identity, Nature, and Play in the West

Finding a copy of the latest Sundance Catalog in my mailbox is one of my guiltier pleasures. It's one of the few mail-order catalogs I receive in which I can find a decent pair of hiking boots in the same issue with a pair of cosmic cowboy boots. The catalog easily taps into my own sense of "being western," offering up Eco totes that appeal to my environmentalist bent, along with Kokopelli salt and pepper shakers and Indian warrior kinetic wall sculptures, whose presence in my home somehow reinforces my sense of place, identity, and regional consciousness. These obvious and taken-for-granted representations of the West just seem naturally to belong together. That they appear so perfectly suited to one another may be one reason the catalog, and indeed Redford's West, is so appealing. Historical actors with complicated and tumultuous relationships become reconciled through commodification in the Sundance Catalog. After all, the catalog unselfconsciously peddles the Sioux ceremonial drum handcrafted by Native American artisans in Taos, the Comanche end table, and the Sacred Being "No Place to Roam" Buffalo Sculpture on the same page with the "How Wire Won the West" antique barbed-wire mirror, a reconciliation that is no small feat.

In its fetishizing of "western" products, the catalog rather ingeniously harmonizes the conflicting meanings given the West by cowboys and environmental recreationalists, Sioux Indians, and wealthy second home owners. "Like many of you," the catalog quotes Redford, "I feel a special connection to the heritage and the beauty of the American west. The open range, the wildness of the environment, the history and culture of the Native Americans and the indomitable spirit of the pioneers have all become imbedded in our national character. In this catalog, we try to celebrate some of that heritage."[1]

This symbiosis of western identity and meaning reflects Redford's sense of the West as a whole, in which varying groups, often with vastly different political and environmental beliefs, nonetheless cooperatively fuse into the aesthetically and morally pure West he requires. And it is this view of the West as a nostalgic and reconciled space that undergirds Redford's vision of the region as ultimately a place of play.

The goods hawked by the Sundance Catalog seem so perfectly symbiotic mainly because of the connotations of primitivism they share, and of which the catalog makes full use. The Art of the Anasazi ceramic urn, the beaded moosehide moccasins (handmade by the Manitoba Indians in Canada), the African necklace carved from camel bone, the Appalachian twig side table, and the Country Calico quilt are all infused with cultural meanings of simplicity, purity, and nostalgia. One issue quotes Redford: "In our catalog, we honor the land that came before us. Our hope is to bring you handcrafted items that reflect a harmony with the earth. We strive to connect each material, color and fabric to the land from which it came."[2] The merchandise in the Sundance Catalog seems to tease us into believing that if we capture some remnant of the identities it represents, we can reconnect to an earlier and less corrupted version of our society. The presentation basket handwoven by village women in Pakistan, the Wild Horse letter holder, and the American frontier lamp all seem to transcend the mundane order of life, to take us home to something less urban and crowded. "Tea sipped from a hand-thrown mug probably tastes the same," Redford admits in one issue, "but the sensation of the rough clay surface on your hand and the visual enjoyment of a uniquely carved design all enhance the experience of drinking the tea."[3] The catalog skillfully interprets the meanings of these items and determines what's authentic, what's real, and what's western. "The West has long been favored in literature, film and fashion," Redford explains. "Very often when a subject reaches such dimensions, it can border on myth. Fortunately, much of the real heritage and environment of the real West endures. A true American classic."[4] In Redford's West, the "real West" and its past are turned into morality lessons; Redford is usually the chief tutor, and the catalog is one of his primers.

Redford's perception of the West's "real" inhabitants neatly corresponds with the value he places on the western landscape they inhabit. The "real" westerners Redford champions and interprets he also views as less corrupted and, perhaps not coincidentally, more endangered than the urban dwellers from whom he distinguishes them; and Redford in turn transfers the meanings he gives to these "real westerners" to the wares he sells in the catalog. "Some of my best teachers have been Hopi Indians," Redford commented in a 1982 interview: "These people are living up here and the more you get into their culture, the more you understand their rituals and their dances and ceremonies, the more impressive it becomes to me that their respect for nature has been the mainstay of their ability to remain alive. The Hopi Indians defy gravity. I believe it's a steadfast and almost mystical knowledge and use of nature." Redford noted, "I found more important value in being with the Indians accepting and knowing the fact that you could never be an Indian, you could never be completely of them, but you could be with them and begin to absorb some of their ways and some of their processes and find out what meaning they have for you as a western person, as a Caucasian or non Indian and apply that meaning to yourself."[5] The "naturalness" of Redford's authentic westerners fixes them beyond history, their worth determined by nature and their imminent demise.[6] By Redford's evaluation, the Hopis' "western" value and their primitive magical ability to dissolve difference *depends* on their difference: their ability to "defy gravity," to live at one with nature, to exist in a separate world—and it is this aspect of them that Redford privileges in the Sundance Catalog.

Native Americans are not the only true westerners who are familiarly lionized, differentiated, and commodified in Redford's West.[7] Even the cowboy and rancher, though often antagonistic to Redford's environmental stances and viewpoints, are nonetheless rendered cooperative and environmentally harmless—perhaps because, like the Hopi Indian, they too, in Redford's view, are on the verge of extinction. Redford said of his 1998 role as Zen rancher Tom Booker in *The Horse Whisperer*, "Booker was an older Sundance Kid, aware that history was bearing down on his way of life," he lamented. "I know enough to know that that character is a vestige of what once was a way of life. . . . He is in such low numbers, yet he is almost constantly mythologized as the western man. . . . There are fewer and fewer of them as other forces push them out. . . . Theirs is a tradition that is slowly fading."[8] In Redford's eyes, noted an interviewer, he wasn't Booker so much as Booker was someone he would like to be. "Maybe I, too, am aiming for the security of a simple life," he admitted to the reporter.[9]

If Redford reads values such as simplicity into these authentic westerners, they are values that the suburbanites who buy the Sundance products lack and crave. Like their symbols in the catalog, Redford uses these human vestiges of westernness to teach lessons to a modern world. "Silence is in the very grain of American ranch life. Understatement is part of the deal," he explains.[10] But if Redford's authentic westerners look good on the land, their presence doesn't actually seem to affect it. His West provides us with a "natural" state and "natural" inhabitants, without ever having to reconcile the human impact on the environment. In an interview following the release of *The Horse Whisperer*, Redford commented:

> Unquestionably one of the things that appealed to me about doing [*The Horse Whisperer*] was the opportunity to show the lives of people on a ranch, still connected to the land. People who operate the land for their livelihood. . . . It's not always that romantic. It's no longer an agricultural time, no longer an industrial time. It's information now. So we're already two ages away from the lifestyle that's hanging on there. It's on its way to vanishing because . . . [a] lot of the leadership that should be preserving the land for our children and grandchildren are taking a short term view, not thinking about generations to come, particularly corporations. So it'll be gone, like the extinction of animals. I think it'll be sad to lose something that special. That kind of mourning maybe I put into my work.[11]

If the ranching lifestyle itself edges toward oblivion, the Sundance Catalog nonetheless provides its vestiges for purchase, including the Boot Scootin' Wall Sampler, the Horse Whisperer shirt, Tom Booker's bracelet, and the Range Roving hat, "inspired by the heroes and heroines of the American West." The departure of the West's past residents from the "New West" renders them largely innocuous, if not more precious, and perhaps more malleable as pedagogical tools for the present. Redford appropriates and commodifies symbols of the "Old West" and thereby acts as interpreter and translator, even fashion director, for residents of the "New West," a powerful role indeed. "I live in both East and West," he told one interviewer, "so I can put my knowledge of both on screen."[12]

The nostalgic meaning he reads into these doomed westerners is, in effect, what Redford sells; in the Sundance Catalog the pioneer, the Hopi Indian, the cowboy, and western nature itself are all present outside linear time, separate from the urban, distinct from the vast majority of consumers.[13] Redford views the western man, the "authentic" western man, as "someone who is deeply feeling, who embraces life as something he doesn't try to control, a larger order that he's a part of." And if there is a western man, untainted and morally uncorrupt, there must be his opposite. "Urban man, on the other hand," notes Redford, "he was someone who believes he can control things."[14] In the Sundance Catalog the West and its rural authentic becomes Redford's natural "Other" to the urban artificial, and that distinction is largely what compels his customers to buy that Sioux ceremonial drum for $135.00.

Redford's ambition to connect urban consumers to a natural, primitive, and distinctive western space through "real work" and its premodern vestiges is hardly novel. His impulse is continuous with an antimodernist tradition counterposed to the impersonal nature of bureaucracy and urbanization and to work viewed as divorced of meaning. As far back as Thomas Carlyle, writers have warned of the dangers of the industrial revolution and its effects on the human soul and have admonished that machines would replace the traditional standards of beauty with those of economy and profit. Redford is thus part of a long line of critics of the modern age who seek regeneration and renewal in the glories of the past.[15] But his own concerns about the modern world and his desire for a personal connection to a nostalgic and primitive past perhaps most closely echo the sentiments of the antimodernists at the end of the nineteenth century and beginning of the twentieth.

During the 1880s both Europeans and Americans began to fear that life had become overcivilized and unreal and that moral impotence had infested modern culture. They fervently sought to reconstruct personal identities, which they feared had fallen victim to a modern world. Between 1880 and 1920 the antimodernists reached back to remnants of the republican tradition of agrarian labor and the childlike, rustic, and simple life of the premodern character to "rekindle possibilities for authentic experience—possibilities they felt had existed once before, long ago."[16] The Arts and Crafts movement formed a major part of this crusade.

The Arts and Crafts movement was a material manifestation of the antimodernist reaction to urbanization, the growth of the bureaucratic corporate structure, and the limited variety of products available to consumers in an increasingly standardized market.[17] In a quest to form a more simple and virtuous life its enthusiasts harked back to the premodern artisan, whose work they believed to be rooted in the genuine community and "real life." Craftsmen thus emphasized the imprint of tools and hand processes on their wares and stressed simplicity, utility, and the democratization of art.[18] Crafts' writers attacked the general character of a modern civilization that they believed associated money with happiness, produced goods for trade and not for the life of the people, and replaced tradition with fashion. They instead sought to "ennoble labor to free workmen from the tyranny of mass production." Redford no doubt would have found a kindred spirit in Gustav Stickley, one of the most influential leaders of the Arts and Crafts movement in America. Stickley opened the United Crafts furniture workshop in 1898 and edited *The Craftsman* magazine. Stickley spoke for many antimodernists when he expressed his forebodings about the era: "Originally intended to make simpler and easier the doing of necessary things, the introduction of machinery with its train of attending evils has so complicated and befuddled our standards of living that we have less and less time for enjoyment, growth, and nervous prostration is the disease of the age."[19] In a 1997 issue of the Sundance Catalog Redford echoes Stickley: "Digital technology and innovation have come to the arts, but with a cost. . . . We lose the sense of immediacy and connection to raw materials and the human touch. In our catalog we concentrate on maintaining that connection, which is why we offer so many items that are handcrafted."[20]

Like Redford, the Arts and Crafts reformers believed that rural life represented a path to moral regeneration and a rejuvenating work ethic.[21] Stickley in particular advocated nature's moral virtue and sought to associate the craftsman ideal with agrarianism. "The backbone of the nation is working people, especially those who work for themselves and gain at least part of their living from the soil," he commented in 1908. "On the farm or in village life a man controls to some extent his own identity and is responsible for his success and failure to provide his family with the necessities of life."[22] Local nature also showed up in Arts and Crafts products, from gnarled tree bookends to flowered decorative cigar boxes. Many Craft reformers reduced the simple life to a cottage or rustic suburban home filled with handcrafted, natural items that drew from the rural and primitive, and looked to Appalachia and the Italian and Russian peasantry for models. Rural Europeans, like Native Americans, became the picturesque "objects of social uplift, alternatives to modern industrial life." Stickley's suggestion that Indian rugs and Navajo blankets "turn any porch into a peaceful outdoor living room" certainly evokes images in the Sundance Catalog.[23]

Not unlike the suburban dweller of today whose front closet bulges with cross-country skis, snowshoes, and climbing gear, many of the antimodernists enthralled with the Crafts movement believed that experience was not genuine unless it was physically demanding, and they longed for the imagined premodern past of physically rigorous and authentic work—of "real life." Perhaps not surprisingly, the movement especially appealed to the ranks of professional people who felt most cut off from "real life" and its moral and cultural regeneration of manual labor.[24] The Arts and Crafts movement used the past, nature, and idealized work separated from modern reality to salve the woes of the confused identities of suburban dwellers. And this, perhaps, is how *The Craftsman* magazine connects to the Sundance Catalog, how Redford's longing for a simplified West links us to the premodern agrarian ideals of turn-of-the-century Americans, and perhaps most important, how the unresolved longings of the antimodernist past are instructive of our own yearnings in the antimodern present.

But if the Craft reformers' movement and the Sundance Catalog share a devotion to craftsmanship, primitivism, and nature, they differ significantly in their consideration of work and consumption. Stickley and the Craft revivalists offered a critique of consumer culture that envisioned the ennobling of work as a path to moral regeneration and even as an oppositional model of a capitalist society. The antimodernists critiqued industrial capital for degrading work and alienating people from themselves and their natural world—the very things that Redford's commodified West seems to accomplish, however unintentionally.[25] If the agenda of the antimodernists was to free workmen and craftsmen from the tyranny of mass production, the Sundance Catalog accomplishes just the opposite; it commodifies artisans' wares for a global urban consumer and turns its featured artisans into a sort of endangered species, remnants of a lost world akin to Redford's heroic perishing ranchers and Native Americans. And unlike the Craft reformers' solution, regeneration in Redford's West is accomplished not through work but through leisure, recreation, and consumption, often at odds with the kind of work *in* nature that the Arts and Crafts movement advocated.

And perhaps this is the peril of buying into Redford's West. Redford reconciles western symbols but not the relationships implicit in them: work and play, the natural and the artificial. The reconciliation of harmonious western cultural symbols and meanings comes at the price of separation and distance—urban dwellers from rural inhabitants, East from West, humanity from nature, work from the environment—a separation on which the appeal of Sundance and its products depends.

In many ways Redford's West both constructs and is constructed by the New West of recreation—of SUVs, of Patagonia and North Face gear. The rural operates primarily as scenery or as pedagogy in this "New West," with the realities of even rural work and its relationship to nature largely ignored. Rather than view the West as an escape, the cowboy heroes Redford both portrays and idolizes *use* nature, after all, and affect it by their livelihood, an inconvenience Redford adroitly sidesteps because in his West, rural work is ultimately a thing of the past, a loss to be mourned, its value commemorated in western knickknacks.

Redford's commodification of Montana in his films reveals the fated relationship between work and play in his vision of the West. In A *River Runs Through It* (dubbed "A Realtor Runs Through It" by disgruntled locals) and *The Horse Whisperer* the director presents the state's breathtaking scenery to the world and assigns the "leading role to Montana," as one reviewer noted.[26] "The director presents Montana as if he were worshiping some mythical, mystical promised land," observed another.[27] Redford advertises the West's natural glory in his movies but in so doing, promotes not a West of work but ultimately a place of play. "There's a movie opening this week that makes fly fishing look so wonderfully seductive, even non-fishermen who see it will want to rush out and buy one of those funny hats festooned with flies and fish hooks," *Sports Illustrated* maintained in 1992. "Montana couldn't ask for a better ad campaign to promote tourism," noted *People* magazine of *The Horse Whisperer*.[28] The aesthetic West that moviegoers take in through Redford's films is a cultural place of beauty to be preserved for play, not a utilitarian space to sustain the Tom Bookers of the world. And Redford, however unwittingly, presents a West that draws those who can afford to ante up the money to invest in the mythic, aesthetic West he, in effect, sells.[29]

It is difficult for the West of play, valued for its aesthetic attributes, to coexist with the West of rural work. "We wanted to buy eight hundred acres adjoining our ranch," one ranching family in southwestern Montana commented to *Forbes* magazine. "But some stockbroker bought it for $800,000; we could offer $100,000."[30] After the release of *The Horse Whisperer* cattle prices fell while land prices surged, a shift that turned many a "Tom Booker" into an erstwhile river guide for those who furnish their vacation homes with the Sundance Catalog's Wild West lodgepole pine bed for $1,600. In 1996 *Forbes* noted that "Montana has become an in place for people who enjoy active outdoor activities. Vail-weary folks see it as an escape to nature and the simpler life."[31] And the appeal is due in no small part to the gloriously filmed western vistas Redford revealed to urbanites seeking nature and the "real" West. Redford's sanctioning of Montana in his movies no doubt helped legitimize the state as an "in" Zip code for people who can afford to view the natural and pristine West as a place of leisure removed from economic necessity.[32] (Perhaps this cultural sanctioning is nowhere better demonstrated than the Fall Collection inspired by *The Horse Whisperer* created by designer Michael Kors or the recent "guidelines" outlined by *Harper's Bazaar* on how to dress for Montana, including Claudie Pierlot leather jacket, Fendi leather satchel, and Ralph Lauren denim bikini.)[33] And yet in his films Redford nonetheless resolutely laments the replacement of the "true" westerners by their inauthentic urban substitutes. "The immensity of the landscape overpowers the petty mortal doings within the story. He puts before us some reaches of Montana that are more than gorgeous; they haunt us with loss," said one reviewer of *The Horse Whisperer*.[34] Redford seems to acknowledge the paradoxical relationship between his reverence and desire for the aesthetic West he so wonderfully depicts and the demise of the "genuine" westerner, simpler times, and purer lifestyles—based on utilitarian land usage—that he mourns. In showcasing Montana's aesthetics, Redford places himself in the somewhat peculiar role of helping destroy the very thing for which he pines.

In Redford's West, then, nature has become an escape, a fantasy, an arena for human play and leisure; this change is a victory for leisure and a defeat for work, as Richard White writes.[35] Redford's West suggests that the proper usage of public lands is as sites of public play, as places to mimic the pre-modern past with physically rigorous outdoor exertions—albeit hiking a nature trail rather than chopping down trees. The West of work, where Redford's stoic, heroic ranchers graze their herds on Forest Service and BLM allotments, has often been at battle with this West of play that he seeks to protect. "Our western lands cannot be taken for granted," he writes to his Sundance Catalog clientele. "Even mountains and valleys need constant protection. . . . I believe that we all have a special responsibility to preserve [them] to secure a place where our children can go to recapture the spirit that is so much a part of America."[36] Redford's vision of the West illustrates White's argument that environmentalists identify nature with play and make it by definition a place where leisured humans come only to visit and not to work, stay, or live, a reality Redford seems to accept in his catalog: "More and more Americans are living in cities and suburbs which are rapidly spreading across lands that were once family farms or woodlands. We have to face the problem of the environment being crowded out of our lives. To live in close proximity to nature is becoming a luxury most Americans cannot afford. . . . We need to use our creativity to bring the outdoor environment into indoor and urban places."[37] Redford's association of "living in close proximity to nature" with luxury clearly indicates that in his view, nature's modern function is to be a playground and certainly not to be a place of work or sustenance.

The Sundance Catalog's merchandise illustrates this presumption of separation of work from nature: the hand-carved Tarahumara wooden bowls it sells, "carried out of the canyons on the back of a donkey," were once used by the Indians to roll dough, but the catalog now markets them as perfect for "filling with dried flowers, pine cones, whatever you like." (Pine cones sold separately for $15 per bag.) The catalog sells old-time hayforks for $119, "to hang on your wall"; weathered denim workshirts, "raised to new heights of sophistication" (with updated Navajo designs, $115); African pack baskets, "marvelous for storing so many things: video tapes, cassettes, books, cards, games, even toiletries in the bath," for $159; hand-hewn coatracks, "a great choice for your entry, cabin or summer house"; "backpack to take around the world," $129; country barn jackets "to keep you warm while hiking," $195; aspen walking staffs from aspen from the Jemez Mountains for $65; and, God forbid, the distressed leather fanny pack "to carry around your waist for a day of skiing, biking and hiking in the woods or the urban jungle."[38]

It is our use of these commodities—as instruments of play and leisure, not work—that provides us glimpses of the "proper relations" implied in

Redford's West between humans and nature: in which humans live but somehow do not touch nature, where we can frolic but not sustain ourselves within its boundaries. In Redford's West the only way work connects to nature is through commodities marketed as frivolities, an indicator of the privileged position held by those who "buy" his West. And as White points out, in sustaining a belief of a connection with nature through play, we detach modern work from the land and nature, forever divorcing most of our lives and existence from the place we live and work and from the place we play and escape to. The products in the Sundance Catalog sell a West in which it is difficult to imagine a way to reconcile modern work and modern living with the environment—except perhaps to purchase the Majestic Forest Floor Lamp for $495. For Redford to create a reconciled West, he must mournfully bury the past's inhabitants and then sell their vestiges in his catalog.

This rather adroit act, however, unfortunately denies Redford's western icons a place within the "New West." In his reconciled West they cooperatively become instructive memories. After all, there is simply no role for a Web-savvy Hopi or a wolf-averse rancher in Redford's New West. Their history, presence, and work have no place there, other than as instruments for pedagogy or archetypes for commodification. In his reconciliation of western symbols through commodification, as symbols of difference and escape, Redford sells us the illusion that the "Old West" and the "New West"—that the wild and the tame, work and play, our ideas of public land use—are reconciled. In the end, this removed and endangered view of the West distances us not only from the things and people who exist in that imagined, mythic, separate space but, as William Cronon writes, from the very things it teaches us to value—home, the place where we actually live.[39] And so, although I do love my new Zuni mantel clock, Western Roundup afghan, Nostalgic Teepee light, and Rustic Moose key fob, I have to continually remind myself that Redford is a master of reconciliation and that these remnants of the past truly reconcile nothing; if only those real western problems and identities could in fact be resolved with a telephone and credit card, the West would be just the kind of place Redford has for so long been searching.

NOTES

1. Sundance Catalog, Fall 1993, no. 18.

2. Sundance Catalog, Fall 1997, no. 42. Marianna Torgovnick, *Gone Primitive: Savage Intellects, Modern Lives* (Chicago: University of Chicago Press, 1990). Torgovnick writes that the "creation of specific versions of the primitive often depends on and is conditioned by a sense of disgust or frustration with western values. . . . The

primitive becomes a convenient locale for the exploration of western dullness or degeneracy, and of ways to transcend it, and thus functions as a symbolic entity. . . . It becomes grist for the western fantasy mill" (153).

3. Holiday Sundance Catalog, 1994, no. 25.

4. Sundance Catalog, March 1991, no. 6.

5. Gordon F. Sander, "Sundance to a Different Drummer," *Omni* (April 1982): 78.

6. Stuart Hall, "The Spectacle of the Other," in *Representation: Cultural Representations and Signifying Practices*, ed. Stuart Hall (London: Sage Press, 1997), 236–49.

7. Torgovnick points out that "frequently, the working class or other subordinated segments of a population become associated or identified with primitives" (*Gone Primitive*, 18).

8. Louis B. Parks, "Romancing the West: Robert Redford Takes Mythic Journey in *Horse Whisperer*," *Houston Chronicle*, 10 May 1998, 8.

9. *New Yorker*, 18 May 1998, 71.

10. *New Yorker*, 18 May 1998.

11. Jay Carr, "The Redford Way," *Boston Globe*, 10 May 1998, 1.

12. Desmond Ryan, "Screen Icon Directs Himself for the First Time in 'Horse Whisperer,'" 13 May 1998, Knight Ridder Newspapers. Torgovnick points out that "to identify with others is to invoke a hierarchy: humans exist in relations of mastery, rather than reciprocity, with other humans and with the world. In studying primitive societies or in inventing versions of them, Westerners pretend to learn about or to create alternative, less oppressive ways of knowing, all the while establishing mastery and control over those ways of knowing" (*Gone Primitive*, 173).

13. Torgovnick observes that "the belief that primitive societies reveal origins or natural order depends on an ethnocentric sense of existing primitive societies as outside of linear time, and on a corresponding assumption that primitive societies exist in an eternal present which mirrors the past of Western civilization" (*Gone Primitive*, 46).

14. *New Yorker*, 18 May 1998. Torgovnick writes, "Primary sites of primitivism in the West are most often urban spaces, associated with the processes of industrialization and the concentration of population that gave rise to the features of modern culture we know best" (*Gone Primitive*, 191).

15. Martin Iedelberg, David A. Hanks, and Susan Otis Thompson, eds., *The Arts and Crafts Movement in America* (Princeton: Princeton University Press, 1972), 9.

16. T. J. Jackson Lears, *No Place of Grace: Anti-modernism and the Transformation of American Culture, 1880–1920* (New York: Pantheon, 1981), 57.

17. The Arts and Crafts movement originated in England with the philosophy of John Ruskin and William Morris. Ruskin and Morris believed that handicrafts would provide an alternative mode of production that would permit worker creativity and revive beauty, merging art with daily life and reeducating the consumer. In the United States the Arts and Crafts style served as a counterpart to Progressive reform. See Eileen Boris, *Art and Labor: Ruskin, Morris, and the Craftsman Ideal in America* (Philadelphia: Temple University Press, 1986), xii.

18. Elizabeth Cumming and Wendy Kaplan, *The Arts and Crafts Movement* (London: Thames and Hudson, 1991), 146.

19. Lears, *No Place of Grace*, 69.

20. Sundance Catalog, January 1997, no. 38.

21. Lears, *No Place of Grace*, 75–90.

22. Boris, *Art and Labor*, 157.

23. Boris, *Art and Labor*, 125, 77.

24. Lears, *No Place of Grace*, 61; Boris, 77.

25. On the Arts and Crafts movement's view of work, see Boris, *Art and Labor*, xv, 28; Lears, *No Place of Grace*, 70–77.

26. John Sedgewick, "The Californication of Montana," *GQ* (December 1995): 245; Stanley Kauffmann, review of *The Horse Whisperer*, *New Republic*, 15 June 1998, 26.

27. Parks, "Romancing the West," 8.

28. Review of *A River Runs Through It* in *Sports Illustrated*, 12 October 1992, 10; review of *The Horse Whisperer* in *People*, 25 May 1998, 1.

29. Sedgewick writes that to newcomers drawn by celebrity sanctification and movies, "Montana is just another item for consumption . . . they want to look at agriculture, but they don't want to smell it." He observes about the Bozeman area, which Redford showcases: "The cowboy hat, the horse, the ranch, the mountains, even the dust and the high wide sky, all of these have somehow lost their original urgent meaning and become little more than design elements for a few transients eager for a change of scene" ("Californication," 243).

30. *Forbes*, 21 October 1996, 73.

31. *Forbes*, 21 October 1996, 73.

32. Pierre Bourdieu, "The Aristocracy of Culture," in *Media, Culture and Society: A Critical Reader*, ed. Richard Collins (Beverly Hills, Calif.: Sage Press, 1986). Bourdieu writes that "nothing more rigorously distinguishes the different classes than the disposition objectively demanded by the legitimate consumption of legitimate works, the aptitude for taking a specifically aesthetic point of view of objects already constituted aesthetically, and therefore put forward for the admiration of those who have learned to recognize the signs of the admirable" (182). The West and Montana are examples of places that are consumed as legitimate works, distinguishing one class from another: those who see the West as ordained to a higher function—either as a preserved aesthetic site or a "style of life"—and those who still view it as a site of economic necessity. The "aesthetic disposition," writes Bourdieu, unites all those who are the product of similar conditions but only by distinguishing them from all others; in this case, those who can afford to view the "natural" as freed from economic necessity and those who are bound by material necessity.

33. *Harper's Bazaar* (May 1998): 76.

34. Kauffmann, review of *The Horse Whisperer*, 26.

35. Richard White, "'Are You an Environmentalist or Do You Work for a Living?'

Work and Nature," in *Uncommon Ground: Rethinking the Human Place in Nature*, ed. William Cronon (New York: W. W. Norton, 1995).

36. Sundance Catalog, Fall 1993, no. 18.

37. Sundance Catalog, March 1997, no. 39.

38. Sundance Catalog, Fall 1989, no. 1; March 1991, no. 6; March 1997, no. 39.

39. William Cronon, "The Trouble with Wilderness," in *Uncommon Ground*, ed. Cronon, 87.

Thomas J. Harvey

THE SUNDANCE KID AND SUNDANCE

The West as Nature

> I suppose I've gone through all the religions and rejected them and in the end, this is what I come back to. The god of this landscape, of this nature, is the one who speaks to me.
>
> Robert Redford

Robert Redford's Sundance development in Utah's Wasatch Mountains is a ski resort, conference center, mountain recreational retreat, and upscale housing development. It offers lodging and restaurants, skiing and snowboarding in the winter, and hiking, mountain biking, and horseback riding in the summer. It has up to ten thousand square feet of meeting space. It plays host to workshops for playwrights, movie makers, and artists; it has a children's theater and a summer theater; and it sponsors concerts as well as Native American Heritage Day. The development takes up only a small percentage of available land, and the buildings are spaced relatively far apart and hidden among trees. No overhead power lines are visible. A tumbling stream of pure water glides between the buildings. The structures themselves are made of rough-hewn lumber or logs, resembling American pioneer buildings or mining structures. The interiors of the main resort buildings are decorated with western Americana, Kachina dolls, Navajo blankets, baskets, rustic furniture, cowboy artifacts, and photographs of Redford in his various western movie roles. The Owl Bar houses a varnished wood counter from a Wyoming bar where the real Old West outlaws Butch Cassidy and the Sundance Kid once reputedly hung out. Redford wants to call Sundance a community and not a resort, and he holds it out as a model of ecologically sensitive development.[1]

Redford uses the resort to circulate knowledge about the West. In their resemblance of nineteenth-century frontier structures, Sundance's buildings enshrine a western past that Redford values for its supposed pureness of person and environment. A statue of an Indian in premodern dress in a spiritual pose over a placid pond gives a kind of native legitimacy to the area, blessing it as promoting a purer relationship with nature. The various photographs of Redford in "Old West" movie roles interspersed with old saddles and other western objects and artifacts blend a popular-culture version of the West and the "real" thing, valuing a certain construction of the past of men closer to nature and their true selves. Sundance is a collage of objects and images torn from historical and social context and repositioned and displayed as a narrative of a particular version of the Old West come home to a new place in nature.

Intersecting at Sundance are the twentieth-century discourses of antimodernism and antiurbanism, ensconced in a specific idea of nature and of the "Old West" of popular culture—all reified in a postindustrial economy of consumption. What binds these discourses together and makes Sundance a coherent whole is their collection into a narrative we can label the "wilderness plot." William Cronon traced the twentieth-century idea of wilderness to an anxiety over the closing of the frontier of the Old West, the site where white men uncomfortable with the encroachments of civilization went to rejuvenate themselves. The myth of the frontier, of wilderness or free land, was combined with the nineteenth-century romantic vocabulary of the sublime to produce the notion of wilderness. That wilderness carries with it the American cultural history of "nature" and the "Old West." Literary scholar Krista Comer defines the "wilderness plot" as a love of wide-open wild spaces, a penchant for the mystical that includes the "natural" American Indian, the suggestion of redemptive possibilities, a disavowal of the industrial and technological, and representations of women as nature. It is an antiurban discourse intended to serve as a critique of and alternative to the displacements of modern or postmodern life. The wilderness plot also permeates much of New West discourses, narrating its styles, recreation, design, placemaking, and politics. Sundance records the intersections of these Old West and nature narratives, their construction revealed through a review of Redford's long record of environmental activism, where his "nature" is most clearly articulated.

Redford's role as the Sundance Kid provided him capital: the money that allowed him and partners to buy five thousand acres of land in Provo Canyon that included an old ski resort, and the social and cultural kind to speak out on environmental issues and back politicians and causes. Redford's then wife,

Lola, introduced her husband to activism in 1969 with her founding of the group Consumer Action Now. His Sundance persona gave him a forum by attracting invitations to speak, interviews in major publications, and appearances on television. It got out the crowds and the interest from viewers and readers even as it also gave Redford a basis for a particular construction of nature and the West.[2]

Redford's first major issue was a plan by the state of Utah for a four-lane highway through Provo Canyon past the entrance road to Sundance. He credits the thirty-year political and legal conflict with providing him an education in activism. Over the years he has become involved in any number of issues, from nuclear waste disposal to the advocacy of wilderness areas to protection of cougars.

Redford has a core narrative, a story he has told over and over again in various forums to explain his rise to environmental consciousness and activism:

> My own involvement with the environment began before I ever knew it, when I was growing up in Los Angeles at the end of the Depression and during and after World War II. . . . I watched as the green, open space turned into concrete malls and freeways, and the clean, pure air turned into smog alerts. I watched as unbridled development became the order of the day. Oil drills appeared off the beaches, along with oil spills in the water and hunks of tar in the sand. The smell of orange blossoms turned into exhaust fumes.
>
> I felt my home being taken away from me. I felt my roots being pulled out from under me. And I took it personally. I had to go further and further away to find places where the natural environment still existed.[3]

For Redford, the environment is an abstract idea and space outside his own early experience. He even places his own body outside nature ("before I ever knew it") when he equates an environmental consciousness with his later intellectual and social understanding and his activism. He laments the postwar boom of development in the Los Angeles area of his youth and equates it with the loss of "home." What is expressed in this Genesis tale is a state of "transcendental homelessness,"[4] the solution to which is to retreat into a primitive nature, to go "further and further away to find places where the natural environment still existed," to find a new home in the wild spaces of the interior West.

In 1962 the Redfords bought a few acres of land and constructed a cabin in Provo Canyon in the Wasatch Mountains of Utah. Redford narrates this small purchase, which later was to grow into his Sundance resort, in the form of a discovery: "I found this place and what drew me was the incredible physical appeal of this place and it was totally virginal at that time."[5] Redford empties the landscape by making it "virgin" and begins to fill it with a story of "discovery." A wall in a Sundance resort building in 1999 quoted Redford: "I fell in love with this canyon the first time I saw it. To me it was special to the point of having mystical properties. There was a little sheepherders' camp up top and a guy put a little j-bar [ski] lift in. There was no development to speak of. And I thought, 'This will be the last outpost. I'll be safe here for a long time.'"[6]

The emptied land becomes an "outpost" under Redford's command, evoking the western of popular culture with its images of Euro-American males on the frontier. The outpost in this case is built to hold off not dangerous Indians but the city. At Sundance the antiurban or countermodern response of flight to nature is narrated as the West. The "Old West" is equated with nature.

Redford's opposition in the mid-1970s to a power plant proposed for the remote Kaiparowits Plateau in southern Utah in the vicinity of several national parks first brought him a large national audience for his activism. The power plant was proposed in 1964 but delayed, and by the mid-1970s opposition was strong. Redford's role was low-key until he appeared on "60 Minutes" on 21 March 1976 in a segment called "Robert Redford and the Electric Company." Dan Rather was the CBS correspondent.

> *Rather:* How did you get into all of this? You were raised in southern California?
>
> *Redford:* Yeah. Well, southern California, it wasn't a place to live anymore. There was no air to breathe. You couldn't look any which way without seeing concrete and freeways. And—and life started centering around the automobile, which was not my idea of a way to live. So I started coming more and more out into this country that—where I felt more comfortable.
>
> *Redford:* . . . when I—when I think of the—the land that we're talking about—of all places to be putting a plant--that is so beautiful. If we remove the air quality surrounding the scenic parks, if we degrade the land with roads and transmission lines, then—then obviously, that space that has scenic value is gone, and we've just removed yet another spot for man to go and—and feel nature and feel space and feel in touch with himself.[7]

In the role of environmental activist Redford repeats his Genesis story of the loss of home, the flight from the city to the emptiness of the West, where a man is regenerated and can breathe "and feel nature and feel space and feel in touch with himself." It is an argument for a particular kind of space, one emptied of the visual trappings of an advanced, industrialized economy and seemingly disconnected from the city. On 14 April, a few weeks after the

CBS broadcast, the power plant consortium abruptly canceled its plans. Redford was burned in effigy in Kanab, Utah, near the proposed site for the plant, by residents angry over the loss of promised jobs and an economic boost for the rural area.[8]

The anger directed at him by plant supporters and politicians affected Redford's views of himself as an environmental activist and the direction of his activism. To be sure, he remained active in the public arena, supporting political candidates, giving graduation speeches, testifying before Congress, advocating solar power, and speaking out on other issues. Yet his activism was tempered. He began to question labels such as *environmentalist* and even supported construction of a coal-fired power plant in remote central Utah, far from national parks or other designated scenic areas.[9]

He wrote of the Kanab incident:

> . . . to my amazement and hurt, I was burned in effigy by the local citizens. They had a different point of view. They wanted the jobs the plant would provide, and thought of me as an interloper.
>
> That experience taught me an important lesson, one that led to the creation of the Institute for Resource Management.[10]

The institute, founded in 1983, brought together leaders in industry, environmental groups, and governments to search out a balanced approach to development and environmental problems. Even Howard Allen, head of Southern California Edison, the sponsor of the Kaiparowits Plateau power plant, at one time sat as chairman of the IRM board.[11] Although Redford touted the institute as a mediator, it represented a retreat from a dialogue with "locals" over environmental issues, in favor of an elite, more conservative and corporate organizational approach.[12] Most of the budget of the institute came from foundations and corporate sponsors. One reporter described the IRM conferences as resembling college mixers, "the 'players' schmoozing over gin-and-tonic and barbecued chicken on the well-groomed grounds of Sundance."[13]

If on the one hand Redford retreated to the more exclusive atmosphere of the IRM, he also used the medium of film to reinforce the popular status of the local environmental activist to a national audience. In the *Milagro Beanfield War*, directed by Redford and released in 1988, Milagro is a quaint Mexican-American village whose water is going to a new golf development. Some of the townspeople, including the mayor, are happy to see the development because it means a boost for the local economy. But Joe Mondragon plants a beanfield and uses resort water in an act of defiance. Ruby, the local mechanic and activist, uses the beanfield as a rallying point to convince residents that the new development means an end to a way of life and a rejection of shared roots. The project is canceled and the activists are heroes after directing the local people to realize what is in their own best interests and to preserve their rustic way of life.

In the 1990s Redford's activism turned less openly political and public. He dropped his affiliation with the Institute for Resource Management, and his appearances and public role in environmental causes became more sporadic. But on 18 September 1996 Redford appeared with President Clinton at the edge of the Grand Canyon in Arizona as Clinton announced, in the midst of his reelection bid, the creation by proclamation of the Grand Staircase–Escalante National Monument, some 1.8 million acres, including those on which the Kaiparowits Plateau power plant had been proposed thirty-two years earlier. The previous month, Redford had written Clinton urging him to save the area: "Protecting the Kaiparowits Plateau and wild lands of Southern Utah, which exist nowhere else on earth, would be a stunning legacy of the Clinton presidency for generations to come."[14]

On that day in 1996 Redford's wilderness plot had, in part at least, come to fulfillment. Indeed, it seems that Redford's basic story line of the West as nature and countermodern balm is widely accepted.[15] His Sundance resort displays that plot in a rather seamless way, melding so naturally the traces of the Old West in a modern idea of nature. But Sundance also is riddled with troubling questions: about Native American and Hispanic communities held in some pure premodern state of the past that would deny them a complicated environmental history and their present social realities; as a "virginal" place open to men's conquest; as part of a plot of open spaces that denies a place for the stories of contemporary urban women; as an elite residential colony where that particular relationship to nature is available only to those with high incomes; as a place of play within nature that denies the way of knowing nature through work.[16] Yet from the standpoint of political activism, what seems most troubling is Sundance as an "outpost" holding off the aesthetic indignities, environmental pollutants, and complicated social relations of the city. Sundance creates an oppositional dualism of nature and the city. It says, "Here is nature, not there in Los Angeles." If one shares the environmentalist critique of capitalism's destructive relationship to nature, then one should be disturbed by the disconnections Sundance makes between nature and the city. "Any political movement," geographer David Harvey reminds us, "that does not embed itself in the heart of the urban process is doomed to fail in advanced capitalist society."[17] Nature as "Out There" says little about how residents of the city are immersed in nature and use it every day. As Jennifer Price has written, "The definition of nature as a place apart doesn't merely allow you to ignore your economic connections to nature . . . it also actively *erases* them."[18] Sundance and its discourses of the West and Nature are modern artifacts themselves, telling a tale of alienation not just from the city but also from nature.

NOTES

1. Christopher Smith, "Belly up, Folks, to the Outlaws' Old Bar at Sundance," *Salt Lake Tribune*, 5 August 1996, D3; Jim Fergus, "Bob's World: If Life Were Like Sundance . . ." *Outside* (December 1989): 49.

2. William Cronon, "The Trouble with Wilderness; or, Getting Back to the Wrong Nature," in *Uncommon Ground: Toward Reinventing Nature*, ed. William Cronon (New York: W. W. Norton, 1995), 69–90. The wilderness plot is found in Krista Comer, *Landscapes of the New West: Gender and Geography in Contemporary Women's Writing* (Chapel Hill: University of North Carolina Press, 1999), 127.

3. Robert Redford, "Taking It Personally," in *Heaven Is Under Our Feet*, ed. Don Henley and Dave Marsh (Stamford, Conn.: Longmeadow Press, 1991), 68. For other places where Redford tells this story, see Minty Clinch, *Robert Redford* (Seven Oaks: New English Library, 1989), 157; Robert Redford, "Save the Earth," in *Save the Earth*, ed. Jonathon Porritt (Atlanta: Turner Publishing, 1991), 10; and Margaret Traub-Aguirre, "Talking the Environment with the Sundance Kid," *Salt Lake City* 4 (March/April 1993): 78.

4. Marianna Torgovnick, *Gone Primitive: Savage Intellects, Modern Lives* (Chicago: University of Chicago Press, 1990), 188, 191–92.

5. Steven Smith, "Robert Redford: Hollywood Outlaw," dir. Steven Smith, in *Biography* (Arts & Entertainment Network, 29 October 2000). Annette Kolodny, *The Lay of the Land: Metaphor as Experience and History in American Life and Letters* (Chapel Hill: University of North Carolina Press, 1975), 10–25, writes that such masculine labeling of land as *virginal* has a history in American discourse, producing images of a feminine nature awaiting conquest and exploitation.

6. From notes taken by the author on a 1999 visit to Sundance.

7. CBS, "Robert Redford and the Electric Company," 21 March 1976, transcript (New York: CBS), 15, 18.

8. Reed Madsen, "Actor, Others 'Burned' by S. Utahns," *Deseret News*, 19 April 1976, B1.

9. George Raine, "Robert Redford Objects to 'Environmentalist' Label," *Salt Lake Tribune*, 3 May 1978; Clinch, *Robert Redford*, 159.

10. Robert Redford, introduction to *Greenhouse Glasnost: The Crisis of Global Warming* (New York: Ecco Press, 1990), xix.

11. David Foster, "Redford Is Real-Life Star of an Environmental Epic," *Deseret News*, 7 January 1990, Worldwide Web edition, desnews.com.

12. Mark Dowie, *Losing Ground: American Environmentalism at the Close of the*

Twentieth Century (Cambridge: MIT Press, 1995), describes how mainstream environmental groups retreated into less democratic, corporate organizational models and forms of activism.

13. Fergus, "Bob's World," 108.

14. Robert Redford to William J. Clinton, 5 August 1996, photocopy obtained from Jim Woolf of the *Salt Lake Tribune*.

15. After Redford and Utah senator Orrin Hatch squared off in commentaries in *USA Today* over setting aside millions of acres as wilderness in Utah, an unscientific poll showed that of some 25,000 respondents, 22,922 sided with Redford whereas only 1,772 agreed with Hatch. David Diamond, "Duel for the West: What's Best for the West?" *USA Weekend* (5 November 1995), 4; Jim Woolf, "Redford Clobbers Hatch on Wilderness Ideas," *The Salt Lake Tribune*, 6 December 1995, A14.

16. These questions were influenced by the following works: Kolodny, *Lay of the Land*; Comer, *Landscapes of the New West*; Philip Joseph Deloria, *Playing Indian* (New Haven: Yale University Press, 1998); and Richard White, "'Are You an Environmentalist or Do You Work for a Living?' Work and Nature," in *Uncommon Ground*, ed. Cronon, 171–85.

17. Quoted in Comer, *Landscapes of the New West*, 67.

18. Jennifer Price, *Flight Maps: Adventures in Nature in Modern America* (New York: Basic Books, 1999), 118.

CONTRIBUTORS

Michael A. Amundson is an assistant professor of history at Northern Arizona University in Flagstaff, where he teaches courses on the American West, the Southwest, and occasionally sports history. He is a coeditor of the series Atomic History and Culture, published by the University Press of Colorado. His book *Yellowcake Towns: Uranium Mining Communities in the American West* examines the nuclear past of Moab and other towns.

Elaine M. Bapis is a doctoral candidate in American history at the University of Utah, where she also received her master of arts degree in English and film. She is currently working on a dissertation on American film, identity, and culture, 1965–75. She is an adjunct instructor at Westminster College in Salt Lake City.

Alicia Barber is a doctoral candidate in American studies at the University of Texas at Austin, where she is completing her dissertation, "Living It Up, Living It Down: Civic Reputation and Sense of Place in Reno, Nevada." She has written on natural and cultural landscapes throughout the West for the University of Utah's American West Center and the National Park Service.

Lawrence Culver is a doctoral candidate in the Department of History at the University of California at Los Angeles, specializing in the cultural, urban, and environmental history of the nineteenth- and twentieth-century United States. His essay is based on his master's thesis, completed at Utah State University. His dissertation is a study of regional promotion, tourism, and resort development in Los Angeles and southern California.

Robert R. Dykstra, emeritus professor of history and public policy at the State University of New York, Albany, is the author of two prizewinning books on the trans-Mississippi West, *The Cattle Towns* and *Bright Radical Star*. He has twice previously collaborated with his coauthor here, Jo Ann Manfra.

Thomas J. Harvey is a doctoral candidate in history at the University of Utah, where he is expected to graduate in spring 2003. His dissertation is tentatively titled "The Storehouse of Unlived Years: Producing the 'Old West' as Modern Space." He holds a bachelor's degree in journalism from the University of Montana and has been a journalist for more than twenty years. He and his wife, Joan O'Brien, live in Salt Lake City, where he is a news editor of government and education at the *Salt Lake Tribune*.

Karen Jones is a teaching fellow in the history of the United States at the University of Essex, United Kingdom. Her first book, *Wolf Mountains: A History of Wolves Along the Great Divide*, was published in 2002.

Michael Lundblad is the Sara Shallenberger Brown Fellow in Environmental Literature at the University of Virginia, where he is completing a doctoral degree in English. He holds a master's degree in literature and environment from the University of Nevada, Reno.

Jo Ann Manfra is a professor of history at Worcester Polytechnic Institute in Massachusetts. Her publications include essays on the antebellum Catholic hierarchy and on anti-Catholicism. Her first collaboration with Robert R. Dykstra, "Serial Marriage and the Origins of the Black Stepfamily," 1985, won the Binkley-Stephenson Award from the Organization of American Historians.

Liza Nicholas lives, works, and teaches in Bozeman, Montana. She earned her doctorate in history at the University of Utah in 2001. She is the author of the forthcoming *Becoming Western: Stories of Culture and Identity in the Cowboy State*. Her latest project is a book about horse racing in the Midwest and West in the 1920s and 1930s.

Ken Owens is professor emeritus of history and ethnic studies at California State University, Sacramento, and founder of the CSUS Capital Campus Public History Program. His publications include *The Wreck of the Sv. Nikolai: Two Narratives of the First Russian Expedition to the Oregon Country, 1808–1810*, *John Sutter and a Wider West*, and *Riches for All: The California Gold Rush and the World*. He fishes some.

Amanda Rees is a visiting assistant professor in the Department of Geography at the University of Wyoming. She earned her doctorate in 1998 at the

University of Kansas. Her primary research interests are regionalism, the Great Plains, and the New Urbanism.

Wendy Rex-Atzet is a doctoral candidate in the Department of History at the University of Colorado at Boulder. Her primary area of research involves American environmental history, cultural history, and the history of the American West. She received a master's degree in history from San Diego State University in 1999.

Gordon Sayre is an associate professor of English at the University of Oregon. He is a member of the Obsidians Club of Eugene and has climbed Hood, Rainier, Shasta, and many other Cascades peaks. His other research and writing has been in colonial American literature and on interdisciplinary topics in literature and natural history. He is the author of *Les Sauvages Américains: Representations of Native Americans in French and English Colonial Literature.*

Joseph E. Taylor III is an associate professor in the Department of History at Iowa State University. His first book, *Making Salmon: An Environmental History of the Northwest Fisheries Crisis*, won the American Society for Environmental History's George Perkins Marsh Prize for best book in environmental history. He is currently working on a history of Yosemite rock climbing that traces the links between recreation and environmental culture in the American West.

Meredith Wiltsie earned her master's degree in earth sciences from Montana State University at Bozeman in 1998. Her research interests focus on the historical geography of the West, particularly the changing economies and cultures of small, amenity-rich western towns. The author of many outdoor- and travel-related magazine articles, Wiltsie runs a business licensing photographic rights and enjoys living in the northern Rockies.

William Wyckoff earned a doctorate in geography from Syracuse University in 1982. His research and writing centers on the changing historical and cultural geography of the American West. Recent books include an edited collection (with Lary Dilsaver) titled *The Mountainous West: Explorations in Historical Geography* and *Creating the Colorado: The Making of an American Landscape, 1860–1940*. He is a professor of geography in the Department of Earth Sciences at Montana State University at Bozeman.

INDEX